Altogether Elsewhere

Altogether Elsewhere

Writers on Exile

Edited by Marc Robinson

A Harvest Book
Harcourt Brace & Company
SAN DIEGO NEW YORK LONDON

A Harvest Book
Harcourt Brace & Company
SAN DIEGO NEW YORK LONDON

Library of Congress Cataloging-in-Publication Data
Altogether elsewhere : writers on exile / edited by Marc Robinson.—1st Harvest ed.
p. cm. — (A Harvest book)
Originally published: Boston : Faber and Faber, 1994.
ISBN 0-15-600389-9
1. Exiles' writings. 2. Authors, exiled. I. Robinson, Marc. 1962–
PN6069.E94A47 1996
808.8'9920694—dc20
95-26324

Printed in the United States of America

First Harvest edition

ACEFDB

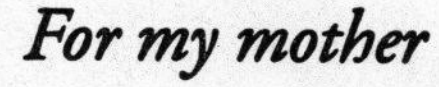
For my mother

Altogether elsewhere, vast
Herds of reindeer move across
Miles and miles of golden moss,
Silently and very fast.

—W. H. Auden
"The Fall of Rome"

Contents

Introduction

A LARGE PORTRAIT of my grandfather hangs near my desk, and as I arranged and rearranged the pieces of this anthology, I often welcomed the distraction of looking up at him. My grandfather, a Czech Jew, is only six years old in the painting, so it's unlikely that I would have found any guidance in his dark eyes. Those eyes don't even look at me, but instead stare blankly toward a vague horizon as though, untouched by his surroundings, he anticipates some future destination. Only my knowledge of his later exile leads me to see prescience in that gaze, the same detachment that absorbed the shock of leaving Prague in 1938—his wife and two-month-old daughter, my mother, in tow—just missing the German annexation by three months.

My family thought they would certainly return to Prague after a few weeks, so it's odd that this portrait should be among the few belongings they packed for the trip to Budapest, then Trieste and Switzerland, and finally London, Toronto, and New York. I'm sure that the armchair in which my grandfather sat for his portrait and the large illustrated book he held in his lap were left behind, along with the house's rugs, tables, china, and silverware, as well as a full library of more books and paintings. Perhaps in the uncertainty of exile the family wanted some tangible reminder of home, of itself *as* a family, and found it in this painting. I often try to imagine their last day in Prague: In my romanticized view, my mother's widowed grandmother sits magisterially amid sheet-cloaked furniture, gripping (of all things) this bulky, life-sized portrait of her only son as she waits for her daughters to choose the few personal belongings they themselves can't do without.

No one from the family did return to Prague, of course, and the portrait has moved circuitously among various relatives for the past fifty years. When I rescued it from my mother's basement several years ago, it had lost its frame, started to sag in its blocking, and acquired scratches, nicks, and enough dust to muddy the blues and whites of Grandpa's sailor suit. It was also beginning to mildew. Yet, despite its wear-and-tear, it quickly became for me a link with the past as powerful as it had been for my great-grandmother, seeming at times even to spark memories I couldn't possibly have.

In 1985 I traveled to Prague for the first time. My grandfather had been back only once, in 1967, and was so disappointed with the change in the city that he vowed never to return. My mother once made it as far as Czechoslovakia's border with what was then West Germany, but she couldn't get an entry visa. So, with no small amount of self-importance, I saw my trip as a compensation, a return to Prague for those who will not or cannot go themselves. For I was not only visiting the city. I knew that I could also visit my grandfather's former house, now (in a complicated twist of fate) owned and used by the United States government, and would see all the family possessions it still holds.

I took numerous pictures of every room in the house. Looking at my photographs after I came home, my grandfather told me what had happened on his visit to Prague, twenty years earlier. Traveling through this house preserved much the way he had left it, he noticed many objects that called up sharp recollections of his early life—a pair of vases, for instance, monogrammed with his sisters' initials—and with the memories came an equally painful understanding that he couldn't take these items, now government property, back home with him. But when he browsed among the library shelves he came across a book on economics that he asked the official with him to let him have. In its margins were annotations my grandfather's father had scribbled in the twenties. My grandfather's request was honored—what use, after all, would a defaced volume of antiquated fiscal theory have for the government?—but everything else, including the hundreds of other books that my grandfather and his family once read, remain in Prague.

Something in those marginal notes—vague, arcane markings in German, the family language—allows my grandfather to measure his distance from his past, enables him to connect his childhood in Prague with his adulthood in American exile. The volume sits now among newer books, mostly histories of the war, on his shelves in New York, making continuity out of a fragmented, interrupted life, a literary binding. It is his exile reader.

The literary enthusiasms of another family figure, my mother's mother, also led me to assemble this anthology. Her children's anxious questions, accumulating unanswered over many years, have forced my grandmother to begin writing makeshift memoirs, long letters she sends to my mother, who photocopies and circulates them around the family. What began as one epic letter explaining how an English-born woman came to live in Madrid, Prague, New York, and finally California has since become an enormous undertaking: It is now ten years since she began chronicling her multiple displacements and she's only up to my mother's birth. But what has already emerged is a portrait of a woman accustomed to sequential emigrations and skilled in the task of adaptation. Now in her late eighties, long divorced from her husband and outliving her American friends, she talks of returning to Europe—not to England, she says, but perhaps Andorra, that tiny, anonymous border country made up of people from other countries.

This absence of uniform cultural identity is well suited to a woman who has never settled long in any home. And she proudly insists that her trip wouldn't constitute an exile's return but only another displacement, another challenge to her adaptability. Like my grandfather, reimagining Prague in the margins of an old book, she finds her only continuity, and perhaps her only residence, in prose, the letters she writes telling of coerced or welcomed trips abroad.

The writing I've collected in *Altogether Elsewhere* serves the same function. Like one relative's marginalia and another's epistolary chronicles, these essays, letters, journal entries, excerpts from memoirs, and random jottings are mere traces, notes written on the sides of literary careers usually devoted to fiction, poetry, criticism, or philosophy. But without them, much of that larger, more public, more ambitious work would lack a context. For it is in this occasional prose that these exiles write their history, place themselves, and orient their other writing. This writing is conjunctive, filling the interstices between the literary activity of two homes, one lost, one not yet familiar, neither of which they can occupy as natives. These pieces provide more portable shelters, prose in which the authors pass the time until larger homes, bigger books, are ready for their arrival.

I have organized this anthology with an elastic understanding of exile, and the writers I've selected address (and represent) a variety of displacements. Exile usually means political banishment: A person leaves his or her country to avoid harassment by the state; the state expels an individual for real or imaginary crimes. My Jewish grandfather escaping Prague embodies one segment in a spectrum of political exile that begins with the Babylonians and includes those in flight from the French Revolution, the revolutions of 1848, the Partitions of Poland, the Russian Revolution and Stalin's Great Terror, Franco and the Spanish Civil War, the regimes of Peron and Pol Pot, Budapest in 1956, Chile in 1971, South Africa, Palestine, Iraq, and Bosnia in recent years.

But my British grandmother represents another, equally prevalent style of exile. Her voluntary expatriation has its own long tradition, encompassing figures like Rousseau, Calvin, the English Romantic poets in Italy, Beckett, Joyce, the American writers in Paris, Auden in New York, Paul Bowles in Tangiers. As Mary McCarthy (another voluntary expatriate) observes in her own taxonomy of exile included here, these two forms of displacement have spawned their own variations, each of which tailors the abstract idea of exile to fit the shape of individual histories. The émigré settles into a permanence and optimism that elude the refugee. The restlessness of the nomad has greater purpose than the wanderings of the stateless. The inner exile retreats to the dark recesses of his or her own country, while the colonizer lays bare the darkness of foreign countries. The traveler moves with a surer gait and follows a looser rhythm than the tourist.

The meaning of exile expands as the terms denoting it proliferate, each label suggesting a slightly different cause of displacement and response to its rigors. Countries in which a simple world view saw only natives and visitors now also contain illegal aliens, migrant workers, "population transfers," pilgrims, emissaries, the "disenfranchised," loners, and even a few straggling descendants of Erasmus's militant Christian soldier. Often one figure moves through several stages of exile. My family followed the familiar path of those who start as travelers, following an itinerary with home as both origin and final destination. They soon found themselves stateless—and were considered refugees. Then they chose to regain some dignity by calling themselves exiles. Finally, resigned to their fate, they settled into being émigrés. Salman Rushdie has experienced one of the most harrowing variations on this pattern. He began by freely emigrating from India to England; now, in hiding from Muslim fundamentalists, he is an exile from his exile.

The circumstances and styles in which natives devolve into exiles may differ widely, but the dilemmas they confront are often the same for all displaced figures. Each loses the ability (or prerogative) to live comfortably at home, and must work more industriously than natives to fashion a sense of placement out of forbidding places. For many exiles, the first task is to determine just what kind of exile they have experienced. What brought them to this place? How far have they traveled, geographically and psychologically? Where, exactly, are they? Some search for models from whom they might learn answers to these questions, and on whose experiences they can base their own plans for the future. In the loneliness of exile, one welcomes a sense of fellowship wherever it is available. Many times, the most helpful and inspiring kindred spirits are long gone—Ovid, for instance, or Pushkin, or maybe even Hemingway—yet to the suspended contemporary writer they are the most accessible. Once an exile chooses to take a place alongside them, he or she enjoys a fresh sense of purpose and significance. A writer's private distress, especially troubling because so solitary, now seems an almost comforting variation on a theme. Exile cuts one off from familiar history, that of a native country and culture; in its place surfaces a history of exile. This history is steadily extended by new exiled writers, as they respond with their own experiences to ancient sadnesses, frustrations, and tales of the occasional epiphany.

Altogether Elsewhere begins with a section of essays that make such connections. In the public and private statements gathered under the rubric "Definitions," the writers orient themselves—and, I hope, orient readers of this anthology. Personal experience, in these pieces, becomes a springboard for general meditations on the subject of displacement; and the broad commentary, in turn, helps each writer clarify the confusion surrounding his or her private history. As these writers propose different categories of exile, they are giving structure to their own lives as well. Once they have achieved a sense of kinship with fellow exiles and erected a context for their experience, they are able to make the next important rescue: to distinguish their own displacements from those of others—and so restore their individuality. Banishment, and even less brutal forms of displacement, can turn lives into statistics. An exile's life, which at home was distinct and one of a kind, now matters less than the condition he or she shares with millions of others: One is an "exile" first and foremost. The shrewdest among the writers collected here emerge from the act of making definitions with a new sense of community that urges them to create a new sense of self.

Subsequent sections of *Altogether Elsewhere* address the various challenges facing exiles after they announce their arrival and then resume artistic work, participate in the rituals of declaring loyalties and forging friendships, and fulfill all the petty obligations of day-to-day living. In a sense, all the sections of this anthology show writers continuing to make definitions: Exiles expand their understanding of their condition and their new identities in public and domestic spheres, renovating their beliefs under the pressures of a strange land. In the high thin air of exile, one learns to see multiple significances in even the smallest sensation. A private moment of remembering a favorite site back home, for instance, can resonate in political, historical, psychological, and artistic chambers. The questions spill forth unbidden from such a meditation: Where will you place your loyalties? What will inspire you? In what culture will you participate? As exile continues, the blurred impressions about the new home coalesce into "viewpoints"; fleeting memories lead to more considered declarations of patriotism, or quiet fidelity, or outright renunciation; the many small encounters in the give-and-take of living in exile become the material from which the exile can, if he or she wishes, develop a code of behavior. This process is the subject of the second section, "Allegiances."

Most of the selections in this section are expansive and declamatory, addressed, in some cases, more to natives than to exiles. From Victor Hugo's indignant manifesto through the exultantly patriotic testimony of Mary Antin to the more anguished meditations of Marina Tsvetaeva and Hilde Domin, these pieces work through matters of social responsibility. Many exiles see their lives as emblematic of a nation's fate, their own mistreatment a symptom of something larger and malignant. In these writings, they forge a new relationship with their forsaken country. Often they indict the cause of their humiliation (if that is what they feel); sometimes they wave the image of their new freedom back toward those who would deny it and ahead to those who, in the exiles' new home, take such privilege for granted. In many of these pieces, the writers seem to be tearing up old, cruel laws and laying down new ones, creating an ethics of exile, or at least a protocol. It's as though they need the security of dogma, in the shape of opposition or commitment, in order to make their way through the less traveled corridors of their private lives—their evenings away from the crowd of admirers in the new country, and also away from the waiting eyes and ears of those back home. Both audiences seem eager to claim the exiles as their country's conscience.

When faced with their own consciences, some exiles panic: The desolation is too great, the image of all that has been lost overwhelms whatever new challenges present themselves. For some exiles, their natural sadness softens into self-pity; the exiles sink into themselves further as natives offer added pity for such a sorry state. In "Lessons and Opportunities," the third section, several writers try to reverse this inward spiral. Few of them have much patience with the standard response to exile: despair. They wrench an exile away from a fixed stare at the past and redirect attention to the busy, challenging present and wide-open future. The experience of exile teaches a particular kind of discipline and adaptability—an awareness of what is essential in life, and what is mere decor. Exiles are also less prone than most natives to provinciality and purblind nationalism; as Edward Said writes, they "break barriers of thought and experience" that most natives can't even see. Unfettered by old obligations, unswayed by cultural assumptions, blissfully unheedful (at least for a moment) of the customs of the country, the most energetic exiles have the opportunity to see things from an unvisited perspective—to enjoy a degree of sensitivity and acuity unavailable to most non-exiles. They also regularly enjoy the pleasure of surprise—often at the least consequential things. (Such frequent surprise has long since faded for most non-exiles, who must turn to the "exotic" to enjoy wonder.)

In *The Book of Laughter and Forgetting,* Milan Kundera describes how his heroine, Tamina, begins to cope with life in exile. She writes compulsively, longing "to fill in the fragile framework of events in a new notebook, give it walls, make it a house she can live in." The section in *Altogether Elsewhere* about "Speaking and Writing" shows how several other writers make their own houses out of writing. For some, one's first language becomes an essential, protective shell in a forbidding new world. For others, such as Eva Hoffman, the new language offers continuous pleasures despite its mysteries: As each phrase is mastered another whole world comes into view. Whatever language exiles favor, writing offers them territory that they alone can legislate. The page becomes one of the few spaces where others aren't telling them how to behave. Writing also allows a return home: Exiles can travel back and forth between two languages, or two versions of the same language, retrieving ideas left behind (those that can only be expressed in native speech) and venturing deeper into a new land than they could on foot. During the labor of translating what they remember and encounter on these journeys, they are also translating themselves.

The constant threat of solitude in exile increases the value of language as a sustaining link to old and new worlds. Many exiles implicitly suggest that, for them, writing can no longer be private or inward-looking, no matter how much they would like it to be. From even the most reserved writer, some words written in exile can't help but sound like poignant, embarrassed pleas for attention—ways of reaching toward an indifferent group of people, potential readers who might anchor the writer with their interest. Other words are hopeful reachings-back to readers no longer known. Many exiles start magazines and presses that publish in their language or feature their culture. (Mary McCarthy discusses some of the most prominent.) Several contributors to this anthology wouldn't have survived as writers were it not for journals like the Paris-based *transition* (which published Kay Boyle and Harry Crosby), Josef Skvorecky and Zdena Salivarova's Czech-language Sixty-Eight Publishers in Toronto (which distributed in Canada and spirited into Prague clandestine novels by Jan

Novak), or the Ardis firm in Michigan (which makes available to émigrés many banned Russian classics, among them the works of Tsvetaeva).

An exile's native language lives in these publications, and he or she uses them to organize entire regions of a lost heritage inside the otherwise impenetrable new country. Magazines spawn readings, which in turn lead to discussion groups. As discussion proliferates, and the exile's living room becomes too crowded, restaurants and bars open, serving native specialities to accompany native controversies. Then cultural centers emerge, followed soon by businesses, political blocs, and, in some cases, governments-in-exile. An entire surrogate society evolves and replaces the one left behind. It fortifies the exiles, ensures that they won't lose their natural identities amid the seductions of a foreign culture.

But does the exile's solitude ever really lift? Most contributors to *Altogether Elsewhere* imply that it doesn't; some see their detachment most clearly at the moment of meeting someone new. The essays occasioned by these self-interrogations (and gathered in the section called "Solitudes") are, to some degree, correctives. They correct an exile's own illusions, as James Baldwin's does, and also the misapprehensions of the witnesses to exile. Exile rarely makes for good melodrama or *Sturm und Drang*. As with every writer, the lows are usually banal, the highs depend more on hard work than dreamy inspiration. After the shock of arrival subsides, many exiled writers find mundane schedules and conventional habits reassuring, if they're lucky enough to acquire them. All else in their lives may be topsy-turvy, but at least the same hour late at night can be reserved for tinkering on a poem; the morning coffee can always be brewed to the desired strength; and the garden grows as planned. Many of the pieces in "Solitudes," written in a minor key, isolate meditative moments of little apparent significance to anyone but the authors, happening far from the public stage where an exile's every action seems symbolic. Whatever lessons are to be learned come accidentally.

For Rousseau and Petrarch, the solitude is glorious; for others, it is disorienting, if not agonizing. One writer's chance encounter with a stranger throws into sudden relief an aspect of his own temperament, revealing convictions and long-ignored anxieties. Amid the rushing self-importance on a city's streets, or in the secluded corners of a bar where intimacies never seem untoward, other exiles see for the first time the true dimensions of their lives, and understand finally that exile will forever be shuttling them from anonymity to celebrity and back again—day in, day out. There is little glamour in this, but then why should there be? Only when the business of "being in exile" subsides can they start doing what they have been meaning to do all along, and what probably sent them into exile in the first place: writing. The art won't be glamorous either: These writers record all the betrayals that, as Baldwin reminds us, make up the bulk of exile—the slow realization that what the exiles thought they were seeking in a new country wasn't available, that what they hoped to escape was inescapable, and that what they never dreamed of getting, they got.

Altogether Elsewhere ends with a selection of writings that raises the inevitable subject of return. If these pieces are any indication, few exiles, no matter how fully they assimilate into new societies, ever succeed in muffling their own persistent questions about what is going on "back home," and what it would feel like to see for themselves. In several of these chronicles of return trips, the illusions about one's native land shatter as quickly as did those about exile. The climate has changed, the mores shifted, the tone in which people talk sounds different, the usual direction in which they think has detoured, the objects of their faith and the fruits of their imagination are no longer what they once were. Or at least this is how things seem. Those homelands where nothing has changed are even more disconcerting: Didn't the exile's departure disrupt anything? Didn't it force a reassessment of general social principles? Didn't anyone notice that someone was missing?

Clichés along the lines of "you can't go home again" don't begin to respond to the mix of distress and pride, wonder and disgust, fear and unexpected anger that overtakes an exile at the moment of return. Nor do they explain why many exiles choose to remain abroad even when they can freely return home. Furthermore, for every exile who painstakingly lays a foundation of friendships and builds up a new home resistant to political storms, there is another kind of exile who refuses any home, even when its doors are flung open wide and the comforts are ample. Uprooting can be habit-forming, the only constant in a life defined by inconstancy. The sharpened sensitivity that one experiences after the first displacement is addictive. The attention span of this kind of exiled writer is short; the blood-pressure high; the longing for startling sensations insatiable. These exiles feel most present when presence is only temporary, when they are on the move. Their returns are always followed by fresh departures; their exile is regularly reaffirmed.

The writing of the perpetual wanderers in this final section strives to retain their fervor. Each sentence seems to burst with anticipation about the next sentence; each paragraph or stanza marks a momentary layover, followed by a quick intake of breath, on a racing excursion without destination. The writing, and the writer, don't stop long enough to become recognizable—and so achieve what every exile wants: an identity that cannot be compared to others; work that forever eludes categories (and anthologies); a style that scorns national habits of glibness and never matches the common pitch—a writing life, in short, that keeps its observers looking to see when the nomad will next burst forth, then greeting him or her with all the earnest concern they reserve for new arrivals and rare visitors.

It's probable that readers who, like me, are not exiles themselves will come to this anthology conditioned to respond with awe at the exiles' endurance and civic-minded compassion for their plight. How could we not, given their often heroic stories? Yet once the luster of those stories wears off, something vexing remains. The very impressiveness of the exiles' example can stir us to leave off pitying them, and instead to almost envy them their opportunity, and then to consider ourselves. The lessons of exile, they imply, can profitably be studied by natives, too. For the native writer, such lessons have particular force: They challenge the central assumptions of his or her craft.

As one begins to count just how many hundreds of valued writers have been in exile of one form or another, an attractively neat formula begins to take shape: Is writing itself a form of exile? It's tempting to say yes, and then feel suitably aggrieved and noble. Yet the equation isn't specific enough. Most writing happens too far inside society's magic circle of fashion and received wisdom to recall an exile's distinctive voice. Closer to the truth might be an inversion of the formula. As an expatriate writer said to me, "one isn't in exile merely because one writes; one writes because one is in exile." She might have added, "one *must* write." (How many native writers could sincerely echo Kay Boyle and title a collection *Words That Must Somehow Be Said*?) The necessity of writing is often palpable in an exile's words, and distinguishes his or her work from most other literature. From a native's perspective, this sense of necessity is also enviable—differently inflected from even his or her most engaged and urgent writing about exile: For the exile, the commitment is not voluntary.

In the best work by exiles, one senses that the poem or story is doing more than just capturing an object of the writer's scanning eye. Each piece also honors the continuation of writing itself. Exiled writers remind readers (and themselves) that their imagination and craft haven't been mortally damaged by the uprooting; each new piece is a gesture of defiance, a spiting of the odds. Some exiled writers seem to hover over their writing even after it has been published, loath to be severed once again from something intimately known and thus exiled from their art. Each work is also something of a mapping device. As they write, exiles resemble blind bats who emit chirps in order to hear them bounce against buildings and trees: From the echoes they can determine where they are. In making their own acts of verification, many exiles seem to believe that by recording what they imagine in a place, they will know the place, prove that they are there, and maybe even learn how to move on to the next stop.

The business of verification is unending, and so demands from exiles an astonishing degree of patience. William Gass, not an exile by conventional definitions, nonetheless feels lost in a culture that is itself in a kind of exile from its own language—or, more precisely, from the thrill of being amazed by words, a thrill that many "literal" exiles are lucky to experience every day. Most native speakers, he implies in an essay collected here, use words unthinkingly. They toss them around in predictable rhythms, organize them in dull, time-honored arrangements—and rarely pause long enough over their phrases, or stop and listen to the sound of their voices, at least not with the sensitivity exiles must learn if they are to make their art live for others. One rarely senses in the work of non-exiles, no matter how "alienated" they feel, the same anxiety over simple constructions, or sees so clearly the evidence of multiple revisions, or hears so distinctly the small sigh of satisfaction as each thought makes it out of the imagination one at a time—intact and intelligible. As I read over the essays collected here, particularly those in which the writer uses English as a second language, I read also a long history of effort behind even the pronouns and articles. Unlike many of their native colleagues, these writers actually earn their pride of authorship. After showing such care in committing ideas to print, they truly can feel that one more mystery has been faced squarely, if never quite solved. For just as they can no longer take for granted the basics of language, neither can they take for granted the essential aspects of, say, narrative. The old metaphors don't quite capture the same experiences when they happen in the new setting. A story or a conversation among characters unfolds at a different pace. Everything must be renamed.

One doesn't need to be a writer, of course, to feel humbled by an exile's persistence and patience. And the lessons that these writers teach by example need not be applied only in the act of writing. Writing may provide exiles with a refuge, but it also becomes a training ground in which they can master the skills necessary to sort through the confusion outside. As they renegotiate their relationship with words, they are also renegotiating their relationship with the world. Many of the exiles gathered here invite their readers to make the same connection: As we read their words, the exiles seem to ask, shouldn't we also be rethinking the way we "read"—or experience—our own world?

Their question is something of a dare; the difficulty of answering it accounts for my ongoing obsession with exile. In principle, one certainly would wish to emulate an exile's acute consciousness and share his or her innate understanding that each moment is weighted with significance. The exile has much at stake with just about every breath and glance. Each movement seems like a statement of principles, one more proposal in a lengthy deliberation over how best to live. Many exiles seem mesmerized by the simplest daily routines, as though they believe that buried in each day's experience lies another key to their future, one that they will discover only through unblinking awareness. Of course, many exiles are on their guard (against abandonment and others' indifference, among other things) at the same time as they are pleasurably engrossed in the moments as they pass. But then, the writers in *Altogether Elsewhere* have found an opportunity in that nervousness, too.

George Steiner has identified the border as one of the most powerful inventions shaping the modern mind. Its variants are everywhere we look: thresholds, fences, bridges, and tollbooths; doormen and ticket-takers; air-rights and "glass ceilings"; the layers of the psyche and the class system. For exiles, the border is their only reliable home: They are never able to settle fully on either side. Standing forever on the frontier, exiles seem frozen at the moment of arrival—wide-eyed and feverish. Yet their stance could also mark the expectant moment of departure. The border instructs exiles in readiness: They peer ahead, yet look back over their shoulders. They hold their ground, yet ponder the many available directions. They feel the fullness of the earth supporting their weight—there is so little earth to call their own—yet they also could float away at any moment. On the border, exiles make their lives over from scratch. They don't have any choice. Observing them, the natives among us begin to develop our own sense of readiness—to join the exiles on the border, and for a moment to feel nowhere at home, if only to see better where we've been living. I hope that *Altogether Elsewhere* expands the dimensions of those borders, and returns them to the map not only as tools that define places, but also as places of their own—always filling with settlers too busy asking questions to unpack.

I
Definitions

Emigrés: earn living by teaching guitar and waiting on tables.

—Gustave Flaubert
Dictionary of Accepted Ideas

The Condition We Call Exile

An Address

Joseph Brodsky

AS WE GATHER HERE, in this attractive and well-lit room, on this cold December evening, to discuss the plight of the writer in exile, let us pause for a minute and imagine some of those who, quite naturally, didn't make it to this room. Let us imagine, for instance, Turkish *Gastarbeiters* prowling the streets of West Germany, uncomprehending or envious of the surrounding reality. Or let us imagine Vietnamese boat people bobbing on high seas or already settled somewhere in the Australian outback. Let us imagine Mexican wetbacks crawling the ravines of southern California, past the border patrols into the territory of the United States. Or let us imagine shiploads of Pakistanis disembarking somewhere in Kuwait or Saudi Arabia, hungry for menial jobs the oil-rich locals won't do. Let us imagine multitudes of Ethiopians trekking some desert on foot into Somalia—or is it the other way around?—escaping the famine. Well, we may stop here because that minute of imagining has already passed, although a great many could be added to this list. Nobody ever counted these people and nobody, including the UN relief organizations, ever will: coming in the millions, they elude computation and constitute what is called—for want of a better term or a higher degree of compassion—migration.

Whatever the proper name for these people, whatever their motives, origins, and destinations, whatever their impact on the societies which they abandon and to which they come may amount to—one thing is absolutely clear: they make it very difficult to talk about the plight of the writer in exile with a straight face.

Yet talk we must; and not only because literature, like poverty, is known for taking care of its own kind, but more because of the ancient and perhaps as yet unfounded belief that should the masters of this world be better read, the mismanagement and grief that make millions take to the road could be somewhat reduced. Since there is not much on which to rest our hopes for a better world, since everything else seems to fail one way or another, we must somehow maintain that literature is the only form of moral insurance a society has; that it is the permanent antidote to the dog-eat-dog principle; that it provides the best argument against any sort of bulldozer-type mass solution—if only because human diversity is literature's lock and stock, as well as its raison d'être.

We must talk because we must insist that literature is the greatest—surely greater than any creed—teacher of human subtlety, and that by interfering with literature's natural existence and with people's ability to learn literature's lessons, a society reduces its own potential, slows down the pace of its evolution, ultimately, perhaps, puts its own fabric in peril. If this means that we must talk about ourselves, so much the better: not for ourselves, but perhaps for literature.

Whether he likes it or not, *Gastarbeiters* and refugees of any stripe effectively pluck the carnation out of an exiled writer's lapel. Displacement and misplacement are this century's commonplace. And what our exiled writer has in common with a *Gastarbeiter* or a political refugee is that in either case a man is running away from the worse toward the better. The truth of the matter is that from a tyranny one can be exiled only to a democracy. For the old gray mare of exile ain't what it used to be. It isn't leaving civilized Rome for savage Sarmatia anymore, nor is it sending a man from, say, Bulgaria to China. No, as a rule what takes place is a transition from a political and economic backwater to an industrially advanced society with the last word on individual liberty on its lips. And it must be added that perhaps taking this route is for an exiled writer, in many ways, like going home—because he gets closer to the seat of the ideals that inspired him all along.

If one would assign the life of an exiled writer a genre, it would have to be tragicomedy. Because of his previous incarnation, he is capable of appreciating the social and material advantages of democracy far more intensely than its natives are. Yet for precisely the same reason (whose main byproduct is the linguistic barrier) he finds himself totally unable to play any meaningful role in his new society. The democracy into which he has arrived provides him with physical safety but renders him socially insignificant. And the lack of significance is what no writer, exile or not, can take.

For it is the quest for significance that very often constitutes the rest of his career. To say the least, it is very often a literary career's consequence. In the case of an exiled writer, it is almost invariably the cause of his exile. And one is terribly tempted to add here that the existence of this desire in a writer is the conditioned response on his part to the vertical structure of his original society. (On the part of a writer living in a free society, the presence of this desire bespeaks the atavistic memory every democracy has of its unconstitutional past.)

In this respect, the plight of an exiled writer is indeed much worse than that of a *Gastarbeiter* or the average refugee. His appetite for recognition makes him restless and oblivious to the superiority of his income as a college teacher, lecturer, little magazine editor, or just a contributor—for these are the most frequent occupations of exiled authors nowadays—over the wages of somebody doing menial work. That is, our man is a little bit corrupt, almost by definition. But then the sight of a writer rejoicing in insignificance, in being left alone, in anonymity is about as rare as that of a cockatoo at the Polar Circle, even under the best possible circumstances. Among exiled writers, this attitude is almost totally absent. At least it is absent in this room. Understandably so, of course, but saddening nonetheless.

It is saddening because if there is anything good about exile, it is that it teaches humility. One can even take it a step further and suggest that the exile's is the ultimate lesson in that virtue. And that it is especially priceless for a writer because it puts him into the longest possible perspective. "And thou art far in humanity," as Keats said. To be lost in mankind, in the crowd—crowd?—among billions; to become a needle in that proverbial haystack—but a needle somebody is searching for—that's what exile is all about. Pull down your vanity, it says, you are but a grain of sand in the desert. Measure yourself not against your fellow penmen but against human infinity: it is about as bad as the inhuman one. Out of that you should speak, not out of your envy or your ambition.

Needless to say, this call goes unheeded. Somehow a commentator on life prefers his position to his subject and, when in exile, he considers that position grim enough not to aggravate it any further, and such calls inappropriate. He may be right, although calls for humility are always timely. For the other truth of the matter is that exile is a metaphysical condition. At least, it has a very strong, very clear metaphysical dimension, and to ignore or to dodge it is to cheat yourself out of the meaning of what has happened to you, to doom yourself to remaining forever at the receiving end of things, to ossify into an uncomprehending victim.

It is because of the absence of good examples that one cannot describe an alternative mode of conduct (although Milosz or Musil come to mind). Maybe this is just as well, because we are here evidently to talk about the reality of exile, not about its potential. And the reality of it consists of an exiled writer constantly fighting and conspiring to restore his significance, his poignant role, his authority. His main consideration, of course, is the folks back home; but he also wants to rule the roost in the malicious village of his fellow émigrés.

Playing ostrich to the metaphysics of his situation, he concentrates on the immediate and tangible. This means besmirching colleagues in a similar predicament; bilious polemics with rival publications; innumerable interviews for the BBC, *Deutsche Viele*, ORTF, and the Voice of America; open letters; statements for the press; going to conferences—you name it. The energy previously spent in food lines or petty officials' musty anterooms is now released and gone rampant. Unchecked by anyone, let alone by his kin (for he is himself now a Caesar's wife, as it were, and beyond suspicion—how could his maybe-even-literate-but-aging spouse correct or contradict her certified martyr?), his ego grows rapidly in diameter and eventually, filled with CO_2, lifts him from reality—especially if he resides in Paris, where the Mongolfiere brothers set up the precedent.

Traveling by balloon is always precipitous and, above all, unpredictable: too easily one becomes a plaything of winds, in this case, of political winds, which are anything but *Passete* [tradewinds]. Small wonder then that our navigator keenly listens to all the forecasts, and on occasion ventures to predict the weather himself. That is, not the weather of wherever he starts or finds himself en route, but the weather at his destination, for our balloonist is invariably homebound. And perhaps the third truth of the matter is that a writer in exile is by and large a retrospective and retroactive being. In other words, retrospection plays an excessive role—compared with other people's lives—in his existence, overshadowing his reality and dimming the future into something thicker than its usual pea soup. Like the false prophets of Dante's *Inferno*, his head is forever turned backward and his tears, or saliva, are running down between his shoulder blades. Whether or not he is of elegiac disposition by nature is beside the point: doomed to a limited audience abroad, he cannot help pining for the multitudes, real or imagined, left behind. The way the former fills him with venom, the latter fuels his fantasy. Even having gained the freedom to travel, even having actually done some traveling, he will stick in his writing to the familiar material of his past, producing, as it were, sequels to his previous works. Approached on this subject, an exiled writer will most likely evoke Ovid's Rome, Dante's Florence, and—after a small pause—Joyce's Dublin.

Indeed, we've got a pedigree, and a much longer one than that. If one wants, one can trace it all the way back to Adam. And yet we should be careful about the place it tends to occupy in the public's and our own minds. We all know what happens to many a noble family over generations or in the course of a revolution. Family trees never make or obscure the forest; and the wood is now advancing. I am mixing metaphors here, but perhaps I can justify my doing this by remarking that to expect for ourselves the kind of future that we associate with the above-mentioned few is imprudent rather than immodest. Of course a writer always takes himself posthumously: and an exiled writer especially so, inspired not so much by the artificial oblivion to which he is subjected by his former state as by the way the critical profession in the free marketplace enthuses about his contemporaries. Yet one should go carefully about this type of self-estrangement, not for any other reason than the realization that, with the population explosion, literature, too, took on the dimensions of a demographic phenomenon.

There are today simply too many writers around per reader. A couple of decades ago a grown man thinking about books or authors as yet to be read would come up with thirty, forty names; nowadays these names will run in the thousands. Today one walks into a bookstore the way one enters a music shop stuffed with recorded groups and soloists, listening to whom would take more than a lifetime. And very few among those thousands are exiles or particularly good. But the public will read them, and not you, in spite of your halo, not because it is perverse or misguided but because statistically it is on the side of normalcy and trash. In other words, it wants to read about itself. On any street of any city in the world at any time of night or day there are more people who haven't heard of you than those who have.

The current interest in the literature of exiles has to do, of course, with the rise of tyrannies. Herein perhaps lies our chance with the future reader, though that's the kind of insurance one would like to do without. Partly because of this noble caveat, but mainly because he can't think of the future in any other than the glowing terms of his triumphant return, an exiled writer sticks to his guns. But then why shouldn't he? Why should he try to use anything else, why should he bother probing the future in any other fashion, since it is unpredictable anyhow? The good old stuff served him well at least once: it earned him exile. And exile, after all, is a kind of success. Why not try another tack? Why not push the good old stuff around a bit more? Apart from anything else, now it constitutes ethnographic material, and that goes over big with your Western, Northern, or (if you run afoul of a right-wing tyranny) even Eastern publisher. And there is always the chance of a masterpiece when you go over the same turf twice, a possibility that doesn't escape the eye of your publisher, either, or at least it may provide future scholars with the notion of a "myth-making" element in your work.

But however practical sounding, these are secondary or tertiary among the reasons that keep an exiled writer's eyes firmly trained on his past. The main explanation lies in the aforementioned retrospective machinery that gets unwittingly triggered within one by the least evidence of one's surroundings' strangeness. Sometimes the shape of a maple leaf is enough, and each tree has thousands of these. On an animal level, this retrospective machinery is constantly in motion in an exiled writer, nearly always unbeknown to him. Whether pleasant or dismal, the past is always a safe territory, if only because it is already experienced; and the species' capacity to revert, to run backward—especially in its thoughts or dreams, since there we are generally safe as well—is extremely strong in all of us, quite irrespective of the reality we are facing. Yet this machinery has been built into us not for cherishing or grasping the past (in the end, we don't do either), but more for delaying the arrival of the present—for, in other words, slowing down a bit the passage of time. See the fatal exclamation of Goethe's Faust.

The whole point about our exiled writer is that he, too, like Goethe's Faust, clings to his "fair," or not so fair, "moment," not for beholding it but in order to postpone the next one. It's not that he wants to be young again; he simply doesn't want tomorrow to arrive because he knows that it may edit what he beholds. And the more tomorrow presses on him, the more obstinate he becomes. There is terrific value in this obstinacy: with luck, it may amount to intensity of concentration and then, indeed, we may get a great work of literature (the reading public and the publishers sense that, and therefore—as I've already said—they keep an eye on the literature of exiles). More often, however, this obstinacy translates itself into the repetitiveness of nostalgia, which is, to put it bluntly, simply a failure to deal with the realities of the present or the uncertainties of the future.

One can of course help matters somewhat by changing one's narrative manner, by making it more avant-garde, by spicing the stuff with a good measure of eroticism, violence, foul language, etc., after the fashion of one's free-market colleagues. But stylistic shifts and innovations greatly depend on the condition of the literary idiom "back there," at home, the links with which have been severed. As for the spice, a writer, exiled or not, never wants to appear to be influenced by his contemporaries. Perhaps an additional truth about the matter is that exile slows down one's stylistic evolution, that it makes a writer more conservative. Style is not so much the man as the man's nerves, and on the whole exile provides one's nerves with fewer irritants than the motherland does. This condition, it must be added, somewhat worries an exiled writer, not only because he regards existence back home as more genuine than his own (by definition, and with all attendant or imagined consequences for normal literary process), but because in his mind there exists a suspicion of a pendulum-like dependency, or ratio, between those irritants and his mother tongue.

One ends up in exile for a variety of reasons and under a number of circumstances. Some of them are better sounding, some worse, but the difference ceases to matter already by the time one reads an obituary. On the bookshelf your place will be occupied not by you but by your book. And as long as they insist on making a distinction between art and life, it is better if they find your book good and your life foul than the other way around. Chances are, of course, that they won't care for either.

Life in exile, abroad, in a foreign element, is essentially a premonition of your fate in book form, of being lost on the shelf among those with whom all you have in common is the first letter of your surname. Here you are, in some gigantic library's reading room, still open. . . . Your reader won't give a damn about how you got here: in a certain perspective, all that he reads merges. To keep yourself from getting closed and shelved you've got to tell your reader who thinks he knows it all something qualitatively novel—about his world and himself. If this sounds a bit too suggestive, so be it, because suggestion is the name of the entire game anyhow, and because the distance exile puts between an author and his characters indeed sometimes begs for the use of astronomical or ecclesiastical symbols.

This is what makes one think that "exile" is, perhaps, not the most apt term to describe the condition of a writer forced (by the state, by fear, by poverty, by boredom) to abandon his country. "Exile" covers, at best, the very moment of departure, of expulsion; what follows is both too comfortable and too autonomous to be called by this name, which so strongly suggests a comprehensible grief. The very fact of our gathering here indicates that if we indeed have a common denominator, it lacks a name. Are we suffering the same degree of despair, ladies and gentlemen? Are we equally severed from our public? Do we all reside in Paris? No, but what binds us is our book-like fate, the same literal and symbolic lying open on the table or the floor of that gigantic library, at its various ends, to be trampled on or picked up by a mildly curious reader or—worse—by a dutiful librarian. The qualitatively novel stuff we may tell that reader about is this autonomous, spacecraft-like mentality, which, I am sure, visits every one of us but whose visitations most of our pages choose not to acknowledge.

We do this for practical, as it were, or genre considerations. Because this way lies either madness or the degree of coldness associated rather with the paleface locals than with a hot-blooded exile. The other way, however, lies—and close, too—banality. All of this may sound to you like a typically Russian job of issuing guidelines for literature, while, in fact, it is simply one man's reactions to finding many an exiled author—Russian ones in the first place—on the banal side of virtue. That is a great waste, because one more truth about the condition we call exile is that it accelerates tremendously one's otherwise professional flight—or drift—into isolation, into an absolute perspective: into the condition in which all one is left with is oneself and one's own language, with nobody or nothing in between.

Exile brings you overnight where it normally would take a lifetime to go. If this sounds like a commercial, so be it, because it is about time to sell this idea. Because I indeed wish it had more takers. Perhaps a metaphor will help: to be an exiled writer is like being a dog or a man hurtled into outer space in a capsule (more like a dog, of course, than a man, because they will never bother to retrieve you). And your capsule is your language. To finish the metaphor off, it must be added that before long the passenger discovers that the capsule gravitates not earthward but outward in space.

For one in our profession, the condition we call exile is, first of all, a linguistic event: an exiled writer is thrust, or retreats, into his mother tongue. From being his, so to speak, sword, it turns into his shield, into his capsule. What started as a private, intimate affair with the language, in exile becomes fate—even before it becomes an obsession or a duty. A living language, by definition, has a centrifugal propensity—and propulsion; it tries to cover as much ground as possible—and as much emptiness as possible. Hence the population explosion, and hence your autonomous passage outward, into the domain of the telescope or a prayer.

In a manner of speaking, we all work for a dictionary. Because literature *is* a dictionary, a compendium of meanings for this or that human lot, for this or that experience. It is a dictionary of the language in which life speaks to man. Its function is to save the next man, a new arrival, from falling into an old trap, or to help him realize, should he fall into that trap anyway, that he has been hit by a tautology. This way he will be less impressed—in a way, more free. For to know the meaning of life's terms, of what is happening to you, is liberating. It would seem to me that the condition we call exile is due for a fuller explication; that, famous for its pain, it should also be known for its pain-dulling infiniteness, for its forgetfulness, detachment, indifference, for its terrifying human and inhuman vistas for which we have no yardstick except ourselves.

We must make it easier for the next man, if we can't make it safer. And the only way to make it easier for him, to make him less frightened of it, is to give him the whole measure of it—that is, as much as we ourselves can manage to cover. We may argue about our responsibilities and loyalties (toward our respective contemporaries, motherlands, other-lands, cultures, traditions, etc.) ad infinitum, but this responsibility, or rather, opportunity to set the next man—however theoretical he and his needs may be—a bit more free shouldn't become a subject for hesitation. If all this sounds to you a bit too lofty and humanistic, then I am sorry about it. It is actually not so much humanistic as deterministic, although one shouldn't bother about making such subtle distinctions. All I am trying to say is that, given an opportunity, in the great causal chain of things, we may as well stop being just its rattling effects and try to play at causes. The condition we call exile gives exactly that kind of opportunity.

Yet if we don't use it, if we decide to remain effects and play at exile in an old-fashioned way, that shouldn't be explained away as *nostalgie de la* boot. Of course it has to do with the necessity of telling about oppression, and of course our condition should serve as a warning to any thinking man toying with the idea of an ideal society. That is our value for the free world. That is our function.

But perhaps our greater value and greater function lie in our being unwitting embodiments of the disheartening idea that a freed man is not a free man, that liberation is just the means of attaining freedom and is not synonymous with it. This highlights the extent of the damage that can be done to the species, and we can feel proud of playing this role. However, if we want to play a bigger role, the role of a free man, then we should be capable of accepting—or at least imitating—the manner in which a free man fails. A free man, when he fails, blames nobody.

A Letter from Exile, to Don Espejuelo

Breyten Breytenbach

Dear Don,

YOU HAVE ASKED ME several times now what it is like to be living in exile. Let us then, as the saying goes, bring light to bear upon the matter. That is, let us be absolutely clear (I am eaten alive by the need to become clear): I am not an exile. I am not even an expatriate. I may be considered, I suppose, an *émigré*.

Why I say that? For several reasons. First because technically and legally I am not. No longer am I a political refugee: since December 1983 I have been a naturalized French citizen. For the first time in my adult life I can now live somewhere without being a 'foreigner' needing a *carte de séjour*: and I can cross most borders without the hassle of obtaining visas or worrying whether my forged documents will pass close scrutiny. I can be poor if I want to; I can go to Africa; I could even vote! No political refugee any more, but should we not look closer at the notion of 'cultural refugee'?

You see, I feel quite at ease in Paris. You mustn't forget that I had been living 'abroad' for well on fourteen years before going on extended leave into South Africa's intestines, and that returning from there on the fifth day of December 1982 was very much like 'coming home'. Remember too that I had been formed—or deformed if you wish—from an impressionable age, by the Parisian way of life, by European culture. Recently I came across a poem by a Latin American cosmopolitan, one of the *métèques* of many nations living in the capital, which said more or less: 'La France aux Français; Paris est à nous!'

Even now I am writing in the language of the hereditary enemy—English. With the consoling knowledge that in so doing I go to sea in a basket like all the other non-Anglos: the Indians and the Nigerians and the many-tongued Americans . . . I also write in French. Primly and properly so. With the requisite 'redundant' demagogic phraseology, stylishly crafted. I have caught on to the tune even if the words still elude me. In fact, a Ghanaian writer reviewing *Confessions* criticized me for using Gallicisms . . . Nevertheless, I remain the only Afrikaans-writing French poet.

Is the *émigré* author a parrot? You could say that I ought to be able to give a passable imitation of the European. Exiled? But then, can you imagine a more pleasant place of exile, had that been my fate, than Paris?

The implication, you may wish to remark, seems to be that my sojourn in No Man's Land burned me clean of any attachment to that ancestral earth. Yes and no. It is true that I experience a profound revulsion, shot through with pity, when I think of the Afrikaners, when I even hear Afrikaans! (The pity comes from seeing them foundering apathetically in the mire of their own making—a compassion one senses, for different reasons, for other population groups also. But disgust and pity remain debilitating sentiments.) And yet I feel that my entanglement with the continent has become more complex, my rooting more painful, my involvement deeper, my concern more acute. The hills, the smells, the birdflight, the boom of breakers and the rustle of wind through frost-crystallized grass, the pairing dance of cloud and sky—these and all the other shadings of memory have entered unto me; they are the ground of my being. John Coetzee, in a rather querulous review I came across, remarks upon the Afrikaner's attachment to the land. He implies that the Afrikaner writer's passionate and mystical descriptions of flatland and hillock exclude the non-Afrikaners, and in fact aver: this is our land, you don't belong here. An interesting point (forgetting for the time being that his own books are essentially a communion with the surroundings), and upsetting when you remember the Teutonic obsession with *Blut und Boden.* And it is indeed curious that the White African writer should be so acutely aware of the landscape, as if he needs to reaffirm his puny presence, or exorcize its cruelty or its hostility, or lay claim to it, or tame it by words—whereas the Black African writer quite obviously accepts the land as his natural and unquestioned dimensions.

But more than the land I have a sense of closeness with the people. Not an exclusive sentiment: I feel I can identify from within with all the poor bastards of that ravaged country—the cocky but obtuse White peasant boy, the insufferable captain of industry brimming over with charitable comprehension, the snooty city Jew, the tattooed Brown *skollie* or the prissy Coloured intellectual, the Indian coolie or the silly chap in business, the low-profiled Chinaman, the Black *tsotsi* or the African migrant labourer. Prison has destroyed the barriers and broken the stays.

More than any of these I feel an association with the human forces battling for betterment, projecting revolution—when that is the transformation of a stultified and fear-frozen society to one of greater social justice. I can identify with the good, with the potential good (the generosity, the solidarity, the tenderness, the will to resist, the respect for the other) to be found in some measure in any South African; knowing at the same time that the percentage of rottenness in that individual, as in me (the corruption, the collaboration, the hate, the despair, the dumbness and the numbness, the apathy, the hypocrisy), will be preponderant. I am the syntax of the people. The tense and the tenseness.

And beyond the borders of terror I feel at one with Africa, with the African peoples, with the resilience and the absurdity and the fragility and the poverty and the decadence and inadaptability and the garishness of her cultures. With the swaggering dictator twirling his fly-whisk, the strutting murder-man toting his weapon, the gun-on-hip soldier, the poacher, the goatherd, the marabout, the beggar all heel and elbow. Africa humiliated. Africa in exile. Africa with rotten and greedy rulers, and beggar economies.

There are a few obvious remarks that need to be made. The history of exile, of people being displaced or being forced to become refugees, is as old as that of organized communal life, as ancient as the mountains. Or that of property and of power. Yet, despite the legalistic distinction made between 'forced' and 'voluntary' exile, I don't think anyone in his right mind will by choice prefer to live away from the intimate communication with his own people. Abdellatif Lâabi who, more than most, must have been prompted to leave Morocco, says that it is vital to stay 'home' for as long as you have the possibility of operating effectively. Crisp new words, he says, are being coined daily on the streets of Casablanca, and for the wordsmith it is terrible to be deprived of the enrichment. Language, for the writer, is of the essence of the equation; it is to the writer what religion or superstition or traditional cooking must be to others: root-nourishing security. Besides, it is important that there should be present alternative models for the youth particularly to look up to, in opposition to symbols of authority promoted or imposed by the government. Of course, when the choice is either prison or silence, then you move off to fight the silence by other ways, or to go and measure yourself against other shapes of muteness.

There are specific problems relating to 'exile'. Each nation state, conditioned by its history and the level of its moral reflection, has its own attitude to 'the foreigner within the gates'. The situation is complicated when the host nation hearkens back to a long-lost position of colonial ascendancy, which was often rationalized in terms of supposed ethnic superiority. It becomes especially bitter when the exile or the refugee originates from a country that has booted out the colonists. The right to asylum is not yet a universally recognized and practised conquest. The legitimacy and therefore the prerogatives and the privileges of the state (without which totalitarianism ultimately cannot develop) still take precedence over the rights and the protection of the individual. 'New' composite national communities—the Americans, the Canadians—seem to thrive on the influx of new citizens. Older nations, often in decline, are more hidebound, less accommodating to 'the other', despite their own chequered histories made up of different tribes and languages.

France, for instance, is not really a *terre d'accueil.* Maybe its claim to international cockiness is still too much alive to accommodate the foreigner, particularly if he is an ex-subject. Maybe its culture is too centrifugal, too codified, to recognize the extent to which it has sagged on the world market. And instead of admitting to the enrichment of *métèques* writing and painting in French, it is developing a relationship of cultural provincialism *vis-à-vis* America (borrowing from it, without really understanding or sharing the sources, striving for the *look*, trying to be *cool*, and simultaneously reacting against it). There is in France, worst of all, a latent—and less and less latent!—racism, compounded by conditions of economic stress. For instance, a Black person hunting for an apartment in Paris will not find it as difficult as in Pretoria, but every bit as hard as in London. The authorities do not combat the endemic racism vigorously enough. (Its timid policy concerning the immigrant families and its reluctance to do away with blatant White exploitation of New Caledonia, for instance, do not help at all.)

Still, *Dieu merci*, there is the tradition of tolerance of political dissidents exiled in France, of which every Frenchman could rightly be proud. There is also a strong minority awareness of the benefits accruing to France from the contributions of foreign artists and authors—from the East to Middle Europe to Africa to the Americas—having been grafted on to French culture. Less élitist: what a dreary place France would have been to live in were it not for the variety of minority cultures and culinary arts!

When I lay claim to not being an exile or an uprooted drifter (although I am a vagabond), it is also because I abhor the concept of exile, which goes clothed in a myth of romantic lamentation. I have seen too many of them—drenched in self-pity; at odds with themselves and blaming invariably 'the oppressors' or history; petrified in a time warp where the reference points are a rosily remembered past; victims to the corruption of suffering; up to their necks in dog-eat-dog exile politics. And too often have I observed the relations between exile and host: the slightly patronizing attitude of the master of the mansion to his unfortunate guest, suspending the critical faculties when judging his work . . . Only to tear him to pieces once the exotic aura has faded, especially once the intruder starts wanting to be treated on an equal footing . . . And the exile takes refuge in the comforting knowledge that he will 'never be understood'.

But, to return to the subject, what is it really like to be exercising the 'dur métier de l'exil', to be 'climbing up and down other people's staircases', to be 'changing countries more often than changing your shoes, despairing whether the revolt can ever bring injustice to an end'?

It is, when you are a writer, to be living *elsewhere* (*ailleurs*), to be writing *differently* (*autrement*). You live in an acquired linguistic zone like going dressed in the clothes of the husband of your mistress. It may be said that you are caught in a cleft mouth. You live and you write in terms of absence, of absent time (or in terms of a questioned present time). Not an imagined or remembered existence: more an absent presence. A state of instant reminiscence. With your tongue you keep searching for the aftertaste of remembered delicacies, and you may well imbue the tasteless fibres with an unexpected refinement. But the tongue keeps clacking against areas of dead palate. Your relationship with the world around you is that of the foreign observer. Or you turn in upon yourself, turn yourself over, observe the albino insects scurrying away from the light. And you taste a distaste, bloated as the tongue in its orifice of saying.

You risk the rupture of silence: either because the break with your milieu is finally too traumatic (you can't stand being painted into a corner), and the awareness of your declining faculties wears the few existing links down to nothingness; or (which is the same problem seen full face) you lose the sense of inevitability, you stop believing in the magic-making, you break with yourself. Writing, after all, is like breathing. Only more painful.

True, you never really relax. You never completely 'belong'. And yet—your situation is probably a blessing in disguise. Freedom, because that is where you're at, is a nasty taskmaster. You have so much more to learn. You are conscious of the *étrangeté* of life, and your senses are sharpened to needles with which you skewer the grey flesh of dull daily acceptances. Your head too is crammed with clichés and stereotypes, but at least you recognize them for what they are—in several languages! For better or for worse you are an outsider. You may be a mutant, for all you know—like a Jew in Poland or a Palestinian in Egypt or a Black in America! If so you are privileged. And, in a century of Displaced Persons and exiles and those fleeing famine or torture, you are in the position to share in and contribute to a historically important, and vital, human experience. (Not to say experiment.)

Take heart then. Lady Luck has smiled upon you!

With greetings from house to house,
Breytenbach
Girona, May 1985

How I Got Over

Darryl Pinckney

JAMES BALDWIN WAS the most famous black writer of my youth and also the most famous black expatriate, more so than the jazz musicians, actors, opera singers, painters, or unforgiven refugees from McCarthyism. As an adolescent in the late 1960s, I carried *Notes of a Native Son* around as if it were a training manual. Though Baldwin was very clear in his essays about where he was, I wasn't. I had no experience, at least none I valued or was not ashamed of as a child of the Indianapolis suburbs. I had poses, which I did not learn until much later was not always the same as recreating the self.

Baldwin was skeptical about the "fried chicken and jazz" tradition of African-Americans in Paris and scornful of veterans lingering there on the GI Bill, but when he accused them of being so incoherent in their reasoning that they'd come to a city that existed only in their minds, I believed more in the fears and temptations of his prose than I did in the suffering that informed his meaning. The deliberate isolation and "depthless alienation" struck me as glamorous, as the privileges of the impertinent and the lost.

However, Baldwin's tone about his situation changed very quickly in his essays. *Nobody Knows My Name* spoke to me less about where he was sitting and more about where he and the rest of the U.S. were headed. There were sweeping phrases about the realizations to which his journey had been tending, the high price of self-delusion haven dwellers pay, and his having overcome his reluctance to go home. Published in 1961, *Nobody Knows My Name* was in its fifteenth printing when I first read it in 1970. Elsewhere, Baldwin had already begun to describe himself as a commuter, not an expatriate. I thought he was talking about the cheapness, for him, of air fares.

In the summer of 1971, I went to Europe for the first time. I was seventeen years old and traveling alone. The entire cabin seemed to want to play cards all night. We disembarked; everything happened. On the return flight, a woman next to me said loudly that there was no better place than the good old U.S.A. Those were expressive days, when transatlantic passengers applauded after a safe landing. The woman fixed me with an expectant look. I had the uncomfortable sensation that everyone digging around in overhead compartments had stopped to dare the thin black teenager with the dirty Afro to disagree. I'd thought of Baldwin when a child on a train to Cherbourg peeked over the seat to touch my hair. I thought of Baldwin again as I smiled at the woman on the 747.

Patriotism was a coercive force and so were other kinds of tribal belonging. I soon realized that when Baldwin said he was a commuter, he was defending himself against the charge leveled most frequently by black militants: that he was cut off from the struggle. He wanted to say that he had not forgotten, that there was, for him, not only as a black man but as an American, no getting away from it all. *Nobody Knows My Name* included Baldwin's uneasy memoir of Richard Wright in exile—estranged from other blacks, playing pinball alone in a cafe, "wandering in a no-man's land between the black world and the white." The irony was that what Baldwin said blacks had said about Wright—that he was out of touch—a new generation was beginning to say about him.

Baldwin, like Wright before him, stood in the light as a spokesman and, because he was obliged to interpret the civil-rights era, perhaps he dreaded becoming as obsolete as he felt Wright had, dreaded the paradoxical cognitive partition that goes on when the freight of the past appears to have no relevance to immediate events. The reinvigoration of the marketplace of discussion about race has always depended on a passing on of the torch, on another generation coming along as a corrective to the one before it, the assumption being that the next generation will be more real and finally tell it like it is. When Baldwin fretted about obsolescence, he was not only worried about being far away from the highways the Freedom Riders traveled, he was also talking about becoming older, about falling out of touch with the streets and no longer speaking their language of desire. This was particularly urgent in Baldwin's day because the civil-rights movement had become a youth movement.

Baldwin's memoir did not introduce me to Richard Wright, but it had the effect of backing up what my father had gone on and on about. When I was growing up, Wright was, in our house at least, the preeminent writer of the migration, the writer who vivified why blacks left the tired fields of the South and what happened to them in the slums of the North. As my father saw it, the higher protest tradition was a straight line from Victor Hugo to Richard Wright. But this work, *Uncle Tom's Children, Native Son,* and *Black Boy,* was accomplished before Wright went into voluntary exile. The lesson of my adolescence was that Richard Wright was a brilliant man who couldn't take racism in the United States anymore and so, like Paul Robeson, he went away.

Wright went to France in 1947 and died there in 1960. At first he had trouble getting a passport. Gertrude Stein and Lévi-Strauss intervened with an official invitation, which the State Department could not ignore without scandal. In his letters, Wright wanted to see himself as following the Lost Generation of Hemingway, but the picture of him in exile that emerged in subsequent biographies was that of a figure trapped in Foucault's panoptical prison. His actions were watched, his remarks reported. Wright's decision to live in France was a criticism of the United States and the U.S. government took it as such.

Because of his fame and that of his subject matter, Wright was called upon to make statements about the racial situation in the U.S., which, because of the Cold War, displeased white officials, white intellectuals, and some of his fellow black Americans in Paris, not all of whom were above envy. In 1950, *Ebony*, a black glossy, declined to publish his volatile essay, "I Choose Exile." Critics began to hint that he was ungrateful, that he had made a fabulous career in the U.S. and then went abroad to say things satisfying only to friends of the Soviet Union. As the political crisis deepened in France in 1958, Wright had to be circumspect: a foreigner too outspoken about domestic affairs could be deported. According to one biographer, Wright, weakened by fever, kept a loaded revolver on his person in the last year of his life and talked about FBI and CIA conspiracies against him.

For a long time it was the fashion to talk about the books Wright wrote in France as failures, to say that he succumbed to the influence of Sartre and de Beauvoir, misplaced the particular of black oppression in the general of the human condition, and ended up with an enervating fatalism. The personal relief of self-exile was said to have been paid for by a loss of inspiration. Baldwin was one of the few to praise *Eight Men*, Wright's last book of stories. There were elements of anti-intellectualism and condescension in the criticism of Wright, as if his interest in Existentialism, his wanting to explore through the use of white characters some of the themes that gripped him as a black man who wrote, were a form of forgetting himself, of getting above himself; as if he didn't need to write from anything other than what he knew as a black man in the U.S. and could only make a spectacle of himself in the realm of ideas; as if writing about race did not require profound ideas.

In a sense, Wright went to Europe to unmake himself as an activist—he was disappointed that anti-fascist solidarity did not survive the war—just as Baldwin had to go to Europe in order to become one—radical politics in the U.S. were ruinous for a black man in the war's aftermath. Nevertheless, they were both connected to a tradition that went back to the late nineteenth century, when sons and daughters of the "Talented Tenth" began to study abroad. Life on the other side of the ocean as a paradise of equality became spectacular lore after World War I. Among the black soldiers who stayed when the troops went home were the musicians who ignited the Jazz Age in Europe, an era celebrated by the writers of the New Negro movement in the 1920s. They were, for the most part, champions of Negritude and Pan-Africanism, and they put the Paris garret and the champagne breakfast into African-American literature.

World War II brought another generation of black soldiers, among them Ralph Ellison, who tired of hearing that life in Paris was good because blacks were served in its restaurants and black men could sit in public with white women. Both Wright and Baldwin reflected on the discrepancy between the way the French treated them as black Americans—writers at that—and the manner in which the French handled Algerians. African independence movements made it impossible not to question the mask of European tolerance and enlightened culture. Wright argued that France was no utopia, but compared to the U.S. the difference in his daily life amazed him. The French may not have been free of racism, but Paris was free of Jim Crow. It irked Baldwin that Wright insisted on looking at Paris as the "city of refuge," though he, too, savored the detachment of being away. He expressed it as a search for identity, whereas for Wright it was a social question. Wright believed that in France he was free, though he was not, and Baldwin wrote of the entrapment of living in Europe as an American, even though he was at liberty.

Baldwin was twenty-four when he got away to Paris in 1948. He used the funds from a literary fellowship to pay for the airplane ticket and stayed broke for the next nine years. The awful hotels taught him why so much Parisian life took place in cafes. By the time Baldwin reached Deux Magots, Wright had turned forty, and had arrived a year earlier under circumstances that were Jamesian in comparison to Baldwin's—with his Oldsmobile in the ship's hold. Wright was internationally acclaimed and had his family with him; Baldwin was unknown and navigated with longings that had no settled object. Perhaps the distance between forty and twenty-four meant more then than it does now, but Wright, in the Paris he shared with Baldwin, seemed to me a much older man, possibly because Baldwin so effectively cast him as such. Wright's expatriate experience was remote, historical, but Baldwin's inspired me because it seemed possible, within reach, contemporary.

I had yet to find out that scrounging around was the opposite of liberating. Baldwin, penniless in a Europe of postwar scarcity, followed the ghosts of Langston Hughes and Claude McKay, who had been young vagabonds in their time: jumping steamers and washing dishes and combing waterfronts. To me, the "allowed irresponsibility" that Baldwin talked about was the romance of deracination. Expatriatism was an earlier, culturally sanctioned version of dropping out and finding yourself. In my teenage days—the late 1960s—classmates of my sisters could make my parents blink by announcing that they were quitting college to found a Harriet Tubman Brigade in Georgia, that they were selling vitamins in order to get some money together to join a commune in India—anything to avoid the traps of what they confidently referred to as bourgeois existence, the compromised life. It wasn't Jim Crow they were worried about.

Baldwin's voyage of discovery was sexual and ruthlessly self-centered, a pilgrimage that suited the ideology of youth. I did not know that youth was the most transient of social categories. Most important, Baldwin's exile was literary, a quest for voice. I imagined a narrow, ill-lit room with an overflowing ashtray, the props of composition, and the sounds that went with concentration: muffled street life, weather, hearts pounding or records playing down the corridor, and no parent anywhere to hammer on the locked door. I was convinced that the stranger in a strange land lived in a state of grace. You could behave toward where you came from as someone just passing through. You could look at where you ended up as someone invisible. The observer, I told myself, is by temperament an outsider, an infiltrator, a traitor. Three things the writer needs, Joyce said: silence, exile, and cunning.

Baldwin, as a civil-rights spokesman, could age, and he did, in talk show after talk show. But James Baldwin in Paris remained, like Werther, a youth forever seeking his conversion experience. My misinterpretation was shameless, which I can only explain by remembering how in need of character I was when I first read *Notes of a Native Son.* But it meant that the expatriate heaven I wanted to look for would be impossible to find because it was already nostalgic fantasy. Some books you never get over, like a first love. Some books that made an enormous impression on you when you were young you are afraid to read again years later, like being sorry you met that former love for coffee, because you couldn't see what you once saw. But there are those few books that can still move you in the old, throbbing way.

When I was growing up, Europe and Africa, as cultural ideals, were like Chi-Chi and An-An, the giant pandas of the London and Beijing zoos that failed to mate. Though Africa became during my youth once again Mother Africa, my interest in the Third World was political, not literary. It was an opportunity for engagement, but I preferred disengagement. Eldridge Cleaver in Algiers and Huey Newton in Havana did not conjure up an image to rival that of Baldwin and Wright quarreling in Paris. I grew up before the vogue for retracing the stages of the Middle Passage, from the Caribbean to the slave prison in the harbor at Dakar, when Europe was safe, psychologically close, simply because you didn't need a string of vaccinations to go there. Culturally, Africa did not present itself to me as being especially urban or big-city. I did not know the Lagos novels of Ekwensi. There wasn't much literary testimony about expatriate life in Africa. I couldn't see Accra in Maya Angelou's autobiography, because she never got off stage, so to speak.

When, at the end of his life, W. E. B. Du Bois couldn't stand where he lived anymore, he left the United States. Du Bois moved to Ghana and renounced his citizenship. He was ninety-five years old when he died, shortly before the March on Washington in 1963. It seemed that every black of a certain age during my childhood had a memory of the revered Dr. Du Bois wielding his gold-tipped cane. My grandparents went to his public lectures. My mother grew up seeing him every day as she walked to the Oglethorpe School and then to high school, the Atlanta University Lab School. My father remembered being too intimidated to venture a greeting. Whenever Du Bois's name came up, it was like talking about someone who had fallen off the edge of the earth. I thought it was because he who had been a student at the University of Berlin in the 1890s had chosen Africa instead of Europe, but Du Bois's becoming a non-person was really the result of his membership in the Communist Party late in his life. He was harassed by the State Department and ignored by wary black intellectuals and civil-rights leaders.

Though Du Bois was received in Ghana like Herod in Rome, the final chapter of his life had the scandalous quality of the great man cheated of honor in his own country. The bitterness behind his exile was irrevocable, a scar that could not be quieted. Because of his example, I have this anxiety that old age for African-Americans is not marked by forgiveness or by a vision of triumph on the other side of the mountain, but by a wild grief that all the patience has been for nothing. Du Bois dedicated his last energies to compiling an *Encyclopedia Africana.* Then he yielded to the heat, listened to the roar from the Gulf of Guinea. If there was an accusation in his affirmation of the "African personality," after the liberators had been supplanted by tyrants or been turned into dictators themselves, its force needed a suspension of disbelief, a wilfulness similar to the Stalinoid obtuseness that once led a black activist to explain the gulag to me by praising the sight of a schoolroom of nine-year-olds playing chess in Moscow.

In the long history of black people being rejected by the United States and of black people rejecting the United States in turn, emigration to Africa had always been projected as a mass rather than an individual solution. Thomas Jefferson advised that free blacks ought to be removed "beyond the reach of mixture" because they contradicted the institutionally defined relationship between blacks and whites. In 1789, the Free Africa Society of Newport, Rhode Island, embraced, for reasons of wounded esteem, the call for removal as the only way to escape discrimination. Sierra Leone was founded in 1787, Liberia in 1822, but in between, in 1804, rose Haiti, which transformed the meaning of leaving the United States. Going away was no longer admitting defeat or showing acquiescence to the propaganda that the territory of the U.S. belonged to the white man. Departure became heroic, a verdict delivered against the unredeemed.

The Fugitive Slave Act of 1850 denied to blacks the protection of the Sixth Amendment—involving the right to trial—and the Dred Scott decision of 1857 held that blacks had not been citizens of the U.S. when the Constitution was written and had not become citizens since. Though the abolitionist movement became thoroughly confrontational, blacks despaired that they would ever enjoy their rights, even in non-slaveholding states. A black physician, Martin R. Delaney, declared in 1852 that emigration was absolutely necessary for political elevation. Delaney tried to set up a black state in Nicaragua. A similar plan took him to the Niger River Valley in 1859. As cold waters to a thirsty soul, so is good news from a foreign country, the Old Testament proverb has it.

The early dreams of getting out were conceived in terms of repatriation, but as connections to Africa dropped away emigration schemes looked to the New World. There were so many places to go and you didn't have to cross oceans to get to them, though the obstacles were formidable enough. Escaped slaves established a colony in Vera Cruz, Mexico. The number of runaway slaves living in Canada at the outbreak of the Civil War was said to be 40,000. As early as 1855, there were 4,000 blacks in California, and after Reconstruction's demise Oklahoma became a popular location for the founding of all-black towns.

For most blacks, however, the Promised Land was not a distant country. The Promised Land was release from bondage. The legacy of Emancipation was that the language of freedom was Biblical, that black people in the U.S. were for the most part integrationists, and that the coming up out of Egypt was therefore the attainment of equal rights. A sharp distinction was made between moving on, seeking the better life, and going back. Go back to where? "Abide in the ship, or you cannot be saved." A black Quaker merchant had transported thirty-eight blacks to Sierra Leone after the War of 1812, and a Haiti Emigration Society existed in 1818, but from the very beginning the majority of free blacks resisted voluntary emigration, saying that it would mean abandoning those blacks still in slavery and that they as a people were too altered for West Africa. They also resented the implication of inferiority in colonization schemes: that they would never be at home in the U.S., though their ancestors had been the "first cultivators of its wilds"; that they would never make good, though their "blood and sweat had manured its fields." By the time the Liberian Exodus and Joint Stock Company collapsed in 1877 and the African Emigration Association went under in 1886, such schemes were dismissed as crackpot.

The call to emigrate was a manifestation of black nationalism, which was itself a high or low fever depending on conditions. The fever was raging in the 1920s, and it only needed Marcus Garvey to take advantage of it. Garvey's very theatrical Back to Africa movement was particularly successful among working-class blacks who had come North in search of jobs and safety from lynching. The self-proclaimed President of Africa, Garvey opened negotiations with Liberia, whose government feared he would take over the country. Garvey was abused for meeting with the Ku Klux Klan, just as blacks had distrusted antebellum colonization schemes because secessionists like John C. Calhoun favored them. The feeling was that if whites—even Lincoln—wanted blacks to go so badly, perhaps blacks should stay. Then, too, Garveyism, like its predecessors, overlooked as much as any colonialist venture the fact that these lands were already inhabited. Garvey, who disclosed that God was black, eventually failed, but Garveyism restored Africa in the popular imagination as the original link in the chain of identity. Emigration's message was absorbed by separatists who rediscovered Garveyism in the 1960s, by which time going back to Africa was an inward journey. Africa ceased to be a destination and became a symbol.

Baldwin pointed to "the fury of the color problem" as his reason for leaving the United States, as had every black exile from the U.S. since the eighteenth century. He said that blacks born in the South could at least move North, but if you were already living in the North the only place left to go was out of the country. I remember my father saying that if he had stayed in Georgia after he got out of university, he would have been killed. Though I had no way of knowing what it was like to live every day with this sense of imminent danger, of being hemmed in on every corner, I did know what Baldwin meant by the long exile blacks endured in their own country. The fury had not abated.

The historic complex of the African-American was a postulation of simultaneous doubleness, as defined by Du Bois in *The Souls of Black Folk*, published in 1903. The dual consciousness of the black, Du Bois said, was that of "two warring ideals in one dark body," two thoughts, two souls, "two unreconciled strivings." African-Americans, according to Du Bois, possessed a second sight that let them see themselves through the revelation of the other world. The African-American was never without the sense of "always looking at one's self through the eyes of others, of measuring one's soul by the tape of a world that looks on in amused contempt and pity."

Six decades after *The Souls of Black Folk*, the duality of African-American consciousness was no longer spoken of as an inner struggle. It was described in terms of divided loyalty. Given the political climate of the time, the atmosphere of conspiracy that stretched from the Nixon White House to the Black Panther headquarters in Oakland, love of country and love of race represented extremes. Duality of soul was unacceptable, as if only scorched ground lay between the two fortresses of national and racial identity. The moment refused to allow the holding of two passports. Whose side are you on? Angela Davis was to describe her decision to give up her studies in Frankfurt in 1967 in much the same way that Baldwin reinvented himself as a commuter. By the time Dr. King and Senator Kennedy had been assassinated, the contempt and pity that so galled Du Bois belonged to the black world to aim at the white world. Black Power encouraged African-Americans to see themselves primarily as blacks, as part of a vast diaspora.

I hadn't been brought up to think of the African-American as oscillating between two poles, as if being both black and American were a contradiction. I always knew that my heritage was my homeland—my family, other relatives, their friends, people like them, people instantly recognizable to one another, like aliens in science-fiction films. My country was a phantom to the uninitiated. It was an archipelago superimposed on a map of the continental United States, with the heaviest cluster of islands falling in the South, the Old Country.

In my youth, everyday life for the black male teenager was a series of tests to gauge how black you were. Back then, as now, what constituted authentic blackness was determined by the plight of the majority, which meant the poorest. If you did not live on The Avenue, then you were at a remove from the Black Experience. If you did not walk the walk and talk the talk, then you were vulnerable to a kind of bullying. Not being down with it was perceived as weakness. It was feeble sport, because the black middle class was so available as a target—as was the white middle class, the phrase being evocative of the repressed and the repressive.

Being of the black middle class could make you defensive. You were accused of trying to act white, of not knowing who you were. You were warned that one day soon it would be proven to you that you were black. Whites would reject you, and because of the monotonous predictability of oppression, the inevitability of betrayal, you were therefore really no different from the toughs you tried not to heed on the moveable basketball courts of apprenticeship macho. You had a lot to prove. After all, you could look forward to university and to exemption from the draft. Only poor blacks and poor whites were getting sent to Vietnam as privates. Robert McNamara, secretary of defense, was excoriated in 1965 when he suggested that the War on Poverty could be won if 35,000 black men joined the army.

In the late 1960s, the black bourgeoisie was synonymous with Uncle Tom. The black bourgeoisie was depicted as light-skinned, clubbish, collaborationist, materialistic; and yes, there was too much of that. But the image of a black middle class created by federal anti-poverty programs and corrupted by patronage has obscured the historical truth of a sector of the black population that defined itself more by political and social objectives than it did by income. Not all of the physicians, ministers, or businessmen of my grandparents' day were preoccupied solely with driving blatant Packards. The old black middle class knew more than it wanted to about the front line. There was no refuge in success. A cousin of my mother's, a student at Atlanta University, was lynched in 1931. The old black middle class, walking to Jerusalem, never doubted that it was truly black and the true America.

There was, consequently, a vengeful pleasure in confounding whites, in exasperating those who were eager to grant me a license of approval, probationary membership as one of them, or nearly like them—middle class, decipherable, reliable. I had no wish to be accepted. Acceptance meant conformity, and falling-in was for cheerleaders, jocks, the living dead. Snobbery went into the disdain: those bumper stickers proclaiming "America: Love It or Leave It" were vulgar, like too many Christmas lights. The flag was at most a consolation to families at the funerals of sons who died in Vietnam.

I remember the summer day in 1969 when astronauts first landed on the moon. A white high-school classmate of mine confessed that in spite of the Vietnam War the moon landing made him proud to be an American. My shock extinguished the glow of his liberalism for the day. That same afternoon, my parents said I had to get my hair cut. At the barbershop in the black neighborhood a customer said that the moon walk had been faked, that The Man was just trying to distract us. Not everyone agreed that the moon shot was a hoax, but there were mutterings of assent that the money would have been better spent on earth. It was my turn to shut up.

The barbershop was the only forum of black populist feeling I knew, and I was careful to avoid conversation that might reveal I did not fit in, in case it was taken to mean that I did not want to fit in. My double consciousness was not that as expressed by Du Bois, but the elementary dual existence Edmund Gosse remembered in *Father and Son.* While he kneeled and prayed, a captive of his rigid upbringing, there was another self, unsuspected by anyone in his religious life, who managed to thrive on imaginative scraps. Gosse found a companion and confidant in himself. A secret could belong to him and to the somebody who lived in the same body with him. The two of them, Gosse and the sympathizer in his breast, could talk to each other and offer solace. There is a rapture on the lonely shore.

Sometimes I think that Anglophilia was the first foreign language I learned. However, I couldn't pick up a royal history without my parents reminding me that the British were among the most racist people on earth, second only to the Japanese. Elizabeth Tudor had issued a proclamation intended to expel blacks from her kingdom. Everyone except the immigration officials at Heathrow knew that more people were trying to leave Britain than were trying to get into it. My parents' disapproval of my fanciful reading matter bore the traces of their brief careers as dissenters on black campuses back during World War II.

After Ethiopia, Spain, and Roosevelt's refusal to lift immigration controls, there had been a sort of murky coolness toward the war effort among some black students, a private withholding of support for the anti-fascist rhetoric, because the democracies they were being exhorted to defend were, to them, imperialist powers. Then, too, the U.S. Army was segregated and, in spite of Joe Louis, my father dodged the troop ships for as long as he could.

Murray Kempton, who served in New Guinea and the Philippines during World War II, once told me that for most white boys the war had been their only chance to go someplace and meet people different from themselves. On the other hand, the stories I heard from my father featured white second lieutenants putting at risk the black squads they loathed being in command of—which had an echo during the Vietnam War in rumors of white officers being fragged by their men—and mobs waiting outside dance halls in not-so-small Italian towns to try to punish black soldiers for flirting with local girls.

My father tried to tell me as he slipped a package of condoms in my shaving kit when I packed for my first trip abroad that I would do well not to take Europe too seriously, and certainly not at its own word. The Grand Tour was fine as a sowing of wild oats, but the solutions I sought were not in going away, and the away I was looking for was not Europe. Never mind the beguiling tales of unstable relatives—great uncles who'd lit up Paris during the Jazz Age or elderly cousins teaching school in Munich. And yet, in those days, a black kid going to study in Europe was spoken of as having achieved something in the white world. A black kid going to study in Africa was whispered about as having a mysterious vocation. My father left out mention of that aunt in Chad.

I was just going on holiday and the ambivalence my parents felt was akin to being unsure about having given permission for an unsupervised camping trip. I suppose for blacks of my mother and father's generation, letting your kids go off to Europe was a kind of doing the right thing, giving them the same advantages white kids had, though their duty and wish to be protective also put them in the position of having to be the bad guys, the ones who warned that Europe wasn't just old buildings and art, it was also history and people, and racism didn't disappear at passport control at JFK.

My father's attitude was typical, I thought, of his generation, as VE-Day and out of date as condoms, silk stockings, or telling recalcitrant children at the dinner table to meditate on starving children in Europe. Vietnam and the American Century hadn't absolved Europe of its past, but compared to the policies of the U.S. government, the villainies of Europe were receding, regardless of the bashing of Pakistanis in Britain. Draft dodgers in Sweden, De Gaulle's humiliation in '68—liberal culture appeared to be flourishing in Europe. One day I would realize that the image of Europe that I imbibed as a teenager, nurtured through university, and had recourse to as a young adult was just as old-fashioned, incomplete, and limited, as much a relic of postwar arrangements, the Occupation, and the Marshall Plan as the image of black soldiers distributing chocolate and chewing gum to grimy blond waifs.

I left Indiana in the early 1970s, went to university in New York City, and stuck around for a decade or so. The moves—or the not moving, the passivity—were as casual and chaotic as the times could make them. The searing dinner-table battles with those who had kept a futile vigil over my development, the classroom analyses, the late-night dormitory vows—all that high-mindedness about life was lost in an unsurprising kind of molting. Not too long ago I asked a friend from those new wave days, a black woman who had spent some of that time in Paris, what had happened to all those years. "We smoked up quite a few of them," she said. Because I was from the Midwest, New York offered the eroticism of a foreign country. Every dive was crammed with the flying dutchmen of internal exile. As Langston Hughes said of the Harlem Renaissance, I had a swell time while it lasted.

What was not casual were the shifts in the city under my feet: the real-estate squeeze, the "semantic adventurism" of neo-conservatives, the coming of crack cocaine, the terror of AIDS. Once, in 1983, I got off the plane from Amsterdam and took the subway into Manhattan. I read the *Village Voice* over the shoulder of another passenger. I saw a photo of a downtown rock star whose band I often went to hear. The story wasn't the interview I'd expected. It was an obituary saying he'd died of AIDS. I sometimes think of a line from Peter Handke's *A Sorrow Beyond Dreams*, about the game the girls in his mother's village played based on the stations of a woman's life: "tired / exhausted / sick / dying / dead."

Whenever I could get abroad for a summer holiday—if I had the time, I didn't have the money; if I had the money, I didn't have the time— I was testing places, auditioning places, imagining the shape of old habits pursued through endless days in new places. When you are a visitor you make the mistake of thinking the life you're visiting would be the life you'd have if you lived there. I became afraid of getting stuck, of not being able to get out before it was too late, before I was too old for the marginal life, which was the only one I could afford. I was waiting for the fleeting notion that would lead me somewhere, for the fortuitous meeting that would look in retrospect like destiny.

I was jealous of the nurse who quit her job to open an herbal medicine shop in Jamaica, of the graduate students who packed unfinished dissertations for permanent vacation in Belize, of the musicologist last heard of in the rain forest of the Central African Republic. "The man who loves his homeland is a beginner; he to whom every soil is as his own is strong; but he is perfect for whom the entire world is a foreign country," Hugo of St. Victor said. For the brave, the possibilities were wide; for the timid, those of us dependent on all-night delis, neon, and telephones, the choices were limited.

I said the point was to make yourself up as you went along, but I was interested in where it was possible to reproduce the way I already lived: side streets where everyone wore black, danced all night, or marched in the mornings in favor of disarmament, and tucked within that bohemian zone of commiseration a room from which I could contemplate the variousness of the world and congratulate myself for doing so. I had the provincial's belief that an interesting life could take place only in a great metropolis. What I needed from a city were enough corners to lose myself in. Cultural fantasy is as escapist as any other.

Because whole peoples, countries, and cities were not knowable, I considered where I could go with as much gravity as discussing the merits of clubs: the more popular it was the less attractive it was. Paris, like the Mudd Club, was overrun, and as a place to implode it had long been a cliché for blacks, a dream that had made as many comebacks as Josephine Baker. Amsterdam, like the Michael Todd Room upstairs at the Palladium, had also been done to death. An Irish trumpet player on his way back to Abidjan almost convinced me that it had become the new capital of chill. A Nigerian taxi driver didn't know how enticing it was to hear that Lagos was the most dangerous city on earth. I'd taken an advanced placement exam in high school and been excused from German classes in college. That was a mistake because my German was embarrassing. But the hardest thing about Berlin, in 1987, was getting there. Isherwood's *Berlin Stories* was one of those books I had not gotten over.

Your historical moment, the era that forged your consciousness, sets you up, makes you out a chump, a fall guy. It means everything to my circumstances that the Cold War is over. On the night of November 9, 1989, when I climbed onto the Berlin Wall, when I walked under the Brandenburg Gate, I realized, watching the drunken scenes of reunion all around me, that the postwar occupation of Berlin had come to an end. Your troops can go home, the tears said. I was one of the camp followers of the army that had dug in too deeply. I felt like an American for the first time in my life. That is, I was not entirely pleased to have the arrogance of my passport diminished. And then Berlin became a German town. The sophisticated, hard-edged, international city dissolved into nothing.

The attacks on Turks began that very night, behind the main train station, in the cold dark of the Tiergarten, away from the glare of the camera lights. Earlier, in October, on the day when 6,000 students marched in Leipzig to demand free speech, 200,000 people assembled in Rome to demonstrate against racist attacks, one of which, in southern Italy, had resulted in the deaths of six Africans. The troubles in France had long been in the news. Sometimes, after German unification, when alone in the cobalt of a summer night, I surprised myself that I hurried. The overnight seriousness of change exposed as irrelevant certain postures of alienated sensibility. I could be vulnerable to assault, but I was not an exile. Though I'd been very solemn with myself about my flight from the policies of successive Republican administrations, I had no right to the term, and I'd learned from people I met—writers from South Africa and Yugoslavia, pianists from Russia, historians from Chile, students from Iran, engineers from Ghana, actors from Uganda, farmers from Bangladesh—that it was not a status I should have been in a rush to claim.

Long before anyone thought the Wall would fall so easily, a man from South Africa, an Afrikaner, a member of the ANC who had been in prison, looked out at the Berlin streets and said to me, "Forget Europe, brother. Africa's the place." I took his advice as an expression of passionate homesickness on his part—and hope: he had information that Mandela was to be released in a few months' time. But he'd turned the tables on me. That was my line and he was white. It was okay for me to talk about Herder, but it wasn't okay for a white to hold forth about Fanon, in the way that my presence in a white environment was merely testing its egalitarianism, but a white person's presence in a black environment signaled yet another agent, however hip, of exploitation, because integration seldom worked both ways. I was surprised to hear an Afrikaner, even a radical one, speak as though he really thought of himself as an African. I'd always thought that Africa was mine, even when I wasn't using it, and didn't know how to take his offer to share it with me.

The moral intensity of his cause made it impossible for me to think that he was telling me to go back and help my people, in the way white professors used to tell black students to go back and teach in the cotton fields of the South, as if their black students would never be happy up North. It was harder not to feel that he had confronted me with one of those challenges of loyalty and identification I sometimes faced back in the U.S., back when there were the beginnings of that aura of vindication of everything having to do with Africa, which was sometimes a form of not taking the subject as seriously as it deserved. I had an inkling of how frustrated Wright must have been when people told him that intellectually there was nothing for him in Europe; how impatient Baldwin became when his critics said he'd gone to Europe to forget that he was black.

Meanwhile, as I sat brooding in a cafe, trying to identify some old song, Europe changed, or went back to something it had been before the NATO–Warsaw Pact lid was clamped on. I was appalled to hear a Czech diplomat, one of the early dissidents from Charter 77, insist—admittedly, this was after the euphoria of the Velvet Revolution had been dissipated—that while watching a group of children at play in Prague she noticed that a girl from India, adopted when a baby, behaved differently from the others and that the girl did so because she was answering some cultural siren in her genes. I'd never liked that way of assigning to whole nations or groups innate behavioral characteristics. The work of every serious black social scientist militated against it. Now that even the prettiest claims of ethnicity have helped to erode belief in the possibility of secular, non-racial society, I feel I can't find a place for myself in the world anymore.

On the night in 1993 when it was announced that Berlin had lost the competition to host the Olympics in the year 2000, I ran into an acquaintance, a black from the U.S. He was standing under a lit awning, with a beer in his hand. He always seemed to have a magical beer, one that never emptied no matter how long the night, unless you were buying. I asked him what he was up to and went on automatic pilot as his convoluted explanation revealed that he was up to what he had been up to when I was first introduced to him five years before. Back then he was three years older than I was. In the meantime he somehow had become two years my junior.

In the halcyon days when the Berlin Wall made the city a cushioned cradle for some, one of the things American artists said about other American artists was that they'd come to Berlin, that subsidized island of the avant garde, to have the careers they'd been unable to make back in the States. Everyone accused everyone else of running a con. But that night, with much gloating being indulged in by members of several anti-Olympics groups, looking at the black American sipping his bottomless beer and tugging at his X cap that hid his hairline, I wondered if the con wasn't actually a self-deception.

Youth was already a very extended period for middle-class Americans and going abroad was a way of keeping this trouble-free phase going a bit longer. When young, you are in a state of becoming, always on the verge.

Knocking a few years off his age was, for my fellow countryman, a way of reassuring himself that what he would become—his having to become something—was still comfortably in the distance, off somewhere around the corner. He had postponed that moment when you wake up and face the fact that the life to come is no longer in the misty future, when you sit up and have to tell yourself that you have indeed made a life, that you are in it, that it is what it is. Nothing is more infantile-making of a man than his organizing his life around the avoidance of suffering, because of course that is the one thing you cannot avoid.

We got on, the old youngster and I, because we were both African-American, and there was between us something of what Baldwin said about a black not spoiling another black's hustle in front of whites. A big part of the old youngster's act had been to remind the Germans how German they were, and so when we reviewed the latest report of a fight between Neo-Nazis and refugees, he repeated with a shrug, "They're German." I was sure that the bored expressions in East Berlin techno clubs were also visible in London, in Marseilles, in Bensonhurst, New York. I started to say that I didn't understand this new generation—and sounded like every adult who'd ever thought every kid was the same. More of my sentences began, "In my day. . . ." It was like the faint tolling of a bell.

Some Pakistanis satisfied with life in New Jersey once told Salman Rushdie that they knew there was racism in the U.S., but they weren't the objects of it. This had ceased to be the contract between black Americans and Europe ages ago, except in enclaves that could not have been mistaken for anything else. Black Americans could trust the evidence of their own eyes: that these countries weren't exclusively white anyway. This is the defining aspect of postwar Europe, however slow or melancholy the recognition has been for some. A black German friend—her mother was born in Berlin, her father in Liberia—told me that white Germans didn't like it when she returned their compliments and said they also spoke excellent German.

In *Afrolook,* the newsletter of an Afro-German awareness group, I read an interview with Ollie Harrington, a black American who, because of his political past, had slipped into East Berlin in the 1950s. He managed to survive by hosting a radio jazz show that became the favorite of black soldiers over in West Berlin. I felt sorry for him: the door had been blown off his deep freeze, leaving him exposed. Where will he go? Being away from the United States has changed since that old hand's day—if your "away" is Western Europe and not, say, a prawn farm in the Philippines. Telephones, fax machines, CNN, film, the prevalence of English as a tool, and international newspaper distribution have made being cut off a conscious choice. These days being away, in Europe, requires determined immersion, an illusionist's trick, one accomplished by dropping out twice: leaving the U.S. and then burying yourself when you land in your someplace else. And you are not as stranded as you used to be, unless you are really busted.

Being away has also changed in the universality of shopping mall, boutique, and McDonald's culture, though, as Susan Sontag has pointed out, modernization is no longer synonymous with Americanization. American culture doesn't have the influence in Europe that it once had. European youth don't defer to American tastes and ideas, not even in music. You no longer carry the authority of coming from where you do, and blacks have lost the stardom of the exotic as well. A young Briton recently accused of rape claimed that not only were his relations with the girl in question consensual, he'd asked her whether she'd ever slept with a black man, because he didn't want to contract AIDS.

The decline in U.S. prestige was accelerated by the dollar's slide after 1985. Exchanging dollars used to be like collecting Lotto winnings. Virgil Thomson concluded a preface to a volume of memoirs about his charmed circle by reminding his readers that he was talking about a time when their pennies were like dollars. Read it and weep, he said. The age of young Americans going to Europe to live cheaply and to fill their heads with things that have no utilitarian value is fading. The new generation of American expatriates is largely entrepreneurial. They are driving up prices in Prague, jogging in Ho Chi Minh City, publishing collegiate-bright English-language newspapers in Moscow, and making deals to import butter in the lobbies of hard-currency St. Petersburg hotels. Concurrently, the places to get away to have seemingly multiplied. I listened to a young man describe the job he'd accepted at an economics institute in Kazakhstan and felt like an old man rocking on a porch.

I hardly think of the expatriate's distance anymore, except when there is a story in the U.S. that everyone I phone there has been following on cable court channels day in and day out. When pressed, I call myself nomadic, because I move from country to country on a fixed cycle during the year. Susan Sontag once tried to put her foot down with me, saying that home was wherever my books were. Most of my books are in storage in a barn in New Jersey. The rest are in Oxford, London, Berlin, New York, Indianapolis, and my suitcase. I live without papers, employment, assets, or permanent address. The most valuable part, Brecht called his passport. Sometimes I wonder how long I can go on roaming from room to room.

The other day I tried to pick blanket fluff from my beard and found that I was pulling at gray hair. I am protected in a way that makes me think I have no right to be alive. I don't know how long I can continue to elude the suffering, but for the time being home is the place where there is someone who does not wish you any pain.

Notes on Exile

Czeslaw Milosz

He did not find happiness, for there was no happiness in his country.
—Adam Mickiewicz

Usage

EXILE ACCEPTED AS a destiny, in the way we accept an incurable illness, should help us see through our self-delusions.

Paradigm

He was aware of his task and people were waiting for his words, but he was forbidden to speak. Now where he lives he is free to speak but nobody listens and, moreover, he forgot what he had to say.

Commentary to the Above

Censorship may be tolerant of various avant-garde antics, since they keep writers busy and make literature an innocent pastime for a very restricted elite. But as soon as a writer shows signs of being attentive to reality, censorship clamps down. If, as a result of banishment or his own decision, he finds himself in exile, he blurts out his dammed-up feelings of anger, his observations and reflections, considering this as his duty and mission. Yet that which in his country is regarded with seriousness as a matter of life or death is of nobody's concern abroad or provokes interest for incidental reasons. Thus a writer notices that he is unable to address those who care and is able to address only those who do not care. He himself gradually becomes used to the society in which he lives, and his knowledge of everyday life in the country of his origin changes from tangible to theoretical. If he continues to deal with the same problems as before, his work will lose the directness of captured experience. Therefore he must either condemn himself to sterility or undergo a total transformation.

New Eyes

New eyes, new thought, new distance: that a writer in exile needs all this is obvious, but whether he overcomes his old self depends upon resources which he only dimly perceived before.

One possibility offered him is to change his language, either literally, by writing in the tongue of the country of his residence, or to use his native tongue in such a manner that what he writes will be understandable and acceptable to a new audience. Then, however, he ceases to be an exile.

Another, much more difficult choice consists of preserving his postulated and imagined presence in the country he comes from. Imagined: for he must visualize the history and literature of his country as one organism developing in time and assign to his work a function in a movement which leads from the past to the future. This implies a constant reassessment of tradition in search for vital roots as well as critical observation of the present. Certain literary genres (the realistic novel, for instance) and certain styles cannot, by definition, be practiced in exile. On the other hand, the condition of exile, by enforcing upon a writer several perspectives, favors other genres and styles, especially those which are related to a symbolic transposition of reality.

Despair

Despair, inseparable from the first stage of exile, can be analyzed, and then it would probably appear as resulting more from one's personal shortcomings than from external circumstances. There are three main causes of such despair: loss of name, fear of failure and moral torment.

A writer acquires a name through a complex interchange with his readers, whether he appeals to a large audience or to a narrow circle of sympathizers. He elaborates an image of himself as reflected in the eyes of those who react to his writings. When he emigrates, that image is suddenly annihilated and he makes up an anonymous member of the mass. He no longer even exists as a person whose virtues and faults were known to his friends. Nobody knows who he is, and if he reads about himself in the press, he finds that the data concerning him are grotesquely distorted. Then his humiliation is proportionate to his pride, and that is perhaps a just punishment.

He has good reasons to fear failure, for only a few possess the resilience necessary to oppose the corroding effects of isolation. He belonged to a community of writers committed to a certain ritual and occupied with distributing praise and blame to one another. Now, no community, no ritual, no sweet games of satisfied ambition. He suffers because he has contracted collectivistic habits, which means perhaps that he has never learned to stand on his own feet. He may win, but not before he agrees to lose.

Exile is morally suspect because it breaks one's solidarity with a group, i.e., it sets apart an individual who ceases to share the experience of colleagues left behind. His moral torment reflects his attachment to a heroic image of himself and he must, step by step, come to the painful conclusion that to do morally valid work and to preserve an untarnished image of himself is rarely possible.

Acclimatization

After many years in exile one tries to imagine what it is like not living in exile.

Space

Imagination, always spatial, points north, south, east and west of some central, privileged place, which is probably a village from one's childhood or native region. As long as a writer lives in his country, the privileged place, by centrifugally enlarging itself, becomes more or less identified with his country as a whole. Exile displaces that center or rather creates two centers. Imagination relates everything in one's surroundings to "over there"—in my case, somewhere on the European continent. It even continues to designate the four cardinal points, as if I still stood there. At the same time the north, south, east and west are determined by the place in which I write these words.

Imagination tending toward the distant region of one's childhood is typical of literature of nostalgia (a distance in space often serves as a disguise for a Proustian distance in time). Although quite common, literature of nostalgia is only one among many modes of coping with estrangement from one's native land. The new point which orients space in respect to itself cannot be eliminated, i.e., one cannot abstract from one's physical presence in a definite spot on the Earth. That is why a curious phenomenon appears: the two centers and the two spaces arranged around them interfere with each other or—and this is a happy solution—coalesce.

Shadows on the Wall

It is being said that our planet is slowly but inexorably entering an era of unification brought about by technology, hygiene and literacy. And yet the opposite opinion may be advanced as well, and only in exile can its validity be fully understood. A writer who lives in a foreign country brings a thorough knowledge of the geographical area from which he comes—its history, economy, politics, et cetera. He is sensitive to any information about what he knows so well, whether it is provided by books, newspapers or television. This leads him to discover how new divisions between men come about. A hundred years ago average people not familiar with remote regions of the globe quietly relegated them to the realm of the legendary or at least the exotic. Today, however, they feel they are offered the means to embrace places and events of the whole Earth simultaneously. But when confronted with a newcomer's firsthand knowledge, news and reports on the land of his origin prove to be completely misleading. Multiplied, the sum of similar disparities between the message and the fact reaches astronomical proportions. Plato's parable of the cave, which until now has been discussed only in philosophy classes, acquires a more practical meaning as well. As we remember, the prisoners chained there cannot move their necks and are able to see only the wall facing them. Shadows are projected on that wall and they take them for reality. An outsider wonders whether he could convince newspaper readers and television viewers that they are in error, but arrives at the conclusion that he neither could nor should. Were deception due merely to ignorance or political bias, the predicament of modern cave dwellers would offer some hope. But what if—and this should not be excluded in advance—deception resides in the very nature of the media, i.e., of mediation?

Self-Examination

Here is a draft of a speech which may be addressed by a writer in exile to himself. "Are you certain that your colleagues here who move in a world familiar to them from childhood fare better than you do? It is true that they write in their own tongue. But do art and literature correspond to what we have learned about them in school and at the university? Couldn't they have changed so rapidly in these last decades that their names are now no more than empty shells? Don't they perhaps become an exercise in solitude, a signal sent forth by the disinherited? How many of these people are rewarded by love and respect in their hometowns, the only kind of love and respect that are really worth seeking? They share the same language with their audience, but do they see a gleam of comprehension on the faces of their listeners? Isn't the same tongue just an illusion where uncountable individual languages fill space with a jamming noise? Are your colleagues listened to or read by the public at large, or do they read only each other? Can you even be sure that they read each other? After all, it is possible that you are better off: your exile is legitimized.

"You have always believed that the true goal of writing is to reach all the people of the world and to change their lives. And what if such a goal is unattainable? Does it cease to be valid? Don't you believe that every one of your colleagues here has in his heart remained faithful to that, yes, childish dream? Yet haven't you witnessed their defeat?

"And if you cannot save the world, why should you care whether you have a large or a small audience?"

Language

A writer living among people who speak a language different from his own discovers after a while that he senses his native tongue in a new manner. It is not true that a long stay abroad leads to withering of styles, even though the vivifying influence of everyday speech is lacking. What is true, however, is that new aspects and tonalities of the native tongue are discovered, for they stand out against the background of the language spoken in the new milieu. Thus the narrowing down in some areas (street idioms, slang) is compensated for by a widening in others (purity of vocabulary, rhythmic expressiveness, syntactic balance). Rivalry between two languages is not necessarily typical of literature written in exile. For a couple of centuries in several European countries the literati were bilingual, their vernacular being modified by their Latin and vice versa.

The Philosophy of Travel

George Santayana

HAS ANYONE EVER considered the philosophy of travel? It might be worth while. What is life but a form of motion and a journey through a foreign world? Moreover locomotion—the privilege of animals—is perhaps the key to intelligence. The roots of vegetables (which Aristotle says are their mouths) attach them fatally to the ground, and they are condemned like leeches to suck up whatever sustenance may flow to them at the particular spot where they happen to be stuck. Close by, perhaps, there may be a richer soil or a more sheltered and sunnier nook; but they cannot migrate, nor have they even eyes or imagination by which to picture the enviable neighbouring lot of which chance has deprived them. At best their seed is carried by the wind to that better place, or by some insect intent on its own affairs: vegetables migrate only by dying out in one place and taking root in another. For individual plants it is a question of living where they are or not living at all. Even their limbs can hardly move, unless the wind moves them. They turn very slowly towards the light, lengthening and twisting themselves without change of station. Presumably their slumbering souls are sensitive only to organic variations, to the pervasive influence of heat or moisture, to the blind stress of budding and bursting here, or the luxury of blooming and basking and swaying there in the light. They endure in time and expand vaguely in space, without distinguishing or focussing the influences to which they are subject; having no occasion to notice anything beyond their own bodies, but identifying the universe, like the innocent egoists they are, with their own being. If ever they are forced into a new pose, which might be of permanent advantage to them, they revert to the perpendicular when the force is relaxed; or if the pressure has been brutal, they may remain permanently a little bent, as if cowed and humbled by the tyrant into a life-long obliquity. Often all the trees in a row lean to the prevalent leeward, like a file of soldiers petrified on the march, or a row of statues unanimously pointing at nothing; and perhaps their crookedness may prove merciful to them, and enable them more comfortably to weather the storm, in forgetfulness of perfection. If it were not that the young shoots still tend to grow up straight, I would almost believe that distortion had become their proper ideal and was no longer distortion but character. Certainly among mankind, when vices become constitutional, they turn into worldly virtues; they are sanctioned by pride and tradition, and called picturesque, sturdy, and virile. Yet to a wider view, when their forced origin is considered, they still seem ugly and sad. Sin is sin, though it be original, and misfortune is misfortune so long as the pristine soul stirs within the crust of custom, tortured by the morality which is supposed to save it.

The shift from the vegetable to the animal is the most complete of revolutions; it literally turns everything upside down. The upper branches, bending over and touching the ground, become fingers and toes; the roots are pulled up and gathered together into a snout, with its tongue and nostrils protruding outwards in search of food; so that besides the up-and-down and inwards-and-outwards known to the plant, the animal now establishes a forward-and-back—a distinction possible only to travellers; for the creature is now in perpetual motion, following his own nose, which is itself guided and allured by all sorts of scents and premonitions coming from a distance. Meantime the organs of fertility, which were the flowers, sunning themselves wide open and lolling in delicious innocence, are now tucked away obscurely in the hindquarters, to be seen and thought of as little as possible. This disgrace lies heavy upon them, prompting them to sullen discontent and insidious plots and terrible rebellions. Yet their unrest is a new incentive to travel, perhaps the most powerful and persistent of all: it lends a great beauty to strangers, and fills remote places and times with an ineffable charm. Plants had no such possibilities; they could not make a chance acquaintance, they could not fall in love, and I am not sure that in their apparent placidity they were really happier. There is something dull in the beauty of flowers, something sad in their lasciviousness; they do not crave, they do not pursue, they wait in a prolonged expectation of they know not what, displaying themselves to order like a child decked out for a holiday, vaguely proud, vaguely uncomfortable, vaguely disappointed. The winds are impatient wooers, and a shower of gold-dust is a poor embrace. They fade, thinking they are still virgins; they drop their petals in sadness, and shrink nun-like into a withered stalk; there is an acrid savor in their elderly sweetness: they believe they have missed something which they pretend to despise. Yet they are mistaken; they have altogether fulfilled their function: they are grandmothers without knowing it. They were married long ago, with only a faint sense of being present at their own wedding; they have borne children as is consonant with their nature, painlessly and in quite other places; they have marched unawares, veiled and honoured as mothers, in the procession of time.

In animals the power of locomotion changes all this pale experience into a life of passion; and it is on passion, although we anaemic philosophers are apt to forget it, that intelligence is grafted. Intelligence is a venture inconceivably daring and wonderfully successful; it is an attempt, and a victorious attempt, to be in two places at once. Sensibility to things at a distance, though it may exist, is useless and unmeaning until there are organs ready to avoid or pursue these things before they are absorbed into the organism; so that it is the possibility of travel that lends a meaning to the images of the eye and the mind, which otherwise would be mere feelings and a dull state of oneself. By tempting the animal to move, these images become signs for something ulterior, something to be seized and enjoyed. They sharpen his attention, and lead him to imagine other aspects which the same thing might afford; so that instead of saying that the possession of hands has given man his superiority, it would go much deeper to say that man, and all other animals, owe their intelligence to their feet. No wonder, then, that a peripatetic philosophy should be the best. Thinking while you sit, or while you kneel with the eyes closed or fixed upon vacancy, the mind lapses into dreams; images of things remote and miscellaneous are merged in the haze of memory, in which facts and fancies roll together almost indistinguishably, and you revert to the vegetative state, voluminous and helpless. Thinking while you walk, on the contrary, keeps you alert; your thoughts, though following some single path through the labyrinth, review real things in their real order; you are keen for discovery, ready for novelties, laughing at every little surprise, even if it is a mishap; you are careful to choose the right road, and if you take the wrong one, you are anxious and able to correct your error. Meantime, the fumes of digestion are dissipated by the fresh air; the head is cleared and kept aloft, where it may survey the scene; attention is stimulated by the novel objects constantly appearing; a thousand hypotheses run to meet them in an amiable competition which the event soon solves without ambiguity; and the scene as a whole is found to change with the changed station of the traveller, revealing to him his separate existence and his always limited scope, together with the distinction (which is all wisdom in a nutshell) between how things look and what they are.

A naturalist who was also a poet might describe the summer and winter tours of all the animals—worms, reptiles, fishes, birds, insects, and quadrupeds—telling us what different things they travel to see or to smell, and how differently they probably see and smell them. A mere moralist is more cramped in his sympathies and can imagine only human experience. And yet, when once the biped has learned to stand firmly on his hind legs, the human mind, more agile if less steady than a camera on its tripod, can be carried nimbly to any eminence or *Aussichtsthurm*; and if the prospect is unpleasing, it can scamper down again and perhaps change its chance environment for a better one. It is not the eye only that is consulted in surveying the panorama, and choosing some striking feature or hill-top for the end of the journey. The eye knows very well that it is only a scout, a more dignified substitute for the nose; and most of the pleasures it finds are vicarious and a mere promise of other satisfactions, like the scent of game. A search for the picturesque is the last and idlest motive of travel. Ordinarily the tribes of men move on more pressing errands and in some distress.

The most radical form of travel, and the most tragic, is migration. Looking at her birthplace the soul may well recoil; she may find it barren, threatening, or ugly. The very odiousness of the scene may compel her to conceive a negative, a contrast, an ideal: she will dream of El Dorado and the Golden Age, and rather than endure the ills she hath she may fly to anything she knows not of. This hope is not necessarily deceptive: in travel, as in being born, interest may drown the discomfort of finding oneself in a foreign medium: the solitude and liberty of the wide world may prove more stimulating than chilling. Yet migration like birth is heroic: the soul is signing away her safety for a blank cheque. A social animal like man cannot change his habitat without changing his friends, nor his friends without changing his manners and his ideas. An immediate token of all this, when he goes into a foreign country, is the foreign language which he hears there, and which he probably will never be able to speak with ease or with true propriety. The exile, to be happy, must be born again: he must change his moral climate and the inner landscape of his mind. In the greatest migration of our time, that of Europeans to America, I know by observation how easily this may be done, at least in the second generation; but a circumstance that makes the transformation easy is this: there need be no direct conversion of mind or heart, or even of language, but only an insensible exchange of old habits for new, because the new are more economical and soon seem easier. The adaptation, like all the creative adaptations of nature, is imposed by external influences, by compulsory material arrangements, by daily absorption in the prevalent forms of thrift and management, and yet it seems to come from within. The old habits may thus be soon shed completely and without regret. Colonists, who move in masses into lands which they find empty or which they clear of their old inhabitants, have this advantage over straggling immigrants worming their way into an alien society: their transformation can be thorough and hearty, because it obeys their genuine impulses working freely in a new material medium, and involves no mixture of incompatible traditions. America is a vast colony, and it still seems such to people who migrate even into those prosperous parts of it, like the United States or the Argentine, which have long-established constitutions and manners. The newcomers make themselves at home; they adapt themselves easily and gladly to the material environment, and make a moral environment of their own on that solid basis, ignoring or positively condemning the religion and culture of the elder Americans. Perhaps the elder Americans are assimilated in spirit to the new ones more readily than the new Americans to the old. I do not mean that any positively German, Italian, Jewish, or Irish ingredients are incorporated into American traditions: on the contrary, the more recent immigrants are quick—much quicker than the British colonists were—to shed all their memories and start afresh, like Adam in paradise: and for that very reason they stand out as naked Americans, men sharply and solely adapted to the present material conditions of the world: and in this sense their Americanism is louder and bolder than that of the old Yankees or the old Southerners, to whom the merely modern world seems perhaps a little deafening and a little unprincipled.

Compared with the emigrant the explorer is the greater traveller; his ventures are less momentous but more dashing and more prolonged. The idea of migration is often latent in his mind too: if he is so curious to discover new lands, and to describe them, it is partly because he might not be sorry to appropriate them. But the potential conqueror in him is often subdued into a disinterested adventurer and a scientific observer. He may turn into a wanderer. Your true explorer or naturalist sallies forth in the domestic interest; his heart is never uprooted; he goes foraging like a soldier, out in self-defence, or for loot, or for elbow room. Whether the reward hoped for be wealth or knowledge, it is destined to enrich his native possessions, to perfect something already dear: he is the emissary of his home science or home politics. Your rambler, on the contrary, is out on the loose, innocently idle, or driven by some morbid compulsion; his discoveries, if he makes any, will be lucky chances, to be attributed to sheer restlessness and fishing in troubled waters. The inveterate wanderer is a deluded person, trying like the Flying Dutchman to escape from himself: his instinct is to curl up in a safe nook unobserved, and start prowling again in the morning, without purpose and without profit. He is a voluntary outcast, a tramp. The maladaptation from which he suffers and which drives him from society may not be his fault: it may be due to the closeness of the home atmosphere, the coldness there, the intolerable ache of discords always repeated and right notes never struck. Or it may express an idiosyncrasy by no means regrettable, a wild atavistic instinct, or a mere need of stretching one's legs, or a young impulse to do something hard and novel. The mountain-climber, the arctic explorer, the passionate hunter or yachtsman, chooses his sport probably for mixed reasons: because he loves nature; because having nothing to do he is in need of exercise and must do something or other; or because custom, vanity, or rivalry has given him that bent; but the chief reason, if he is a genuine traveller for travel's sake, is that the world is too much with us, and we are too much with ourselves. We need sometimes to escape into open solitudes, into aimlessness, into the moral holiday of running some pure hazard, in order to sharpen the edge of life, to taste hardship, and to be compelled to work desperately for a moment at no matter what.

In the wake of the explorer another type of traveller is apt to follow, the most legitimate, constant, and normal of all: I mean the merchant. Nowadays a merchant may sit all his life at a desk in his native town and never join a caravan nor run the risk of drowning; he may never even go down into his shop or to the ship's side to examine or to sell his wares. This is a pity and takes half the humanity and all the poetry out of trade. If a merchant may be sedentary, it should be at least in one of those old mansions in Amsterdam where the ships came up the canal to the master's door, and the bales of merchandise were hoisted into the great lofts at the top of his house by a pulley that, like a curious gargoyle, projected from the gable. There the comforts and good cheer of family life could be enjoyed under the same roof that sheltered your wealth and received your customers. But if the merchant now will not travel, others must travel for him. I know that the commercial traveller is a vulgar man, who eats and drinks too much and loves ribald stories; he, like his superior, has been robbed of his natural dignity and his full art by the division of labor, the telegraph, and the uniformity of modern countries and modern minds; nevertheless I have a certain sympathy with him, and in those provincial inns where he is the ruling spirit, I have found him full of pleasant knowledge, as a traveller should be. But commerce has also its seafaring men, its engineers, its surveyors, its hunters and its trappers: all indefatigable travellers and knowers of the earth. My own parents belonged to the colonial official classes, and China and Manila, although I was never there, were familiar names and images to me in childhood; nor can I ever lose the sense of great distances in this watery globe, of strange amiable nations, and of opposed climates and ways of living and thinking, all equally human and legitimate. In my own journeys I have been enticed by romantic monuments and depth of historical interest rather than by geographical marvels; and yet what charm is equal to that of ports and ships and the thought of those ceaseless comings and goings, by which our daily needs are supplied? The most prosaic objects, the most common people and incidents, seen as a panorama of ordered motions, of perpetual journeys by night and day, through a hundred storms, over a thousand bridges and tunnels, take on an epic grandeur, and the mechanism moves so nimbly that it seems to live. It has the fascination, to me at least inexhaustible, of prows cleaving the water, wheels turning, planets ascending and descending the skies: things not alive in themselves but friendly to life, promising us security in motion, power in art, novelty in necessity.

The latest type of traveller, and the most notorious, is the tourist. Having often been one myself, I will throw no stones at him; from the tripper off on a holiday to the eager pilgrim thirsting for facts or for beauty, all tourists are dear to Hermes, the god of travel, who is patron also of amiable curiosity and freedom of mind. There is wisdom in turning as often as possible from the familiar to the unfamiliar: it keeps the mind nimble, it kills prejudice, and it fosters humour. I do not think that frivolity and dissipation of mind and aversion from one's own birthplace, or the aping of foreign manners and arts are serious diseases: they kill, but they do not kill anybody worth saving. There may be in them sometimes a sight of regret for the impossible, a bit of pathetic homage to an ideal one is condemned to miss; but as a rule they spring not from too much familiarity with alien things but from too little: the last thing a man wishes who really tastes the savour of anything and understands its roots is to generalise or to transplant it; and the more arts and manners a good traveller has assimilated, the more depth and pleasantness he will see in the manners and arts of his own home. Ulysses remembered Ithaca. With a light heart and clear mind he would have admitted that Troy was unrivalled in grandeur, Phaeacia in charm, and Calypso in enchantment: that could not make the sound of the waves breaking on his own shores less pleasant to his ears; it could only render more enlightened, more unhesitating, his choice of what was naturally his. The human heart is local and finite, it has roots: and if the intellect radiates from it, according to its strength, to greater and greater distances, the reports, if they are to be gathered up at all, must be gathered up at that centre. A man who knows the world cannot covet the world; and if he were not content with his lot in it (which after all has included that saving knowledge) he would be showing little respect for all those alien perfections which he professes to admire. They were all local, all finite, all cut off from being anything but what they happened to be; and if such limitation and such arbitrariness were beautiful there, he has but to dig down to the principle of his own life, and clear it of all confusion and indecision, in order to bring it too to perfect expression after its kind: and then wise travellers will come also to his city, and praise its name.

A Guide to Exiles, Expatriates, and Internal Emigrés

Mary McCarthy

FIRST LET ME SAY what I think these terms signify in common speech. An expatriate is different from an exile. In early use an exile was a banished man, a wanderer or roamer: *exsul.* "For I must to the greenwood go, alone, a banished man." In ancient Greek times, a man with a price on his head unable to return home until he had ransomed his blood guilt. The Wandering Jew, I suppose, is the archetypal exile, sentenced to trail about the earth until the Second Coming. Or Dante, a *fuoruscito,* waiting for a Second Coming in the shape of the German emperor who would make it safe for him to return to Florence. Ovid, banished by Augustus and writing his *Tristia.*

The exile is essentially a political figure, though the offense he has committed may have been in the sphere of morals. He has incurred the displeasure of the state by some sort of levity of conduct or looseness of tongue—a political crime in a tyranny, ancient or modern. Or he is an unhealthy element sent to lonely quarantine in some remote spot, like Prometheus on his rock.

Though the term easily lends itself to metaphorical inflation—"I am in exile here, in this unsympathetic environment into which fate has cast me," as Mme Bovary might have sighed to the notary's clerk—it has not lost its primary, political sense. The exile waits for a change of government or the tyrant's death, which will allow him to come home. If he stops waiting and adapts to the new circumstances, then he is not an exile any more. This condition of waiting means that the exile's whole being is concentrated on the land he left behind, in memories and hopes. The more passive type, summed up in the banished poet, lives on memories, while the active type, summed up in the revolutionist, lives on hopes and schemes. There is something of both in every exile, an oscillation between melancholy and euphoria.

More than anybody (except lovers), exiles are dependent on mail. A Greek writer friend in Paris was the only person I knew to suffer real pain during the events of May 1968, when the mail was cut off. In the absence of news from Greece, i.e., political news, he was wasting away, somebody deprived of sustenance. They are also great readers of newspapers and collectors of clippings. The fact that the press of their country is censored (a corollary, evidently, of their exile) makes them more hungry for scraps of rumor and information which they can piece together.

Classically, exile was a punishment decreed from above, like the original sentence of banishment on Adam and Eve, which initiated human history. Today deportation of native-born citizens is illegal, so far as I know, in most Western countries, where the opposite punishment—refusal of a passport—is meted out to political undesirables, and assignment to forced residence, which is really a form of imprisonment, is practiced most notably by the colonels' regime in Greece and by the Soviet Union, as in the case of Solzhenitsyn. Today a man may be an exile from his homeland even though he left voluntarily—the Jews who managed to get out of Nazi Germany, defectors from the East, Cuban runaways, American draft-resisters and deserters.

A person who cannot return home without facing death or jail for acts committed against the government is an exile. Eldridge Cleaver in Algiers. Or for acts he may commit if he remains true to himself, a whole being. Or for no acts at all, if he belongs to a proscribed category owing to his race, class, or religion. But in recent times, it is worth noticing, a new word, "refugee," describes a person fleeing from persecution because of his category. Taken from *refugie,* it was first used in England in 1685 of the Huguenots seeking asylum after the Revocation of the Edict of Nantes.

The exile is a singular, whereas refugees tend to be thought of in the mass. Armenian refugees, Jewish refugees, refugees from Franco Spain. But a political leader or artistic figure is an exile: Thomas Mann yesterday, today Theodorakis. Exile is the noble and dignified term, while a refugee is more hapless. At one point in your flight you may be a refugee and later, covered with honors, turn into an exile. If a group of Greek writers draws up a manifesto, they are writers-in-exile, but if we are trying to raise money to help them, they are refugees. The Vietnamese, Cambodian, and Lao peasants fleeing from the war zones are, of course, refugees; former Vietnamese politicians living in Paris are exiles.

What is implied in these nuances of social standing is the respect we pay to choice. The exile appears to have made a decision, while the refugee is the very image of helplessness, choicelessness, incomprehension, driven from his home by forces outside his understanding and control. We speak of flood refugees, earthquake refugees, persecuted by nature on account of the place they live in, war refugees harried by men for no other reason than that. Since refugees are seen as a mass the immediate thought is to process and resettle them. After first aid and minimal feeding. But no bureaucrat or social worker would dream of resettling exiles. The whole point about them is their refusal to put down new roots.

They are more like birds than plants, perching wherever they are, ready for homeward flight. Even when they have funds to buy a little house, take a long lease on a flat, they prefer transient accommodations—bed-sitters or hotel rooms, like Nabokov at the Hotel Montreux-Palace in Montreux. If an exile buys a house or takes a long lease on a flat, it's a sign that he's no longer a true exile.

An expatriate is almost the reverse. His main aim is never to go back to his native land or, failing that, to stay away as long as possible. His departure was wholly voluntary. An exile can be of any nationality, but an expatriate is generally English or American. The type was not seen in any numbers until the Romantic period. His predecessor was the eighteenth-century traveler, someone like Lady Mary Wortley Montagu, but the true expatriate is not a gadabout. Nor a wanderer like the exile. He tends to take up residence in some fixed spot (which he may change definitively, as Henry James did when he moved from France to England) and to buy property or lease it. In fact, the acquisition of desirable property, also in the form of furniture, paintings, statues, bibelots, seems to be one of the motives for expatriation. This is clear enough in James's novels.

The expatriate is a hedonist. He is usually an artist or a person who thinks he is artistic. He has no politics or, if he has any, like the Brownings he has acquired them from the country he has adopted. The average expatriate thinks about his own country rarely and with great unwillingness. He feels he has escaped from it. The expatriate is a by-product of industrialism. The Industrial Revolution sent him abroad, in headlong flight from ugliness. At the same time, of course, he owes his presence abroad to the prosperity induced by the factories and manufactures he is fleeing from. This too is clearly, though somewhat coyly, stated by James.

The expatriate's need is to locate as far as possible from the source of his capital and to be free of the disapprobation of the administrators of the same. He is somewhat less compromised if he is "only" receiving checks, like Scott Fitzgerald, from the *Saturday Evening Post* or royalties from Scribner's, like Hemingway. Least compromising of all is to find work in the adopted country, like the poet Allen Tate acting as a janitor in a Paris basement, but the expatriate is seldom willing to work at a job, since the nine-to-five routine is part of the spiritual oppression he is escaping from.

Dependence on money from a despised source tends to demoralize any but very young people. This demoralization is felt all through expatriate literature.

The exile too is dependent on money remitted from the homeland and other doubtful sources. The draft-resister's parents send checks; relations of the East European defector smuggle out icons and bits of jewelry which he can offer for sale. Without papers, the political refugee may have trouble finding work; if he is an author, he has exiled himself from his audience: at home his books are banned. But since he is not a hedonist money is not very important to him. As soon as he gets any, he is likely to share it with others or start a magazine.

Magazines are very important to exiles, and for literary expatriates they are morale-builders. To start a magazine—e.g., *transition, Blues, Broom*—is to start a sort of literary government-in-exile; up to then, you were just expatriates sitting in cafés. For the genuine exile, a magazine in the native language, like Herzen's *The Bell* or today's Polish *Kultura,* is almost as vital as mail. It is not only a forum for discussion but also a transmission belt to the home underground. Texts and news of secret trials, assassination attempts, purges, executions are smuggled out of the mother country, and copies of the magazine are then smuggled back in, to circulate in clandestinity.

The expatriate writers of the twenties and early thirties, mainly located in Paris, mainly rather poor or at any rate struggling, were also mainly American. Hemingway, Scott Fitzgerald, Henry Miller, Djuna Barnes, and so on. And of course Gertrude Stein and Edith Wharton, who were not poor. T. S. Eliot, Pound, and Conrad Aiken were living in England. The Irishmen Joyce and Beckett were living in Paris, Joyce having moved on from Trieste and Zurich. Norman Douglas and Percy Lubbock were in Italy. D. H. Lawrence and Katherine Mansfield had died in some awful combination of exile and expatriation, since their health forbade England to them. She was already an expatriate from New Zealand to England.

But when the dollar dropped in value during the thirties, after the crash, the Americans, by and large, went swiftly home, proving that even those who like Malcolm Cowley (author of a book called *Exile's Return*) had imagined themselves to be exiles were only expatriates. The few who stayed were driven back to the United States as refugees after the fall of France in 1940. Those few were the ones who returned when the war ended: the others had "refound their roots."

Today the expatriate writer is mainly a memory. In Paris, so far as I know, there are only Graham Greene, Beckett (unless he counts as French), James Jones, Nancy Mitford, Lesley Blanch, Italo Calvino, though there is a rumor that Lawrence Durrell is around. S. J. Perelman in England. A few live in Tangiers, a few still in Athens; in Rome, Gore Vidal and Muriel Spark. James Baldwin, in the south of France and before that in Turkey, is more of an exile than an expatriate. That is true of Burroughs too.

Expatriate writing, a potpourri of the avant-garde and the decadent, has almost faded away. In fiction, Henry James had set the themes once and for all. Everything that followed can be seen as a variation, however grotesque. *South Wind, The Sun Also Rises, Nightwood, The Alexandria Quartet, The Merry Month of May,* even *Tropic of Cancer.* From James on too, there is a certain Jackie-and-Ari color-supplement flavor to most of this fiction. The characters, from Isabel Archer to Henry Miller's hero, have come abroad to lead the beautiful life in one form or another. They are impersonating figures in a work of art—something few people dare to do at home.

The great exception is Joyce. But he considered himself an exile, not an expatriate. He proclaimed it in the title of his single play, *Exiles,* and in Stephen Dedalus's famous vow of silence, exile, and cunning. Of course, this was rhetoric: it was only in his own mind that Joyce was driven into exile by the tyranny at home. He could have come back without risk whenever he wanted and did several times. Yet he willed his rhetoric so fiercely that it commands belief, particularly since the difficulties of publication pitted him against the forces of order in the shape of censors wherever his native language was spoken. He was able to go home freely, but his books could not. In this, he differed from expatriates like Hemingway and Fitzgerald, who never had any problems with censors or customs.

Moreover, Joyce was no hedonist, though fond of white wine and song. He had come abroad with a purpose: "to forge in the smithy of my soul the uncreated conscience of my race." He was engaging himself in a conspiracy against the ruling forces of Ireland, and the infernal machine was to be his literary work. It was a plot, to be executed with the typical methods of the revolutionary: silence (i.e., secrecy) and cunning.

As an exile and a conspirator, he had no moral shrinking from accepting money from his hard-up brother, from his rich patron, Miss Weaver, from any available source. It was as impersonal as raising money to buy a mimeograph machine or material for making bombs. Unlike other exiles, he was a real loner, a conspiracy of one, yet he had great organizational talent and was always able to recruit a staff of collaborators: Herbert Gorman, Stuart Gilbert, the Jolases, Sylvia Beach, Samuel Beckett, Frank Budgen, Robert McAlmon, Padraic Colum, not to mention typists, copiers, miscellaneous helpers. In London his chief agent, Pound, was active. In Paris there was a small cell of Frenchmen, headed by Valéry Larbaud. The expatriates who helped him fabricate the big bomb, first known as *Work in Progress*, became, as it were, honorary exiles, and the organization did not dissolve with his death.

He had the exile's characteristic restlessness: the Joyces were constantly moving. Yet he regarded his exile as permanent and definitive and was rather upset when the Irish finally got their freedom, which he feared might suggest that he no longer had any reason to stay away. He was making a *literary* revolution, whose strategy required his physical absence to foster mental concentration. True to form, he was nourishing himself on memories. Nothing could be farther from the expatriate "international novel" than his careful reconstruction of Bloomsday—June 16, 1904—with its remembered Dublin containing real streets and real people, like the scale model of some famous battle with all the generals, foot soldiers, and artillery pieces in place. *Finnegans Wake* is still set in Dublin with a cast of native characters, seemingly pre-World War I, who have become eternal.

Ada, you might say, is Nabokov's *Finnegans Wake*, polylingual, full of puns and linguistic jokes, placed in an imaginary future-past, where America and Russia have merged and annexed bits of France and Switzerland into their author's sovereign territory. The characters, like the Earwicker nuclear family, are closely related and prone to split and fuse; though not primordial or eternal, they attain patriarchal ages without taking leave of adolescence, as though playing naughty tricks on time. If the self-banished Joyce was making a one-man literary revolution, Nabokov, a genuine displaced person, has been trying throughout his career to make a one-man literary restoration, using his prodigious memory to undo the present. "Speak, Memory," he commands royally, in a title, and the masque begins.

Though he has the reputation of a modernist, his language is antique Mandarin, like his life style, and he is probably the greatest enemy of modernism extant. He is against psychoanalysis, every kind of "new" politics, atom bombs, avant-garde art. He is not just any White Guard exile but a dethroned monarch, like Charles the Beloved, in *Pale Fire*, traveling under the incognito of Kinbote-Botkin, a poor mad refugee. Nabokov's relations with English are often highly autocratic: witness his controversy with

Edmund Wilson over his Pushkin translation—an international incident. He has written a long poem—and some shorter ones—to the Russian language, which he treats as a national treasure the usurper Bolsheviks appropriated from him, to turn over to the rabble.

Ada is his supreme revenge. There he at last reinstates himself in a supra-national, supercilious palace of culture, with a queen by his side; the mirror pair of children, like the Ptolemys, are brother and sister. "A Family Chronicle" is the subtitle; "Dynastic" would be better. Nothing could be more remote from the Family of Man or Here-Comes-Everybody of *Finnegans Wake*, which takes place in a pub.

Ada, in my view, is a failure, a misfired *coup d'état*, and this, I think, is not unrelated to the crows of triumph that shrill through it. The theme of need in all its sad and threadbare forms (Gogol's overcoat), so characteristic of the author, has here been cast aside or molted, like last year's set of feathers. But this theme and the allied one of insuperable distance, which everybody has experienced, if only when in love, have up to now supplied a human element, compensating for a great deal of extravagance and foppery in Nabokov's writing. We forgive the vanity and arrogance of the Pretender exile because, like Pnin, like Humbert Humbert, like Botkin, he is at least half a refugee. In *Ada*, there is no shared mass misery of furnished rooms, German boarding-houses and park benches, underpaid language lessons, *émigré* magazines and newspapers, sectarian bickering all leading on to American lectureships, missed trains, common-room snubs, motels. One of the chief interests, instead, is genealogy. It is as if the author, once a Russian exile in America, with all that implies of loss and grieving, had metamorphosed into an American expatriate living on a Swiss mountaintop "above it all."

Nabokov insists that he is indifferent to current Russian events, but that is only his way of snubbing the Soviet Union, just as his pose of being indifferent to politics is a snub to *engagé* literature. Actually, he is far from apolitical and continues to feud in books and interviews with left-wingers as a body and with Russian left-wingers in particular, including Chernyshevsky, author of *What is to be done?*, who died in 1889. More peculiar is his malice toward Pasternak, whom he half admired as a poet and who was dead too, and disgraced when *Ada* came out, in which Nabokov cites, among other repellent titles, *Les Amours du Docteur Mertvago*—i.e., *mertv* (death plus *merde*). This must be a case of novelist's jealousy. Nabokov, an exile, envied Pasternak, an "internal *émigré*"—a Soviet term of abuse often applied to Pasternak and meaning something like an internal expatriate, if that can be conceived.

As novelists, Nabokov and Pasternak were in rivalry for "the Russian land," a legacy they had from Tolstoy and Aksakov. They belonged to the same milieu, the old educated class—what the Soviets called "former persons," like ghosts—though Pasternak's family were lower on the tsarist social scale, artists and bohemians, city people and apartment-dwellers, rather than well-to-do landowners. And the external exile, despite his much greater worldly success, envied the internal exile—the man-in-possession.

Perhaps it was sometimes mutual. In *Dr. Zhivago* (page 312 of the English edition) Pasternak appears to be emitting a signal of some kind to the other writer. "Folding and unfolding like a scrap of coloured stuff, a brown speckled butterfly" flies in and out of the story for the length of a paragraph, giving rise to some reflections on mimicry and protective coloring. Yury Zhivago, says Pasternak, has alluded to this subject in his medical publications. But Nabokov too, as a professional lepidopterist, has published on protective mimicry—a fact probably known to Pasternak, who certainly was aware of him as a butterfly-hunter. Yet if the passage was intended as a fraternal greeting, it got a cold response.

The characters in *Dr. Zhivago,* many of them exiles from their former way of life, are swept up by the storm of the Revolution and become refugees. Sooner or later, everybody is in flight or hiding—refugees from war, from the Red terror, from the White terror, peasants who have lost their homes, townspeople driven into the countryside by hunger. The long and beautiful train trip across the Russian land into the Ural Mountains, which recalls a trip in Aksakov's memoirs, is the great major sequence of the book, combining an idyl with an epic trek. The revolutionary storm spares nobody, not even the commissar Antipov, who is found toward the end hiding in a farmhouse encircled by wolves. With one big exception, the evil genius Komarovsky, Lara's seducer. He is last seen riding off in a *wagon-lit* to become, not an exile, for he has never been "political," but a true expatriate, doubtless smoking a cigar and heading for Manchuria. Another exception, another immune figure—who does not belong, though, to the naturalistic plane of the novel and who, like Komarovsky, is not even listed among the principal characters—is Yury's half-brother and miraculous protector, Yevgraf, the Angel of Death. According to Nadezhda Mandelstam, in her book *Hope against Hope,* the mysterious Yevgraf is simply some high-up bureaucrat whose miracles are worked by knowing "the right people," that is, by having a transmission belt to Stalin.

Pasternak's own situation varied between periods of internal exile and official favor and protection. With Solzhenitsyn, you get internal exile at its bleakest and in nearly all its forms and stages. Deportation, forced labor in a camp, forced residence, confinement in a cancer ward—in his novel of that name the sick are treated by the staff and people outside rather as if they were wilful exiles from a healthy society. His books take place in a climate so frozen and immobile that Pasternak's orphans in the storm, by comparison, are enjoying the wildest liberty. The revolution described by Pasternak still has something of a Tolstoyan natural force, awesome and fierce, but in Solzhenitsyn, the savage natural is replaced by the universal ordinary. He does not write about former people but about Soviet people and about Soviet society, almost as if there had never been any other kind. Nobody is homeless or buffeted by circumstance, since everyone must be registered. There are no outlaws hiding in the forest: Pasternak's red rowanberry trees have probably been leveled by a bulldozer to make a detention camp.

Nor is there any refuge in memory. For most writers-in-exile—e.g., Joyce, Nabokov, the internal exile Pasternak—recollections of childhood are a literary food source and have been hoarded, squirrel-wise, against the winter; it does not appear to matter whether the childhood was happy, like Nabokov's, or dingy, like Joyce's. Solzhenitsyn, a Soviet man (born in 1918), seems to have had no childhood to look back to for sustenance. That other dimension, the past, is seldom glimpsed in his books up to now, unless it is through the old peasant woman Matriona, who is herself a reminiscence, a piece of stout material left over from some prehistoric eon.

Unlike Pasternak, he has no influential connections, which would relate him to a sphere "higher up." At present he is being sheltered by the cellist Rostropovich, who is risking his passport by harboring him. His only "outlet" seems to have been teaching mathematics. One of the most interesting things about the drama of his getting the Nobel Prize award was the official threat not to let him back into the country if he went to Stockholm to receive it. They knew their man: Solzhenitsyn did not go to Stockholm. But he accepted the prize. He chose internal exile against the other kind—a decision some Westerners found mysterious since so many Soviet citizens are doing their best to get out. Solzhenitsyn insisted on his right to stay *and* to receive the prize.

The decision was typical of today's internal exiles in the Soviet Union, not only writers but scientists. Probably Mme Mandelstam, Sinyavsky, and Daniel would respond in the same way in the circumstances, and

Akhmatova too, if she were alive. It is a question of politics and of pride—in fact, of national pride. The internal exiles seem to have made it a principle to behave toward the Soviet Union as if it were a normal country, with an operative constitution. As though by their determination they could oblige the "as if" to come true. To go into exile, on the one hand, or conform, on the other, would be to give up any hope of that happening and to accept the Soviet Union as some sort of clinical monstrosity outside the norms of law. This notion they refuse. And they do not compare Soviet justice with U.S. justice or English justice or tsarist justice, but with articles in the Soviet constitution and laws in the statute books. Thus their frame of reference is Soviet reality, which they also occupy with their bodies rather like sit-in strikers.

This political determination is clear in Solzhenitsyn's books. He writes as coolly as if there were no censorship and no conceivable interference with publication. His books appear as simple statements of fact, without exaggeration or fantasy. That may be why memory of the distant kind ("the laundryman in the lavender flannels") has no place in them. One of the few rhetorical reminders of anything "outside," of a larger frame, is the title of *The First Circle*, which refers to Dante's Hell. The prisoners there are relatively privileged spirits, like Dante's virtuous heathen, the First Circle being Limbo. Their punishment is light, compared to Ivan Denisovich's, and consists simply of exclusion, but it has the hellish characteristic of permanence. A better metaphor for internal exile might be Purgatory, a place where you wait, like exiles in a foreign land, to go home. Solzhenitsyn *is* home, and yet he declines to recognize the immediate political geography as permanent. This might be a definition of the internal exile: a man who has taught himself to behave as if he had already crossed a frontier while refusing to leave his house.

Exile

Austin Clarke

GEORGE LAMMING'S BRILLIANT analysis of his life in Britain as an immigrant during the 1950s bears the title *The Pleasures of Exile.* There is obvious irony in this title to his essay on cultural and social dislocation, made all the more significant because Lamming is addressing his disapproval of Britain's treatment of him, a black Briton, a black Barbadian. His disappointment is understandable. A mother, even an oppressive, heartless one, does not treat her children in this unredeeming, brutal manner and remain a mother. What is more, the child-victim can no longer embrace this former familial relationship without cynicism. The relationship ceases to be pleasurable, if it could ever have been described in that way.

For these reasons, I have always felt that "exile" cannot be a pleasure. But more importantly, I do not consider my life in Canada for the last thirty-eight years to be one of "exile." For I am not escaping from any form of political oppression or social persecution in Barbados. And even though a critical look at our social and class differences, and the way in which it apportions privilege and reward, might, at first glance, be termed oppressive and disadvantageous to some who suffer under its complicated application, still it cannot be said that the society from which I came propelled me because of its heinousness to seek social, cultural and political redress and refuge in Canada.

If it can be argued that the material benefits are greater here than they are in Barbados, I still do not qualify under the aegis of "exile." But these very material benefits must be evaluated fairly and compared with the standards that are Barbadian before I can even argue that this society offers more benefits that did Barbados.

I admit that, intellectually and politically, my presence here can be termed an "exile." And the term takes on an added currency of sophistication because I am an author, a Barbadian writer who lives in Canada. In blunt terms, reflecting Frantz Fanon's "psycho-existential complex" as a means of measuring black-white relations in a white society, a black writer working in a white environment—I am tempted to say in a white culture, but to do so is to ascribe to "white" and to "culture" a pre-eminence that is undeserved and that from my experiences in Canada and my knowing

Canada does not exist—applying Fanon's measurement, the term "exile" is inapplicable in my case.

The term "exile" when used in the case of the black writer living in a white society has the implication that the writer is better off in this environment, that this environment gives him objectivity, if not a greater grasp on his creative skill, and that were this environment, this "exile," not possible, were there not this extension of hospitality and the provision of a climate suitable for work and existence, the black writer would be lost, or dead, or stifled amidst the memories of his former inhospitable native climate. There is also an insidious implication in the term that suggests a banishment and a cultural surgery carried out on the psyche of the writer. And therein lies its other inference of required gratitude towards the country that has saved you from your former inhospitable state.

If the term could be applied, as it was, to Richard Wright and to James Baldwin, who sought refuge in Paris from the exigencies of racism in America, their county of birth, it was properly applied in their cases, since it is doubtful that either of them could, in the context of the forties and fifties, have had the leisure and the protection from that racism so necessary for them to develop their art. They had no protection from their own government when as young writers they left that country. And it is doubtful that at this stage of their careers, had not the French government extended to them, both officially and privately, a climate suitable for the creation of works of fiction—and nonfiction—their artistic development might have been curtailed by the brutality of racism in America. At least, this is their word.

It must also be said that today in America, in spite of lingering racism, no black writers would in Baldwin's or Wright's terms seek to be "exiles" in a foreign country as a pre-condition of their creative development or of their objective or subjective critical judgement in America.

Gratitude, one of the aspects of "exile" in its most traditional sense, is exemplified by a silence of criticism of the country offering this "exile." It is debatable whether in Paris racism was not so pronounced as it had been in America. If this is the case, why did not either of them, Baldwin or Wright, make comment on this subject? Perhaps they were deluded into feeling that French *égalité* was less abstract than it was, and could be applied to them. The fact is, they did not make this comment about French racism. And they did not, and could not, because cognizant as they had to be of gratitude and guided by the principle of decency, they, as "beggars," could not be "choosers."

The "exile" is a beggar in the most sophisticated sense that he must know his place. And he himself contributes to whatever deprecation of his native culture, his mores, his native view is implied, which he is forced to evaluate through foreign eyes and using a foreign sensibility. He is, most of all, a man who lives in two cultures; and when one culture is underpinned by a language he does not speak, his existence during his "exile" becomes, at least, schizophrenic.

Denying therefore the characterization of my life in this country as that of an "exile," I have to say now how I look upon my time here, after I arrived in 1955. I would have to say first what was the purpose of coming here, what my expectations were and how the mere act of arrival transformed me. My purpose in coming was to attend university. It was not to become a writer, for in 1955 my ambitions were not literary, even though I had tried my hand at schoolboy poetic ventures. Had I retained any of that literary adventurousness, I would have followed other West Indians, such as George Lamming, Samuel Selvon, V. S. Naipaul and Aubrey Williams, to England. The choice would have been appropriate as England was then, and perhaps still is now, the Mother Country and any literary tradition to which we were exposed through our education was English. It is an aspect of the disappointment of those writers in their social lives there that has caused so many of them to define their time in England during the 1950s understandably as an "exile."

In spite of their contribution, now acknowledged to have been significant, still the exigencies of English racism cut them out of any meaningful role they could have played as men. And to varying extents their lives became alienated from precisely that font of creativity and the possibility of objectivity in viewing their respective islands that their going to England had promised.

My expectations about Canada were not so traumatic in their rupture, precisely because I had wanted nothing more than a university education from the place of my choice. My choice was mine (though it was not the primary one). And my expectations, even though tinged by aspects of discrimination and racism, were never dulled because my intention was to return to Barbados after having crossed the Atlantic to read Law in England. And my demands were furthermore not entirely frustrated because I had made no commitment to Canada so far as applying for any status other than that of the periodic, investigated one of student. There was, therefore, no bargain, no negotiation, no promise, no exacting of loyalty. As a matter of fact, I was, by the definition of being a student, expected to make no transaction. Get your education and run back where you came from: that was the unspoken individual and official relationship ingrained into us.

I have always insisted that my arrival in this country did not bring about a shock of culture. We had known Canada, in our geography books, in the importation of cod fish, potatoes, Canadian Healing Oil, apples at Christmas, sardines, canned salmon and the lady boats which trafficked in Caribbean waters. And Canadians had always considered the sun and the blue water of Barbados to be a spa of rejuvenation. In those days, unless you lived close to the Marine Hotel, the bastion of segregation and tourists' eccentricities; unless your mother, aunt, uncle or brother was in the hotel business, those Canadians were hidden from us, and we were protected from their enjoyment of our sea and sun by a line of defined exclusion: them from us, but more importantly, us from them.

Barbados is older though not richer than Canada. And if the first veneer of awe and spectacle, wonder and envy at the bigness of things, buildings and streets, cars and houses, is worn off, even at that first meeting a critical spirit was able to see more quality in the older, more established society of Barbados than in the newness of Canada at that time, also a colony of the Mother Country. There was nothing spiritual, nothing culturally compelling to make one want to embrace Canada as a place of redemption. This is not to say that I may not be grateful for Canada as the place where, physically and psychologically, I have written my novels. But they could have been written in Italy or in Germany. Ironically, they could not have been written in Barbados. So there is some decency in acknowledging this, and in being grateful, but without the deeper spiritual gratitude of the "exile."

We have a true spirit of multiculturalism here. I can, as I have done, become a Canadian citizen. And in a real sense, I am regarded as a Canadian. Not so the predicament of emigrants living in England. Those from amongst us who went to England were never regarded as Englishmen. Not even black Englishmen, unless the term was used with political cynicism. How then could "exile" be considered seriously as a definition of my time, spent either as a foreigner or as a writer? And it cannot, because I have retained the ethnic and cultural flavour of Barbados, and the winters here can do nothing to transform them through a drop in the enthusiasm of my Barbadian-ness. But the impossibility of that is more subjective. It was my choice not to permit this freezing of my expectation, to have me swallowed up culturally during my long temporary sojourn here.

In the month of August, when Toronto is transformed into colours of the Caribbean and there is music and a new pulse to the activities of men and women, an incident I witnessed, simple in its social significance, perhaps, brought home to me that the time had come for me to consider seriously the extent to which my senses had been numbed by too long a stay in this city, in this country. A store was playing calypso music through its loudspeakers, spewing the refreshing, pulsating beat onto the street filled with people, filled with their own business. It was a reminder of Barbados. The music was. And it was beautiful. It was loud because the bus had stopped outside the door of the store. I could breathe some of that memory. And relive the long past. But a woman, not West Indian, said disapprovingly, "Why do they have to play *that* music?"

The rejection was not only euphemistic, it was not only that many animosities were barely buried in her voice, which came close to being hysterical; nor was it the dismissal of this aspect of my culture, used in this city to enrich merchants during the annual Caribana Parade season. It was a declaration of subordination to things which she wanted to be Canadian: an intrusion upon her more bland consciousness. She would have no jerk-seasoning in her chicken that night.

Her voice and her manner in the voice killed the music. But the beat had already been made indelible. And I yearned for the first time in thirty-eight years to hear that sound, that noise, that pounding of steel on steel, of wood on tightened skin, once more, more often in its native, disturbingly loud, jungled environment.

I packed my bags, in that deep spiritual way, and removed myself from further assaults upon my true culture, assaults made by a declaration whose impact was probably not known by the woman making it. But it was made. And intent, motive and cause were now irrelevant. If I had ever thought of "exile," of the cutting off from known and accustomed ways, it happened that beautiful, bright afternoon in August.

II
Allegiances

homesick, my desire
crawled across snow
like smoke, for its lost fire

—Derek Walcott
"A Village Life"

What Exile Is

Victor Hugo

I

LAW INCARNATE IS the citizen; law crowned is the lawmaker. The ancient republics thought of law as sitting in a curule chair, with a scepter in hand, the law, and dressed in purple, authority. This figure was true, and the ideal remains the same today. All regular societies must have at their summit sacred and armed law, sacred by justice, armed by freedom.

In what has just been said, the word force was not mentioned. Force exists, however; but it does not exist outside of law; it exists within law.

Whoever says law says force.

What then is there outside of law?

Violence.

There is only one necessity, truth; that is why there is only one force, law. Success outside of truth and law is an appearance. The short view of tyrants is mistaken here; a successful ambush gives them the impression of a victory, but this victory is full of ashes; the criminal thinks that his crime is his accomplice; mistake; his crime is his punisher; the murderer always cuts himself on his own knife; treason always betrays the traitor; offenders, without realizing it, are ensnared by their offense, an invisible specter; an evil deed never lets go of you; and inevitably, through an inexorable path ending in cesspools of blood for glory and in abysses of mud for shame, without fail for the guilty, the Eighteenth Brumaire leads great men to Waterloo and the Second of December leads the small to Sedan.

When they strip and dethrone law, men of violence and traitors of the state do not know what they are doing.

II

Exile is law laid bare. Nothing is more terrible. For whom? For the one who is subjected to exile? No, for the one who inflicts it. The torture turns around and bites the torturer.

A dreamer walking alone on a shore, a desert surrounding the contemplative, an aged, calm face circled by birds surprised by the storm, the assiduity of a philosopher at the reassuring break of morning, God called to witness from time to time in the presence of rocks and trees, a reed that not only thinks but meditates, hair that goes from black to gray and from gray to white in solitude, a man who feels himself gradually becoming a shadow, the long passage of years on the one who is absent but who is not dead, the gravity of this deprived man, the nostalgia of this innocent man, nothing is more fearsome for the crowned criminals.

Whatever the temporarily all-powerful do, the eternal depths resist them. They have only the surface of certainty, what is beneath belongs to thinkers. You exile a man. Very well. And afterwards? You can pull a tree up by its roots, you cannot wrest the daylight from the sky. Tomorrow, dawn.

Yet, in fairness to the exilers, let us say they are logical, perfect, abominable. They do all that they can to destroy the exile.

Will they achieve their goal? Will they succeed? No doubt.

A man so ruined that he has nothing but his honor, so stripped that he has nothing but his conscience, so isolated that he has nothing but impartiality, so disowned that he has nothing but truth, so thrown into darkness that he has nothing left but the sun, this is what an exile is.

III

Exile is not a material thing, it is a moral thing. Any corner of the globe is as good as any other. *Angulus ridet.* Any place one can daydream is good, provided the corner is dark and the horizon vast.

The archipelago of the Channel is particularly attractive; it is not difficult to liken to the fatherland, being France. Jersey and Guernsey are pieces of Gaul, broken in the eighth century by the sea. Jersey had more coquetry than Guernsey; she won for being prettier and less beautiful. In Jersey the forest has made itself a garden; in Guernsey the boulders have remained colossal. More grace here, more majesty there. In Jersey one is in Normandy, in Guernsey, one is in Brittany. Jersey is a bouquet as large as the city of London. All is perfume, sunlight, smiles; which does not prevent storms. The one who is writing these pages has somewhere described Jersey as "an idyll in the middle of the sea." In pagan times, Jersey was more Roman and Guernsey more Celtic; one senses Jupiter in Jersey and Teutates in Guernsey. In Guernsey, the ferocity has disappeared, but the unsociability has remained. In Guernsey, what was once druidic is now Huguenot; it is no longer Moloch, but Calvin; the church is cold, the landscape austere, the religion ill-humored. All in all, two charming islands; one pleasant, the other surly.

One day the queen of England, more than the queen of England, the duchess of Normandy, venerable and sacred six days out of seven, went, with salvo, smoke, din and ceremony, to visit Guernsey. It was a Sunday, the only day of the week that was not hers. The queen, having suddenly become "that woman," disturbed the Lord's rest. She descended to the quay in the middle of a silent crowd. Not a person took off his hat. One man greeted her, the exile speaking here.

He did not greet a queen, but a woman.

The devout island was surly. This puritanism has its grandeur.

Guernsey was made to leave the exile with only good memories; but exile exists outside of the place of exile. From the interior point of view, one can say: there is no beautiful exile.

Exile is a severe land; everything is knocked down, uninhabitable, demolished and recumbent, except for duty, standing alone, like a church steeple in a collapsed town that seems even taller amidst the rubble.

Exile is a place of punishment.

Of whom?

Of the tyrant.

But the tyrant defends himself.

IV

Expect everything, you who are exiled. You are flung away, but you are not set free. The banisher is curious and he will cast many eyes over you. He will visit you in ingenious and varied ways. A respectable Protestant pastor will sit in your foyer, this Protestantism draws its salary from the Tronsin-Dumersan cashbox; a jabbering foreign prince introduces himself, it is Vidoçq who has come to see you; is he a real prince? Yes, he is from royal blood, and also from the police; a gravely doctrinaire professor gains entry to your home, you catch him reading your papers. They will take all sorts of liberties against you; you are outside of the law, that is, outside of justice, outside of reason, outside of respect, outside of plausibility; they will claim to be authorized by you to publish your conversations, and they will make sure that they are stupid; they will attribute to you words that you have not said, letters that you have not written, deeds that you have not done. They will draw near only to choose more effectively where they will stab you; exile is openwork; they look through it as into an animal's den; you are isolated and watched.

Do not write to your friends in France; your letters can be opened; the Supreme Court consents to this; beware of your relations as an exile, they will end in obscure things; the man who smiled at you in Jersey will tear you apart in Paris; the one who greets you under his name insults you under a pseudonym; the one in Jersey writes pages against exiled men that are worthy of being offered to men of the empire, and dedicates them to Pereire bankers. All of this is so simple, you understand. You are in quarantine. If someone honest comes to see you, woe to him. The border awaits him, and the emperor will be there in the form of military police. They will strip women bare to find one of your books on them, and if they resist, if they become indignant, they will be told: *this is not for your skin.*

The master, who is the traitor, surrounds you with whom he sees fit; the banisher has the quality of the banished; he adorns his agents with it; there is no security; watch out for yourself; you are speaking to a face, it is a mask that listens; your exile is haunted by this specter, the spy.

A mysterious stranger approaches you, saying softly in your ear that, if you like, he will arrange to have the emperor assassinated; it is Bonaparte offering to kill Bonaparte for you. At your banquets of brotherhood, someone in the corner will shout: *Long live Marat! Long live Hébert! Long live the guillotine!* With a bit of attention you will recognize the voice of Carlier. Sometimes the spy begs; the emperor asks you for alms through his Piétri; you give them, he laughs; the gaiety of the torturer. You pay for the inn of this exile, he is an agent; you pay for the trip of this fugitive, he is a henchman; you walk down the street, you hear someone say: *There is the real tyrant!* He is speaking of you; you turn around; who is this man? He answers you: he is an exile. Hardly. He is a state employee. He is ferocious and paid. He is a republican with *Maupas* written all over him. Coco disguised as Scaevola.

As for the subterfuge, the deception, the baseness, accept them. These are the projectiles of the empire.

Above all, do not complain. They would laugh. After the complaint, the abuse would start again, same as before, without any variation; why bother to change slime? Yesterday's is as good.

The insults will continue, relentlessly, every day, with the tireless ease and satisfied conscience of the wheel turning and venality lying. No retaliations; insult is protected by its vileness; *la platitude sauve l'insecte.* The crushing of zero is impossible. And slander, sure of impunity, has a great time of it; it descends to such inane indignities that the degradation of refuting it goes beyond the distaste of enduring it.

The insulters have imbeciles as their audience. This makes a loud laugh.

They are surprised that you do not find it quite natural to be slandered. Are you not there for that? O naive man, you are a target. Such and such person is in the academy for having insulted you; this other received the cross for the same act of bravery, the emperor decorated him on the field of honor of the slander; this other, who also distinguished himself through brilliant affronts, has been named prefect. To offend you is lucrative. People have to make a living. Indeed! Why are you exiled?

Be reasonable. You are in the wrong. Who forced you to think badly of the coup d'état? What possessed you to fight for the law? What passing fancy made you revolt? Can the law be defended when there is no one left in favor of it? These are the demagogues! To be stubborn, to persevere, to persist is absurd. A man stabs law, assassinates law. He probably has his reasons. Be with this man. Success makes him just. Be with success since success becomes law. Everyone will be grateful to you. We will sing your praises. Instead of being exiled you will be a senator, and you will not look like an idiot.

Do you dare doubt this man's rights? But you see that he has succeeded! You see that the judges who have accused him pledge oaths to him! You see that priests, soldiers, bishops, generals are with him! You think you have more virtue than all this! You want to defy all this! Come now! On the one hand, all that is respected, all that is respectable, all that is venerated, all that is venerable; on the other, you! This is inept; and we deride you, and we are right to do so. To lie against a brute is allowed. All the decent people are against you; and we, the slanderers, we are with the decent people. Listen, think, look within yourself. Society had to be saved. From whom? From you. Was there anything you did not threaten it with? No more war, no more scaffold, abolition of the death penalty, free and obligatory education, everyone knowing how to read! It was horrible. And what a lot of abominable utopias! The underage woman made of age, this half of the human species allowed universal suffrage, marriage liberated by divorce; the poor child instructed like the rich child, equality resulting from education; taxes lowered at first, then abolished altogether by the destruction of parasites, by the construction of national edifices, by the sewer transformed into fertilizer, by the repartition of communal goods, by cultivating the fallow, by exploiting social capital gain; lowered cost of living by stocking the rivers with fish; no more classes, no more boundaries, no more ligatures, the republic of Europe, continental monetary unity, increased circulation increasing wealth tenfold; nothing but folly?

We had to steer clear of all of this! What! Peace will be made among men, there will be no more army, there will be no more military service!

What! France will be cultivated so that it will be able to nourish two hundred fifty million men; there will be no more tax, France will live off its profits! What! Women will vote, children will have rights before their fathers, mothers of families will no longer be subjects and servants, husbands will no longer have the right to kill their wives! What! The priest will no longer be the master! What! There will be no more battles, there will be no more soldiers, there will be no more executioners, there will be no more gallows and guillotines! This is appalling! We had to save ourselves. The president did it! Long live the emperor! You are resisting him; we are tearing you apart; we are writing whatever we want about you. We know that what we say is not true, but we are protecting society, and slander that protects society is state-approved. Since the magistracy is with the coup d'état, justice is as well; since the clergy is with the coup d'état, religion is as well; religion and justice are immaculate and holy figures; slander that is useful to them is part of the honor that we owe them; slander is a prostitute, perhaps, but she serves virgins. Respect her.

Thus reason the insulters.

The best thing that the exile can do is to think of other things.

V

Since he is at the seaside, he should take advantage of it. May this movement beneath the infinite give him wisdom. May he meditate upon the eternal riot of waves against the shore and of deceptions against the truth. Diatribes are convulsive in vain. May he watch the wave spit upon the rock and ask himself what it gains and what this rock loses.

No. No revolt against insult, no expenditure of emotion, no retaliation. Maintain a severe calm. . . .

May the tracked down, betrayed, booed, barked at, bitten exile be quiet.

This is the great silence.

To want to extinguish insult is to fan its flames. Everything thrown onto slander is fuel for it. It uses its own shame. To refute it is to satisfy it. Actually, slander profoundly values the slandered. Slander is the one that suffers; it dies of disdain. It aspires to the honor of a refutation. Do not accord it one. To be slapped would prove to it that it is perceived. It will show its hot cheek, saying: Thus I exist!

VI

Besides, why and of what would exiles complain? Look at all of history. Great men are even more insulted than they.

Insult is an old human habit; idle hands take pleasure in throwing stones; woe to all who go beyond this level; those at the summits make lightning come from above and stones from below. It is almost their fault; why are they at the summits? They attract attention and affront. The envious passerby is ever present in the street and hatred is his function; and one always encounters him, small and furious, in the shadow of tall buildings.

The specialists should research the causes of insomnia in great men. Homer sleeps, *bonus dormitat;* this sleep is roused by Zoilos. Aeschylus feels on his skin the firing of Eupolis and Cratinus; these infinitely small men abound; Virgil has Moevius on top of him; Horace, Licilius; Juvenal, Codrus; Dante has Cecchi; Shakespeare has Greene; Rotrou has Scudéry, and Corneille has the academy; Molière has Donneau de Visé, Montesquieu has Desfontaines, Buffon has Labeaumelle, Jean-Jacques has Palissot, Diderot has Nonotte, Voltaire has Fréron. Glory, a golden bed where there are bugs.

Exile is not glory, but there is this resemblance with glory, vermin. Adversity is not left in peace. To see the just exile sleep displeases those who collect crumbs beneath the table of Nero or of Tiberius. What, he is sleeping! He must be happy! Let us bite him!

A man knocked down, lying down, and swept away (which is very simple; when Vitellius is the idol, Juvenal is the filth), a man expelled, deprived, vanquished, people are jealous of this. How bizarre, exiles make people envious. This could be understood of great virtues envying great misfortunes, of Caton envying Régulus, of Thraséas envying Brutus, of Rabbe envying Barbès. But no. The vile are jealous of the lofty; what is troublesome about the proud protests of the vanquished is their utter futility. Gustave Planche is jealous of Louis Blanc, Baculard is jealous of Milton, and Jocrisse is jealous of Aeschylus.

The ancient insulter only followed the chariot of the victor, the modern insulter follows the hurdle of the vanquished. The vanquished bleeds. The insulters add their mud to this blood. Very well. May they have this joy.

This joy seems all the more real when it is not hated by the master and when it is regularly paid. Secret funds come out in public insult. Despots, in their war against exiles, have two auxiliaries: first, envy, second, corruption.

To speak of what exile is, one must go somewhat into detail. Part of this subject is the indication of certain peculiar worms, and we have had to penetrate this entomology.

VII

These are the small aspects of exile, here are the larger ones:

To dream, to think, to suffer.

To be alone and to feel one is with everyone; to loathe the success of evil, but to bemoan the happiness of the evil man; to strengthen oneself as a citizen and purify oneself as a philosopher; to be poor, and to make up for one's ruin by one's work; to meditate and premeditate, to meditate on the good and intend better; to have no other anger but public anger, to ignore personal hate; to breathe the vast alive air of the solitudes, to become lost in grand absolute reverie; to look at what is above without losing sight of what is below; never to push the contemplation of the ideal as far as forgetting the tyrant; to observe in oneself the magnificent mixture of increasing indignation and increasing appeasement; to have two souls, one's own and one's country.

One thing is sweet, pity in advance; to have clemency for the guilty man when he is brought down and on his knees; to say to oneself that one would never turn away clasped hands. One feels an august joy in giving the vanquished of the future, whoever they be, and unknown fugitives, promises of hospitality. Anger is disarmed when the enemy is overcome. The one who is writing these lines has accustomed his companions in exile to hearing him say: *If ever there is a revolution and the fleeing Bonaparte knocks on my door to ask me for asylum, not a hair of his head will fall.*

These meditations, complicated by all the torrents of adversity, are pleasing to the exile's conscience. They do not prevent him from fulfilling his duty. Far from it. They encourage him. Be more severe today so that you can be all the more sympathetic tomorrow; strike down the powerful while waiting to rescue the supplicant. Later, you will only apply one condition to your amnesty, repentance. Today you are in the midst of a happy crime. Strike.

To dig the chasm for the victorious enemy, to prepare the sanctuary for the vanquished enemy, to fight with the hope of being able to pardon, this is the great effort and great dream of the exile. Add to this a devotion to universal suffering. The exile has the magnanimous satisfaction of not being useless. Hurt himself, bleeding himself, he forgets himself and bandages as best he can the human wound. It seems he is daydreaming; no; he is seeking reality. What is more, he finds it. He roams the desert and he dreams of cities, commotion, swarms, miseries, of all those who work, of thought, of the plow, of the needle in the red fingers of the seamstress with no fire in the attic, of the evil that grows there where goodness is not sown, of the father's unemployment, of the child's ignorance, of the growth of bad weeds in heads left uncultivated, of the streets in the evening, of the pale street lamps, of the offers made to passersby that hunger inspires, of social extremes, of the sad girl who is prostituting herself, men, through our fault. Painful and useful surveys. Sit on a problem, the solution will hatch. He dreams without respite. His footsteps along the sea are not lost. He fraternizes with this power, the abyss. He looks at the infinite, he listens to the unknown. The great somber voice speaks to him. All of nature in a mass offers itself to this solitary figure. Harsh analogies instruct and advise him. Fated, persecuted, pensive, he sees before him clouds, breezes, eagles; he notes that his destiny is thunderous and black like the clouds, his persecutors vain like the breezes, and his soul free like the eagles.

An exile is kindly. He likes roses, bird nests, the to-and-fro of butterflies. In the summer he blossoms in the sweet joy of living things; he has unshakeable faith in secret and infinite goodness, being childish enough to believe in God; he makes of springtime his house; the interlacing of branches, full of charming green lairs, are the dwelling place of his mind; he lives in April, he inhabits the Floreal; he looks at gardens and prairies, profound emotion; he watches intently the mysteries of a tuft of grass; he studies these republics, the ants and the bees; he compares the various melodies jousting for the ear of an invisible Virgil in the poem of the woods; he is often moved to tears because nature is beautiful; the wildness of the thickets entices him, and he emerges from them mildly alarmed; the positions of the rocks occupy him; he sees through his daydream the little three-year-old girls run on shore, their bare feet in the sea, their skirts held up with two arms, showing the immense fertility of their innocent stomachs; in the winter, he crumbles bread on the snow for the birds. From time to time, someone writes him: You know, this penalty was abolished; you know, so-and-so's head will not be cut off. And he raises his arms to the sky.

VIII

Against this dangerous man governments come to each other's assistance. They agree reciprocally among themselves on the persecutions of exiles, internments, expulsions, sometimes extraditions. Extraditions! Yes, extraditions. It was a question of this in Jersey, in 1855. The exiles could see, on

October 18, moored to the Saint-Hélier quay, a ship of the imperial navy, *Ariel,* that came to get them; Victoria would offer the exiles to Napoleon; from one throne to another these courtesies are exchanged.

The gift did not take place. The English royalist press applauded, but the people of London took it badly. They started to rumble. These people are like that; their government can be a poodle, they are a mastiff. The mastiff is a lion in a dog; majesty in integrity, this is the English people.

This good and proud people showed their teeth; Palmerston and Bonaparte had to content themselves with expulsion. The exiles were not particularly upset. They accepted the official notification with a smile, a bit tongue-tied. Very well, said the exiles. *Expulshun.* This pronunciation satisfied them. . . .

IX

Does the exile hate the exiler? No. He fights him; that's all. All out? Yes. Always as a public enemy, never as a personal enemy. The anger of the honest man does not go beyond the necessary. The exile abhors the tyrant and ignores the person of the exiler. If he knows it, he only attacks it in proportion to his duty.

If need be, the exile does the exiler justice; if, for example, the exiler is in some measure a writer and has a sufficient body of work, the exile willingly acknowledges it. It is indisputable, let it be said in passing, that Napoleon III was an adequate academician; the academy under the empire had, through politeness no doubt, sufficiently lowered its standards so that the emperor could be one; the emperor was able to believe himself among his literary peers there, and his majesty in no way detracted from that of the forty others.

At the time that the emperor's candidacy was announced for a vacant chair, an academician of our acquaintance, wanting to do justice to the historian of Caesar and to the man of December, had written his voting ballot in advance: *I vote for the admission of Monsieur Louis Bonaparte to the academy and to the penal colony.*

As one can see, all concessions are possible, the exile has made them.

He is uncompromising only in terms of principles. There his inflexibility begins. There he ceases to be what in political jargon is called "a practical man." Hence, his resignation to everything, to violence, to insult, to ruin, to exile. What do you expect him to do? Truth comes out of his mouth, despite him, when necessary.

To speak through truth and for it, this is his proud happiness.

The true has two names; philosophers call it the ideal, statesmen call it idle fancy.

Are the statesmen right? We do not think so.

To listen to them, all the advice that an exile might give is "fanciful."

Admitting, they say, that this advice has truth in its favor, it has reality against it.

Let us examine this.

The exile is a fanciful man. Very well. He is a blind seer; a seer in terms of the absolute, blind in terms of the relative. He practices good philosophy and bad politics. If one were to listen to him, one would founder in the abyss. His advice is the advice of honesty and perdition. Principles make him right, but facts make him wrong.

Let us look at the facts.

John Brown is defeated at Harper's Ferry. The statesmen say: Hang him. The exile says: Respect him. John Brown is hanged; the Union is dismantled, the war of the South erupts. John Brown spared would be America spared.

In terms of the fact, who was right, the practical men, or the fanciful man?

Second fact. Maximilian is seized at Querétaro. The practical men say: Shoot him. The fanciful man says: Pardon him. Maximilian is shot. This is enough to make an immense thing seem smaller. The heroic struggle of Mexico loses its supreme luster, the lofty clemency. Maximilian pardoned would be Mexico henceforth inviolable, it would be this nation, which had declared its independence through war, declaring its sovereignty through civilization; it would be, on the heads of the people, after the helmet, the crown.

This time again, the fanciful man saw accurately.

Third fact. Isabella is dethroned. What will Spain become? Republic or monarchy? Monarchy! say the statesmen. Republic! says the exile. The fanciful man is not listened to, the practical men prevail; Spain is made a monarchy. It falls from Isabella to Amédée, from Amédée to Alphonse, while waiting for Carlos; this concerns only Spain. But here is what concerns the world: this monarchy in search of a monarch gives a pretext to Hohenzollern; hence the ambush of Prussia, hence the engorgement of France, hence Sedan, hence shame and darkness.

Suppose Spain had become a republic, no pretext for a surprise attack, Hohenzollern would not be possible, no catastrophes.

Thus the exile's advice was sage.

What if by chance we discovered one day that this strange thing known as truth was not idiotic, that the spirit of compassion and deliverance was good, that a strong man was a just man, and that reason was right!

Today, in the midst of disaster, after the foreign war, after the civil war, in the presence of liabilities incurred on both sides, the former exile thinks of the exiles of today, ponders the banishments, he wanted to save John Brown, this past sheds light on the future, he would like to close the wound of the fatherland and he asks for amnesty.

Is he a blind man? Is he a seer?

X

In December 1851, when the one who is writing these lines arrived on foreign land, life was somewhat hard at first. It is particularly in exile that the *res augusta domi* makes itself felt.

This brief sketch of "what exile is" would not be complete if the material side of the exile's existence were not pointed out, in passing, and moreover, with the proper sobriety.

Of everything this exile had owned, he had seven thousand francs left in annual income. His theater, which brought him sixty thousand francs per year, was done away with. The hasty sale by auction of his furniture had produced a little less than thirteen thousand francs. He had nine people to feed.

He had to provide for moving, travel expenses, new accommodations, the displacements of a group of which he was the center, for the unexpected aspects of an existence henceforth pulled from the earth and swayed by the winds; an exile is someone uprooted. It was necessary to preserve the dignity of life and make sure that no one around him was suffering.

Hence the immediate necessity of work.

Let us say that the first house of exile, Marine-Terrace, was rented at the very moderate price of fifteen hundred francs per year.

The French market was closed to his publications.

His first Belgian editors published all his books without giving him the least compensation, among others, the two volumes of *Oeuvres oratoires. Napoléon le Petit* was the sole exception. As for *Châtiments,* they cost the author two thousand five hundred francs. This sum, entrusted to the editor Samuel, was never reimbursed. The total product of all the editions of *Châtiments* was confiscated for eighteen years by foreign editors.

The English royalist newspapers extolled English hospitality, mixed, one remembers, with nocturnal attacks and expulsions, like Belgian hospitality, by the way. What English hospitality had to a fuller degree was a tenderness for exiles' books. It reprinted these books and published them and sold them with the most cordial eagerness to the benefit of English editors. The hospitality for the book went so far as to forget the author. English law, which is part of British hospitality, allows this sort of oversight. The duty of a book, Chatterton attests, is to allow its author to die of hunger and its editor to grow rich. *Châtiments* in particular was sold and is still sold to this day in England to the sole profit of the Jeffs bookshop. English theater was no less hospitable to French plays than English bookshops to French books. No author's rights whatsoever were ever paid for *Ruy Blas,* performed more than two hundred times in England.

It is not without reason, one can see, that the royalist-Bonapartist press of London reproached exiles for abusing English hospitality.

This press often called the one who is writing these lines *greedy.*

It also called him a "drunkard," an abandoned drinker.

These details are part of exile.

XI

This exile did not complain about anything. He worked. He rebuilt his life for himself and for his family. All is well.

Is there merit in being exiled? No. This amounts to asking: Is there merit in being a decent man? An exile is a decent man who persists in decency. That is all.

There are certain periods when this persistence is rare. Very well. This scarcity takes something away from the period, but adds nothing to the decent man.

Decency, like virginity, exists outside of praise. You are pure because you are pure. Ermine has no merit in being white.

A representative exiled for the people accomplishes an act of integrity. He promised to do so, and keeps his promise. He keeps it even beyond the promise, as all scrupulous men should. This is why the imperative mandate is useless; the imperative mandate makes the mistake of placing a degrading word upon a noble thing, which is the acceptance of duty; moreover, it omits the essential, which is sacrifice; sacrifice—that which must be made, that which cannot be imposed. There is reciprocal commitment, the hand of the elected in the hand of the elector, the voter and the representative give each other their word, the representative to defend the voter, the voter to support the representative, two rights and two mingled powers, this is truth. This being so, the representative must do his duty, and the people theirs. This is the debt of the settled conscience of both sides. But must one devote oneself to the point of exile? No doubt. Then it is beautiful; no, it is simple. All that one can say of the exiled representative is that he has not deceived anyone on the quality of the thing promised. A mandate is a contract. There is no glory in not selling at false weight.

The honest representative carries out the contract. He must go, and he goes, to the ends of honor and of conscience. There he finds the precipice. Very well. He falls in. Perfectly.

Does he die there? No, he lives there.

XII

Let us sum up.

This sort of existence, exile, has, one can see, a variety of aspects.

This is the life, agitated if one looks at destiny, calm if one looks at the soul, that, from 1851 to 1870, from December Second to September Fourth, the absent person lived, who today is giving an account of his absence to his country through the publication of this book. This absence lasted nineteen years and nine months. What did he do during these long years? He tried not to be useless. The only beautiful thing about this absence was that, miserable himself, miseries came to find him; shipwrecks asked for help from this shipwrecked person. Not only individuals, but peoples; not only peoples, but consciences; not only consciences, but truths. It was given to him to hold out his hand from the top of his stumbling block to the ideal fallen into the abyss; it seemed at times that the future in distress tried to reach his rock. Yet what was it? Not much. A living effort. In the presence of conjured and triumphant evil forces, what is will? Nothing, if it represents selfishness; everything, if it represents what is right.

The most inexpugnable positions result from the most profound collapses; it is enough that the collapsed man be a just man; this must be emphasized—if this man is right, he is good whether he is condemned, ruined, despoiled, expatriated, ridiculed, insulted, repudiated, slandered and whether he epitomizes all forms of defeat and weakness; then he is all-powerful. He is invincible in being upright; he is unconquerable in having reality on his side. What strength this is: to be nothing! To have nothing left to you, to have nothing on you, this is the best condition for combat. This absence of armor proves unassailable. There is no position higher than this, to have fallen for justice. In the face of the emperor the exile stands erect. The emperor damns, the exile condemns. One possesses codes and judges; the other possesses truths. Yes, it is good to have fallen. The fall of what was prosperity makes a man's authority; your power and your wealth are often your obstacle; when this leaves you, you are unburdened, and you feel free and masterful: nothing can bother you from now on; by taking everything from you, they give you everything; all is permitted to whom all is forbidden; you are no longer forced to be academic and parliamentary; you have the formidable affluence of truth, wildly superb. The power of the exile is composed of two elements; one is the injustice of his destiny, the other is the justice of his cause. These two contradictory forces rely on one another; a tremendous situation that can be summed up in two phrases:

Outside of law, in the right.

The tyrant who attacks you first encounters the opponent of his own iniquity, that is, himself, and then the opponent of your conscience, that is, God.

An unequal battle, certainly. The certain defeat of the tyrant. Go before yourself, judge.

These are realities that, in the first pages of this introduction, we have tried to express in this line:

Exile is law laid bare.

XIII

This is why the one who is writing this has been happy and sad for nineteen years; happy with himself, sad for others; happy to feel honest, sad for the crime extended indefinitely that from soul to soul swayed public opinion and ended up calling itself the satisfaction of interests. He was indignant and overcome by this national disaster that is called the prosperity of the empire. The joys of the orgy are miseries. A prosperity that is the gilding of an infamy and hatches disaster. The egg of December Second is Sedan.

These were the sorrows of the exile, sorrows full of duty. He sensed the future and denounced in the giddiness of celebration the approach of catastrophe. He heard the footstep of the events to which the happy are deaf. The catastrophes came, having in them the double force of impulse that came to them from Bonaparte and Bismarck, from a surprise attack of one on the other. In sum, the empire fell and France will lift itself up again. Ten million and two provinces, this is our ransom. It is expensive, and we have the right to a reimbursement. While waiting, let us remain calm; less of the empire is more honor. The current situation is good. It is better that

France be mutilated by an assault than lessened by a dishonor. It is the difference between a wound and a virus. One recovers from a wound, one dies from a plague. France was dying of the empire. Lost to shame, France dies. Today the shame is vomited, France will live. The people are healthy and robust, now that the Eighteenth Brumaire and the Second of December are spit out.

In the solitude in which he pondered the future, the preoccupations of the exile were harsh, but serene; his despair was mingled with hope. He had, we have just seen, the melancholy of the public disaster and at the same time the lofty joy to feel himself exiled. Exile was a joy for this man, because it was a power. The decree of Luther, excommunicated but undaunted: *Stat coram pontifice sicut Satanas coram Jehovah.* The comparison is just, and the exile who speaks here recognizes it. Over the silence created in France, over the grovelling tribune, the gagged press, the exile, free as the Satan of truth before the Jehovah of falsehood, could speak and did. He defended universal suffrage against plebiscite, the people against mobs, glory against the military ruffian, justice against the judge, the torch against the pyre, and God against the priest. Hence this long cry that fills this book. From all sides, it has just been said and in this book it will be seen, anguish addressed him, knowing that he would not shrink from any duty. The oppressed saw in him the public accuser of the universal crime. To accept this mission, it is enough to be a soul, and, to fulfill this function, to be a voice. An honest soul and a free voice, he was that. He heard the calls on the horizon, and from the depths of his isolation he replied. This is what one will read here. All the rulers' persecutions were unleashed on him, and there was, and there still is, an inexpressible accumulation of hatred upon his name; but what does that matter, and who cares? He nevertheless had the proud happiness of being exiled twenty years, and of holding his head up, he, alone before the multitudes; he, disarmed before legions; he, a dreamer before murderers; he, banished before despots; he, an atom before giants, having in him only this single force, a ray of light.

This light was, we have said, law, the eternal law.

He thanks God. During all the time that it takes for a brow of forty to become a forehead of sixty, he lived this lofty life. He was the expelled, the tracked down, the hunted one. He was abandoned by all and abandoned no one. He came to know the greatness of the desert; in the desert there is the echo. There one can hear the clamor of peoples. While the oppressors worked at evil beneath his fixed stare, he endeavored to work for good. He let all the tyrants unleash their wrath over his head, he was concerned only with the public disaster. He lived in a pitfall, he dreamed, meditated, contemplated, calm beneath a cloud of anger and threats; and he declares himself satisfied; for what can one complain of when one has had close to oneself and with oneself for twenty years justice, reason, conscience, truth, law and the sea with its immense noise?

And in all this darkness he was loved. Hatred was not alone upon him; a somber love shone forth into his solitude; he felt the profound warmth of the gentle and sad people, the opening of hearts was made on his side, he thanks the immense human soul. He was loved from afar and from nearby. Around him were intrepid, tested companions, obstinately dutiful, stubbornly just and true, indignant and smiling combatants; the illustrious Vacquerie, the admirable Paul Meurice, the stoic Schoelcher, and Ribeyrolles, and Dulac, and Kesler, these valiant men, and you, my Charles, and you, my Victor . . . I will stop. Let me remember.

XIV

He will not finish these pages, however, without saying that during this long night made by exile, he did not lose sight of Paris for a single instant.

He notes it, and he who for so long dwelled in obscurity has the right to note it, even in the darkening of Europe, even in the overshadowing of France, Paris is not eclipsed. This is because Paris is the frontier of the future.

A frontier visible by the unknown. All the quantity of Tomorrow seen in Today. This is Paris.

Whoever seeks Progress sees Paris.

There are black cities; Paris is a city of light.

The philosopher makes it out at the bottom of his dreams.

XV

To see this city live, to witness this grandeur, is a heartrending feeling. No place is vaster; no view is more unsettling and more sublime. Those who, through the random chance of life, have left the sight of Paris for the sight of the ocean have not felt, in changing spectacles, any increase in the infinite. Besides, to go from the horizon of men to the horizon of things erases nothing. This dream backwards, which memory pursues, floats like a cloud, but persists. Surroundings have nothing to do with it. The wind goes through it day and night, the four hurricanes that alternate forever, the North winds, the squalls, the gusts, do not carry away the silhouette of the twin towers, and do not disperse the Arc de Triomphe, the gothic belfry, and the high colonnade around the sovereign dome; and, in the most remote distance of the abyss, above the upheaval of foam and ships, in the midst of the rays, clouds and winds, at the bottom of the haze is outlined the immense phantom of the immobile city. A majestic apparition to the banished. Paris, an idea as much as a city, is ubiquitous. Parisians have Paris, and the world has it. One would like to take out of it what one cannot; Paris is breathable. Whoever sees it, even without knowing it, has it within. All the more so for those who have known it. The wild distraction of the ocean becomes complicated in this memory, equal to storms. Whatever storms the sea has, Paris has '93. The evocation suggests itself on its own, the roofs seem to emerge among the waves, the city is reconstructed on all this water, and this infinite trembling is added. In the crush of the swelling waves one thinks one can hear the murmur of the anthill of the streets. A ferocious charm. One looks at the sea and one sees Paris. The great peace that these spaces are composed of do not thwart this daydream. The vast oblivion that surrounds you can do nothing; the thought arrives in calmness, but a calmness that admits this turmoil; the thick envelope of shadows lets a glimmer through that comes from behind the horizon, and that is Paris. One thinks of it, thus one possesses it. It mingles, indistinct, with the muted emanations of contemplation. The sublime soothing of the starry sky is not enough to dissolve this grand figure of the supreme city at the bottom of a mind. These monuments, this history, these people at work, these women who are goddesses, these children who are heroes, these revolutions beginning with anger and finishing with a masterpiece, this sacred all-powerfulness of a whirlwind of intelligences, these tumultuous examples, this life, this youth; all of this is present to the one who is absent; and Paris remains unforgettable, and Paris remains indelible and unsinkable, even for the ruined man in the dark who spends his nights in contemplation before the eternal serenity, and who has in his soul the profound astonishment of the stars.

Translated by Jeanine Herman

The Émigrés and the Begrudgers

Miguel de Unamuno

CASTILIAN—THE CASTILIAN of Castile, I mean—does not have a word which corresponds point by point with the Portuguese *saudade*, the Galician *morriña*, the Asturian *señardá*, the Catalan *anyoransa*, or even the Andalusian *soledad*. The Andalusian *soledades* are not Castilian. The Castilian does not die of solitude. Perhaps because he lives in it like a fish in water. Nor does the land hold him very strongly. At least this is true of the plains Castilian, for the sierra Castilian is another matter. Roots are put down only by the side of the sea or in the lap of the mountains. Perhaps roots in such places are peregrine roots, migratory, but roots they are.

And nevertheless, when My Cid Ruy Díaz the Castilian—which he was par excellence—was forced to leave his home, in Cardeña, banished by King Alfonso VI of León and Castile, all because of schisms and ill-will from "evil begrudgers" ("malos mestureros": v. 267 of the *Poem of the Cid*), he turned his head, with his eyes full of tears, to look at the palaces he was leaving empty and "disinherited," and he sighed with the burden of his great cares. Around the figure of this exile, around this departed outcast, the nascent patriotism of Castile first crystallized in poetry. An exile, an outcast, became the first poetic symbol of *castellanidad*—"Castilinity." He created the fatherland outside his native territory. Most especially he formed it in Valencia the Major, Valencia of the Cid. Indeed, for his caste, patriotism was a work of reconquest, not of conservation.

And as for Spain herself in her entirety: where but outside herself has she forged herself? Where can she live her life in her own image more faithfully than in the score of republics she has brought forth, and in their future democracies?

As for this old ancestral manse . . .

Spain herself is an outcast nation, or better, an outcast people, a people cast out into exile. Our land itself is an outland, an outland of expatriation. Every Spaniard who has a live and clearheaded notion of his Spanishness feels himself to be exiled and is forced to tell himself unceasingly: "Our kingdom is not of this world!" Or if you prefer: "Our republic is not of this world!" No, our community is not of this world. Of what other world, then, is it? I, the Spaniard who now speak these sorrowful words, regret intimately, in the marrow of my Spanish soul, that I am not some twenty years younger so I could quit this ancestral home handed down to us through primogeniture. I would leave as soon as the war of the civilized world is concluded. For then, when the lacerated and weary nations must rebuild, materially and spiritually, Spain, too, will have to remake herself—but outside herself. She will have to be remade, but from outside. And, like the Cid, future Spaniards will have to quit their ancestral home so as to win the battle of Spain, and they will leave behind in the old homestead Alfonso VI and his court of meddlesome begrudgers.

"So many people are leaving!" goes the cry. And we think: And those still to go . . . ! Those who still must go . . . ! Those who should go . . . ! Emigration will become the deepest form of patriotism. But: Spain will become depopulated! Well, what is there to do about that? It will not be the fault—if fault it is—of those who go, of the emigrants, but of those who made them go, of the begrudgers. These are the only ones who can live, like moss, on the ancestral rocks, clinging to the cliffsides.

Oh to be young! To be young so as to quit Spain in order to dream her! Because . . . how handsome must our country be when seen and felt from outside!

Now, scenting the coming harvest, some of those men have returned who went out to do peaceful chores on the foreign lands whose owners went marching off to war; but those who have come back to Spain will again go out one day, for gain, and they will be right to do so. And it is not only hunger for bread that drives them out; it is, perhaps without their even knowing it, hunger for sweeter dreams in softer lands, far from the maternal rocks.

No, our patriotism cannot be territorial. Grandsons of nomadic shepherds, we no longer tend flocks of meat and wool, but dreams and beliefs, and so must take them where the pasture is richer. Wide is the path of peoples. And it is not here, in the land of our origin, that our bread will flourish. The native pasture land is exhausted now. Spain will live again, but not in the Iberian Peninsula, and perhaps not even in a land with the kind of earth one can take in one's hand or tread with one's feet.

Why is it that every Spaniard who has cultivated the sacred orchard of his Spanishness with love and care feels himself, as he reaches a certain age—that fearful "certain age"—feels himself exiled, expatriated? Especially if on one of his life's paths he encountered the begrudgers and did not get out of their way or make way so they might not fall behind in their career. In Spain, the sunset of life for a patriot is one long large sadness.

Don Quixote died at home, in the house of his birth, in the very bed in which he had been born, and in which his father—who could his father have been?—had died; but Don Quixote died tragically sane and amid the ruins of his spiritual fatherland, of the enchanted land of castles, of his Castile. And meanwhile, its highroads and inns witnessed the idle wanderings of Guzmán de Alfarache and Lazarillo de Tormes and Marcos de Obregón and Rinconete and Cortadillo and all the politicians of the day.

Very well. And who was Don Quixote's father? We must find out. We must discover and invent him. The Knight had no children. Is it possible that he had no father either? Then neither did he have a fatherland.

He certainly did not have one in this world. Don Quixote's empire was not of this world. He went out—another émigré!—from his hearth, his plot of land, the old ancestral manse, and he went to seek his true fatherland. He did not attempt to fix up that place in La Mancha whose name Cervantes did not wish to remember—Cervantes, another eternal expatriate! He left behind in that place the begrudgers: the parish priest, the barber, Samson Carrasco, Tomé Cecial, the authorities, the politicians. And Don Quixote, the émigré, conquered spiritual lands. Lands? Lands . . . no! He conquered heavens—for Spain, for celestial Spain.

And every Spaniard who bears within himself the soul of the Cid or of Don Quixote, the soul of the symbolic émigrés, must go to the conquest of the heavens of the spirit, must go out to embody the Castilian Word, to give body to ideas of human universality, while leaving all the begrudgers, served by Guzmán and Lazarillo and Marcos and Rinconete and Cortadillo and living off the favors of King Alfonso, to pasture their mangy donkeys in these plains owned by the first-born elders.

What a shame not to be twenty years younger so as to "go out" like the Cid and Don Quixote! But at least one can go out in spirit, and by spreading one's wings, rise above this land of bald rock, up and over the hills, the sierras, and see the sea round about washing up against the shores of numberless peoples, and seek out in the sky the reflection—cleared of impurities—of this land.

The fatherland of any Spaniard worthy of the name, of every brother to Don Quixote, is not here, where the begrudgers wax fat at Court and Capital. Our fatherland is in exile.

Translated by Anthony Kerrigan

My Country

Mary Antin

THE PUBLIC SCHOOL has done its best for us foreigners, and for the country, when it has made us into good Americans. I am glad it is mine to tell how the miracle was wrought in one case. You should be glad to hear of it, you born Americans; for it is the story of the growth of your country; of the flocking of your brothers and sisters from the far ends of the earth to the flag you love; of the recruiting of your armies of workers, thinkers, and leaders. And you will be glad to hear of it, my comrades in adoption; for it is a rehearsal of your own experience, the thrill and wonder of which your own hearts have felt.

How long would you say, wise reader, it takes to make an American? By the middle of my second year in school I had reached the sixth grade. When, after the Christmas holidays, we began to study the life of Washington, running through a summary of the Revolution, and the early days of the Republic, it seemed to me that all my reading and study had been idle until then. The reader, the arithmetic, the song book, that had so fascinated me until now, became suddenly sober exercise books, tools wherewith to hew a way to the source of inspiration. When the teacher read to us out of a big book with many bookmarks in it, I sat rigid with attention in my little chair, my hands tightly clasped on the edge of my desk; and I painfully held my breath, to prevent sighs of disappointment escaping, as I saw the teacher skip the parts between bookmarks. When the class read, and it came my turn, my voice shook and the book trembled in my hands. I could not pronounce the name of George Washington without a pause. Never had I prayed, never had I chanted the songs of David, never had I called upon the Most Holy, in such utter reverence and worship as I repeated the simple sentences of my child's story of the patriot. I gazed with adoration at the portraits of George and Martha Washington, till I could see them with my eyes shut. And whereas formerly my self-consciousness had bordered on conceit, and I thought myself an uncommon person, parading my schoolbooks through the streets, and swelling with pride when a teacher detained me in conversation, now I grew humble all at once, seeing how insignificant I was beside the Great.

As I read about the noble boy who would not tell a lie to save himself from punishment, I was for the first time truly repentant of my sins. Formerly I had fasted and prayed and made sacrifice on the Day of Atonement, but it was more than half play, in mimicry of my elders. I had no real horror of sin, and I knew so many ways of escaping punishment. I am sure my family, my neighbors, my teachers in Polotzk—all my world, in fact—strove together, by example and precept, to teach me goodness. Saintliness had a new incarnation in about every third person I knew. I did respect the saints, but I could not help seeing that most of them were a little bit stupid, and that mischief was much more fun than piety. Goodness, as I had known it, was respectable, but not necessarily admirable. The people I really admired, like my Uncle Solomon, and Cousin Rachel, were those who preached the least and laughed the most. My sister Frieda was perfectly good, but she did not think the less of me because I played tricks. What I loved in my friends was not inimitable. One could be downright good if one really wanted to. One could be learned if one had books and teachers. One could sing funny songs and tell anecdotes if one travelled about and picked up such things, like one's uncles and cousins. But a human being strictly good, perfectly wise, and unfailingly valiant, all at the same time, I had never heard or dreamed of. This wonderful George Washington was as inimitable as he was irreproachable. Even if I had never, never told a lie, I could not compare myself to George Washington; for I was not brave—I was afraid to go out when snowballs whizzed—and I could never be the First President of the United States.

So I was forced to revise my own estimate of myself. But the twin of my new-born humility, paradoxical as it may seem, was a sense of dignity I had never known before. For if I found that I was a person of small consequence, I discovered at the same time that I was more nobly related than I had ever supposed. I had relatives and friends who were notable people by the old standards—I had never been ashamed of my family—but this George Washington, who died long before I was born, was like a king in greatness, and he and I were Fellow Citizens. There was a great deal about Fellow Citizens in the patriotic literature we read at this time; and I knew from my father how he was a Citizen, through the process of naturalization, and how I also was a citizen by virtue of my relation to him. Undoubtedly I was a Fellow Citizen, and George Washington was another. It thrilled me to realize what sudden greatness had fallen on me; and at the same time it sobered me, as with a sense of responsibility. I strove to conduct myself as befitted a Fellow Citizen.

Before books came into my life, I was given to stargazing and daydreaming. When books were given me, I fell upon them as a glutton pounces on his meat after a period of enforced starvation. I lived with my nose in a book, and took no notice of the alternations of the sun and stars. But now, after the advent of George Washington and the American Revolution, I began to dream again. I strayed on the common after school instead of hurrying home to read. I hung on fence rails, my pet book forgotten under my arm, and gazed off to the yellow-streaked February sunset, and beyond, and beyond. I was no longer the central figure of my dreams; the dry weeds in the lane crackled beneath the tread of Heroes.

What more could America give a child? Ah, much more! As I read how the patriots planned the Revolution, and the women gave their sons to die in battle, and the heroes led to victory, and the rejoicing people set up the Republic, it dawned on me gradually what was meant by *my country*. The people all desiring noble things, and striving for them together, defying their oppressors, giving their lives for each other—all this it was that made *my country*. It was not a thing that I *understood*; I could not go home and tell Frieda about it, as I told her other things I learned at school. But I knew one could say "my country" and *feel* it, as one felt "God" or "myself." My teacher, my schoolmates, Miss Dillingham, George Washington himself could not mean more than I when they said "my country," after I had once felt it. For the Country was for all the Citizens, and *I was a Citizen*. And when we stood up to sing "America," I shouted the words with all my might. I was in very earnest proclaiming to the world my love for my new-found country.

I love thy rocks and rills,
Thy woods and templed hills.

Boston Harbor, Crescent Beach, Chelsea Square—all was hallowed ground to me. As the day approached when the school was to hold exercises in honor of Washington's Birthday, the halls resounded at all hours with the strains of patriotic songs; and I, who was a model of the attentive pupil, more than once lost my place in the lesson as I strained to hear, through closed doors, some neighboring class rehearsing "The Star-Spangled Banner." If the doors happened to open, and the chorus broke out unveiled—

O! say, does that Star-Spangled Banner yet wave
O'er the land of the free, and the home of the brave?—

delicious tremors ran up and down my spine, and I was faint with suppressed enthusiasm.

Where had been my country until now? What flag had I loved? What heroes had I worshipped? The very names of these things had been unknown to me. Well I knew that Polotzk was not my country. It was *goluth*—exile. On many occasions in the year we prayed to God to lead us out of exile. The beautiful Passover service closed with the words, "Next year, may we be in Jerusalem." On childish lips, indeed, those words were no conscious aspiration; we repeated the Hebrew syllables after our elders, but without their hope and longing. Still not a child among us was too young to feel in his own flesh the lash of the oppressor. We knew what it was to be Jews in exile, from the spiteful treatment we suffered at the hands of the smallest urchin who crossed himself; and thence we knew that Israel had good reason to pray for deliverance. But the story of the Exodus was not history to me in the sense that the story of the American Revolution was. It was more like a glorious myth, a belief in which had the effect of cutting me off from the actual world, by linking me with a world of phantoms. Those moments of exaltation which the contemplation of the Biblical past afforded us, allowing us to call ourselves the children of princes, served but to tinge with a more poignant sense of disinheritance the long humdrum stretches of our life. In very truth we were a people without a country. Surrounded by mocking foes and detractors, it was difficult for me to realize the persons of my people's heroes or the events in which they moved. Except in moments of abstraction from the world around me, I scarcely understood that Jerusalem was an actual spot on the earth, where once the Kings of the Bible, real people, like my neighbors in Polotzk, ruled in puissant majesty. For the conditions of our civil life did not permit us to cultivate a spirit of nationalism. The freedom of worship that was grudgingly granted within the narrow limits of the Pale by no means included the right to set up openly any ideal of a Hebrew State, any hero other than the Czar. What we children picked up of our ancient political history was confused with the miraculous story of the Creation, with the supernatural legends and hazy associations of Bible lore. As to our future, we Jews in Polotzk had no national expectations; only a life-worn dreamer here and there hoped to die in Palestine. If Fetchke and I sang, with my father, first making sure of our audience, "Zion, Zion, Holy Zion, not forever is it lost," we did not really picture to ourselves Judæa restored.

So it came to pass that we did not know what *my country* could mean to a man. And as we had no country, so we had no flag to love. It was by no far-fetched symbolism that the banner of the House of Romanoff became the emblem of our latter-day bondage in our eyes. Even a child would know how to hate the flag that we were forced, on pain of severe penalties, to hoist above our housetops, in celebration of the advent of one of our oppressors. And as it was with country and flag, so it was with heroes of war. We hated the uniform of the soldier, to the last brass button. On the person of a Gentile, it was the symbol of tyranny; on the person of a Jew, it was the emblem of shame.

So a little Jewish girl in Polotzk was apt to grow up hungry-minded and empty-hearted; and if, still in her outreaching youth, she was set down in a land of outspoken patriotism, she was likely to love her new country with a great love, and to embrace its heroes in a great worship. Naturalization, with us Russian Jews, may mean more than the adoption of the immigrant by America. It may mean the adoption of America by the immigrant.

On the day of the Washington celebration I recited a poem that I had composed in my enthusiasm. But "composed" is not the word. The process of putting on paper the sentiments that seethed in my soul was really very discomposing. I dug the words out of my heart, squeezed the rhymes out of my brain, forced the missing syllables out of their hiding-places in the dictionary. May I never again know such travail of the spirit as I endured during the fevered days when I was engaged on the poem. It was not as if I wanted to say that snow was white or grass was green. I could do that without a dictionary. It was a question now of the loftiest sentiments, of the most abstract truths, the names of which were very new in my vocabulary. It was necessary to use polysyllables, and plenty of them; and where to find rhymes for such words as "tyranny," "freedom," and "justice," when you had less than two years' acquaintance with English! The name I wished to celebrate was the most difficult of all. Nothing but "Washington" rhymed with "Washington." It was a most ambitious undertaking, but my heart could find no rest till it had proclaimed itself to the world; so I wrestled with my difficulties, and spared not ink, till inspiration perched on my penpoint, and my soul gave up its best.

When I had done, I was myself impressed with the length, gravity, and nobility of my poem. My father was overcome with emotion as he read it. His hands trembled as he held the paper to the light, and the mist gathered in his eyes. My teacher, Miss Dwight, was plainly astonished at my performance, and said many kind things, and asked many questions; all of which I took very solemnly, like one who had been in the clouds and returned to earth with a sign upon him. When Miss Dwight asked me to read my poem to the class on the day of celebration, I readily consented. It was not in me to refuse a chance to tell my schoolmates what I thought of George Washington.

I was not a heroic figure when I stood up in front of the class to pronounce the praises of the Father of his Country. Thin, pale, and hollow, with a shadow of short black curls on my brow, and the staring look of prominent eyes, I must have looked more frightened than imposing. My dress added no grace to my appearance. "Plaids" were in fashion, and my frock was of a red-and-green "plaid" that had a ghastly effect on my complexion. I hated it when I thought of it, but on the great day I did not know I had any dress on. Heels clapped together, and hands glued to my sides, I lifted up my voice in praise of George Washington. It was not much of a voice; like my hollow cheeks, it suggested consumption. My pronunciation was faulty, my declamation flat. But I had the courage of my convictions. I was face to face with twoscore Fellow Citizens, in clean blouses and extra frills. I must tell them what George Washington had done for their country—for *our* country—for me.

I can laugh now at the impossible metres, the grandiose phrases, the verbose repetitions of my poem. Years ago I must have laughed at it, when I threw my only copy into the wastebasket. The copy I am now turning over was loaned me by Miss Dwight, who faithfully preserved it all these years, for the sake, no doubt, of what I strove to express when I laboriously hitched together those dozen and more ungraceful stanzas. But to the forty Fellow Citizens sitting in rows in front of me it was no laughing matter. Even the bad boys sat in attitudes of attention, hypnotized by the solemnity of my demeanor. If they got any inkling of what the hail of big words was about, it must have been through occult suggestion. I fixed their eighty eyes with my single stare, and gave it to them, stanza after stanza, with such emphasis as the lameness of the lines permitted.

He whose courage, will, amazing bravery,
Did free his land from a despot's rule,
From man's greatest evil, almost slavery,
And all that's taught in tyranny's school,
Who gave his land its liberty,
Who was he?

'Twas he who e'er will be our pride,
Immortal Washington
Who always did in truth confide.
We hail our Washington!

The best of the verses were no better than these, but the children listened. They had to. Presently I gave them news, declaring that Washington

Wrote the famous Constitution; sacred's the hand
That this blessed guide to man had given, which says, "One
And all of mankind are alike, excepting none."

This was received in respectful silence, possibly because the other Fellow Citizens were as hazy about historical facts as I at this point. "Hurrah for Washington!" they understood, and "Three cheers for the Red, White, and Blue!" was only to be expected on that occasion. But there ran a special note through my poem—a thought that only Israel Rubinstein or Beckie Aronovitch could have fully understood, besides myself. For I made myself the spokesman of the "luckless sons of Abraham," saying—

> Then we weary Hebrew children at last found rest
> In the land where reigned Freedom, and like a nest
> To homeless birds your land proved to us, and therefore
> Will we gratefully sing your praise evermore.

The boys and girls who had never been turned away from any door because of their father's religion sat as if fascinated in their places. But they woke up and applauded heartily when I was done, following the example of Miss Dwight, who wore the happy face which meant that one of her pupils had done well.

The recitation was repeated, by request, before several other classes, and the applause was equally prolonged at each repetition. After the exercises I was surrounded, praised, questioned, and made much of, by teachers as well as pupils. Plainly I had not poured my praise of George Washington into deaf ears. The teachers asked me if anybody had helped me with the poem. The girls invariably asked, "Mary Antin, how could you think of all those words?" None of them thought of the dictionary!

If I had been satisfied with my poem in the first place, the applause with which it was received by my teachers and schoolmates convinced me that I had produced a very fine thing indeed. So the person, whoever it was—perhaps my father—who suggested that my tribute to Washington ought to be printed, did not find me difficult to persuade. When I had achieved an absolutely perfect copy of my verses, at the expense of a dozen sheets of blue-ruled note paper, I crossed the Mystic River to Boston and boldly invaded Newspaper Row.

It never occurred to me to send my manuscript by mail. In fact, it has never been my way to send a delegate where I could go myself. Consciously or unconsciously, I have always acted on the motto of a wise man who was one of the dearest friends that Boston kept for me until I came. "Personal presence moves the world," said the great Dr. Hale; and I went in person to beard the editor in his armchair.

From the ferry slip to the offices of the "Boston Transcript" the way was long, strange, and full of perils; but I kept resolutely on up Hanover Street, being familiar with that part of my route, till came to a puzzling corner. There I stopped, utterly bewildered by the tangle of streets, the roar of traffic, the giddy swarm of pedestrians. With the precious manuscript tightly clasped, I balanced myself on the curbstone, afraid to plunge into the boiling vortex of the crossing. Every time I made a start, a clanging street car snatched up the way. I could not even pick out my street; the unobtrusive street signs were lost to my unpractised sight, in the glaring confusion of store signs and advertisements. If I accosted a pedestrian to ask the way, I had to speak several times before I was heard. Jews, hurrying by with bearded chins on their bosoms and eyes intent, shrugged their shoulders at the name "Transcript," and shrugged till they were out of sight. Italians sauntering behind their fruit carts answered my inquiry with a lift of the head that made their earrings gleam, and a wave of the hand that referred me to all four points of the compass at once. I was trying to catch the eye of the tall policeman who stood grandly in the middle of the crossing, a stout pillar around which the waves of traffic broke, when deliverance bellowed in my ear.

"Herald, Globe, Record, *Tra-avel-er!* Eh? Whatcher want, sis?" The tall newsboy had to stoop to me. "Transcript? Sure!" And in half a twinkling he had picked me out a paper from his bundle. When I explained to him, he good-naturedly tucked the paper in again, piloted me across, unravelled the end of Washington Street for me, and with much pointing out of landmarks, headed me for my destination, my nose seeking the spire of the Old South Church.

I found the "Transcript" building a waste of corridors tunnelled by a maze of staircases. On the glazed-glass doors were many signs with the names or nicknames of many persons: "City Editor"; "Beggars and Peddlers not Allowed." The nameless world not included in these categories was warned off, forbidden to be or do: "Private—No Admittance"; "Don't Knock." And the various inhospitable legends on the doors and walls were punctuated by frequent cuspidors on the floor. There was no sign anywhere of the welcome which I, as an author, expected to find in the home of a newspaper.

I was descending from the top story to the street for the seventh time, trying to decide what kind of editor a patriotic poem belonged to, when an untidy boy carrying broad paper streamers and whistling shrilly, in defiance of an express prohibition on the wall, bustled through the corridor and left a door ajar. I slipped in behind him, and found myself in a room full of editors.

I was a little surprised at the appearance of the editors. I had imagined my editor would look like Mr. Jones, the principal of my school, whose coat was always buttoned, and whose finger nails were beautiful. These people were in shirt sleeves, and they smoked, and they didn't politely turn in their revolving chairs when I came in, and ask, "What can I do for you?"

The room was noisy with typewriters, and nobody heard my "Please, can you tell me." At last one of the machines stopped, and the operator thought he heard something in the pause. He looked up through his own smoke. I guess he thought he saw something, for he stared. It troubled me a little to have him stare so. I realized suddenly that the hand in which I carried my manuscript was moist, and I was afraid it would make marks on the paper. I held out the manuscript to the editor, explaining that it was a poem about George Washington, and would he please print it in the "Transcript."

There was something queer about that particular editor. The way he stared and smiled made me feel about eleven inches high, and my voice kept growing smaller and smaller as I neared the end of my speech.

At last he spoke, laying down his pipe, and sitting back at his ease.

"So you have brought us a poem, my child?"

"It's about George Washington," I repeated impressively. "Don't you want to read it?"

"I should be delighted, my dear, but the fact is—"

He did not take my paper. He stood up and called across the room.

"Say, Jack! here is a young lady who has brought us a poem—about George Washington.—Wrote it yourself, my dear?—Wrote it all herself. What shall we do with her?"

Mr. Jack came over, and another man. My editor made me repeat my business, and they all looked interested, but nobody took my paper from me. They put their hands into their pockets, and my hand kept growing clammier all the time. The three seemed to be consulting, but I could not understand what they said, or why Mr. Jack laughed.

A fourth man, who had been writing busily at a desk near by, broke in on the consultation.

"That's enough boys," he said, "that's enough. Take the young lady to Mr. Hurd."

Mr. Hurd, it was found, was away on a vacation, and of several other editors in several offices, to whom I was referred, none proved to be the proper editor to take charge of a poem about George Washington. At last an elderly editor suggested that as Mr. Hurd would be away for some time, I would do well to give up the "Transcript" and try the "Herald," across the way.

A little tired by my wanderings, and bewildered by the complexity of the editorial system, but still confident about my mission, I picked my way across Washington Street and found the "Herald" offices. Here I had instant good luck. The first editor I addressed took my paper and invited me to a seat. He read my poem much more quickly than I could myself, and said it was very nice, and asked me some questions, and made notes on a slip of paper which he pinned to my manuscript. He said he would have my piece printed very soon, and would send me a copy of the issue in which it appeared. As I was going, I could not help giving the editor my hand, although I had not experienced any handshaking in Newspaper Row. I felt that as author and editor we were on a very pleasant footing, and I gave him my hand in token of comradeship.

I had regained my full stature and something over, during this cordial interview, and when I stepped out into the street and saw the crowd intently studying the bulletin board I swelled out of all proportion. For I told myself that I, Mary Antin, was one of the inspired brotherhood who made newspapers so interesting. I did not know whether my poem would be put upon the bulletin board; but at any rate, it would be in the paper, with my name at the bottom, like my story about "Snow" in Miss Dillingham's school journal. And all these people in the streets, and more, thousands of people—all Boston!—would read my poem, and learn my name, and wonder who I was. I smiled to myself in delicious amusement when a man deliberately put me out of his path, as I dreamed my way through the jostling crowd; if he only *knew* whom he was treating so unceremoniously!

When the paper with my poem in it arrived, the whole house pounced upon it at once. I was surprised to find that my verses were not all over the front page. The poem was a little hard to find, if anything, being tucked away in the middle of the voluminous sheet. But when we found it, it looked wonderful, just like real poetry, not at all as if somebody we knew had written it. It occupied a gratifying amount of space, and was introduced by a flattering biographical sketch of the author—the *author!*—the material for which the friendly editor had artfully drawn from me during that happy interview. And my name, as I had prophesied, was at the bottom!

When the excitement in the house had subsided, my father took all the change out of the cash drawer and went to buy up the "Herald." He did not count the pennies. He just bought "Heralds," all he could lay his hands on, and distributed them gratis to all our friends, relatives, and acquaintances; to all who could read, and to some who could not. For weeks he carried a clipping from the "Herald" in his breast pocket, and few were the occasions when he did not manage to introduce it into the conversation. He treasured that clipping as for years he had treasured the letters I wrote him from Polotzk.

Although my father bought up most of the issue containing my poem, a few hundred copies were left to circulate among the general public, enough to spread the flame of my patriotic ardor and to enkindle a thousand sluggish hearts. Really, there was something more solemn than vanity in my satisfaction. Pleased as I was with my notoriety—and nobody but I knew how exceedingly pleased—I had a sober feeling about it all. I enjoyed being praised and admired and envied; but what gave a divine flavor to my happiness was the idea that I had publicly borne testimony to the goodness of my exalted hero, to the greatness of my adopted country. I did not discount the homage of Arlington Street, because I did not properly rate the intelligence of its population. I took the admiration of my schoolmates without a grain of salt; it was just so much honey to me. I could not know that what made me great in the eyes of my neighbors was that "there was a piece about me in the paper"; it mattered very little to them what the "piece" was about. I thought they really admired my sentiments. On the street, in the schoolyard, I was pointed out. The people said, "That's Mary Antin. She had her name in the paper." *I* thought they said, "This is she who loves her country and worships George Washington."

To repeat, I was well aware that I was something of a celebrity, and took all possible satisfaction in the fact; yet I gave my schoolmates no occasion to call me "stuck-up." My vanity did not express itself in strutting or wagging the head. I played tag and puss-in-the-corner in the schoolyard, and did everything that was comrade-like. But in the schoolroom I conducted myself gravely, as befitted one who was preparing for the noble career of a poet.

An Insistence of Memory

Marina Tsvetaeva

ONE'S HOMELAND IS NOT a geographical convention, but an insistence of memory and blood. Not to be in Russia, to forget Russia—you fear that only if you think Russia is outside yourself. Whoever has Russia inside will lose it only along with his life.

Writers like A. N. Tolstoy, i.e., pure social ethnographers, must—if they treasure writing above all else—by all means *be* in Russia, to take in through eye and ear the details of the passing hour.

But lyricists, epic poets, and storytellers, far-sighted by the very nature of their craft, can see Russia better from far away—all of it, from Prince Igor to Lenin—than they can bubbling in the dubious, steaming cauldron of the present.

Besides, a writer is better off where he is bothered less while writing (breathing).

The question of returning to Russia is the question of love-up-close and love-from-afar, between love-in-sight, even when it distorts the visage beyond recognition, and spiritual love, which it resurrects. Of impassioned love, prepared for anything, and impatient love—that ruins what you love.

"But if there's a fire, you can't help out!" The writer's only agency is the word. All other deeds are patriotic deeds (Gumilev). So if the *man* is strongest in a writer, there's work for him to do in Russia. And heroic work! But if the artist in him rules, he will fall silent; better, he'll decline to speak; and in the best instance (morally) he will speak out within the walls of the Cheka.

"But they're writing in Russia!"

Yes, with cuts by the censor, under the threat of literary denunciation, and one can only marvel at the heroic resourcefulness of these so-called Soviet writers, writing the way grass pushes up through prison floors—regardless and despite.

As for me, I will return to Russia not as a sanctioned "social relic," but as a desired and awaited guest.

Translated by Catherine Ciepiela

The Exiled Writer's Relation to his Homeland

An Address

Thomas Mann

IT WAS A SPLENDID and generous decision on the part of the heads of this Congress that, in the course of the discussions of the problems of the writer in wartime, the literary exiles should also have their say and should be invited to express their opinions concerning the relation of the emigrant intellectuals to their own country in this war and, looking into the future, after this war. But I do not know whether to be pleased that this task has been assigned to me; these are painful and complicated matters about which I am to write—experiences which one can scarcely communicate in words to you who, in these times, live with your own people, in complete harmony with them, in unshakable faith in their cause, and are permitted to fight enthusiastically for that cause. This perfectly natural good fortune is denied us; not the enthusiasm, only the battle is ours. We also battle; these times permit no one to retreat to an ivory tower, to an existence of a peaceful cult of beauty. But it is our destiny to carry on this battle against our own land and its cause of whose corruptness we are convinced; against the land whose speech is the spiritual material in which we work, against the land in whose culture we are rooted, whose tradition we administer, and whose landscape and atmosphere should be our natural shelter.

You will say to me: "We are all fighting for the same cause, the cause of humanity. There is no distinction between you and us." Certainly, but it is your good fortune to be able to identify yourselves more or less with the cause of your people, of your fighting forces, of your government, and when you see the emblem of American sovereignty, the Stars and Stripes, you are perhaps not naïvely patriotic enough that your heart beats with pride in your throat and that you break into loud hurrahs. You are critical people and you know that these colors must conceal many human weaknesses and inadequacies and perhaps even corruption and yet you look upon this emblem with a feeling of home, with sympathy and confidence, with calm pride and heartfelt hopes, while we ———. You can scarcely conceive the feelings with which we look upon the present national emblem of Germany, the swastika. We do not look upon it, we look away. We would rather look at the ground or at the sky, for the sight of the symbol under which our people are fighting for their existence, or rather delude themselves that they are fighting for that existence, makes us physically ill. I speak as a German; the Italians may have similar feelings at the sight of their national fasces. You do not know how horribly strange, how detestable, how shocking it is for us to see the swastika-ornamented entrance to a German consulate or embassy. Here I have this experience only in the cinema; but when I lived in Zürich I often came into the neighborhood of the house of the German representative with the ominous flag upon it, and I confess that I always made a wide detour as one would about a den of iniquity, an outpost of murderous barbarism, extending into the realm of a friendly civilization under whose protection I lived.

Germany—a great name, a word which carries with it hundreds of homely and respected, pleasant and proud associations. And now, this word, a name of terror and of deadly wilderness, into which even our dreams do not dare to transport us. Whenever I read that some unhappy person has been "taken to Germany," as were recently the party leaders from Milan who had signed the anti-Fascist manifesto, or as was Romain Rolland, who is said to be in a German concentration camp, cold shudders run up and down my back. To be "taken to Germany" is the worst. To be sure, Mussolini has also been taken to Germany but I doubt whether even he is happy under Hitler's protection.

What an abnormal, morbid condition, abnormal and morbid for anyone, but especially for the writer, the bearer of a spiritual tradition, when his own country becomes the most hostile, the most sinister foreign land! And now I wish to think not only of us out here in exile, I finally wish to remember also those people who are still there, the German masses, and to think of the cruel compulsion which destiny has forced upon the German spirit. Believe me, for many there the fatherland has become as strange as it has for us; an "inner emigration" of millions is there awaiting the end just as we. They await the end, that is the end of the war, and there can be only one end. The people in Germany, in spite of their strangled isolation, are well aware of it, and yet they long for it, in spite of their natural patriotism, in spite of their national conscience. The ever-present propaganda has deeply impressed upon their consciousness the pretended permanently destructive results of a German defeat, so that in one part of their being they cannot avoid fearing that defeat more than anything else in the world.

And yet there is one thing which many of them fear more than a German defeat, that is a German victory; some only occasionally, at moments which they themselves regard as criminal, but others with complete clarity and permanently although with pangs of conscience. Imagine that you were forced with all your wishes and hopes to oppose an American victory as a great misfortune for the entire world; if you can imagine that you can place yourself in the position of these people. This attitude has become the destiny of uncounted Germans and it is my deep conviction that this destiny is particularly and unimaginably tragic. I know that other nations have been put into the position of wishing for the defeat of their government for their own sake and for the sake of the general future. But I must insist that in view of the all-too-great credulousness and innate loyalty of the German character the dilemma in this case is especially acute, and I cannot resist a feeling of deepest resentment against those who have forced the German love of country into such a position.

These people have been deluded and seduced into crimes that cry to high heaven. They have begun to atone for them and they will atone even more severely; it cannot be otherwise; common morality or, if you wish, divine justice demands it. But we out here, who saw disaster coming, we, who, ahead of our compatriots intoxicated by a fraudulent revolution, ahead of all the rest of the world, were convinced that the Nazi rule could never bring anything except war, destruction and catastrophe, we see no great difference between that which these scoundrels have done to us and what they have done to our people at home. We hate the destroyers and we long for the day which rids the world of them. But with very few exceptions we are far from being victims of a wretched emigrant hatred against our own land and we do not desire the destruction of our people. We cannot completely deny their responsibility, for somehow man is responsible for his being and doing; but misfortune is a milder and more understanding word than guilt and we feel that it is more appropriate to speak of misfortune and error than of crime.

To my own surprise I became conscious of the indestructibility of the bands which link a man and particularly an intellectual to his home, to the mother soil of his personal culture, when, soon after the outbreak of the war the British Broadcasting Corporation gave me an opportunity to speak to my fellow countrymen with my own voice from time to time. It is no easy fate to be completely severed from the spiritual and moral life of the nation into which one has been born. Emigration in our days has assumed a much more radical form than in earlier times. The exile of Victor Hugo, for example, was child's play compared with ours. To be sure, he sat as an outcast far from Paris on his island in the ocean, but the spiritual link between him and France was never broken. What he wrote was printed in the French press; his books could be bought and read at home. Today exile is a total exile, just as war, politics, world, and life have become total. We are not only physically far from our country but we have been radically expelled from its life both in the purpose and, at least for the present, in the effects of our exile. Our books are outlawed, just as we ourselves are; they exist only in translations, in fact, since the conquest of the European continent by the enemy, they exist only in English. We can count ourselves fortunate that it is still so, that that which we produce exists at all, for every writer will feel with us what it means to exist only as a literary shadow, to live only a translated and denatured life. The English broadcast gave me the only opportunity in these years to break the stupid ban, to exert a direct and original effect in German speech rhythm behind the backs of the dictators; and I have used this opportunity with the greatest satisfaction and have tried once a month to inform those people over there of their situation, to speak to them for their own good and to appeal to their consciences as impressively as possible.

This unfortunately weak and uncertain contact with the people at home I owe to the war; and it is true that without the war those of us who sought refuge in strange lands would have lost all but the most nebulous feeling for our land. Through the war, however, it has again come into more attainable proximity and we now live in hopes of an end of this estrangement. Did we therefore wish for this war? I know that this prejudice existed against us, that we were looked upon as warmongers in a time when the world was still trying to win peace by flattery from the Fascist dictators. We were given to understand that the world could not go to war "pour vos beaux yeux," and I know that even today there still lurks a certain resentment in the regard of many for us, born of the feeling that people who wished the war are in some manner responsible for it. But it is not true that we wished the war. We only know that it would come without fail if the march of Fascism were not interrupted, and we knew it at a time when that was not only possible but easy. We knew that appeasement was the surest means of bringing about the war. Indeed we have suffered from the unwillingness of the world to grasp the fact that domestic and foreign policies are one and the same, and that the sort of policies which the Nazis carried on in their own land were already war even though at the time in domestic form. It required no prophetic gift to see that, one needed only to be a German.

Now that the war is here we support it with all our hearts and we stand firmly on the side of the nations who, for the honor of humanity, had to undertake the difficult and costly struggle. Their final victory is our most urgent prayer, not because we expect revenge against the land which exiled us, but because the defeat of Nazi Germany is the only means of bringing back our country into the community of civilized nations, of taking from the name Germany the horror which now clings to it and of returning to us the spiritual fatherland.

It is an entirely different question whether we intend to take up again our former life in our fatherland after its liberation, no matter how that liberation may occur. This question can only be answered individually, and the answers would vary according to personal circumstances. If I ask myself I must say: No. The idea of returning to Germany, to be reinstated into my property, and to regard these ten years, or how many they may be, as a mere interlude, this thought is far from me and appears to me quite impossible. It is now too late for me, and I say to myself that at my age it is of no consequence in what place one completes the life's work which, on the whole, is already established and which in a certain sense is already history. I am now on the point of becoming an American citizen just as my grandchildren who were born here and are growing up here, and my attachment to this country has already progressed so far that it would be contrary to my sense of gratitude to part from it again. To spend a few months every year in Switzerland where I lived five memorable years would be sufficient for my character as a European. As for Germany, all my wishes would be fulfilled if it were again spiritually open to me and if my work, so closely linked to the German language, again had access there.

Many emigrants may have a similar view with regard to a return home. Many have taken root in the lands of their refuge, have built up a new life and will not wish to start over again. Others perhaps, especially younger ones, await nothing more longingly than the historic moment when the bells will call them back to their home. With the first airplane, with the first ship, with the first train, they will hasten home, anxious to serve as cultural or political leaders in the new Germany. Equipped with the experiences which they have collected in the years of their cosmopolitan life and which have broadened their horizons, they can indeed be very useful to their country; for what Germany needs most is fresh air from the outside, knowledge and understanding of a world in which it has long been alone.

But those who renounce the return home will also have their responsibility and their mission for Germany, for Europe, and for the world. In any case it is an advantage today and a historically appropriate position to be a citizen of two worlds. The world wishes to become unified. Humanity faces the alternative of lacerating itself in one destructive war after another and of seeing civilization perish, or of agreeing upon a form of life which is based upon the idea of union and coöperation, in which the entire world is regarded as the common home of all and in which all are granted a similar right to the enjoyment of its fruits. In such a world and in preparation for such a world it is of small importance to be a German, an American, or an Englishman, in short to be a national in spirit, experience, language, and feeling. The old word "Weltbürger," which, for a time, appeared old-fashioned, will again become honorable, and it is a German word.

We are writers and we claim to be psychologists enough to recognize that this monstrous German attempt at world domination, which we now see ending catastrophically, is nothing but a distorted and unfortunate expression of that universalism innate in the German character which formerly had a much higher, purer, and nobler form and which won the sympathy and admiration of the world for this important people. Power politics destroyed this universalism and brought about its downfall, for whenever universalism becomes power politics then humanity must arise and defend its liberty. Let us trust that German universalism will find the way to its old place of honor, that it will forever renounce the wanton ambition of world conquest and again prove itself as world sympathy, world understanding, and spiritual enrichment.

How closely connected are liberty and peace, and how closely connected the liberty of Germany and peace of the world! We emigrants are deeply ashamed when we think of the sufferings and sacrifices which the world has had to undergo on account of the errors of Germany, but all the more inspiring is the thought that Germany's liberty will be the peace of the world.

On Exile

Madame de Staël

THE POWER TO EXILE without appeal is one of the attributes of authority that predispose it most strongly toward tyranny. The monarchy's use of *lettres de cachet* was certainly a major cause of the French Revolution, as has often been said; but now it was Bonaparte, elected by the people and trampling on all the principles for which the people had revolted, who assumed the power of exiling anyone who displeased him a little, and of imprisoning without benefit of trial anyone who displeased him more than that. I can well understand how most of the former courtiers rallied to Bonaparte's political system. A change of ruler was the only concession they had to make. But the republicans, who must have felt hurt by every word Napoleon's government spoke—every act—every decree: how could they lend themselves to his tyranny?

Many men and women with a variety of opinions have suffered these decrees of exile, giving the sovereign of the state even more absolute authority than he would get from illegal imprisonments; it is harder to use violent measures than a kind of power which is technically benign, however terrible in fact. Insurmountable obstacles always attract the imagination; exile was a source of deep unhappiness to great men like Themistocles, Cicero, and Bolingbroke—especially Bolingbroke, who writes that he finds death itself less terrifying.

To call sending a man or woman away from Paris "sending them off for some country air," as the expression went, is to talk about real suffering with such sweet words that the pain is easy for political flatterers to treat lightly. And yet the simple fear of such exile is enough to bring the entire population of the empire's capital to its knees. Scaffolds may awaken courage sooner or later, but the everyday domestic annoyances of banishment just weaken your resistance and make you afraid of being disgraced in the eyes of a sovereign capable of inflicting this unfortunate existence upon you. To spend a lifetime abroad voluntarily is one thing; if we are forced into it, though, we keep imagining that the people we love might be sick, and we would not be able to go to them, or perhaps ever see them again. Everything is compromised—the affections, social habits, financial interests. Sadder still, these links themselves grow weaker, and we end as strangers in our own homeland.

During the twelve years of exile to which Napoleon condemned me, I often thought that he would be unable to bear the misery of being deprived of France, having no memory of France in his heart. Nothing but the rocks of Corsica retraced his childhood days; Necker's daughter was more French than he. I will speak elsewhere about the circumstances of my exile and the trips I took to the edge of Asia as a result; but I have virtually forbidden myself to portray living people, so I would not have been able to make a personal history interesting in the way such things should be. I will recall here only what will be relevant to the general plan of this work.

I guessed Napoleon's character and political schemes more quickly than most people, and I am proud of that. An infallible instinct enlightens all real friends of liberty about such things. But my position at the beginning of the Consulat was dreadful, because good society in France at the time thought Bonaparte the very man to save them from anarchy or Jacobinism. As a result, my spirit of opposition earned me a lot of disapproval. Anyone who can see as far as tomorrow in politics arouses the wrath of people who can see no farther than today. I must say it took even more strength to bear the persecution of society than to expose myself to the persecution of power.

I have always kept the memory of one of those society tortures (if it is all right to speak that way) that French aristocrats are so good at inflicting whenever it suits them on people who do not share their opinions. A large part of the old nobility had rallied to Napoleon; some, as we have seen since then, trying to recapture their former habits as courtiers, others hoping that the first consul would bring back the old monarchy. Everyone knew I was strongly against the system of government Napoleon was preparing, and the supporters of arbitrary government followed their usual custom of calling opinions that tended to elevate the dignity of nations "antisocial." If anyone were to remind the émigrés who came back under Bonaparte how furiously they blamed the friends of liberty who were still loyal to the same theory, they might learn indulgence from remembering their mistakes.

I was the first woman exiled by Napoleon, though he banished many women of opposing opinions soon afterward. One of the most interesting was the Duchess of Chevreuse, who died of the heart condition brought on by her exile. As she lay dying, she could not get Napoleon's permission to come back to Paris one last time to consult her doctor and see her friends again. Where could such luxuriating in evil come from, if not from a hatred of all independent beings? Women annoyed Napoleon as rebels; they were of no use to his political designs, on the one hand, and were less accessible than men to the hopes and fears dispensed by power, on the other. As a result, he took pleasure in saying hurtful and vulgar things to women. His pursuit of etiquette was matched by his hatred of chivalry: a bad choice to make from the manners of former times. From his early habits of Revolutionary days he also retained a certain Jacobin antipathy to brilliant Paris society, which was greatly influenced by women; he was afraid of the art of teasing which we must admit is characteristic of Frenchwomen. If Bonaparte had been willing to keep to the proud role of great general and first magistrate of the Republic, he would have floated with the height of genius above all the little stinging barbs of salon wit. Once he decided to become a parvenu king, however, the bourgeois gentleman on the throne, he was exposing himself to the kind of society satire which can only be repressed by the use of espionage and terror: and that is how, in fact, he repressed it.

Bonaparte wanted me to praise him in my writings. It is not that one more eulogy would have been noticed in the fumes of incense surrounding him. But he was annoyed that I was the only well-known French writer to publish during his reign without making the least mention of his stupendous existence, and he finally suppressed my book *On Germany* with incredible fury. Until that time my disgrace had merely consisted in having to leave Paris. After that, however, I was forbidden to travel anywhere, and threatened with life imprisonment. The worst aggravation of this distress was the contagion of exile, an invention worthy of the Roman emperors. Anyone who visited banished persons exposed himself to exile in turn; most of my French acquaintances fled as if I had the plague. When it was not too painful, this seemed like a comedy to me; when I happened to meet one of Bonaparte's courtiers in the streets of Geneva I was tempted to frighten him with my courtesy, the way quarantined travelers throw their handkerchiefs to passersby, out of malice, to make them share the trouble of the lazar house.

My great-hearted friend, M. Mathieu de Montmorency, once came to see me at Coppet; four days after his arrival he received a *lettre de cachet* exiling him for having given the consolation of his presence to someone who had been his friend for twenty-five years. I would have done anything at that moment to prevent such a painful thing from happening. At the same time, I received a visit from Mme. Récamier, who had no relationship to politics at all except for her courageous interest in exiled people of various opinions; we had already had several reunions there at Coppet.

Can it be believed? The loveliest woman in France, who could have found champions anywhere in the world for that alone, was exiled because she had entered the château of an unhappy female friend one hundred fifty leagues from Paris. The conqueror of the world found this coalition of two women on the shores of Lake Geneva too threatening, and he made himself look ridiculous by persecuting them. But he had once said, "Power is never ridiculous," and he certainly put this maxim to the proof.

We have seen so many families divided by fear of contact with the exiled! At the onset of tyranny, there are always a few acts of courage, but little by little anxiety alters sentiments, and obstacles become wearisome. People come to believe that their friends' misfortunes are their own fault. The family pundits get together and announce that there is no point in too much communication with M. or Mme. so-and-so; their excellent feelings are not at issue, but they do have such lively imaginations! The truth is that everyone would be willing to proclaim these poor exiles great poets, on condition that their imprudence forbade one's seeing or writing to them. This is the way friendship and even love grow cold in every heart; intimate qualities and public virtues are lost forever; love between oneself and another is no longer possible once one has stopped loving one's country. All one learns is how to use a hypocritical language of sugary blame for those out of favor, adroit apology for the powerful, and the hidden doctrine of egoism.

Bonaparte knew better than anyone else the secret of creating a frozen isolation that presented men to him one by one, never united together. He did not want a single individual of his time to have an independent existence: no one was to get married, or have any kind of fortune, or choose a place to live, or exercise talent, or make any decision at all without his permission. Strange to say, he entered into the least detail of every individual's relationships, combining the empire of a conqueror with the inquisition of a gossip, so to speak, and holding the finest of threads and the strongest of chains in his hands.

In Napoleon's reign, the metaphysical question of man's free will had become completely pointless: no one could follow his own wishes in the most important situations, in the most trivial, in anything at all.

Translated by Vivian Folkenflick

We Refugees

Hannah Arendt

IN THE FIRST PLACE, we don't like to be called "refugees." We ourselves call each other "newcomers" or "immigrants." Our newspapers are papers for "Americans of German language"; and, as far as I know, there is not and never was any club founded by Hitler-persecuted people whose name indicated that its members were refugees.

A refugee used to be a person driven to seek refuge because of some act committed or some political opinion held. Well, it is true we have had to seek refuge; but we committed no acts and most of us never dreamt of having any radical opinion. With us the meaning of the term "refugee" has changed. Now "refugees" are those of us who have been so unfortunate as to arrive in a new country without means and have to be helped by Refugee Committees.

Before this war broke out we were even more sensitive about being called refugees. We did our best to prove to other people that we were just ordinary immigrants. We declared that we had departed of our own free will to countries of our choice, and we denied that our situation had anything to do with "so-called Jewish problems." Yes, we were "immigrants" or "newcomers" who had left our country because, one fine day, it no longer suited us to stay, or for purely economic reasons. We wanted to rebuild our lives, that was all. In order to rebuild one's life one has to be strong and an optimist. So we are very optimistic.

Our optimism, indeed, is admirable, even if we say so ourselves. The story of our struggle has finally become known. We lost our home, which means the familiarity of daily life. We lost our occupation, which means the confidence that we are of some use in this world. We lost our language, which means the naturalness of reactions, the simplicity of gestures, the unaffected expression of feelings. We left our relatives in the Polish ghettos and our best friends have been killed in concentration camps, and that means the rupture of our private lives.

Nevertheless, as soon as we were saved—and most of us had to be saved several times—we started our new lives and tried to follow as closely as possible all the good advice our saviors passed on to us. We were told to forget; and we forgot quicker than anybody ever could imagine. In a friendly way we were reminded that the new country would become a new home; and after four weeks in France or six weeks in America, we pretended to be Frenchmen or Americans. The more optimistic among us would even add that their whole former life had been passed in a kind of unconscious exile and only their new country now taught them what a home really looks like. It is true we sometimes raise objections when we are told to forget about our former work; and our former ideals are usually hard to throw over if our social standard is at stake. With the language, however, we find no difficulties: after a single year optimists are convinced they speak English as well as their mother tongue; and after two years they swear solemnly that they speak English better than any other language—their German is a language they hardly remember.

In order to forget more efficiently we rather avoid any allusion to concentration or internment camps we experienced in nearly all European countries—it might be interpreted as pessimism or lack of confidence in the new homeland. Besides, how often have we been told that nobody likes to listen to all that; hell is no longer a religious belief or a fantasy, but something as real as houses and stones and trees. Apparently nobody wants to know that contemporary history has created a new kind of human beings—the kind that are put in concentration camps by their foes and in internment camps by their friends.

Even among ourselves we don't speak about this past. Instead, we have found our own way of mastering an uncertain future. Since everybody plans and wishes and hopes, so do we. Apart from these general human attitudes, however, we try to clear up the future more scientifically. After so much bad luck we want a course as sure as a gun. Therefore, we leave the earth with all its uncertainties behind and we cast our eyes up to the sky. The stars tell us—rather than the newspapers—when Hitler will be defeated and when we shall become American citizens. We think the stars more reliable advisers than all our friends; we learn from the stars when we should have lunch with our benefactors and on what day we have the best chances of filling out one of these countless questionnaires which accompany our present lives. Sometimes we don't rely even on the stars but rather on the lines of our hand or the signs of our handwriting. Thus we learn less about political events but more about our own dear selves, even though somehow psychoanalysis has gone out of fashion. Those happier times are past when bored ladies and gentlemen of high society conversed about the genial misdemeanors of their early childhood. They don't want ghost-stories any more; it is real experiences that make their flesh creep. There is no longer any need of bewitching the past; it is spellbound enough in reality. Thus, in spite of our outspoken optimism, we use all sorts of magical tricks to conjure up the spirits of the future.

I don't know which memories and which thoughts nightly dwell in our dreams. I dare not ask for information, since I, too, had rather be an optimist. But sometimes I imagine that at least nightly we think of our dead or we remember the poems we once loved. I could even understand how our friends of the West coast, during the curfew, should have had such curious notions as to believe that we are not only "prospective citizens" but present "enemy aliens." In daylight, of course, we become only "technically" enemy aliens—all refugees know this. But when technical reasons prevented you from leaving your home during the dark hours, it certainly was not easy to avoid some dark speculations about the relation between technicality and reality.

No, there is something wrong with our optimism. There are those odd optimists among us who, having made a lot of optimistic speeches, go home and turn on the gas or make use of a skyscraper in quite an unexpected way. They seem to prove that our proclaimed cheerfulness is based on a dangerous readiness for death. Brought up in the conviction that life is the highest good and death the greatest dismay, we became witnesses and victims of worse terrors than death—without having been able to discover a higher ideal than life. Thus, although death lost its horror for us, we became neither willing nor capable to risk our lives for a cause. Instead of fighting—or thinking about how to become able to fight back—refugees have got used to wishing death to friends or relatives; if somebody dies, we cheerfully imagine all the trouble he has been saved. Finally many of us end by wishing that we, too, could be saved some trouble, and act accordingly.

Since 1938—since Hitler's invasion of Austria—we have seen how quickly eloquent optimism could change to speechless pessimism. As time went on, we got worse—even more optimistic and even more inclined to suicide. Austrian Jews under Schuschnigg were such a cheerful people—all impartial observers admired them. It was quite wonderful how deeply convinced they were that nothing could happen to them. But when German troops invaded the country and Gentile neighbors started riots at Jewish homes, Austrian Jews began to commit suicide.

Unlike other suicides, our friends leave no explanation of their deed, no indictment, no charge against a world that had forced a desperate man to talk and to behave cheerfully to his very last day. Letters left by them are conventional, meaningless documents. Thus, funeral orations we make at their open graves are brief, embarrassed and very hopeful. Nobody cares about motives, they seem to be clear to all of us.

I speak of unpopular facts; and it makes things worse that in order to prove my point I do not even dispose of the sole arguments which impress modern people—figures. Even those Jews who furiously deny the existence of the Jewish people give us a fair chance of survival as far as figures are concerned—how else could they prove that only a few Jews are criminals and that many Jews are being killed as good patriots in wartime? Through their effort to save the statistical life of the Jewish people we know that Jews had the lowest suicide rate among all civilized nations. I am quite sure those figures are no longer correct, but I cannot prove it with new figures, though I can certainly with new experiences. This might be sufficient for those skeptical souls who never were quite convinced that the measure of one's skull gives the exact idea of its content, or that statistics of crime show the exact level of national ethics. Anyhow, wherever European Jews are living today, they no longer behave according to statistical laws. Suicides occur not only among the panic-stricken people in Berlin and Vienna, in Bucharest or Paris, but in New York and Los Angeles, in Buenos Aires and Montevideo.

On the other hand, there has been little reported about suicides in the ghettoes and concentration camps themselves. True, we had very few reports at all from Poland, but we have been fairly well informed about German and French concentration camps.

At the camp of Gurs, for instance, where I had the opportunity of spending some time, I heard only once about suicide, and that was the suggestion of a collective action, apparently a kind of protest in order to vex the French. When some of us remarked that we had been shipped there "*pour crever*" in any case, the general mood turned suddenly into a violent courage of life. The general opinion held that one had to be abnormally asocial and unconcerned about general events if one was still able to interpret the whole accident as personal and individual bad luck and, accordingly, ended one's life personally and individually. But the same people, as soon as they returned to their own individual lives, being faced with seemingly individual problems, changed once more to this insane optimism which is next door to despair.

We are the first non-religious Jews persecuted—and we are the first ones who, not only *in extremis*, answer with suicide. Perhaps the philosophers are right who teach that suicide is the last and supreme guarantee of human freedom: not being free to create our lives or the world in which we live, we nevertheless are free to throw life away and to leave the world. Pious Jews, certainly, cannot realize this negative liberty; they perceive murder in suicide, that is, destruction of what man never is able to make, interference with the rights of the Creator. *Adonai nathan veadonai lakach* ("The Lord hath given and the Lord hath taken away"); and they would add: *baruch shem adonai* ("blessed be the name of the Lord"). For them suicide, like murder, means a blasphemous attack on creation as a whole. The man who kills himself asserts that life is not worth living and the world not worth sheltering him.

Yet our suicides are no mad rebels who hurl defiance at life and the world, who try to kill in themselves the whole universe. Theirs is a quiet and modest way of vanishing; they seem to apologize for the violent solution they have found for their personal problems. In their opinion, generally, political events had nothing to do with their individual fate; in good or bad times they would believe solely in their personality. Now they find some mysterious shortcomings in themselves which prevent them from getting along. Having felt entitled from their earliest childhood to a certain social standard, they are failures in their own eyes if this standard cannot be kept any longer. Their optimism is the vain attempt to keep head above water. Behind this front of cheerfulness, they constantly struggle with despair of themselves. Finally, they die of a kind of selfishness.

If we are saved we feel humiliated, and if we are helped we feel degraded. We fight like madmen for private existences with individual destinies, since we are afraid of becoming part of that miserable lot of *schnorrers* whom we, many of us former philanthropists, remember only too well. Just as once we failed to understand that the so-called *schnorrer* was a symbol of Jewish destiny and not a *shlemihl*, so today we don't feel entitled to Jewish solidarity; we cannot realize that we by ourselves are not so much concerned as the whole Jewish people. Sometimes this lack of comprehension has been strongly supported by our protectors. Thus, I remember a director of a great charity concern in Paris who, whenever he received the card of a German-Jewish intellectual with the inevitable "Dr." on it, used to exclaim at the top of his voice, "Herr Doktor, Herr Doktor, Herr Schnorrer, Herr Schnorrer!"

The conclusion we drew from such unpleasant experiences was simple enough. To be a doctor of philosophy no longer satisfied us; and we learnt that in order to build a new life, one has first to improve on the old one. A nice little fairy-tale has been invented to describe our behavior; a forlorn émigré dachshund, in his grief, begins to speak: "Once, when I was a St. Bernard . . ."

Our new friends, rather overwhelmed by so many stars and famous men, hardly understand that at the basis of all our descriptions of past splendors lies one human truth: once we were somebodies about whom people cared, we were loved by friends, and even known by landlords as paying our rent regularly. Once we could buy our food and ride in the subway without being told we were undesirable. We have become a little hysterical since newspapermen started detecting us and telling us publicly to stop being disagreeable when shopping for milk and bread. We wonder how it can be done; we already are so damnably careful in every moment of our daily lives to avoid anybody guessing who we are, what kind of passport we have, where our birth certificates were filled out—and that Hitler didn't like us. We try the best we can to fit into a world where you have to be sort of politically minded when you buy your food.

Under such circumstances, St. Bernard grows bigger and bigger. I never can forget that young man who, when expected to accept a certain kind of work, sighed out, "You don't know to whom you speak; I was Section-manager in Karstadt's [A great department store in Berlin]." But there is also the deep despair of that middle-aged man who, going through countless shifts of different committees in order to be saved, finally exclaimed, "And nobody here knows who I am!" Since nobody would treat him as a dignified human being, he began sending cables to great personalities and his big relations. He learnt quickly that in this mad world it is much easier to be accepted as a "great man" than as a human being.

The less we are free to decide who we are or to live as we like, the more we try to put up a front, to hide the facts, and to play roles. We were expelled from Germany because we were Jews. But having hardly crossed the French borderline, we were changed into "boches." We were even told that we had to accept this designation if we really were against Hitler's racial theories. During seven years we played the ridiculous role of trying to be Frenchmen—at least, prospective citizens; but at the beginning of the war we were interned as "boches" all the same. In the meantime, however, most of us had indeed become such loyal Frenchmen that we could not even criticize a French governmental order; thus we declared it was all right to be interned. We were the first "*prisonniers volontaires*" history has ever seen. After the Germans invaded the country, the French Government had only to change the name of the firm; having been jailed because we were Germans, we were not freed because we were Jews.

It is the same story all over the world, repeated again and again. In Europe the Nazis confiscated our property; but in Brazil we have to pay

30% of our wealth, like the most loyal member of the *Bund der Auslandsdeutschen.* In Paris we could not leave our homes after eight o'clock because we were Jews; but in Los Angeles we are restricted because we are "enemy aliens." Our identity is changed so frequently that nobody can find out who we actually are.

Unfortunately, things don't look any better when we meet with Jews. French Jewry was absolutely convinced that all Jews coming from beyond the Rhine were what they called *Polaks*—what German Jewry called *Ostjuden.* But those Jews who really came from eastern Europe could not agree with their French brethren and called us *Jaeckes.* The sons of these *Jaecke*-haters—the second generation born in France and already duly assimilated—shared the opinion of the French Jewish upper classes. Thus, in the very same family, you could be called a *Jaecke* by the father and a *Polak* by the son.

Since the outbreak of the war and the catastrophe that has befallen European Jewry, the mere fact of being a refugee has prevented our mingling with native Jewish society, some exceptions only proving the rule. These unwritten social laws, though never publicly admitted, have the great force of public opinion. And such a silent opinion and practice is more important for our daily lives than all official proclamations of hospitality and good will.

Man is a social animal and life is not easy for him when social ties are cut off. Moral standards are much easier kept in the texture of a society. Very few individuals have the strength to conserve their own integrity if their social, political and legal status is completely confused. Lacking the courage to fight for a change of our social and legal status, we have decided instead, so many of us, to try a change of identity. And this curious behavior makes matters much worse. The confusion in which we live is partly our own work.

Some day somebody will write the true story of this Jewish emigration from Germany; and he will have to start with a description of that Mr. Cohn from Berlin who had always been a 150% German, a German super-patriot. In 1933 that Mr. Cohn found refuge in Prague and very quickly became a convinced Czech patriot—as true and as loyal a Czech patriot as he had been a German one. Time went on and about 1937 the Czech Government, already under some Nazi pressure, began to expel its Jewish refugees, disregarding the fact that they felt so strongly as prospective Czech citizens. Our Mr. Cohn then went to Vienna; to adjust oneself there a definite Austrian patriotism was required. The German invasion forced Mr. Cohn out of that country. He arrived in Paris at a bad moment and he never did receive a regular residence-permit. Having already acquired a great skill in wishful thinking, he refused to take mere administrative measures seriously, convinced that he would spend his future life in France. Therefore, he prepared his adjustment to the French nation by identifying himself with "our" ancestor Vercingetorix. I think I had better not dilate on the further adventures of Mr. Cohn. As long as Mr. Cohn can't make up his mind to be what he actually is, a Jew, nobody can foretell all the mad changes he will still have to go through.

A man who wants to lose his self discovers, indeed, the possibilities of human existence, which are infinite, as infinite as is creation. But the recovering of a new personality is as difficult—and as hopeless—as a new creation of the world. Whatever we do, whatever we pretend to be, we reveal nothing but our insane desire to be changed, not to be Jews. All our activities are directed to attain this aim: we don't want to be refugees, since we don't want to be Jews; we pretend to be English-speaking people, since German-speaking immigrants of recent years are marked as Jews; we don't call ourselves stateless, since the majority of stateless people in the world are Jews; we are willing to become loyal Hottentots, only to hide the fact that we are Jews. We don't succeed and we can't succeed; under the cover of our "optimism" you can easily detect the hopeless sadness of assimilationists.

With us from Germany the word assimilation received a "deep" philosophical meaning. You can hardly realize how serious we were about it. Assimilation did not mean the necessary adjustment to the country where we happened to be born and to the people whose language we happened to speak. We adjust in principle to everything and everybody. This attitude became quite clear to me once by the words of one of my compatriots who, apparently, knew how to express his feelings. Having just arrived in France, he founded one of these societies of adjustment in which German Jews asserted to each other that they were already Frenchmen. In his first speech he said: "We have been good Germans in Germany and therefore we shall be good Frenchmen in France." The public applauded enthusiastically and nobody laughed; we were happy to have learnt how to prove our loyalty.

If patriotism were a matter of routine or practice, we should be the most patriotic people in the world. Let us go back to our Mr. Cohn; he certainly has beaten all records. He is that ideal immigrant who always, and in every country into which a terrible fate has driven him, promptly sees and loves the native mountains. But since patriotism is not yet believed to be a matter of practice, it is hard to convince people of the sincerity of our repeated transformations. This struggle makes our own society so intolerant; we demand full affirmation without our own group because we are not in the position to obtain it from the natives. The natives, confronted with such strange beings as we are, become suspicious; from their point of view, as a rule, only a loyalty to our old countries is understandable. That makes life very bitter for us. We might overcome this suspicion if we would explain that, being Jews, our patriotism in our original countries had rather a peculiar aspect. Though it was indeed sincere and deep-rooted. We wrote big volumes to prove it; paid an entire bureaucracy to explore its antiquity and to explain it statistically. We had scholars write philosophical dissertations on the predestined harmony between Jews and Frenchmen, Jews and Germans, Jews and Hungarians, Jews and . . . Our so frequently suspected loyalty of today has a long history. It is the history of a hundred and fifty years of assimilated Jewry who performed an unprecedented feat: though proving all the time their non-Jewishness, they succeeded in remaining Jews all the same.

The desperate confusion of these Ulysses-wanderers who, unlike their great prototype, don't know who they are is easily explained by their perfect mania for refusing to keep their identity. This mania is much older than the last ten years which revealed the profound absurdity of our existence. We are like people with a fixed idea who can't help trying continually to disguise an imaginary stigma. Thus we are enthusiastically fond of every new possibility which, being new, seems able to work miracles. We are fascinated by every new nationality in the same way as a woman of tidy size is delighted with every new dress which promises to give her the desired waistline. But she likes the new dress only as long as she believes in its miraculous qualities, and she will throw it away as soon as she discovers that it does not change her stature—or, for that matter, her status.

One may be surprised that the apparent uselessness of all our odd disguises has not yet been able to discourage us. If it is true that men seldom learn from history, it is also true that they may learn from personal experiences which, as in our case, are repeated time and again. But before you cast the first stone at us, remember that being a Jew does not give any legal status in this world. If we should start telling the truth that we are nothing but Jews, it would mean that we expose ourselves to the fate of human beings who, unprotected by any specific law or political convention, are nothing but human beings. I can hardly imagine an attitude more dangerous, since we actually live in a world in which human beings as such have ceased to exist for quite a while; since society has discovered discrimination as the great social weapon by which one may kill men without any bloodshed; since passports or birth certificates, and sometimes even income tax receipts, are no longer formal papers but matters of social distinction. It is true that most of us depend entirely upon social standards; we lose confidence in ourselves if society does not approve us; we are—and always were—ready to pay any price in order to be accepted by society. But it is equally true that the very few among us who have tried to get along without all these tricks and jokes of adjustment and assimilation have paid a much higher price than they could afford: they jeopardized the few chances even outlaws are given in a topsy-turvy world.

The attitude of these few whom, following Bernard Lazare, one may call "conscious pariahs," can as little be explained by recent events alone as the attitude of our Mr. Cohn who tried by every means to become an upstart. Both are sons of the nineteenth century which, not knowing legal or political outlaws, knew only too well social pariahs and their counterpart, social parvenus. Modern Jewish history, having started with court Jews and continuing with Jewish millionaires and philanthropists, is apt to forget about this other trend of Jewish tradition—the tradition of Heine, Rahel Varnhagen, Sholom Aleichem, of Bernard Lazare, Franz Kafka or even Charlie Chaplin. It is the tradition of a minority of Jews who have not wanted to become upstarts, who preferred the status of "conscious pariah." All vaunted Jewish qualities—the "Jewish heart," humanity, humor, disinterested intelligence—are pariah qualities. All Jewish shortcomings—tactlessness, political stupidity, inferiority complexes and money-grubbing—are characteristic of upstarts. There have always been Jews who did not think it worth while to change their humane attitude and their natural insight into reality for the narrowness of caste spirit or the essential unreality of financial transactions.

History has forced the status of outlaws upon both, upon pariahs and parvenus alike. The latter have not yet accepted the great wisdom of Balzac's "*On ne parvient pas deux fois*"; thus they don't understand the wild dreams of the former and feel humiliated in sharing their fate. Those few refugees who insist upon telling the truth, even to the point of "indecency," get in exchange for their unpopularity one priceless advantage: history is no longer a closed book to them and politics is no longer the privilege of Gentiles. They know that the outlawing of the Jewish people in Europe has been followed closely by the outlawing of most European nations. Refugees driven from country to country represent the vanguard of their peoples—if they keep their identity. For the first time Jewish history is not separate but tied up with that of all other nations. The comity of European peoples went to pieces when, and because, it allowed its weakest member to be excluded and persecuted.

Africa in Exile

Es'kia Mphahlele

I

YOU ARE A REFUGEE today. As soon as you find asylum in a country disposed to grant it, you are an exile. Indeed, mentally you already consider yourself an exile as soon as you cross the border of your country in flight. To the extent that you are conscious of what you are fleeing from and of where you are heading to seek a place of refuge, you are an exile.

In his book *The Anatomy of Exile*, Paul Tabori asks us to consider the following points of definition, arrived at after testing an initially tentative definition against the sentiments of several exiles:

1. An exile is a person who is compelled to leave his homeland—though the forces that send him on his way may be political, economic, or purely psychological. It does not make an essential difference whether he is expelled by physical force or whether he makes the decision to leave without such immediate pressure.

2. The status of the exile, both material and psychological, is a dynamic one—it changes from exile to emigrant or emigrant to exile. These changes can be the result both of circumstances altering his homeland and of the assimilation process in his new country. An essential element in this process is the attitude of the exile to the circumstances prevailing in his homeland that are bound to influence him psychologically.

3. The contribution of the exile can be determined by his efforts at assimilation, his desire to become accepted, and by the assets (spiritual and intellectual) he brings with him. That is, he might acquire skills and knowledge in the country of reception that enable him to make such a contribution—or he might cling to his original national and spiritual identity, which makes such a contribution more valuable and more acceptable.

4. While the exile may leave with the full determination to return, this resolve is likely to weaken and fade in direct proportion to the length of absence. It is only exceptional that it survives more than one generation.

5. However eager for assimilation, the exile will always retain an often subconscious interest and affection for his homeland. (He may be watching the Olympic Games and cheer with equal enthusiasm the representatives of his native country and those of his adopted country.)

6. The contribution of the exile to his new country is always likely to be greater than his influence still felt in the land of his birth. His successes abroad are likely to be envied and derided.

There are some variants of his categories, as Paul Tabori readily admits. One can readily think of the following:

1. Essentially, African exiles have left owing to immediate pressure, or out of frustration in the practice of a profession. The frustration may be rooted in considerations of material welfare or spiritual self-fulfillment, or both.

2. The attitude of the exile to the "circumstances prevailing in his homeland" that influence him psychologically varies from person to person, with the possible exception of exiles who leave as a group, bound together by an ideology. Even then, the longer the group stays outside, the greater the likelihood of separation, as the members find avenues for their professional fulfillment separate from one another.

3. Where exiles come as refugees and are accommodated in camps according to their affiliation with exiled political parties, the longer they have been away, the greater the likelihood of internal fighting, splinter factions, even, in extreme cases, killings. This happened to Angola's MPLA (Popular Movement for the Liberation of Angola), Mozambique's FRELIMO (Liberation Front of Mozambique), Zimbabwe's African Peoples Union and African National Union, and South Africa's Pan-Africanist Congress and African National Congress.

4. In countries that provide camps, there may be professionals—teachers, lawyers, doctors, writers—who share a common nationality with the freedom fighters. These professionals are employed by the country of reception under conditions that make assimilation and an immigrant status impossible. Relations between the two groups of exiles are commonly uneasy, and the freedom fighter silently resents his professional countryman. The intellectual most often resigns himself to his personal academic pursuits. Even in relation to the political leadership from his own country, he is gradually made to feel irrelevant, because he is no longer (if he ever was) regarded as a freedom fighter.

5. By and large, because of the shortage of jobs in African countries, and

the propensity of these countries to take care of their own first, Europe, including Britain, and North America have become the main areas of political asylum.

6. There are exiles who return home even if the political situation they left behind may not have changed for the better. The reasons for this are mainly psychological.

7. I would venture to say that there are only a negligible number of African intellectuals who would assert, as so many European exiles do, that they left because of their countries' backwardness and philistinism, the latter being a concern of artists.

8. Of a singular kind, one imagines, is the loneliness of the ruler, or members of the ruling class, who had to flee the retribution that awaits them after a "people's revolution," and for whose blood the masses cry out. They have to go into hiding wherever they can find asylum. They are kept on sufferance, euphemistically called "humanitarian grounds," by the host government. This view, of course, assumes that such people have a high degree of sensitivity and intellect. Even when the host government sympathizes with their cause, owing to its own homegrown tyranny toward the masses, "it can never be like home." And power is sweet: to lose it is to forfeit your whole purpose for living. Amin and Bokassa are among this last category.

The mechanics of living may very well be taken care of for the exile who contributes his skills to his host country. The exiles who live in camps, too, may want for little in material welfare. They may all be provided for by the UN Commission for Refugees, and travel freely on UN documents. But ultimately, it is the individual who is left with the burden of exile as a condition of the mind. He has to face himself and try to resolve this condition. This is especially so among intellectuals. There is a point beyond which the camp leader, the leader of an organization, or the commander in the barracks, where military training is conducted for refugees or freedom fighters, can never reach the individual in his charge.

Beyond this is the exile's private world, a personality loaded with contradictions, riddled with guilt feelings concerning the people who need his services back home. You may perhaps be one in a cluster of exiles in the same city or district thrown together by a common fear. Two insecure persons cannot room together with ease. So you feed on one another's miseries and insecurity. You attend the same parties. Several of these parties are embassy or consulate functions. You move in with a sense of belonging, you have an international status. You are being noticed by the international community. Being there makes you a "legitimate" exile, and exile justifies your being there. Who of your political enemies back home would dare cross that threshold to be graciously received by the ambassador and his wife, and still maintain a normal flow of adrenaline, sail in, and assert a cosmopolitan presence—*who*?

You are thrown together in a house, and Memory Lane takes you all back to your home country. Anecdotes are reeled off. You watch the daily newspapers and look for news about home. You analyze it to death. When, when, *when* will that glorious day come—the return?

"The government's running scared—there's a split in the ruling party. Hear me tell you, boys, it's not long before we march back in."

"Strong people scared—they become brutal, sadistic."

"They say my Ma's very ill."

"Hey, my sister just got married—I should've been there. Me and my sister were close."

"The ancestors will be with you, you've been in touch with your Ma all these years. Think of Kotsi—you know—remember he didn't know his Ma was dead till six years after her burial?"

"Guess who's in the city, fellows?"

"Who?"

"The Chief."

"What's so new about that? He's often here."

"Don't be dumb—the rebels, of course! The gang of eight, man."

"Discipline. Some people don't know we've got to stick together in exile. Either you're nationalist or not—no revisionism in that department. They've got to be disciplined."

"Yes, but what if there's dictatorship in the movement—why should we take the kind of manure from one another we don't want the whites raining on us?"

"You want to join the gang?"

"No, but I just can't stand this any longer!"

"Where would the movement be if we allowed every loudmouth rank-and-file to tell the leaders how to run it? Democracy's a luxury in a freedom movement in exile."

"And don't you be talking subversion, my friend. You forget you're still under a cloud until you're cleared."

"You think I care about being called an informer?"

"You damn well should *care*—I *would."*

"Try me—hey, the world's big, man, call me an informer, persecute me for

it. I'll move elsewhere. It'd still be better than moulding and collecting cobwebs in our brains like we're doing here in a walkie-talkie organization."

"You've no right to speak like that about the Congress."

"What'll you do—assassinate me? Go ahead—what a laugh! The organization's bored because it hasn't got a strategy for the return like FRELIMO and MPLA—so we chew each other's asses off, gun each other down."

"Shut up!"

The words keep coming: sad words, barbed words, venomous words. And the lonely ones keep coming back for more hurt. Suspicions, the guilt, borrowed bravery and stamina, the impotent anger, the vicarious exasperation touched off by events back home, theories insinuated into a home situation and proved later to be quite irrelevant—a home situation that is progressively receding into the hazier areas of memory; the haunting sense of loss and lack of a cultural context that can be intimately felt—all these rush into the vortex of one's person, expand and bubble into a poisonous yeast that can be soul-mutilating.

And when MPLA and FRELIMO and the Zimbabweans shoot their way back home, when Obote returns to Kampala, for better or for worse, those left in exile look on with a mixture of pride, hope, envy, and immobilizing exasperation. And again, some decide to abdicate, stand away for a while, try to better their own educational standing. Several can be found teaching in schools and universities in various parts of the world. For besides teaching, what other escape route or refuge is there for an exile?

As most African exiles are male, the need for female companionship becomes an added problem that extends beyond the basic burden of exile and its political dimensions. Reaching out to the surrounding milieu to find or create female friendships implies the acceptance, conscious or otherwise, of an extragroup commitment. The exile is stepping out of his cultural identity, a process he must contemplate in relation to his future, his plans to return home one day. Numerous things are possible as a result, whether the companion is black or white. On the one hand, she is being asked either to share a life of exile or to ensure the man's negation of it. On the other, this liaison compels him to reckon with his own future as a man and as a political exile.

On what terms will he be assimilated if he wants to raise a family and stay? How will the family adjust if or when that uncertain day comes for the return? Only in very rare cases has a whole African family returned home from exile, because man and wife have considered it unfair to ask that their children exchange a metropolitan life for an underprivileged one, even if this may be under black rule. They have roots in their ancestral soil their children will not necessarily have, hopes for spiritual solace their children cannot share. For them, return will mean the resolution of a condition the children do not psychologically share—exile. And the political imponderables back there are just too many. These are considerations and decisions that lie outside the sanctions of the ideological group, such as one's fellow-exiles may be tempted to project into the situation.

II

My own case history as an exile goes back to September 6, 1957. I have come to know that exile for the writer, or the artist in general, has psychological complexities that only the individual can try to delineate for himself and for others who may care to listen to him. I returned to South Africa in August 1977.

During a social upheaval, a writer is often called upon to give a share of his time to a cause as a social animal rather than as an artist. It seems perfectly natural to make such a distinction when you are on your own homeground. But in exile, you seem to have been thrown into your ego center, as it were, so that to hurt the writer is to hurt the whole man. To use another metaphor, you seem to be living in a rented glasshouse. Vulnerable. You can see clearly only when the rain is gone or when there is no mist. You pray that the lease holds until—who knows?

You and your family press upon one another. There is an extraordinary degree of interdependency among you all, until the children begin to socialize, move in and out of the family circle. For a while you let go, and even if you don't like their peer group, who are acting out another culture or subculture, you feel the relief is worth it. You hope you can manage the peer group influence. In reality, you never fully grasp its influence sufficiently to control it.

As a writer, you seem more than ever before to be monitoring every response you make to what happens to you. You seem to be watching closely the rise and fall of the dial—whatever it is—that you use to measure the intensity and pressure of experience. You are hyperconscious. You are too aware of your mental growth, as if you were contemplating a personality moving in front of your eyes. As if it wouldn't surprise you to have to monitor your own funeral. You seem to be curled up and listening to the juices flow inside you, to every beat of the heart, every pulse in the veins. You think you can even detect the malfunctioning of some part of you that is going to burst into pain. You seem incapable of responding to real-life experience with the ordinary instruments endowed every man, because something compels you to teach as if the experience demanded a literary interpretation, one that has to be sifted through your artistic sensibility and replayed in a verbal medium.

While I absorbed the African environment outside South Africa and felt at home in cultures that were so similar to my own, by turns I consciously and unconsciously resisted assimilation into the local setting during all my nine years in the United States. I was scared of the commitment that would hold me in fee and make return to South Africa more and more difficult. I had no such fear in Africa. I was again thinking of the implications such commitment would have for my writing. One step further into the American setting, I feared, would throw me out of the definition of exile. Unless I sustained an arbitrary definition to assert a nonemigré status, I would be living at least half a lie.

Much has also to do with the circumstances of one's leaving a home country. I did so because I was banned from teaching, having campaigned against the inferior education the authorities were imposing on Africans. I would have continued to teach even in a system I loathed, because I was sure that that very act would give me a purpose—that thing for which one lives when one wants to create beauty out of chaos and make sense out of it. Let the imponderables fall where they might—like the events in 1976 in which schoolchildren revolted against the same inferior system of education—I would be guided by my instinct as a teacher in what to do.

I left on a South African passport, which I abandoned two years after my exit, because it was endorsed only for my initial destination—Nigeria. I registered as a subject of the United Kingdom and Colonies (Nigeria then still being a colony), whose passport facilitated travel for me and my family to any place in the world if its immigration rules allowed. But one day, my wife and I knew, we would want to return. We would cross that bridge when the time came. For the time being, we gloried in the release from the nightmare that those first thirty-seven years of our lives had been in South Africa.

We lived nine years in West, East, and Central Africa, two years in France, and nine years in the United States. For five out of the nine that we lived in the United States, my wife and I kept feeling that we were irrelevant outside Africa. To whom was I teaching black literatures in the United States—people genuinely interested in Africa, or merely students wanting to pick up an exotic grade? Should I not be where black literatures are organized and taught as a functional and organic part of African development, and located, therefore, where there is a living cultural forum for them—on their own native soil? Shouldn't I be spending the rest of my life contributing to this development of the African consciousness?

I had come into a line of tradition in America that had started long ago, and could not grasp the American's cultural goals. I saw them as too fragmented for me to feel part of a unified purpose. I want to teach a community whose cultural goals and aspirations I can comprehend, because education is for me an *agent* of culture at the same time it is culture itself.

I could only identify intellectually and emotionally with the black American's condition, but could not in any tangible, particular way feel his history. To be actively and meaningfully involved in a people's concerns and political struggle as a genuine participant, you *should* feel its history. On the contrary, I kept feeling that *that* river was passing me by. Its complexity defies the oversimplification contained in the assertion, "I am black." And one thing I dislike is intellectual dishonesty, faked involvement that has only repeated slogans to subsist on.

We returned to find most things had not changed, except for the worse. But my wife and I find that we can achieve a number of things in our professions that as long as we were outsiders, we could not. Now we have community. You take your place among the millions of oppressed blacks, you are subjected to the same procedures as they are for restricting movement, choice of jobs, entrances and exits in public places, and so on. You are voteless, regardless of your academic standing. In brief, YOU ARE NOT WHITE. But among the community, YOU ARE POSITIVELY BLACK. There is also the faith that no matter what white people do to us, our ultimate goal is bigger than they are, than even *we* are, and therein lies the moral of a homecoming.

I got to learn, when I was in the United States, that an academic can, if he likes, lose himself in intellectual pursuits, move only in the university community, and be insulated from the rest of the larger community out there, safe, cozy, contented. I didn't want that to happen to me, so that my self-respect hung on the thin thread of long-distance commitment.

I also realized that the longer I was away from South Africa, the angrier, the more outraged, I felt against the sufferings of people here. Out of sheer impotence. In a sense, my homecoming was another way of dealing with impotent anger. It was also a way of extricating myself from twenty years of the compromise that exile itself is. Indeed, exile had become for me a ghetto of the mind.

We left our children in the United States. They will, in their own good time, decide what to do as they grow up. We reckoned that it would be unfair to ask them to accompany or follow us, after having grown up in an atmosphere of relative freedom—relative, but substantial; an atmosphere in which one has a fighting chance to fulfill or equip oneself as a young exile. There is this about exile: there is an age below which it yields tremendous benefits to the individual ego, and there is an age beyond which the local setting can make impossible demands on one's commitment.

Another aspect of my homecoming is that it concludes a cycle in the life of a writer. Like all the other writers in South Africa, I feel the pressure of censorship acutely. But I feel I can deal with this in a way I could not when I was writing outside the context that breeds these tensions. The real sense of community that I feel now helps me understand the nature of my audience better, which must help define the functions of literature at the grass-roots level. In more ways than one, I can deal with something tangible, something real, rather than the shadows and echoes that haunted me in exile, the recurrent dream about people coming after me because they believed I had something of value, which I wasn't sure I possessed. Again, my writing can now be the educational tool I want it to be, according to the needs of the audience.

Heimat

Hilde Domin

"EXILE, IMPOSSIBLE TO LOSE, you carry it with you, a desert, pocket-sized," I once wrote after I had moved back to Heidelberg. *Heimat,** the counterpole to exile? No, that isn't right: Exile is the counterpole, negation. *Heimat* would be a self-evident truth if only it were self-evident. It is no accident that I, asked to speak about "*Heimat,*" begin with exile. As if it were a substitute *Heimat.* Me of all people. And I'm not doing this because exile is an "acceptable"—or even fashionable—word, while *Heimat,* cautiously spoken, has almost become a taboo. Someone like me doesn't adhere to those sorts of "prohibitions." And especially not regarding matters of *Heimat,* and therefore even the word *Heimat.* "Something that shines in everyone's childhood, but where no one has ever been: *Heimat*," says Bloch. He could just as well have said "paradise." He means the immunity to expulsion, the security of square one. Being allowed to belong, *this side* of doubt.

"One can love one's fatherland and grow to eighty years of age and never have known it. But one would have to have stayed home," Heine declared. "One only recognizes the essence of spring in the winter. And so the German love of fatherland only begins at the German border."

The catchphrases have already been uttered. Almost too many. The first—the one with which I began—was "impossible to lose." That thing that couldn't be lost that proved to be so easily lost. And that, ever since, one has known could be disavowed.

"Fatherland," a renowned linguist recently said, "a translation from the Latin. That word will probably sink into oblivion, it has become so discredited." Motherland: earlier that was the metropolis as viewed from the colony. No one thinks about that meaning anymore when using the term. I don't. And no one else I asked thought about it either. The land of one's birth. Mother tongue. "The mother tongue is the language of the mother, inasmuch as the mother speaks the language of the environment," the linguist said to me. But that is what she normally does. Mother tongue is the language of childhood.

For me language is impossible to lose, after everything else has been lost. The last, essential home. Only physical death can take it away from me. The German language, that is. I am a guest in the other languages I speak. A glad and grateful guest. The German language was our foothold, we have it to thank that we were able to hold on to our identities. It is because of the language that I have returned.

Coming home was one of the great excitements of my life. To the country of my birth, where people speak German. Perhaps, yes certainly, even more exciting than leaving, back then. In between lay exile, not-belonging, an experience undergone piecemeal; no one ever sees it stretching out in its entirety. Only upon leaving does one notice how distorted the new condition is, how "out-landish."

When I see the refugees on television, all the ones beginning their trek, all the ones hanging on to airplanes in order to get one stop farther, I already know how dubious their arrival will be. I don't even need to wait for the next report, one week, one month later.

I have experienced "permanent flight" first-hand. And when I had run far enough, I had the good fortune not to be caught. I was even allowed to come back from the edge of the world. To go home.

"You speak of *Heimat*," Enzensberger said back then, it was the early fifties. "And to bring this to us, you crossed oceans. Everything is just a matter of changing backdrops."

That's how it seemed to him, the backdrops had also changed quite a bit for those who stayed home.

Being home, being able to belong, is not a matter of changing backdrops. Or of prosperity. It means sharing the responsibility. Not being a stranger. Being able to mix in, if need be. Having an innate right to have a voice.

Therefore the loss of affiliation is a wound that never completely heals. "Home should never hurt like a cavity or lumbago." But it does hurt, every chance it gets. And these chances have been piling up in recent years. Exemplary expulsion, as exemplary as that of our ancestors: it teaches you everything, absolutely everything about being human, and about "being a fleeting guest." That has stopped being a metaphor heard from the pulpit.

And like home, so love, as soon as one learns that it can be disavowed. Love, perhaps as much a taboo as *Heimat*. Whoever is "in" just talks of sex. Although that is starting to change; love is becoming respectable again. *Heimat* is being discussed. (Meanwhile it has lost the militant aftertaste that the waves of refugees had given it.) Until now it was limited to people like Bloch, like Nelly Sachs, like me. Now it has become topical. We are living in a crisis of affiliations. Also in a crisis of language and speech. Communication crisis, identity crisis. In the not-*Heimat*. These terms are tossed about carelessly like a ball. Whoever really lived through it, whoever is traumatized, can resist it. The language with which I conscientiously name the world, conscientiously communicate it (and in such a way that I am heard), cannot be taken from me, it is my most extreme refuge. I will defend this home to my last breath. Like a farmer used to defend his soil. I can do nothing else.

Everything that I defend, where I dig in my heels, is not on this side of, but beyond doubt. The apple of knowledge was forced down our throats, it can't be revoked. "What would we gain if we were forty today and didn't have this wound!" Grieshaber wrote me shortly before his death. If only we could inoculate the younger generation with our tears.

Translated by Douglas Langworthy

---

*Translator's note: *Heimat* is a German term that, broadly speaking, means one's native country or homeland. But since the word originated long before Germany was a nation, it is more often associated with a region, such as Bavaria or Saxony, distinguished by a particular dialect. A German is connected to his or her *Heimat* by emotional rather than political ties—although Hitler tried to harness the term to his own nationalistic ends, edging the word (which is feminine) toward the masculine *Vaterland.* When Domin discusses the "taboo" surrounding *Heimat,* she is referring to its Nazi associations.

A German Poet

Heinrich Heine

I NEVER BECAME A naturalised Frenchman, and my naturalisation, which has been a notorious fact, is for all that only a German fable. I know not what idle or mischievous brain begat it. Several of my fellow countrymen are supposed to have grubbed my naturalisation up from an authentic source. They reported it in German newspapers and I lent support to this erroneous belief by my silence. My dear literary and political opponents in Germany, and many of my influential enemies in Paris were led astray by it, and believed that I was protected by French citizenship against the many vexations and machinations by which a foreigner, who is subjected to an exceptional jurisdiction here, can so easily be persecuted. Through this profitable mistake I escaped much animosity and much plundering at the hands of commercial people who would have used their privileges in business conflicts, for the position of the unnaturalised foreigner in Paris is difficult and in the long run expensive. He is browbeaten and put upon, and most of all by naturalised foreigners, who are most scurvily sharp in abusing the privileges they have just gained. Once, in dismay and anxiety, I carried out the formalities which imply no obligation and yet do place us in the position of gaining the rights of naturalisation without delay. But I always had a queer horror of the definite act. Through this cautiousness, and my deep-rooted disinclination for naturalisation, I fell into a false position which I must regard as the cause of all my troubles, sorrows and failures during my stay of three and twenty years in Paris. The income of a good poet would have covered amply my domestic expenses and the needs of a way of living not so much capricious as human and free; but without being naturalised I could not take a government post. My friends used to hold up to me enticingly high honours and fat sinecures, and there was no lack of the example of foreigners who had mounted the glittering stairs of power and honour in France. And I may say that I should have had to fight with native jealousy far less than others, for never had a German won to such a degree the sympathy of the French, not only in the literary world but also in society, and the most distinguished man in France sought my company, not as a patron but as a comrade. The chivalrous Prince, who was next the throne, and was not only a distinguished soldier and statesman, but also read the "Book of Songs" in the original, would have been only too glad to have seen me in the French services, and his influence would have been great enough to have set me on the road to such a career. I shall never forget the friendliness with which the great historian of the French Revolution and the Empire, who was then the omnipotent President of the Council, once took my arm in the garden of a Princess who was his friend, and, walking with me, urged me to tell him my heart's desire, so that he could see to it that it was granted. I can still hear the flattering sound of his voice; my nose still smells the scent of the great flowering magnolia which we passed, a tree reaching up to the blue sky, with its splendid flowers white as alabaster, glorious, proud as the heart of the German poet in the days of his happiness!

Yes; I have the word. It was the foolish arrogance of the German poet, which withheld me from becoming a Frenchman, even only *pro forma*. It was an idea, a whim, from which I could not free myself. I have ever been free in mind of what is usually called patriotism, but I could not away with a certain horror if I were to do anything which might appear in any degree to be a renunciation of the Fatherland. Even in the minds of the most enlightened there lurks always a remnant of the old superstition which cannot be expelled; one does not like to speak of it, but in the most secret crannies of his soul it lives on. My marriage with our dear Lady Germany, the blonde Bearskin, had never been happy. I remember lovely moonlight nights when she held me tenderly to her large bosom—but I cannot tell of those sentimental nights, and towards morning there was ever a boredom and a coldness, and then began the endless scolding. In the end we lived apart in both bed and board. But it never came to an actual breach. I have never been able to conquer my heart, or to renounce my domestic cross. I detest disloyalty of every kind, and I could never renounce a German cat or a German dog, however insupportable their fleas and loyalty might be to me. The smallest suckling-pig of my native country cannot complain of me in this respect. In the midst of the distinguished and witty swine of Perigord, who nosed up truffles and battened on them, I did not calumniate the modest grunters who at home in the forest of Teutoburg feed on the fruit of the oak of the Fatherland out of the wooden trough, as once their pious forbears did at the time when Arminius fought Varus. I have not lost a bristle of my Germanity, not a single frill of my German cap, and I have still the vigour to fix on to it the black, red and gold cockade. No; I have not exposed myself to such disgrace. Naturalisation may do for other people: a drunken lawyer, a visionary with a brow of iron and a nose of brass might, in order to snap up a schoolmaster's job, give up his Fatherland which knows nothing of him—but it is not fitting for a German poet, who has written the most beautiful of German songs. It would be a horrible, crazy idea for me if I had to say to myself: I am a German poet and at the same time a naturalised Frenchman. I should seem to myself like one of those abortions with two heads, whom one sees in booths at fairs. It would hamper me terribly in my writing if I were to think that one head was beginning to scan the most unnatural Alexandrines in French turkey-cock pathos, while the other was pouring out its sentiments in its true native metre in the German language. And oh! the verses, like the metre of the French, are insupportable to me, perfumed trifles. I can scarcely put up with their odourless poets. When I consider the so-called *Poésie lyrique* of the French, then I recognise the splendour of German poetry and then I can plume myself on having won my laurels in that realm. We will not give up a leaf of them, and the mason who has to adorn our last resting-place with an inscription will not have to expect any contradiction when he carves there the words: "Here lies a German poet."

Translated by Gilbert Cannan

III

Lessons and Opportunities

For staying is nowhere
—Rainer Maria Rilke
Duino Elegies

Reflections on Exile

Edward Said

EXILE IS STRANGELY compelling to think about but terrible to experience. It is the unhealable rift forced between a human being and a native place, between the self and its true home: its essential sadness can never be surmounted. And while it is true that literature and history contain heroic, romantic, glorious, even triumphant episodes in an exile's life, these are no more than efforts meant to overcome the crippling sorrow of estrangement. The achievements of exile are permanently undermined by the loss of something left behind for ever.

But if true exile is a condition of terminal loss, why has it been transformed so easily into a potent, even enriching, motif of modern culture? We have become accustomed to thinking of the modern period itself as spiritually orphaned and alienated, the age of anxiety and estrangement. Nietzsche taught us to feel uncomfortable with tradition, and Freud to regard domestic intimacy as the polite face painted on patricidal and incestuous rage. Modern Western culture is in large part the work of exiles, émigrés, refugees. In the United States, academic, intellectual and aesthetic thought is what it is today because of refugees from fascism, communism and other regimes given to the oppression and expulsion of dissidents. The critic George Steiner has even proposed the perceptive thesis that a whole genre of twentieth-century Western literature is "extraterritorial," a literature by and about exiles, symbolizing the age of the refugee. Thus Steiner suggests

> It seems proper that those who create art in a civilization of quasi-barbarism, which has made so many homeless, should themselves be poets unhoused and wanderers across language. Eccentric, aloof, nostalgic, deliberately untimely. . . .

In other ages, exiles had similar cross-cultural and transnational visions, suffered the same frustrations and miseries, performed the same elucidating and critical tasks—brilliantly affirmed, for instance, in E. H. Carr's classic study of the nineteenth-century Russian intellectuals clustered around Herzen, *The Romantic Exiles*. But the difference between earlier exiles and those of our own time is, it bears stressing, scale: our age—with its modern warfare, imperialism, and the quasi-theological ambitions of totalitarian rulers—is indeed the age of the refugee, the displaced person, mass immigration.

Against this large, impersonal setting, exile cannot be made to serve notions of humanism. On the twentieth-century scale, exile is neither aesthetically nor humanistically comprehensible: at most the literature about exile objectifies an anguish and a predicament most people rarely experience at first hand; but to think of the exile informing this literature as beneficially humanistic is to banalize its mutilations, the losses it inflicts on those who suffer them, the muteness with which it responds to any attempt to understand it as "good for us." Is it not true that the views of exile in literature and, moreover, in religion obscure what is truly horrendous: that exile is irremediably secular and unbearably historical; that it is produced by human beings for other human beings; and that, like death but without death's ultimate mercy, it has torn millions of people from the nourishment of tradition, family and geography?

To see a poet in exile—as opposed to reading the poetry of exile—is to see exile's antinomies embodied and endured with a unique intensity. Several years ago I spent some time with Faiz Ahmad Faiz, the greatest of contemporary Urdu poets. He was exiled from his native Pakistan by Zia's military regime, and found a welcome of sorts in strife-torn Beirut. Naturally his closest friends were Palestinian, but I sensed that, although there was an affinity of spirit between them, nothing quite matched—language, poetic convention, or life-history. Only once, when Eqbal Ahmad, a Pakistani friend and a fellow-exile, came to Beirut, did Faiz seem to overcome his sense of constant estrangement. The three of us sat in a dingy Beirut restaurant late one night, while Faiz recited poems. After a time, he and Eqbal stopped translating his verses for my benefit, but as the night wore on it did not matter. What I watched required no translation: it was an enactment of a homecoming expressed through defiance and loss, as if to say, "Zia, we are here." Of course Zia was the one who was really at home and who would not hear their exultant voices.

Rashid Hussein was a Palestinian. He translated Bialik, one of the great modern Hebrew poets, into Arabic, and Hussein's eloquence established him in the post-1948 period as an orator and nationalist without peer. He first worked as a Hebrew language journalist in Tel Aviv, and succeeded in establishing a dialogue between Jewish and Arab writers, even as he espoused the cause of Nasserism and Arab nationalism. In time, he could no longer endure the pressure, and he left for New York. He married a

Jewish woman, and began working in the PLO office at the United Nations, but regularly outraged his superiors with unconventional ideas and utopian rhetoric. In 1972 he left for the Arab world, but a few months later he was back in the United States: he had felt out of place in Syria and Lebanon, unhappy in Cairo. New York sheltered him anew, but so did endless bouts of drinking and idleness. His life was in ruins, but he remained the most hospitable of men. He died after a night of heavy drinking when, smoking in bed, his cigarette started a fire that spread to a small library of audio cassettes, consisting mostly of poets reading their verse. The fumes from the tapes asphyxiated him. His body was repatriated for burial in Musmus, the small village in Israel where his family still resided.

These and so many other exiled poets and writers lend dignity to a condition legislated to deny dignity—to deny an identity to people. From them, it is apparent that, to concentrate on exile as a contemporary political punishment, you must therefore map territories of experience beyond those mapped by the literature of exile itself. You must first set aside Joyce and Nabokov and think instead of the uncountable masses for whom UN agencies have been created. You must think of the refugee-peasants with no prospect of ever returning home, armed only with a ration card and an agency number. Paris may be a capital famous for cosmopolitan exiles, but it is also a city where unknown men and women have spent years of miserable loneliness: Vietnamese, Algerians, Cambodians, Lebanese, Senegalese, Peruvians. You must think also of Cairo, Beirut, Madagascar, Bangkok, Mexico City. As you move further from the Atlantic world, the awful forlorn waste increases: the hopelessly large numbers, the compounded misery of "undocumented" people suddenly lost, without a tellable history. To reflect on exiled Muslims from India, or Haitians in America, or Bikinians in Oceania, or Palestinians throughout the Arab world means that you must leave the modest refuge provided by subjectivity and resort instead to the abstractions of mass politics. Negotiations, wars of national liberation, people bundled out of their homes and prodded, bussed or walked to enclaves in other regions: what do these experiences add up to? Are they not manifestly and almost by design irrecoverable?

We come to nationalism and its essential association with exile. Nationalism is an assertion of belonging in and to a place, a people, a heritage. It affirms the home created by a community of language, culture and customs; and, by so doing, it fends off exile, fights to prevent its ravages.

Indeed, the interplay between nationalism and exile is like Hegel's dialectic of servant and master, opposites informing and constituting each other. All nationalisms in their early stages develop from a condition of estrangement. The struggles to win American independence, to unify Germany or Italy, to liberate Algeria were those of national groups separated—exiled—from what was construed to be their rightful way of life. Triumphant, achieved nationalism then justifies, retrospectively as well as prospectively, a history selectively strung together in a narrative form: thus all nationalisms have their founding fathers, their basic, quasi-religious texts, their rhetoric of belonging, their historical and geographical landmarks, their official enemies and heroes. This collective ethos forms what Pierre Bourdieu, the French sociologist, calls the *habitus*, the coherent amalgam of practices linking habit with inhabitance. In time, successful nationalisms consign truth exclusively to themselves and relegate falsehood and inferiority to outsiders (as in the rhetoric of capitalist versus communist, or the European versus the Asiatic).

And just beyond the frontier between "us" and the "outsiders" is the perilous territory of not-belonging: this is to where in a primitive time peoples were banished, and where in the modern era immense aggregates of humanity loiter as refugees and displaced persons.

Nationalisms are about groups, but in a very acute sense exile is a solitude experienced outside the group: the deprivations felt at not being with others in the communal habitation. How, then, does one surmount the loneliness of exile without falling into the encompassing and thumping language of national pride, collective sentiments, group passions? What is there worth saving and holding on to between the extremes of exile on the one hand, and the often bloody-minded affirmations of nationalism on the other? Do nationalism and exile have any intrinsic attributes? Are they simply two conflicting varieties of paranoia?

These are questions that cannot ever be fully answered because each assumes that exile and nationalism can be discussed neutrally, without reference to each other. They cannot be. Because both terms include everything from the most collective of collective sentiments to the most private of private emotions, there is hardly language adequate for both. But there is certainly nothing about nationalism's public and all-inclusive ambitions that touches the core of the exile's predicament.

Because exile, unlike nationalism, is fundamentally a discontinuous state of being. Exiles are cut off from their roots, their land, their past. They generally do not have armies or states, although they are often in search of them. Exiles feel, therefore, an urgent need to reconstitute their broken lives, usually by choosing to see themselves as part of a triumphant ideology or a restored people. The crucial thing is that a state of exile free from this triumphant ideology—designed to reassemble an exile's broken history into a new whole—is virtually unbearable, and virtually impossible in today's world. Look at the fate of the Jews, the Palestinians and the Armenians.

Noubar is a solitary Armenian, and a friend. His parents had to leave Eastern Turkey in 1915, after their families were massacred: his maternal grandfather was beheaded. Noubar's mother and father went to Aleppo, then to Cairo. In the middle-sixties, life in Egypt became difficult for non-Egyptians, and his parents, along with four children, were taken to Beirut by an international relief organization. In Beirut, they lived briefly in a pension and then were bundled into two rooms of a little house outside the city. In Lebanon, they had no money and they waited: eight months later, a relief agency got them a flight to Glasgow. And then to Gander. And then to New York. They rode by Greyhound bus from New York to Seattle: Seattle was the city designated by the agency for their American residence. When I asked, "Seattle?", Noubar smiled resignedly, as if to say better Seattle than Armenia—which he never knew, or Turkey where so many were slaughtered, or Lebanon where he and his family would certainly have risked their lives. Exile is sometimes better than staying behind or not getting out: but only sometimes.

Because *nothing* is secure. Exile is a jealous state. What you achieve is precisely what you have no wish to share, and it is in the drawing of lines around you and your compatriots that the least attractive aspects of being in exile emerge: an exaggerated sense of group solidarity, and a passionate hostility to outsiders, even those who may in fact be in the same predicament as you. What could be more intransigent than the conflict between Zionist Jews and Arab Palestinians? Palestinians feel that they have been turned into exiles by the proverbial people of exile, the Jews. But the Palestinians also know that their own sense of national identity has been nourished in the exile milieu, where everyone not a blood-brother or sister is an enemy, where every sympathizer is an agent of some unfriendly power, and where the slightest deviation from the accepted group line is an act of the rankest treachery and disloyalty.

Perhaps this is the most extraordinary of exile's fates: to have been exiled by exiles: to relive the actual process of up-rooting at the hands of exiles. All Palestinians during the summer of 1982 asked themselves what inarticulate urge drove Israel, having displaced Palestinians in 1948, to expel them continuously from their refugee homes and camps in Lebanon. It is as if the reconstructed Jewish collective experience, as represented by Israel and modern Zionism, could not tolerate another story of dispossession and loss to exist alongside it—an intolerance constantly reinforced by the Israeli hostility to the nationalism of the Palestinians, who for forty-six years have been painfully reassembling a national identity in exile.

This need to reassemble an identity out of the refractions and discontinuities of exile is found in the earlier poems of Mahmud Darwish, whose considerable work amounts to an epic effort to transform the lyrics of loss into the indefinitely postponed drama of return. Thus he depicts his sense of homelessness in the form of a list of unfinished and incomplete things:

> But I am the exile.
> Seal me with your eyes.
> Take me wherever you are—
> Take me whatever you are.
> Restore to me the colour of face
> And the warmth of body
> The light of heart and eye,
> The salt of bread and rhythm,
> The taste of earth . . . the Motherland.
> Shield me with your eyes.
> Take me as a relic from the mansion of sorrow.
> Take me as a verse from my tragedy;
> Take me as a toy, a brick from the house
> So that our children will remember to return.

The pathos of exile is in the loss of contact with the solidity and the satisfaction of earth: homecoming is out of the question.

Joseph Conrad's tale "Amy Foster" is perhaps the most uncompromising representation of exile ever written. Conrad thought of himself as an exile from Poland, and nearly all his work (as well as his life) carries the unmistakable mark of the sensitive émigré's obsession with his own fate and with his hopeless attempts to make satisfying contact with new surroundings. "Amy Foster" is in a sense confined to the problems of exile, perhaps so confined that it is not one of Conrad's best-known stories. This, for example, is the description of the agony of its central character, Yanko Goorall, an Eastern European peasant who, en route to America, is shipwrecked off the British coast:

> It is indeed hard upon a man to find himself a lost stranger helpless, incomprehensible, and of a mysterious origin, in

> some obscure corner of the earth. Yet amongst all the adventurers shipwrecked in all the wild parts of the world, there is not one, it seems to me, that ever had to suffer a fate so simply tragic as the man I am speaking of, the most innocent of adventurers cast out by the sea. . . .

Yanko has left home because the pressures were too great for him to go on living there. America lures him with its promise, though England is where he ends up. He endures in England, where he cannot speak the language and is feared and misunderstood. Only Amy Foster, a plodding, unattractive peasant girl, tries to communicate with him. They marry, have a child, but when Yanko falls ill, Amy, afraid and alienated, refuses to nurse him; snatching their child, she leaves. The desertion hastens Yanko's miserable death, which like the deaths of several Conradian heroes is depicted as the result of a combination of crushing isolation and the world's indifference. Yanko's fate is described as "the supreme disaster of loneliness and despair."

Yanko's predicament is affecting: a foreigner perpetually haunted and alone in an uncomprehending society. But Conrad's own exile causes him to exaggerate the differences between Yanko and Amy. Yanko is dashing, light and bright-eyed, whereas Amy is heavy, dull, bovine; when he dies, it is as if her earlier kindness to him was a snare to lure and then trap him fatally. Yanko's death is romantic: the world is coarse, unappreciative; no one understands him, not even Amy, the one person close to him. Conrad took this neurotic exile's fear and created an aesthetic principle out of it. No one can understand or communicate in Conrad's world, but paradoxically this radical limitation on the possibilities of language doesn't inhibit elaborate efforts to communicate. All of Conrad's stories are about lonely people who talk a great deal (for indeed who of the great modernists was more voluble and "adjectival" than Conrad himself?) and whose attempts to *impress* others compound, rather than reduce, the original sense of isolation. Each Conradian exile fears, and is condemned endlessly to imagine, the spectacle of a solitary death illuminated, so to speak, by unresponsive, uncommunicating eyes.

Exiles look at non-exiles with resentment. *They* belong in their surroundings, you feel, whereas an exile is always out of place. What is it like to be born in a place, to stay and live there, to know that you are of it, more or less forever?

Although it is true that anyone prevented from returning home is an exile, some distinctions can be made between exiles, refugees, expatriates and émigrés. Exile originated in the age-old practice of banishment. Once banished, the exile lives an anomalous and miserable life, with the stigma of being an outsider. Refugees, on the other hand, are a creation of the twentieth-century state. The word "refugee" has become a political one, suggesting large herds of innocent and bewildered people requiring urgent international assistance, whereas "exile" carries with it, I think, a touch of solitude and spirituality.

Expatriates voluntarily live in an alien country, usually for personal or social reasons. Hemingway and Fitzgerald were not forced to live in France. Expatriates may share in the solitude and estrangement of exile, but they do not suffer under its rigid proscriptions. Émigrés enjoy an ambiguous status. Technically, an émigré is anyone who emigrates to a new country. Choice in the matter is certainly a possibility. Colonial officials, missionaries, technical experts, mercenaries and military advisers on loan may in a sense live in exile, but they have not been banished. White settlers in Africa, parts of Asia and Australia may once have been exiles, but as pioneers and nation-builders the label "exile" dropped away from them.

Much of the exile's life is taken up with compensating for disorienting loss by creating a new world to rule. It is not surprising that so many exiles seem to be novelists, chess players, political activists, and intellectuals. Each of these occupations requires a minimal investment in objects and places a great premium on mobility and skill. The exile's new world, logically enough, is unnatural and its unreality resembles fiction. Georg Lukács, in *Theory of the Novel*, argued with compelling force that the novel, a literary form created out of the unreality of ambition and fantasy, is *the* form of "transcendental homelessness." Classical epics, Lukács wrote, emanate from settled cultures in which values are clear, identities stable, life unchanging. The European novel is grounded in precisely the opposite experience, that of a changing society in which an itinerant and disinherited middle-class hero or heroine seeks to construct a new world that somewhat resembles an old one left behind for ever. In the epic there is no *other* world, only the finality of *this* one. Odysseus returns to Ithaca after years of wandering; Achilles will die because he cannot escape his fate. The novel, however, exists because other worlds *may* exist, alternatives for bourgeois speculators, wanderers, exiles.

No matter how well they may do, exiles are always eccentrics who *feel* their difference (even as they frequently exploit it) as a kind of orphanhood. Anyone who is really homeless regards the habit of seeing estrangement in everything modern as an affectation, a display of modish attitudes.

Clutching difference like a weapon to be used with stiffened will, the exile jealously insists on his or her right to refuse to belong.

This usually translates into an intransigence that is not easily ignored. Wilfulness, exaggeration, overstatement: these are characteristic styles of being an exile, methods for compelling the world to accept your vision—which you make more unacceptable because you are in fact unwilling to have it accepted. It is yours, after all. Composure and serenity are the last things associated with the work of exiles. Artists in exile are decidedly unpleasant, and their stubbornness insinuates itself into even their exalted works. Dante's vision in *The Divine Comedy* is tremendously powerful in its universality and detail, but even the beatific peace achieved in the *Paradiso* bears traces of the vindictiveness and severity of judgement embodied in the *Inferno.* Who but an exile like Dante, banished from Florence, would use eternity as a place for settling old scores?

James Joyce *chose* to be in exile: to give force to his artistic vocation. In an uncannily effective way—as Richard Ellmann has shown in his biography—Joyce picked a quarrel with Ireland and kept it alive so as to sustain the strict opposition to what was familiar. Ellmann says that "whenever his relations with his native land were in danger of improving, [Joyce] was to find a new incident to solidify his intransigence and to reaffirm the rightness of his voluntary absence." Joyce's fiction concerns what in a letter he once described as the state of being "alone and friendless." And although it is rare to pick banishment as a way of life, Joyce perfectly understood its trials.

But Joyce's success as an exile stresses the question lodged at its very heart: is exile so extreme and private that any instrumental use of it is ultimately a trivialization? How is it that the literature of exile has taken its place as a *topos* of human experience alongside the literature of adventure, education or discovery? Is this the *same* exile that quite literally kills Yanko Goorall and has bred the expensive, often dehumanizing relationship between twentieth-century exile and nationalism? Or is it some more benign variety?

Much of the contemporary interest in exile can be traced to the somewhat pallid notion that non-exiles can share in the benefits of exile as a redemptive motif. There is, admittedly, a certain plausibility and truth to this idea. Like medieval itinerant scholars or learned Greek slaves in the Roman Empire, exiles—the exceptional ones among them—do leaven their environments. And naturally "we" concentrate on that enlightening aspect of "their" presence among us, not on their misery or their demands.

But looked at from the bleak political perspective of modern mass dislocations, individual exiles force us to recognize the tragic fate of homelessness in a necessarily heartless world.

A generation ago, Simone Weil posed the dilemma of exile as concisely as it has ever been expressed. "To be rooted," she said, "is perhaps the most important and least recognized need of the human soul." Yet Weil also saw that most remedies for uprootedness in this era of world wars, deportations and mass exterminations are almost as dangerous as what they purportedly remedy. Of these, the state—or, more accurately, statism—is one of the most insidious, since worship of the state tends to supplant all other human bonds.

Weil exposes us anew to that whole complex of pressures and constraints that lie at the centre of the exile's predicament, which, as I have suggested, is as close as we come in the modern era to tragedy. There is the sheer fact of isolation and displacement, which produces the kind of narcissistic masochism that resists all efforts at amelioration, acculturation and community. At this extreme the exile can make a fetish of exile, a practice that distances him or her from all connections and commitments. To live as if everything around you were temporary and perhaps trivial is to fall prey to petulant cynicism as well as to querulous lovelessness. More common is the pressure on the exile to join—parties, national movements, the state. The exile is offered a new set of affiliations and develops new loyalties. But there is also a loss—of critical perspective, of intellectual reserve, of moral courage.

It must also be recognized that the defensive nationalism of exiles often fosters self-awareness as much as it does the less attractive forms of self-assertion. Such reconstitutive projects as assembling a nation out of exile (and this is true in this century for Jews and Palestinaians) involve constructing a national history, reviving an ancient language, founding national institutions like libraries and universities. And these, while they sometimes promote strident ethnocentrism, also give rise to investigations of self that inevitably go far beyond such simple and positive facts as "ethnicity." For example, there is the self-consciousness of an individual trying to understand why the histories of the Palestinians and the Jews have certain patterns to them, why in spite of oppression and the threat of extinction a particular ethos remains alive in exile.

Necessarily, then, I speak of exile not as a privilege, but as an *alternative* to the mass institutions that dominate modern life. Exile is not, after all, a matter of choice: you are born into it, or it happens to you. But, provided that the exile refuses to sit on the sidelines nursing a wound, there are things to be learned: he or she must cultivate a scrupulous (not indulgent or sulky) subjectivity.

Perhaps the most rigorous example of such subjectivity is to be found in the writing of Theodor Adorno, the German-Jewish philosopher and critic. Adorno's masterwork, *Minima Moralia,* is an autobiography written while in exile; it is subtitled *Reflexionen aus dem beschädigten Leben* (*Reflections from a Mutilated Life*). Ruthlessly opposed to what he called the "administered" world, Adorno saw all life as pressed into ready-made forms, prefabricated "homes". He argued that everything that one says or thinks, as well as every object one possesses, is ultimately a mere commodity. Language is jargon, objects are for sale. To refuse this state of affairs is the exile's intellectual mission.

Adorno's reflections are informed by the belief that the only home truly available now, though fragile and vulnerable, is in writing. Elsewhere, "the house is past. The bombings of European cities, as well as the labour and concentration camps, merely precede as executors, with what the immanent development of technology had long decided was to be the fate of houses. These are now good only to be thrown away like old food cans." In short, Adorno says with a grave irony, "it is part of morality not to be at home in one's home."

To follow Adorno is to stand away from "home" in order to look at it with the exile's detachment. For there is considerable merit in the practice of noting the discrepancies between various concepts and ideas and what they actually produce. We take home and language for granted; they become nature, and their underlying assumptions recede into dogma and orthodoxy.

The exile knows that in a secular and contingent world, homes are always provisional. Borders and barriers, which enclose us within the safety of familiar territory, can also become prisons, and are often defended beyond reason or necessity. Exiles cross borders, break barriers of thought and experience.

Hugo of St. Victor, a twelfth-century monk from Saxony, wrote these hauntingly beautiful lines:

> It is, therefore, a source of great virtue for the practised mind to learn, bit by bit, first to change about invisible and transitory things, so that afterwards it may be able to leave them behind altogether. The man who finds his homeland sweet is still a tender beginner; he to whom every soil is as his native one is already strong; but he is perfect to whom the entire world is as a foreign land. The tender soul has fixed his love on one spot in the world; the strong man has extended his love to all places; the perfect man has extinguished his.

Erich Auerbach, the great twentieth-century literary scholar who spent the war years as an exile in Turkey, has cited this passage as a model for anyone wishing to transcend national or provincial limits. Only by embracing this attitude can a historian begin to grasp human experience and its written records in their diversity and particularity; otherwise he or she will remain committed more to the exclusions and reactions of prejudice than to the freedom that accompanies knowledge. But note that Hugo twice makes it clear that the "strong" or "perfect" man achieves independence and detachment by *working through* attachments, not by rejecting them. Exile is predicated on the existence of, love for, and bond with, one's native place; what is true of all exile is not that home and love of home are lost, but that loss is inherent in the very existence of both.

Regard experiences as if they were about to disappear. What is it that anchors them in reality? What would you save of them? What would you give up? Only someone who has achieved independence and detachment, someone whose homeland is "sweet" but whose circumstances make it impossible to recapture that sweetness, can answer those questions. (Such a person would also find it impossible to derive satisfaction from substitutes furnished by illusion or dogma.)

This may seem like a prescription for an unrelieved grimness of outlook and, with it, a permanently sullen disapproval of all enthusiasm or buoyancy of spirit. Not necessarily. While it perhaps seems peculiar to speak of the pleasures of exile, there are some positive things to be said for a few of its conditions. Seeing "the entire world as a foreign land" makes possible originality of vision. Most people are principally aware of one culture, one setting, one home; exiles are aware of at least two, and this plurality of vision gives rise to an awareness of simultaneous dimensions, an awareness that—to borrow a phrase from music—is *contrapuntal*.

For an exile, habits of life, expression or activity in the new environment inevitably occur against the memory of these things in another environment. Thus both the new and the old environments are vivid, actual, occurring together contrapuntally. There is a unique pleasure in this sort of apprehension, especially if the exile is conscious of other contrapuntal juxtapositions that diminish orthodox judgement and elevate appreciative sympathy. There is also a particular sense of achievement in acting as if one were at home wherever one happens to be.

This remains risky, however: the habit of dissimulation is both wearying and nerve-racking. Exile is never the state of being satisfied, placid, or secure. Exile, in the words of Wallace Stevens, is "a mind of winter" in which the pathos of summer and autumn as much as the potential of spring are nearby but unobtainable. Perhaps this is another way of saying that a life of exile moves according to a different calendar, and is less seasonal and settled than life at home. Exile is life led outside habitual order. It is nomadic, decentred, contrapuntal; but no sooner does one get accustomed to it than its unsettling force erupts anew.

Advantages of Exile

E. M. Cioran

IT IS A MISTAKE to think of the expatriate as someone who abdicates, who withdraws and humbles himself, resigned to his miseries, his outcast state. On a closer look, he turns out to be ambitious, aggressive in his disappointments, his very acrimony qualified by his belligerence. The more we are dispossessed, the more intense our appetites and our illusions become. I even discern some relation between misfortune and megalomania. The man who has lost everything preserves as a last resort the hope of glory, or of literary scandal. He consents to abandon everything, except his *name*. But how will he impose his name when he writes in a language of which the cultivated are either ignorant or contemptuous?

Will he venture into another idiom? It will not be easy for him to renounce the words on which his past hinges. A man who repudiates his language for another changes his identity, even his disappointments. Heroic apostate, he breaks with his memories and, to a certain point, with himself.

Let us say a man writes a novel which makes him, overnight, a celebrity. In it he recounts his sufferings. His compatriots in exile envy him: they too have suffered, perhaps more. And the man without a country becomes—or aspires to become—a novelist. The consequence: an accumulation of confusions, an inflation of horrors, of *frissons* that *date*. One cannot keep renewing Hell, whose very characteristic is monotony, or the face of Exile either. Nothing in literature exasperates a reader so much as The Terrible; in life, it is too tainted with the obvious to rouse our interest. But our author persists; for the time being he buries his novel in a drawer and awaits his hour. The illusion of a surprise, of a renown which eludes his grasp but on which he reckons, sustains him; he lives on unreality. Such, however, is the power of this illusion that if, for instance, he works in some factory, it is with the notion of being freed from it one day or another by a fame as sudden as it is inconceivable.

Equally tragic is the case of the poet. Walled up in his own language, he writes for his friends—for ten, for twenty persons at the most. His longing to be read is no less imperious than that of the improvised novelist. At least he has the advantage over the latter of being able to get his verses published in the little *émigré* reviews which appear at the cost of almost indecent sacrifices and renunciations. Let us say such a man becomes—transforms himself—into an editor of such a review; to keep his publication alive he risks hunger, abstains from women, buries himself in a windowless room, imposes privations which confound and appall. Tuberculosis and masturbation, that is his fate.

No matter how scanty the number of *émigrés,* they form groups, not to protect their interests but to get up subscriptions, to bleed each other white in order to publish their regrets, their cries, their echoless appeals. One cannot conceive of a more heart-rending form of the gratuitous.

That they are as good poets as they are bad prose-writers is to be accounted for readily enough. Consider the literary production of any "minor" nation which has not been so childish as to make up a past for itself: the abundance of poetry is its most striking characteristic. Prose requires, for its development, a certain rigor, a differentiated social status, and a tradition: it is deliberate, constructed; poetry *wells up*: it is direct or else totally fabricated; the prerogative of cave men or aesthetes, it flourishes only on the near or far side of civilization, never at the center. Whereas prose demands a premeditated genius and a crystallized language, poetry is perfectly compatible with a barbarous genius and a formless language. To create a *literature* is to create a prose.

What could be more natural than that so many possess no other mode of expression than poetry? Even those who are not particularly gifted draw, in their uprooted state, upon the automatism of their exclusion, that bonus talent they would never have found in a normal existence.

In whatever form it happens to take, and whatever its cause, exile—at its start—is an academy of intoxication. And it is not given to everyone to be intoxicated. It is a limit-situation and resembles the extremity of the poetic state. Is it not a *favor* to be transported to that state straight off, without the detours of a discipline, by no more than the benevolence of fatality? Think of Rilke, that expatriate *de luxe,* and of the number of solitudes he had to accumulate in order to liquidate his connections, in order to establish a foothold in the invisible. It is not easy to be *nowhere,* when no external condition obliges you to do so. Even the mystic attains his *askesis* only at the cost of monstrous efforts. To extricate oneself from the world—what a labor of abolition! The exile achieves it without turning a hair, by the cooperation—i.e., the hostility—of history. No torments, no vigils in order for him to strip himself of everything; events compel him. In a sense, he is like the invalid who also installs himself in metaphysics or in poetry without personal merit, by the force of circumstances, by the good offices of disease. A trumpery absolute? Perhaps, though it is not proved that the results acquired by effort exceed in value those which derive from a surrender to the inescapable.

One danger threatens the exiled poet: that of adapting himself to his fate, of no longer suffering from it, of enjoying himself because of it. No one can keep his griefs in their prime; they use themselves up. The same is true of homesickness, of any nostalgia. Regrets lose their luster, wear themselves out by their own momentum, and after the fashion of the elegy, quickly fall into desuetude. What then is more natural than to establish oneself in exile, the Nowhere City, a *patrie* in reverse? To the degree that he revels in it, the poet erodes the substance of his emotions, the resources of his misery as well as his dreams of glory. The curse from which he drew pride and profit no longer afflicting him, he loses, along with it, both the energy of his exceptional status and the reasons for his solitude. Rejected by Hell, he will try in vain to reinstate himself there, to be reinvigorated by it: his sufferings, too mild now, will make him forever unworthy of it. The cries of which he was only yesterday still proud have become bitterness, and bitterness does not become verse: it will lead him beyond poetry. No more songs, no more excesses. His wounds healed, there is no use pointing to them in order to extract certain accents: at best he will be the epigone of his pains. An honorable downfall awaits him. Lacking diversity, original anxieties, his inspiration dries up. Soon, resigned to anonymity and even intrigued by his mediocrity, he will assume the mask of a bourgeois from *nowhere in particular.* Thus he reaches the end of his lyrical career, the most stable point of his degeneration.

"Fixed up," established in the comfort of his fall, what will he do next? He will have the choice between two forms of salvation: faith and humor. If he drags along some vestiges of anxiety, he will gradually liquidate them by means of a thousand prayers; unless he consoles himself with a reassuring metaphysic, pastime of exhausted versifiers. And if, on the contrary, he is inclined to mockery, he will minimize his defeats to the point of rejoicing in them. According to his temperament, he will therefore sacrifice to piety or to sarcasm. In either case, he will have triumphed over his ambitions, as over his misfortunes, in order to achieve a higher goal, in order to become a decent victim, a respectable outcast.

Translated by Richard Howard

A Reply to Cioran

Witold Gombrowicz

CIORAN'S WORDS REEK of a basement coolness and the rot of the grave, but they are too petty. Who is he talking about? Who should one understand to be the "writer in exile?" Adam Mickiewicz wrote books and so does Mr. X, quite correct and readable ones, both are "writers" and, nota bene, writers in exile, but here all parallels end.

Rimbaud? Norwid? Kafka? Slowacki? (There are a variety of exiles.) I believe that none of them would have been too horrified at this category of hell. It is very painful not to have readers and very unpleasant not to be able to publish one's works. It certainly is not sweet being unknown, highly unpleasant to see oneself deprived of the aid of that mechanism that pushes one to the top, that creates publicity and organizes fame, but art is loaded with elements of loneliness and self-sufficiency, it finds its satisfaction and sense of purpose in itself. The homeland? Why, every eminent person because of that very eminence was a foreigner even at home. Readers? Why, they never wrote "for" readers anyway, always "against" them. Honors, success, renown, fame: why, they became famous exactly because they valued themselves more than their success.

And that which is a little Kafka, Conrad, or Mickiewicz in even the smaller caliber writer, that which is genuine talent and real superiority or real maturity, will in no measure fit into Cioran's basement. I would also like to remind Cioran that not only émigré but all art remains in the most intimate contact with decay, it is born of decadence, it is a transmutation of illness into health. All art, generally speaking, borders on silliness, defeat, degradation. Is there an artist who is not, as Cioran says, "an ambitious being, aggressive in his defeat, embittered, a conniving conqueror"? Has Cioran ever seen an artist or writer who was not, who did not have to be, a megalomaniac? And art, as Boy once correctly said, is a graveyard: for every thousand people who were incapable of "coming into existence" and who remained in a sphere of painful insufficiency, barely one or two is capable of really "coming into existence." This dirt, therefore, this venom of unsatisfied ambitions, this tossing and turning in a vacuum, this catastrophe has very little to do with emigration and a lot to do with art. They make up an aspect of every literary café and truly it is a matter of indifference where in the world the writers who are not writers enough in order to really be writers, suffer.

And perhaps it is healthier that they were deprived of doles, applause, all those tiny caresses that the state and society lavished upon them in the good old days in the name of "supporting native creativity." This family playing at greatness and distinction, the sympathetic noise created at one time by the condescendingly smiling press and the half-baked critics, deprived of a feeling for the scale of events, that process of artificially pumping candidates up into a "national writer" . . . didn't all this reek of kitsch? And the result? Nations that at best were capable of producing a few authentic writers nurtured entire hosts of wonders in this incubator, and in this familial warmth, which was a mixture of spinsterish goodness and a cynical disregard for values, all hierarchy disintegrated. Is it surprising then that these hothouse creations, nurtured in the womb of the nation, wilt when out of the womb? Cioran writes about how a writer torn away from his people is lost. If that is the case, this writer never existed in the first place: he was a writer in embryo. Instead, it seems to me that theoretically speaking and bypassing material hardship, the immersing of oneself in the world, that is, emigration, should constitute an incredible stimulus for literature.

For lo and behold the country's elite is kicked out over the border. It can think, feel, and write from the outside. It gains distance. It gains an incredible spiritual freedom. All bonds burst. One can be more of oneself. In the general din all the forms that have existed until now loosen up and one can move toward the future in a more ruthless way.

An exceptional opportunity! The moment everyone has dreamed of! It would seem, therefore, that the stronger individuals, the richer individuals would roar like lions? Then why don't they? Why has the voice of these people faded abroad?

They do not roar because, first of all, they are too free. Art demands style, order, discipline. Cioran correctly underscores the danger of too much isolation, of excessive freedom. Everything to which they were tied and everything that bound them—homeland, ideology, politics, group, program, faith, milieu—everything vanished in the whirlpool of history and only a bubble filled with nothingness remained on the surface. Those thrown out of their little world found themselves facing a world, a boundless world and, consequently, one that was impossible to master. Only a universal culture can come to terms with the world, never parochial cultures, never those who live only on fragments of existence. Only he who knows how to reach deeper, beyond the homeland, only he for whom the homeland is but one of the revelations in an eternal and universal life, will not be incited to anarchy by the loss of his homeland. The loss of a homeland will not disturb the internal order of only those whose homeland is the world. Contemporary history has turned out to be too violent and borderless for literatures too national and specific.

And it is exactly this excess of freedom that inhibits the writer most. Threatened by the enormity of the world and the finality of its affairs, they grasp at the past convulsively; they cling desperately to themselves; they want to remain as they were; they fear even the slightest change in themselves, thinking that everything will then fall apart; and, finally, they cling convulsively to the only hope remaining: the hope of recovering the homeland. Recovering the homeland, however, cannot come to pass without waging a battle, and a battle requires strength and collective strength can be achieved only by giving up one's I. In order to produce this strength, the writer must impose a blind faith, among other deficiencies, on himself and his compatriots and the luxury of objective and free thinking becomes a grievous sin. He does not know how to be a writer without a homeland or in order to regain his homeland, he has to stop being a writer, at least a serious writer.

Though perhaps there is yet another reason for this spiritual paralysis, at least where it is not a matter of intellectuals but artists. I have in mind the very concept of art and the artist, as it has come to be accepted in Western Europe. It does not seem to be that our modern beliefs concerning the essence of art, the role of the artist, the relationship of artist to society have tallied with reality. The artistic philosophy of the West derives from the elite in crystallized societies where nothing interferes with conventional language but there is nothing a man thrown outside the limits of convention can do with such a philosophy. The concept of art forged on that side of the curtain by the victorious bureaucracy of the proletariat is even more elitist and more naive. An artist in emigration, however, is forced to exist not only outside of his people, but also outside of the elite. He confronts the spiritually and intellectually inferior sphere far more directly. Nothing isolates him from this contact, he has personally to endure the pressure of a brutal and immature life. He is like a bankrupt count who sees that the manners of the salon are worthless if there is no salon. Sometimes this pushes people in the direction of "democratic" shallowness, into a kindly ordinariness or into a crude "realism" and sometimes it condemns them to isolation. We have to find a way to feel like aristocrats once again (in the deeper sense of the word).

Therefore, if there is talk about the disintegration and decadence of émigré literature, then this notion of the issue would be closest to me because here, at least, we liberate ourselves for a moment from the vicious circle of trivialities and touch the difficulties capable of destroying authentic writers. I do not deny at all that overcoming these problems requires a great determination and boldness of spirit. It is not easy to be an émigré writer, which means almost total isolation. Why should it be surprising, therefore, that overcome by our own weakness and the enormity of the tasks, we bury our heads in the sand and, organizing parodies of the past for ourselves, we flee the big world to live in our little one?

Yet sooner or later our thought must work its way out of the impasse. Our problems will find people to solve them. At some point, it is no longer a matter of creativity itself, but the recovery of the capacity to create. We have to produce that portion of freedom, boldness, ruthlessness, and even, I would say, irresponsibility, without which creation is impossible. We have to accustom ourselves to a new scale of existence. We will have to treat our most cherished feelings unceremoniously, with sangfroid in order to attain other values. The minute we begin to shape the world in the place where we happen to be and with the means at our disposal, the enormity of the task will shrink, the boundlessness will become delineated, and the turbulent waters of chaos will begin to recede.

Translated by Lillian Vallee

In Consolation

A Letter from Exile to his Mother, Helvia

Seneca

I HAVE DETERMINED to conquer your grief, not to dupe it. And I shall conquer it, I think, if, in the first place, I show that there is nothing in my condition that could cause anyone to call me wretched, still less cause those also to whom I am related to be wretched on my account; and, secondly, if I turn next to you, and prove that your fortune also, which depends wholly upon mine, is not a painful one.

First of all, I shall proceed to prove what your love is eager to hear—that I am suffering no ill. If I can, I shall make it clear that those very circumstances, which your love fancies weigh me down, are not intolerable; but if it will be impossible for you to believe this, I, at any rate, shall be better pleased with myself if I show that I am happy under circumstances that usually make others wretched.

We are born under conditions that would be favourable if only we did not abandon them. Nature intended that we should need no great equipment for living happily; each one of us is able to make his own happiness. External things are of slight importance, and can have no great influence in either direction. Prosperity does not exalt the wise man, nor does adversity cast him down; for he has always endeavored to rely entirely upon himself, to derive all of his joy from himself.

What, then? Do I say that I am a wise man? By no means; for if I could make that claim, I should thereby not only deny that I am unhappy, but should also declare that I am the most fortunate of all men and had been brought into nearness with God. As it is, fleeing to that which is able to lighten all sorrows, I have surrendered myself to wise men and, not yet being strong enough to give aid to myself, I have taken refuge in the Stoic camp—those, clearly, who can easily defend themselves and their followers. They have ordered me to stand ever watching, like a soldier placed on guard, and to anticipate all the attempts and all the assaults of Fortune long before she strikes. Her attack falls heavy only when it is sudden; he easily withstands her who always expects her. For the arrival too of the enemy lays low only those whom it catches off guard; but those who have made ready for the coming war before it arrives, fully formed and ready armed, easily sustain the first impact, which is always the most violent. Never have I trusted Fortune, even when she seemed to be offering peace; the blessings she most fondly bestowed upon me—money, office, and influence—I stored all of them in a place from which she could take them back without disturbing me. Between them and me I have kept a wide space; and so she has merely taken them, not torn them, from me. No man is crushed by hostile Fortune who is not first deceived by her smiles. Those who love her gifts as if they were their very own and lasting, who desire to be esteemed on account of them, grovel and mourn when the false and fickle delights forsake their empty, childish minds, that are ignorant of every stable pleasure; but he who is not puffed up by happy fortune does not collapse when it is reversed. The man of long-tested constancy, when faced with either condition, keeps his mind unconquered; for in the very midst of prosperity he proves his strength to meet adversity.

Consequently, I have always believed that there was no real good in the things that most men pray for; besides, I have always found that they were empty and, though painted over with showy and deceptive colours, have nothing within to match their outward show. Even now in the midst of these so-called evils I find nothing so fearful and harsh as the fancy of everyone foreboded. The very name of exile, by reason of a sort of persuasion and general consent, falls by now upon the ears very harshly, and strikes the hearer as something gloomy and accursed. For so the people have decreed, but decrees of the people wise men in large measure annul.

Therefore, putting aside the verdict of the majority who are swept away by the first appearance of things, no matter what ground they have to trust it, let us see what exile is. It is a change of place. That I may not seem to narrow its force and to subtract the worst it holds, I will admit that this changing of place is attended by disadvantages—by poverty, disgrace, and scorn. These matters I shall cope with later; meanwhile, the first question that I wish to consider is what unpleasantness the mere changing of place brings with it.

"To be deprived of one's country is intolerable," you say. But come now, behold this concourse of men, for whom the houses of huge Rome scarcely suffice; most of this throng are now deprived of their country. From their towns and colonies, from the whole world, in fact, hither have they flocked. Some have been brought by ambition, some by the obligation of a public trust, some by an envoy's duty having been laid upon them, some, seeking a convenient and rich field for vice, by luxury, some by a desire for the higher studies, some by the public spectacles; some have been drawn by friendship, some, seeing the ample opportunity for displaying energy, by the chance to work; some have presented their beauty for sale, some their eloquence for sale—every class of person has swarmed into the city that offers high prizes for both virtues and vices. Have all of them summoned by name and ask of each: "Whence do you hail?"

Pass from the cities that entice very many by their delightful situation and an advantageous position; survey the desert places and the rockiest islands—Sciathus and Seriphus, Gyarus and Cossura; you will find no place of exile where someone does not linger of his own desire. What can be found so barren, what so precipitous on every side as this rock? If its resources are viewed, what is more starved? If its people, what is more uncivilized? If the very topography of the place, what is more rugged? If the character of its climate, what is more intemperate? Yet here reside more foreigners than natives.

So far, therefore, is the mere changing of places from being a hardship that even this place has tempted some from their native land. I find some who say that nature has planted in the human breast a certain restlessness that makes man seek to change his abode and find a new home; for to him has been given a mind that is fickle and restless, it lingers nowhere; it ranges to and fro, and sends forth its thoughts to all places, known and unknown—a rover, impatient of repose and happiest in the midst of new scenes. And this will not make you wonder if you consider its earliest origin. It was not formed from heavy and terrestrial matter, it came down from yonder spirit in the sky; but celestial things by their very nature are always in motion, they ever flee and are driven on in swiftest course.

Behold the planets that light the world; no one of them stands still. The sun glides onward ceaselessly and changes from place to place, and although it revolves with the universe, it moves none the less in a direction contrary to that of the world itself, it runs through all the signs of the zodiac and never halts; its movement is incessant and it shifts from one position to another. All the planets are ever whirling on and passing by; as the inviolable law of Nature has decreed, they are swept from one position to another; when in the course of fixed periods of years they have rounded out their circuits, they will enter again upon the paths by which they came. What folly, then, to think that the human mind, which has been formed from the self-same elements as these divine beings, is troubled by journeying and changing its home, while God's nature finds delight or, if you will, its preservation in continuous and most speedy movement!

Come now, turn your attention from things divine to the affairs of men; you will see that whole tribes and nations have changed their abodes. Why do we find Greek cities in the very heart of barbarian countries? Why the Macedonian tongue among the Indians and the Persians? Scythia and all that great stretch which is peopled with fierce and unconquered tribes show Achaean towns planted on the shores of the Pontic Sea; not by the fierceness of eternal winter, not by the temper of the inhabitants, as savage as their climate, were men deterred from seeking there new homes. A host of Athenians dwell in Asia; Miletus has poured forth in divers directions enough people to fill seventy-five cities; the whole coast of Italy which is washed by the Lower Sea became a greater Greece; Asia claims the Tuscans as her own; Tyrians live in Africa, Carthaginians in Spain; the Greeks thrust themselves into Gaul, the Gauls into Greece; the Pyrenees did not stay the passage of the Germans—through pathless, through unknown regions restless man has made his way. Wives and children and elders burdened with age trailed along.

Some have not settled upon a place from choice, but, tossed about in long wandering, from very weariness have seized upon the nearest; others have established their right in a foreign land by the sword; some tribes, seeking unknown regions, were swallowed up by the sea; some settled in the spot in which a lack of supplies had stranded them. Some, having escaped the destruction of their cities by the forces of the enemy, have been thrust into strange lands when stripped of their own; some have been cast out by civil discord; some have gone forth in order to relieve the pressure from over-crowding caused by an excess of population; some have been driven out by pestilence or repeated earthquakes or certain unbearable defects of an unproductive soil; some have been beguiled by the fame of a fertile shore that was too highly praised. Different peoples have been impelled by different reasons to leave their homes. But at least this is clear—none has stayed in the place where he was born.

The human race is constantly rushing to and fro; in this vast world some change takes place every day. The foundations of new cities are laid, the names of new nations arise, while former ones are blotted out or lost by annexation with a stronger. But all these transmigrations of peoples—what are they but wholesale banishments? The Roman Empire itself, in fact, looks back to an exile as its founder—a refugee from his captured city, who, taking along a small remnant of his people and driven by fear of the victor to seek a distant land, was brought by destiny into Italy. This people, in turn—how many colonies has it sent to every province! Wherever the Roman conquers, there he dwells. With a view to this change of country, volunteers would gladly give in their names, and the old man, leaving his altars, would follow the colonists overseas.

The matter does not require a listing of more instances; yet I shall add one which thrusts itself before my eyes. This very island has ofttimes changed its dwellers. To say nothing of older matters, which antiquity has veiled, the Greeks who now inhabit Marseilles, after leaving Phocis, first settled on this island, and it is doubtful what drove them from it—whether the harshness of the climate, or the near sight of all-powerful Italy, or the harbourless character of the sea; for that the fierceness of the natives was not the cause is clear from the fact that they established themselves in the midst of what were then the most savage and uncivilized peoples of Gaul. Later the Ligurians crossed into the island, and the Spaniards also came, as the similarity of customs shows; for the islanders wear the same head-coverings and the same kind of foot-gear as the Cantabrians, and certain of their words are the same; but only a few, for from intercourse with the Greeks and Ligurians their language as a whole has lost its native character. Still later two colonies of Roman citizens were transported to the island, one by Marius, the other by Sulla; so many times has the population of this barren and thorny rock been changed!

Varro, the most learned of the Romans, holds that, barring all the other ills of exile, the mere changing of place is offset by this ample compensation—the fact that wherever we come, we must still find there the same order of Nature. Marcus Brutus thinks that this is enough—the fact that those who go into exile may take along with them their virtues. Only the most worthless of our possessions falls under the control of another. All that is best for a man lies beyond the power of other men, who can neither give it nor take it away. This firmament, than which Nature has created naught greater and more beautiful, and the most glorious part of it, the human mind that surveys and wonders at the firmament, are our own everlasting possessions, destined to remain with us so long as we ourselves shall remain.

Eager, therefore, and erect, let us hasten with dauntless step wherever circumstance directs, let us traverse any lands whatsoever. Inside the world there can be found no place of exile; for nothing that is inside the world is foreign to mankind. No matter where you lift your gaze from earth to heaven, the realms of God and man are separated by an unalterable distance. Accordingly, so long as my eyes are not deprived of that spectacle with which they are never sated, so long as I may behold the sun and the moon, so long as I may fix my gaze upon the other planets, so long as I may trace out their risings and settings, their periods, and the reasons for the swiftness or the slowness of their wandering, behold the countless stars that gleam throughout the night—some at rest, while others do not enter upon a great course, but circle around within their own field, some suddenly shooting forth, some blinding the eyes with scattered fire as if they were falling, or flying by with a long trail of lingering light—so long as I may be with these, and, in so far as it is permitted to a man, commune with celestial beings, so long as I may keep my mind directed ever to the sight of kindred things on high, what difference does it make to me what soil I tread upon?

"But," you say, "this land yields no fruitful or pleasing trees; it is watered by the channels of no great or navigable rivers; it produces nothing that other nations desire, it scarcely bears enough to support its own inhabitants; no costly marble is quarried here, no veins of gold and silver are unearthed." But it is a narrow mind that finds its pleasure in earthly things; it should turn from these to those above, which everywhere appear just the same, everywhere are just as bright. This, too, we must bear in mind, that earthly things because of false and wrongly accepted values cut off the sight of these true goods. The longer the rich man extends his colonnades, the higher he lifts his towers, the wider he stretches out his mansions, the deeper he digs his caverns for summer, the huger loom the roofs of the banquet-halls he rears, so much the more there will be to hide heaven from his sight. Has misfortune cast you into a country where the most sumptuous shelter is a hut? Truly you show a paltry spirit and take to yourself mean comfort if you bear this bravely only because you know the hut of Romulus. Say, rather, this: "This lowly hovel, I suppose, gives entrance to the virtues? When justice, when temperance, when wisdom and righteousness and understanding of the proper apportionment of all duties and the knowledge of God and man are seen therein, it will straightway become more stately than any temple. No place that can hold this concourse of such great virtues is narrow; no exile can be irksome to which one may go in such company as this."

So far as concerns myself, I know that I have lost, not wealth, but my "engrossments." The wants of the body are trifling. It requires protection from the cold and the quenching of hunger and thirst by food and drink; if we covet anything beyond, we toil to serve, not our needs, but our vices. We have no need to scour the depths of every sea, to load the belly with the carnage of dumb creatures, to wrest shell-fish from the distant shore of farthest sea—curses of gods and goddesses upon the wretches whose luxury overleaps the bounds of an empire that already stirs too much envy! They want game that is caught beyond the Phasis to supply their pretentious kitchens, and from the Parthians, from whom Rome has not yet got vengeance, they do not blush to get—birds! From every quarter they gather together every known and unknown thing to tickle a fastidious palate; the food which their stomachs, weakened by indulgence, can scarcely retain is fetched from farthest ocean; they vomit that they may eat, they eat that they may vomit, and they do not deign even to digest the feasts for which they ransack the whole world.

If a man despises such things, what harm can poverty do him? If a man covets them, poverty becomes even a benefit to him; for he is made whole in spite of himself, and, if even under compulsion he will not take his medicine, for a time at least, while he cannot get them, he is as though he did not want them. Gaius Caesar, whom, as it seems to me, Nature produced merely to show how far supreme vice, when combined with supreme power, could go, dined one day at a cost of ten million sesterces; and though everybody used their ingenuity to help him, yet he could hardly discover how to spend the tribute-money from three provinces on one dinner! How unhappy those whose appetite is stirred at the sight of none but costly foods! And it is not their choice flavour or some delight to the palate that makes them costly, but their rarity and the difficulty of getting them. Otherwise, if men should be willing to return to sanity of mind, what is the need of so many arts that minister to the belly? What need of commerce? What need of ravaging the forests? What need of ransacking the deep? The foods which Nature has placed in every region lie all about us, but men, just as if blind, pass these by and roam through every region, they cross the seas and at great cost excite their hunger when at little cost they might allay it. One would like to say: "Why do you launch your ships? Why do you arm your bands both against man and against wild beasts? Why do you rush to and fro in such wild confusion? Why do you pile riches on riches? You really should remember how small your bodies are! Is it not madness and the wildest lunacy to desire so much when you can hold so little? And so you may swell your incomes, and extend your boundaries; yet you will never enlarge the capacity of your bellies. Nothing will satisfy greed, but even scant measure is enough for Nature's need. Therefore the poverty of an exile holds no hardship; for no place of exile is so barren as not to yield ample support for a man.

"But," you say, "the exile is likely to miss his raiment and his house." Will he desire these also merely to the extent of his need? Then he will lack neither shelter nor covering; for it takes just as little to shield as to feed the body. Nature has made nothing difficult which at the same time she made necessary for man. But if he desires cloth of purple steeped in rich dye, threaded with gold, and damasked with various colours and patterns, it is not Nature's fault but his own if he is poor. Even if you restore to him whatever he has lost, it will do no good; for he who will need to be restored to his native land will still lack more of all that he covets than as an exile he lacked of all that he once had. But if he desires tables that gleam with vessels of gold, and silver plate that boasts the names of ancient artists, bronze made costly by the crazy fad of a few, and a throng of slaves that would hamper a house however large, beasts of burden with bodies over-stuffed and forced to grow fat, and the marbles of every nation—though he should amass all these, they will no more be able to satisfy his insatiable soul than any amount of drink will ever suffice to quench the thirst of a man whose desire arises, not from need, but from the fire that burns in his vitals; for this is not thirst, but disease. Nor is this true only in respect to money or food. Every want that springs, not from any need, but from vice is of a like character; however much you gather for it will serve, not to end, but to advance desire.

He, therefore, who keeps himself within the bounds of nature will not feel poverty; but he who exceeds the bounds of nature will be pursued by poverty even though he has unbounded wealth. Even places of exile will provide necessaries, but not even kingdoms superfluities. It is the mind that makes us rich; this goes with us into exile, and in the wildest wilderness, having found there all that the body needs for its sustenance, it itself overflows in the enjoyment of its own goods. The mind has no concern with money—no whit more than have the immortal gods. Those things that men's untutored hearts revere, sunk in the bondage of their bodies—jewels, gold, silver, and polished tables, huge and round—all these are earthly dross, for which the untainted spirit, conscious of its own nature, can have no love, since it is itself light and unencumbered, waiting only to be released from the body before it soars to highest heaven. Meanwhile, hampered by mortal limbs and encompassed by the heavy burden of the flesh, it surveys, as best it can, the things of heaven in swift and winged thought. And so the mind can never suffer exile, since it is free, kindred to the gods, and at home in every world and every age; for its thought ranges over all heaven and projects itself into all past and future time. This poor body, the prison and fetter of the soul, is tossed hither and thither; upon it punishments, upon it robberies, upon it diseases work their will. But the soul itself is sacred and eternal, and upon it no hand can be laid.

To this one may reply: "Why do you artfully divide things which, if taken separately, can be endured; if combined, cannot? Change of place is tolerable if you change merely your place; poverty is tolerable if it be without disgrace, which even alone is wont to crush the spirit." In reply to this man, the one who tries to frighten me with an aggregation of ills, I shall have to use such words as these: "If you have enough strength to cope with any one phase of fortune, you will have enough to cope with all. When virtue has once steeled your mind, it guarantees to make it invulnerable from every quarter. If greed, the mightiest curse of the human race, has relaxed its hold, ambition will not detain you; if you regard the end of your days, not as a punishment, but as an ordinance of nature, when once you have cast from your breast the fear of death, the fear of no other thing will dare to enter in; if you consider sexual desire to have been given to man, not for the gratification of pleasure, but for the continuance of the human race, when once you have escaped the violence of this secret destruction implanted in your very vitals, every other desire will pass you by unharmed. Reason lays low the vices not one by one, but all together; the victory is gained once for all."

Think you that any wise man can be moved by disgrace—a man who relies wholly upon himself, who draws aloof from the opinions of the common herd? Worse even than disgrace is a disgraceful death. And yet Socrates, wearing the same aspect wherewith he had once all alone put the Thirty Tyrants in their place, entered prison, and so was to rob even prison of all disgrace; for no place that held Socrates could possibly seem a prison. Who has become so blind to the perception of truth as to think that the twofold defeat of Marcus Cato in his candidacy for the praetorship and the consulship was to him a disgrace? It was the praetorship and the consulship, on which Cato was conferring honour, that suffered the disgrace. No one is despised by another unless he is first despised by himself. An abject and grovelling mind may be liable to such insult; but a man who rises up to face the most cruel of misfortunes, and overthrows the evils by which others are crushed—this man's very sorrows crown him, as it were, with a halo, since we are so constituted that nothing stirs our admiration so much as a man who is brave in adversity.

Since you have no reason, my dearest mother, to be forced to endless tears on my own account, it follows that you are goaded to them by reasons of your own. Now there are two possibilities. For what moves you is either the thought that you have lost some protection, or the mere longing for me is more than you can endure.

The first consideration I must touch upon very lightly; for I well know that your heart values nothing in your dear ones except themselves. Let other mothers look to that—the mothers who make use of a son's power with a woman's lack of self-control, who, because they cannot hold office, seek power through their sons, who both spend their sons' inheritances and hope to be their heirs, who wear out their eloquence in lending it to others. But you have always had the greatest joy in the blessings of your children, yet you have used them not at all; you have always set bounds to our generosity, though you set none to your own; you, though a daughter in your father's household, actually made presents to your wealthy sons; you managed our inheritances with such care that they might have been your own, with such scrupulousness that they might have been a stranger's; you were as sparing in the use of our influence as if you were using a stranger's property, and from our elections to office nothing accrued to you except your pleasure and the expense. Never did your fondness look to self-interest. You cannot, therefore, in the loss of a son miss what you never considered your own concern while he was still safe.

So I must direct all my effort at consolation upon the second point—the true source of the power of a mother's grief. "I am deprived," you say, "of the embraces of my dearest son; I may no longer enjoy the pleasure of seeing him, the pleasure of his conversation! Where is he the very sight of whom would smooth my troubled brow, upon whom I unloaded all my anxieties? Where are the talks, of which I could never have enough? Where are the studies, which I shared with more than a woman's pleasure, with more than a mother's intimacy? Where the fond meeting? Where the boyish glee that was always stirred by the sight of his mother?" You add to all this the actual scenes of our rejoicings and intercourse and the reminders of our recent association, which are, necessarily, the most potent causes of mental distress. For Fortune cruelly contrived to deal you even this blow—she willed that you should part from me only two days before I was struck down, and you had no reason for concern nor any fear of such a disaster. It is well that we had been separated before by a great distance, it is well that an absence of several years had prepared you for this misfortune. By returning to Rome, you failed to gain the pleasure of seeing your son, and lost the habit of doing without him. Had you been absent long before, you could have borne my misfortune more bravely, since separation itself lessens our longing; had you not gone away, you would have at least gained the final pleasure of seeing your son two days longer. As it was, cruel Fate contrived that you should neither be with me in the midst of disaster, nor have grown accustomed to my absence. But the harder these circumstances are, the more courage must you summon, and you must engage with Fortune the more fiercely, as with an enemy well known and often conquered before.

Unchastity, the greatest evil of our time, has never classed you with the great majority of women; jewels have not moved you, nor pearls; to your eyes the glitter of riches has not seemed the greatest boon of the human race; you, who were soundly trained in an old-fashioned and strict household, have not been perverted by the imitation of worse women that leads even the virtuous into pitfalls; you have never blushed for the number of your children, as if it taunted you with your years, never have you, in the manner of other women whose only recommendation lies in their beauty, tried to conceal your pregnancy as if an unseemly burden, nor have you ever crushed the hope of children that were being nurtured in your body; you have not defiled your face with paints and cosmetics; never have you fancied the kind of dress that exposed no greater nakedness by being removed. In you has been seen that peerless ornament, that fairest beauty on which time lays no hand, that chiefest glory which is modesty. You cannot, therefore, allege your womanhood as an excuse for persistent grief, for your very virtues set you apart; you must be as far removed from woman's tears as from her vices. But even women will not allow you to pine away from your wound, but will bid you finish quickly with necessary sorrow, and then rise with lighter heart—I mean, if you are willing to turn your gaze upon the women whose conspicuous bravery has placed them in the rank of mighty heroes.

Cornelia bore twelve children, but Fortune had reduced their number to two; if you wished to count Cornelia's losses, she had lost ten, if to appraise them, she had lost the two Gracchi. Nevertheless, when her friends were weeping around her and cursing her fate, she forbade them to make any indictment against Fortune, since it was Fortune who had allowed the Gracchi to be her sons. Such a woman had right to be the mother of him who exclaimed in the public assembly: "Do you dare to revile the mother who gave birth to me?" But to me his mother's utterance seems more spirited by far; the son set great value on the birthdays of the Gracchi, but the mother on their funerals as well.

Rutilia followed her son Cotta into exile, and was so wrapped up in her love for him that she preferred exile to losing him; and only her son's return brought her back to her native land. But when, after he had been restored and now had risen to honour in the state, he died, she let him go just as bravely as she had clung to him; and after her son was buried no one saw her shed any tears. When he was exiled, she showed courage, when she lost him, wisdom; for in the one case she did not desist from her devotion, and in the other did not persist in useless and foolish sorrow.

I know well that this is a matter that is not in our own power, and that no emotion is submissive, least of all that which is born from sorrow; for it is wild and stubbornly resists every remedy. And so I am not going to point you to the expedients that I know many have used, suggesting that you distract or cheer your mind by travel, whether to distant or pleasant places, that you employ much time in diligent examination of your accounts and in the management of your estate, that you should always be involved in some new tasks. All such things avail for a brief space only, and are not the remedies but the hindrances of sorrow; but I would rather end it than beguile it.

And so I guide you to that in which all who fly from Fortune must take refuge—to philosophic studies. They will heal your wound, they will uproot all your sadness. Even if you had not been acquainted with them before, you would need to use them now; but, so far as the old-fashioned strictness of my father permitted you, though you have not indeed fully grasped all the liberal arts, still you have had some dealings with them. Do you return now to these studies; they will render you safe. They will comfort you, they will cheer you; if in earnest they gain entrance to your mind, nevermore will sorrow enter there, nevermore anxiety, nevermore the useless distress of futile suffering. To none of these will your heart be open; for to all other weaknesses it has long been closed. Philosophy is your most unfailing safeguard, and she alone can rescue you from the power of Fortune.

But because you have need of something to lean upon until you can reach that haven which philosophy promises to you, I wish meanwhile to point out the consolations you still have. Turn your eyes upon my brothers; while they live, you have no right to complain of Fortune. Different as their merits are, you have reason to rejoice in both. The one by his energy has attained public honours; the other with wisdom has scorned them. Find comfort in the prestige of one son, in the retirement of the other—in the devotion of both! The secret motives of my brothers I well know. The one fosters his prestige for the real purpose of shedding lustre upon you; the other retired to a life of tranquillity and repose for the real purpose of using his leisure for you. It was kind of Fortune so to arrange the lives of your children that they would bring help and pleasure to you; you can both be protected by the position of the one, and enjoy the leisure of the other. They will vie in their services to you, and the blank that one has caused will be filled by the devotion of two. I can make a confident promise—you will lack nothing except the full number.

From these turn your eyes, too, upon your grandchildren—to Marcus, a most winsome lad, the sight of whom no sorrow can possibly withstand; no one's heart can hold a sorrow so great or so fresh that his embrace will not soothe it. Hold to your bosom Novatilla, who so soon will present you with great-grandchildren, whom I had so transferred to myself, had so adopted as my own, that in losing me she may well seem to be an orphan although her father is still living; do you cherish her for me also! Of your greatest source of comfort I have thus far said nothing—your sister, that heart most loyal to you, upon which without reserve you unload all your cares, who for all of us has the feeling of a mother. To her attach yourself as closely as you can, in her embraces enfold yourself most closely. Those who are in grief are prone to avoid the ones they love most dearly, and to seek liberty for the indulgence of their sorrow. Do you, however, share with her your every thought; whether you wish to retain or to lay aside your mood, you will find in her either the end of your sorrow or a comrade in it. But if I know rightly the wisdom of this most perfect woman, she will not suffer you to be consumed by a grief that will profit you nothing, and she will recount to you an experience of her own, which I myself also witnessed.

In the very midst of a voyage she lost her dearly beloved husband, my uncle, whom she had married when a maiden; nevertheless, she bore up bravely, enduring at the same time both grief and fear, and, overmastering the storm, bore his body safe to land amid the shipwreck. O how many noble deeds of women are unknown to fame! If she had had the good fortune to live in the days of old when men were frank in admiration of heroic deeds, with what rivalry of genius would her praise be sung—a wife who forgetful of her own weakness, forgetful of the sea, which even the stoutest hearts must dread, exposed her own life to peril to give another burial, and, while she planned her husband's funeral, had no fear at all about her own! Alcestis, she who gave herself to death in place of her husband, has fame from the songs of all poets. But for a wife to seek burial for her husband at the risk of her own life is far more; for she who, enduring equal danger, has smaller recompense shows greater love. You must show a courage to match hers, must recall your mind from grief, and strive that no one may think that you regret your motherhood.

But because, though you have done everything, your thoughts must necessarily revert at times to me, and it must be that under the circumstances no one of your children engages your mind so often—not that the others are less dear, but that it is natural to lay the hand more often on the part that hurts—hear now how you must think of me. I am as happy and cheerful as when circumstances were best. Indeed, they are now best, since my mind, free from all other engrossment, has leisure for its own tasks, and now finds joy in lighter studies, now, being eager for the truth, mounts to the consideration of its own nature and the nature of the universe. It seeks knowledge, first, of the lands and where they lie, then of the laws that govern the encompassing sea with its alternations of ebb and flow. Then it takes ken of all the expanse, charged with terrors, that lies between heaven and earth—this nearer space, disturbed by thunder, lightning, blasts of winds, and the downfall of rain and snow and hail. Finally, having traversed the lower spaces, it bursts through to the heights above, and there enjoys the noblest spectacle of things divine, and, mindful of its own immortality, it proceeds to all that has been and will ever be throughout the ages of all time.

Translated by John W. Basore

The Fellowship of Exile

Julio Cortázar

WHAT FOLLOWS IS an attempt to shed some light on the question of the literature of exile and the special problems exile poses for literature. I have no talent for analysis; I limit myself here to a very personal vision. I will not attempt to generalize but merely offer a modest contribution to a multifaceted problem.

As both a fact of life and a literary theme, exile dominates Latin American literature today. As a fact of life, we know only too well the number of writers who have had to leave their countries. As a literary theme, exile obviously shows up in many of the poems, short stories and novels by these writers. A universal theme, at least since the laments of an Ovid or a Dante, exile is a constant in the present-day reality and literature of Latin America, from the countries of the so-called Southern Cone all the way to a good many of the nations of Central America. This anomalous condition of the writer encompasses Argentines, Chileans, Uruguayans, Paraguayans, Bolivians, Brazilians, Salvadorans, Haitians, Dominicans, and the list goes on. By "writer" I mean above all the novelist and short story writer, that is to say, writers of creative prose fiction. Alongside them I include the poet, whom no one has been able to define with precision, but who stands beside the story writer and novelist to the degree that all play their game in a territory dominated by analogy, free-association, expressive rhythms and the tendency to draw directly from experience and personal empathy.

In considering the problem of the exiled writer, I must include myself among the innumerable protagonists of the diaspora. The only difference lies in the fact that my exile has been a forced one only in these last few years. When I left Argentina in 1951, I did so of my own free will and without any compelling political or ideological reasons. That is why for more than twenty years I could frequently travel to my own country, and only since 1974 have I been obliged to consider myself an exile. But there is more to the story and worse: this physical exile has been compounded during the last year by a cultural exile, infinitely more painful for a writer who works in close contact with his national and linguistic heritage. To wit, the Argentine edition of my last collection of short stories was banned by the military junta, which would have authorized it only if I had deleted two stories it considered injurious to itself and what it represents: systematic alienation and repression. One of these stories indirectly referred to the disappearance of people in Argentina. The theme of the other was the destruction of the Christian community of the Nicaraguan poet, Ernesto Cardenal, on the island of Solentiname.

The fact is that today I experience exile all around me, which is to say, paradoxically, within me. Years ago, every time I was called upon to speak on behalf of the victims of any of the dictatorships of our continent at such bodies as the second Russell Tribunal or the Helsinki Commission, it would never have occurred to me to think of myself as a Latin American exile, since I had never considered the distance from my country as exile, not even as voluntary exile. For me at least, exile includes the notion of force, of compulsion. An exile is almost always one who has been expelled, and until recently this was not my case. I would like to make it clear that I have not been the object of any official measure in that sense, and it is very possible that, should I wish to travel to Argentina, I could enter the country without difficulty. What I could not do, however, is leave again, even though the military junta would not be willing to take responsibility for anything that might happen to me. And it is a well-known fact that in Argentina people disappear without any official word of what has happened.

And so, having consciously assumed the identity of an exile, I would like to make a few observations on this matter of such great concern to us as writers. What I intend to perform is not an autopsy but a biopsy. My aim is not to denounce but to respond, as swiftly and effectively as possible, to the cultural genocide increasing daily in so many Latin American countries. At the risk of seeming idealistic, I would like to venture the following: I believe that we writers in exile have the means to transcend the uprooting and separation imposed upon us by the dictatorships, to return in our own unique way the blows we suffer collectively each time another writer is exiled. But to do so we would have to overcome certain misconceptions held over from a romantic, humanistic tradition that is quite frankly obsolete. Instead, we must pose the problem of exile in a way that sees beyond its undeniably negative character, which is by turns terrible, inexorable, stereotyped, sterilizing.

There is, of course, the trauma which follows each blow, each wound. An exiled writer is in the first place a *man* or *woman* who is exiled, someone who has been stripped of everything that he or she has—many times a family and at the very least a way of life, the smell of the air and the color of the sky, the familiarity of the home and the street, of libraries and dogs, of cafés with friends and newspapers and music and walks through the city. Exile marks the end of contact with the leaves and trees, the end of a deep-rooted relationship with the land and the air. It's like an abrupt ending to a love affair, or an inconceivably horrible death in which one continues to be conscious, like the one described by Poe in "The Premature Burial."

This all-too-understandable trauma has always caused and continues to cause a certain number of exiled writers to lapse into something like an intellectual and creative slumber which limits, impoverishes and at times totally annihilates their work. It is sadly ironic to confirm that this is more frequently the case among young writers than among veterans, and that it is here that the dictatorships best achieve their intention of destroying free thought and combative creativity. Over the years I have seen many rising stars extinguished this way in a foreign sky. And even worse is what might be called internal exile; oppression, censorship and fear in our own countries have stopped in their tracks any number of young talents whose early work promised so much. Between 1953 and 1970 I received from young Argentine authors many books and manuscripts that filled me with hope. Today I know little about them, especially the ones who have stayed on in Argentina. This is not just a question of natural selection from generation to generation, but the total or partial abdication on the part of a much larger number of writers than one would expect under normal conditions.

It is sadly ironic to confirm, therefore, that writers who are exiled abroad, whether young or old, are more prolific than those harassed and restricted by conditions at home, which may even reach the extreme of disappearance and death, as in the cases of Rodolfo Walsh and Haroldo Conti in Argentina. But in all its forms the literature of exile is produced as the direct or indirect result of traumatic experiences which are unequivocally reflected, in the majority of cases, in the writer's work.

Faced with this separation from the vital source which neutralizes or unbalances the creative capacity, writers react in a variety of ways. Among the exiles outside the country, a small minority lapses into silence, often obligated by the necessity of readjusting their lives to conditions and activities which lead them away from literature as the essential task. But nearly all the other exiles continue writing, and their reactions are perceptible in their work. There are those who, in almost Proustian fashion, set out from their exile on a nostalgic search for the lost homeland. There are those who dedicate their work to recapturing that homeland, uniting literary effort with political struggle. In both cases, as dissimilar as they may be, we note a common attitude: the tendency to regard exile as a negative value, a humiliation or mutilation against which the exiled writer reacts in one form or another. Up to now I have not had the opportunity to read many poems, stories or novels by Latin American exiles in which the determining factor, the factor of exile, is the subject of an internal criticism which counteracts its negative value and finds a positive way out. Writers almost always begin from the negative (ranging from denunciation to the cry of rebellion which can arise from it) and, balanced on the weak springboard of negative value, they leap forward toward the recovery of what has been lost, focusing on the defeat of the enemy and the return to a homeland free of despots and executioners.

I am fully aware that what follows is perilously close to paradox, but I do not personally believe that this attitude with respect to exile produces the results that could be achieved by another approach which, though irrational at first glance, in fact reflects an absolutely valid awareness of reality. Those who exile intellectuals believe their act to be positive, since it has as its object the elimination of the adversary. But what if exiles were also to take a positive view of exile? This is not a joke in bad taste, since I know full well that I am touching upon an area of open wounds and unimaginable pain. What I am calling for is a deliberate act of distancing; and at the same time, I am making an appeal to those inner resources that have so often saved man from total annihilation, surfacing in various ways, one of them being a sense of humor, the same humor which throughout history has served as a vehicle for ideas and strategies that would otherwise have seemed like madness or delirium. I believe that now more than ever before it is necessary to change the negative sign of exile, which only confirms the triumph of the enemy, to a new awareness of reality, a reality based on positive rather than negative value, a change the writer can achieve by inverting the adversary's program and coming out on top in a way which the latter would never have imagined possible.

I will refer once again to my own personal experience: if my own physical exile is in no way comparable to that of other writers expelled from their countries in recent years, since I left of my own free will and adjusted my life to new realities over a span of more than two decades, my recent cultural exile, on the other hand, which with a single stroke destroyed the bridge uniting me with my fellow countrymen as readers and critics of my books—a bitter blow for one who has always written as an Argentine and loved all that is Argentine—was not for me an altogether negative trauma.

I bounced back from the blow with the feeling that the time had come, that the die was cast, and that now it had to be a fight to the finish. The mere thought of the alienating and impoverishing effect which this cultural exile would have upon thousands and thousands of readers who are my fellow countrymen, as well as upon so many other writers whose works are banned in the country, was enough to cause a positive reaction in me, to send me to my typewriter to get on with my work in support of all the intelligent forms of combat. And if those who have closed off my cultural access to my country think they have thus made my exile complete, they are thoroughly mistaken. They have given me a full-time fellowship, one which will allow me to devote myself more than ever to my work, since my response to this cultural fascism is and always will be to redouble my efforts alongside those who fight for the freedom of my country. Needless to say, I will not thank them for a fellowship of this kind, but I will take full advantage of it and turn the negative value of exile into a positive value with which to fight.

Needless to say, I am not trying to project my own point of view on other exiled writers in the hope that they might share it. Simply stated, I believe it is feasible to invert the stereotyped notion of exile which retains many connotations that we should be rid of by now. The unavoidable fact is that we have been expelled from our countries. Why play into the enemy's hands by treating that expulsion as a misfortune—a response that can only direct our reactions in a negative manner? Why should we harp day after day, in the press and public forums, about our condition as exiles, focusing always on the most painful details when this is precisely what those who close the doors to our countries want us to do? Exiles, yes. Period. Now there are other things to write and do—as exiled writers, of course, but with the emphasis on the word "writers." Because our true effectiveness lies in our ability to profit from exile, to take advantage of these sinister fellowships, to extend and enrich our mental horizons so that when at last we can focus again upon our own realities, we can do so with greater lucidity and effect. Exile and unhappiness always walk hand in hand; but with our free hand let us look for humor: that is what will help us neutralize the nostalgia and despair. Latin American dictatorships don't have writers but scribes: let us not become the scribes of bitterness, resentment or melancholy. Let us truly be free, and let us begin by ridding ourselves from this all too common habit of tears and self-pity. Rather than feeling sorry for ourselves, we should proclaim, mad as it may seem, that the real exiles are the fascist regimes of our continent who are exiled from the true realities of their countries, from social justice, happiness and peace. We are freer, more at home than they. I have spoken of insanity. Like humor, it too is a way of breaking the mold and opening a positive path that we will never find if we continue to adhere to the enemy's cold and calculating rules of the game. Polonius says of Hamlet: "There is method in his madness." And he's right, because by applying his method of madness, Hamlet triumphs in the end. He triumphs as a madman. A sane person would never have been able to bring down the despotic system which was choking Denmark. His own life and the lives of Ophelia and Laertes are the terrible price of that madness, but Hamlet does away with his father's assassins, with power based on terror and lies, with the junta of his time. There *is* method in that madness, and an example we can learn from. Let us invent rather than accept the labels we wear. Let us define ourselves by opposing the predictable, the conventional.

I am sure this is possible, but I am also sure that no one will achieve it without first taking a step backward to take a fresh look at himself, to look at himself as a new person, in order to reap at least that benefit from exile. The awareness of reality to which I earlier referred would not be possible without a self-criticism that strips off the blindfold that covers our eyes.

In this sense any honest writer will admit that it is the uprooting itself which leads to this self-analysis. In brutal but compelling terms, it serves the purpose formerly served in Latin America by the famous "trip to Europe" taken by our fathers and grandfathers. What at present is forced upon us was once a voluntary and pleasurable decision—to approach the mirage of a Europe that would catalyze talents and forces still in embryonic form. That trip by a Chilean or an Argentine to Paris, Rome or London was a voyage of initiation, a push from the nest for which there was no substitute. It provided access to the Holy Grail of Western wisdom. Fortunately, we are gradually coming out of this colonial attitude, which may have had its historical and cultural justification at another time, but which has become an anachronism in an age of instant communication on a shrinking planet. Nonetheless, an analogy remains between that marvelous cultural journey of the past and the merciless expulsion of exile: an opportunity for self-examination as writers torn from our surroundings.

No longer is it a question of learning about Europe, given the fact that we can do this at a great distance by taking advantage of the cultural ubiquity afforded by the mass media, as well as by the media of the "fortunate few." It is a question above all of examining ourselves as individuals who belong to the nations of Latin America, of finding out why we are losing the battle, why we are exiled, why we live badly, why we do not know how to govern ourselves nor topple bad governments, why we tend to overvalue our aptitudes in order to mask our ineptitude. Instead of concentrating on the idiosyncrasies, the behavior and techniques of our adversaries, the first task of exiles should be to bare our souls before the terrible mirror which is the loneliness of a hotel room in a foreign land, and there, no longer supported by the easy alibis of local pride and the lack of terms of comparison, try to see ourselves as we really are.

Many have done so over the years, some even using their writing as the terrain in which to reencounter or to reject their innermost selves. It is easy to identify the writers who have subjected themselves to this merciless examination, since the thrust of their work reflects not only the battle within, but new inflections in their thought and praxis. On one side are those who stop writing in order to enter the domain of personal action, and on the other are those who continue to write as a specific form of action, though now from wider perspectives, along new and more effective lines of fire. In both cases the conception of exile as a negative value is transcended. But those who remain silent and do nothing, or continue writing as they had before, become ineffective, since they approach exile as something negative.

To the degree that we are able to make this difficult critique of all the factors that have led us into exile—factors which it would be only too easy, and hypocritical, to attribute solely to the enemy—let us from this day on prepare to fight against this enemy and return to our homeland. We now know that within our countries little can be done by writers against the machinery of imperialism and the terror of fascism. But it is evident that among readers abroad the repudiation by literary means of that machinery and that terror has achieved a growing impact in the course of the last few years, and as a result this repudiation has achieved greater moral and practical support from the forces of resistance and change. If, on one hand, honest journalism keeps the public more and more informed in this area, something which is certainly true in France, it is the duty of Latin American writers in exile to quicken, to breathe life into this information, to give it the unique corporality engendered by the synthesizing, symbolic powers of fiction: by the novel, the poem or the short story that can incarnate what can never be brought to life in a telex dispatch or in the column of a news analyst. Without a doubt, it is because of this power that the dictatorships in our lands fear, censor and burn the books which are born in exile of both the internal and external varieties. And we can find value even in this action, as we can in exile itself. The book which was censored or burned was not in every way a good one. Let us now write another which is even better.

Translated by John Incledon

The Exile as African

Breyten Breytenbach

"FOR OUR PURPOSES, it matters little what strange thoughts occur to people in Albania or Burkina Faso." This phrase from Francis Fukuyama's arrogant and fatally shortsighted article "The End of History" may for now seem to be apposite. Likewise Milan Kundera, in his *Unbearable Lightness of Being*, may have been right when he chose a war in Africa during the fourteenth century as an example of the most meaningless event in human history. In proposing that any event that happens only once is meaningless, he suggests a life that disappears once and for all, that does not return, is like a shadow, without weight, dead in advance, dead by procuration and procreation; and whether it was horrible, beautiful, or sublime, its horror, sublimity, and beauty mean nothing. He writes: "We need take no more note of it than of a war between two African kingdoms in the fourteenth century, a war that alters nothing in the destiny of the world, even if a hundred thousand blacks perished in excruciating torment." Indeed, one is tempted to ask: Why bother to look back to the fourteenth century? What about now?

On the continent with which I identify, whose cause—however weak—will always be mine, there are at present an estimated thirteen wars being fought: in Angola and Ethiopia and Liberia and Mali and Mauritania and Mozambique and Uganda and Rwanda and the western Sahara and Senegal and Somalia and the Sudan and Chad. (South Africa is not in a war situation; we just have ongoing large-scale slaughter.) Who cares?

For now the rich countries, or the developed world, or the North—call it what you wish—have evidently decided, unilaterally and disdainfully, that developments in the poor countries (by "developments" I mean stages of stagnation and deterioration) can have no bearing on the course of history. But this *realmoral* (the cynical underpinning of *realpolitik*) is ahistorical and brings with it a shrinking of public ethics in the rich world too. Recent events and events to come will show, I am sure, that it is foolhardy for the West or the North to close its eyes and close off its heart behind the pretentious bulwarks of a "new world order." It was the French philosopher Louis Althusser who said, "The future lasts a long time." History may no longer be deterministic or predictable, and it certainly does not progress, but it is never completed. It vomits at unexpected moments.

It is my exile from Africa that has brought home to me that I'm African. If I live in Europe most of the time, it is not as a participant but as an observer, and also as an underground activist for Africa. My pale skin and my Western garb make it possible for me to "pass for white." But my heart beats with the secret rhythm of that continent that seems to have sunk below the perceptual horizon of the North. At night I go out to scribble on the walls of the cold imperial cities: *Africa Lives!* In other words, I consciously try to shape my work, even the expressions of a private or peculiar idiom, so that it contributes to the awareness in Europe of Africa.

Exile is a difficult craft, but the exile hopes that it is also a useful one, that he may be a producer of awareness, even if marginally so. It is another contradiction that exile should be a pointed experience and yet, in a world of specialization, should promote lateral vision and parallel thinking. The exile has to think himself out of a hole.

In the beginning there is the hearth, the ancestral fire, and you are a native of the flames. You belong there and therefore it belongs to you. Then comes exile, the break, the destitution, the initiation, the maiming, which —I think—gives access to a deeper sight, provides a path into consciousness through the mimicry of thinking yourself part of your host environment. Now you can never again entirely relax the belly muscles. You learn, if you're lucky, the chameleon art of adaptation, and how to modulate your laughter. You learn to use your lips properly. Henceforth you are at home nowhere, and by that token everywhere. You learn to live with the flies, and how to slide from death into dream. You learn about creation—because you must compensate—and thus transformation and metamorphosis, although you also come to realize that creation may be only a reordering of existing images.

You husband your weaknesses: These are the souvenirs of your native land. You make sure that you are tougher than "they" are, or you damn well learn how to pretend to be. You never quite master the mysteries of financial transactions. When you are down and out, or when your clothes are not presentable, you keep out of sight. You demand to be treated respectfully; your edges become sharper and your paranoia more acute. In fact, your evaluation of dignity becomes a taut string. You are invited to New York for a conference? Insist upon being put up in the best hotel!

You end up speaking all languages with an accent, even the distant one of your youth, the one you kept for love and anger. You have acquired the knack of fitting in pretty well with any society—you do a good impersonation of the cosmopolitan—but in fact you probably never really penetrate beneath the surface concerns of those around you. You are engaged with an elsewhere that cannot be reached: Isn't that the defining characteristic of exile?

The exiled person is probably marked by a loss that he or she doesn't want to let go of, especially when occasioned by a political situation. But it goes without saying that one can replace, to all intents and purposes, the word "exile" with refugee, misfit, outcast, outsider, expatriate, squatter, foreigner, clandestine, heretic, stranger, renegade, drifter, displaced person, marginal one, the new poor, the economically weak, the dropout. The irony is that if we were to add up all these individuals we'd probably find ourselves constituting a new silent majority!

I dislike the manner in which the subject of exile has been romanticized, with the exiled ones pitied and slobbered over by voyeurs. I abhor feeding the stereotyped expectations of exile as a state of suffering and deprivation. Those who claim to be exiles themselves only too often reinforce the hackneyed perceptions. "Do feel sorry for us," they seem to say. "Blame us on history. Take on the responsibility for our survival." And for too many refugees this condition becomes an easy pretext for milking the sentiments of their hosts. They wallow in self-pity. All experience becomes frozen. On auspicious occasions they bring forth the relics and sing the cracked songs and end up arguing about what "back home" was really like. They are dead survivors waiting for postcards from the realm of the living. The clock has stopped once and for all, the cuckoo suffocated on some unintelligible Swiss sound, and they will continue forever in terms of an absence that, naturally, is now embalmed and imbued with rosy dreams. They lose the language but refuse to integrate the loss, and accordingly will think less, with fewer words and only morbid references from which to suspend their thoughts. They still assume it is possible to hold back the shifting dunes of time. In the meantime, the condition of exile becomes a privileged status from which to morally and emotionally blackmail the world with special pleading. It becomes an excuse for defeat. A meal ticket.

And yet—isn't it true as well that exile is a chance, a break, an escape, a challenge? The courage and the perseverance, the futile quest for survival by these stowaways, wetbacks, throwbacks, and other illegal humans, always astonish me: Tamils with false passports sneaking over the border, Angolans surfacing in Berlin from some "underground railway," Ghanaians passing themselves off as citizens from Zaire or the Ivory Coast, whole families crammed into one room, boat people working like beavers to build dams for a future generation. And nearly always they are starving themselves to help provide for more unfortunate relatives back home.

How resilient they are! See them come to terms with the writ of the rat. See how quickly they pick up the art of negotiating the labyrinths of Administration and Order, how rapidly they snick their tongues around the foreign language, how keen they are to learn! Along the beaches of Europe, on the squares of its cities, you come across the young men from Mali tirelessly unrolling their bundles of African knick-knacks made in Hong Kong, the bangles and the beads and the imitation effigies. They peddle the instantly discardable. They squint at the gray skies and wind up plastic doves, which they throw in the air to flutter and fall. Somehow they survive. Have you noticed the pride and joy when these people manage to afford that first new dress or leather jacket?

History has produced many forgeries, but here—in the seams and folds of adaptation, where history is meandering along many obscure paths into deeper dimensions—the new nomadic man of the future is being forged. To be exiled is to weave in and out of history the way a Charlie Parker or a Sonny Rollins gives a solo edge to a body of sound.

Indeed, the experiences and products of exile could be a dissolvent of border consciousness. It could be a way of reconnoitering, shifting and extending the limits. Somebody will remember having seen on a wall the faded subversive message: *Africa Lives!* In your place of exile you would have introduced a dissonance, a feeling of the texture of awareness. Now, as you return to the past paradise, to your native land (let us imagine it to be South Africa), it may be with scars, but it will also be with precious gifts: the dip and veer of swallows at nightfall over the Niger River, the depth of the seeing without judging in an old man's eyes, the fly-embroidered smile of a child, the musky woman-smell of the loquat flower. Exile teaches you about individual fate with universal implications, because it is eternal and has always been with us: We are all dimly aware of our incompleteness, of the thick veils in which we are draped.

A Letter from Exile

In Protest to a French Friend Who Had Termed Life in Italy an "Exile"

Petrarch

NOW YOU CALL LIFE in Italy a wretched exile, whereas in fact anything outside of Italy might better seem an exile were it not that a strong man's fatherland is everywhere. Hold still while I tell you; your Paris Petit-Pont and its tortoise-shell arch have impressed you too deeply; the murmur of the Seine flowing beneath has too much tickled your ears; too much Gallic dust has settled on your boots. I think you have forgotten the man who, when asked his home, replied: "the world." You are so thoroughly French that you call it exile to overpass the limits of France for any reason whatever. I don't deny that the sweetness of the fatherland is something planted deep in our minds. I know that the very greatest men have been conscious of this affection. I remember in Livy's history that Camillus, the restorer of Rome and its rule, and the equal of its greatest leaders, when in exile at Ardea was moved by memory of his native skies and confessed his homesickness. I remember that Diomedes in Virgil blamed the jealousy of the gods for preventing him from seeing again his Calydon. I can hear Ovid lamenting his absence from Rome, not in a few words but throughout an entire volume. Finally I recollect Cicero bearing his banishment so weakly that the mind of Cicero seems to have lost all its Ciceronian eloquence. But though I know all this and more too, I regard it as petty and mean-minded not to cast off one's shackles without good cause, and to stand upright and subordinate the pleasure of the eyes to manly virtue, which is the pleasure of the mind. A vast number of Roman and other generals and philosophers, whether to gain glory in war or in intellectual achievement, have spent their lives in perpetual wanderings. . . .

To return to your "exile" [Cardinal Gui de Boulogne], about whom you are so worried and anxious, I wish you could see him, more august than ever, advancing starry-eyed among the cities of Italy. You will see a concourse of princes and people assembled to do him honor; you will hear everywhere happy voices raised in cheers and applause. You will be ashamed of your own weak appreciation; you will name your "exile" more properly the author of peace and tranquillity, the savior of the republic. . . .

If indeed experience teaches us, if she is the mother of the arts, what praiseworthy artistic achievement can he hope for who spends his life guarding the house of his fathers? It is a peasant virtue to stay in one's own fields, to know the qualities of one's own soil and cattle, the waters and the trees, and the sowing seasons and rakes and grub-hoes and plows. But it is the mark of a noble, an aspiring mind that one has seen many lands and the customs of many peoples and has reflected on his observations. What you have read in Apuleius is very true. He says: "The divine originator of ancient poetry among the Greeks, wishing to present a man of the utmost wisdom, very justly sang of one who had profited by the vicissitudes of many states and peoples." Our great poet, imitating him, led his Aeneas through numberless cities and shores.

And now you, the one real poet of France, use this Ulysses, this Aeneas of yours as a literary subject to exercise your wit, and you pity him because he has seen something besides your Paris! And you don't realize what a welcome experience it would be, it will be, for him to see with his own eyes what he has already looked upon in his imagination! We have been told the habit of Emperor Hadrian; whatever remarkable places he learned about in his reading or by report, he insisted very eagerly on seeing with his own eyes, and he was not deterred by all the burdens of imperial rule. And as Cicero says in his Tusculan Disputations, if those think they have done something who have seen the outlet of the Black Sea and the straits by which passed the Argo (so called because the picked Argives in her sought the golden fleece), or who have seen the seas where "the cruel wave divides Europe from Libya," what must they think of the feats of Hannibal? Your master, on his travels, saw the Alpine passes, cleared by Carthaginian flames and by vinegar. He measured with his eye the broad, smiling fields of Northern Italy. He saw Milan, that splendid city, founded by your ancestors, and, according to written records, flourishing through so many centuries. He looked on lovely Brescia and Verona, noblest work of men, with Lake Garda, noblest work of nature, lying between. Then he visited Padua, founded by the Trojan Antenor, then Venice, that great, beautiful, most marvelous of all seaboard cities. Then little Treviso, ringed with rivers, the happy center of all summer sports. There he established his headquarters, regarding not so much his own convenience as that of his foreign neighbors, and finding there much delight.

Then to Aquileia, to repress the uprisings to the north. He crossed the Noric Alps, ranged far and wide in the German country, reached the Danube, once, like the Nile, a boundary of the Empire, proud with its thousand springs and swirling with horrible whirlpools. Returning thence loaded with honors, he has now watched the translation of the body of Saint Anthony, called the Less, with the devotion of an immense throng; that no doubt is the reason for his long delay in Padua. Tomorrow he will resume his journeys. As he has seen the stormy Adriatic, he will look on the tempests of the Tyrrhenian Sea. He will cross the Po, king of rivers—with all due respect to the Seine. He will visit Ravenna, most ancient of cities, as they claim. Then Rimini and Perugia, that mighty stronghold, and others on the way. So at last he will come to Rome, the head, the mistress of all. Whoever has not seen her rashly admires any other city.

The fortune of the Roman people disposed that the very aspect of their city should be most beautiful; now the Jubilee year will make it more salutary than ever. He whom you call an exile will seem to me a blest and happy pilgrim. He will cross the thresholds of the Apostles and will tread on soil red with the sacred blood of martyrs; he will see the Holy Face of Our Lord, imprinted on St. Veronica's kerchief and portrayed on the walls of churches dedicated to his Mother. He will see where Christ appeared to St. Peter in flight, and will see his footprints in perdurable stone, ever to be adored by all peoples. He will enter the Sancta Sanctorum, filled with celestial grace. He will explore the Vatican hill and the cave heaped with the blessed bones of St. Calixtus. He will gaze on the cradle and the relic of Our Savior's circumcision and the vial of the Virgin's milk, marvelously white. He will see St. Agnes's ring and will meditate on the miracle of the extinction of her outrager's lust. He will contemplate the lopped head of John the Baptist, and St. Lawrence's grill, and the assembled relics of St. Stephen, brought here so that they may lie contentedly together. He will see where St. Peter died on the cross; where springs of fresh water burst forth when St. Paul's blood was shed; where, at the birth of Christ, a fountain of oil flowed down to the Tiber; where the foundations of a splendid church were laid at the indication of a midsummer snowfall; where, at the Virgin's childbearing, a mighty heathen temple collapsed; where Simon [the Magician], falling from heaven, left his shameful imprint on an innocent stone. And he will be shown the hiding place of St. Silvester, and the place of Constantine's vision and of the divinely-dictated cure of his incurable disease, and innumerable things besides. Some part of them I myself once treated in two long letters to a friend, not exhausting them even then.

But if he should turn his attention from celestial to earthly matters, he will see the palaces stupendous, even in ruins, of Roman leaders and princes, those of the Fabii, the Scipiones, the Caesars, and remains beyond all measure or number. He will gaze in wonder at the seven hills enclosed within a single wall, once supreme over all lands, seas, and mountains; and the broad streets, all too narrow for the hordes of captives. He will look up at the triumphal arches, once loaded with the spoils of subjugated kings and peoples. He will ascend the Capitoline hill, the world's head, the citadel of all lands, where aforetime was Jove's seat, where now stands the *Ara Coeli.* There, they say, the infant Christ was displayed to Caesar Augustus. All this he will see; meanwhile, you will extend your regard from the playing fields of St-Germain to the hill of Ste-Geneviève, and you will think you have seen all that the sun illumines from his rising to his setting. You will be happy in your own conceit, if true happiness can reside in error.

Well, to complete the story, your master has in mind to inspect the Etruscan cities on leaving Rome. He will see Viterbo lying in its green valley, surrounded by springs both warm and cool; and Orvieto, ancient in name, new in its recent splendid structures, sitting at the summit of its high cliff-walls. And Siena, emulous of Rome with its seven hills and its nursing she-wolf. I doubt if any other city rises more beautifully aloft—and I doubt if any beauty of French cities outdoes hers. Next, Florence, the work of Roman rulers. Of her I shall say nothing now, for fear that patriotism may render me suspect to you, or you to me. Then he plans to cross again the Appenines, and, passing through studious Bologna, to return again here to Padua, to attend as Legate a solemn council of all the prelates. So he will at length revisit Milan, and turning to the left will cross the Appenines a third time, and will see Genoa—well worth a visit, for no city is more noble in spirit; none can be more truly called a city of kings, if only it could attain civic peace. Then he will pass along the Ligurian Riviera, sunniest of lands, among groves of cedar and palm, past odoriferous and wave-resounding beaches to the frontier of Italy, and so again to France.

This travel plan is not that of a man in a hurry, or of one who is readily bored. You see how his course twists like that of the Meander River, that his advent may bring joy to many places, that his own well-furnished mind may take pleasure in the most varied sights and scenes. Thus your exile has much cause for rejoicing. He has seen many great and memorable things; and everywhere his presence has exalted his reputation—whereas usually the contrary takes place. And Italy has reason to rejoice, for he has come like a benignant star to pierce the dark clouds of the present and bring her peace. For though she was always, as you know, the most acclaimed of all lands by universal testimony, she now finds in our own time a greater advocate that she had hoped for. For believe me, you will be amazed by his report of his Italian journey.

Translated by Morris Bishop

In Praise of Exile

Leszek Kolakowski

THE FAMILIAR TWENTIETH-CENTURY figure of the "intellectual in exile" can boast an impressive spiritual pedigree, from Anaxagoras, Empedocles, and Ovid, through Dante, Occam, and Hobbes, down to Chopin, Mickiewicz, Herzen, and Victor Hugo. More often than not, however, modern expatriates have been refugees, rather than exiles in the strict sense; usually they were not physically deported from their countries or banished by law; they escaped from political persecution, prison, death, or simply censorship.

This distinction is important insofar as it has had a psychological effect. Many voluntary exiles from tyrannical régimes cannot rid themselves of a feeling of discomfort. They are no longer exposed to the dangers and deprivations that are the daily lot of their friends—or of the entire country with which they identify themselves. A certain ambiguity is therefore unavoidable, and it is impossible to draw up any hard-and-fast rules to distinguish justifiable from unjustifiable self-exile. It is easy to see that nothing would have been gained had Einstein or Thomas Mann remained in Hitler's Germany or had Chagall not left Soviet-ruled Vitebsk. There are, on the other hand, many people living in the Soviet Union or in Poland whom the rulers would love to ship off to a foreign land but who doggedly refuse to move, choosing instead prison, persecution, and misery. Who would dare to say that they are wrong? Solzhenitsyn and Bukovsky had to be handcuffed and kicked out of their country, thus following the sad route of a couple of hundred prominent Russian intellectuals whom the Soviet rulers banished shortly after the Revolution. Many Solidarity leaders were offered freedom at the price of emigration and they refused; some are in jail again; others probably will be soon. Milan Kundera left Czechoslovakia, and Czeslaw Milosz left Poland, and they made of their experiences major works of modern literature; Havel has stayed in his land, and so has Herbert; and we owe a lot to all of them. *Doktor Faustus* and Nabokov's novels are fruits of emigration, as are the works of Conrad, Ionesco, and Koestler, yet *Gulag Archipelago* could not have been produced by an exile. No universal standards can be devised to decide in what condition self-exile, if practicable at all, is preferable.

When we speak of an "intellectual in exile" we almost automatically think of an escapee from such or another form of tyranny and thus assume that exile—even a forcible one—is in some important respects preferable to or better than the alternative. Russia's speciality (arising from her sheer size) is internal exile, which gives people the worst of both worlds: emigration from their homeland together with the same repressive régime as before (here, as everywhere, there are degrees of misery, of course: just compare the exile of Pushkin in Crimea and Odessa with that of Sakharov in Gorky). Leaving this aside, the advantages of exile (freedom) as well as its miseries (uprootedness, intractable difficulties with foreign tongues, etc.) are obvious. Not so obvious is the answer to the question whether exile is merely a lesser evil, or whether it offers privileges unknown to those who are securely settled on their native soil.

We can look for an answer in the vicissitudes of the most experienced exiles, exiles par excellence, the Jews. As long as they lived in ghettos, protecting their identity by an impenetrable shell of highly complicated rituals and taboos (perhaps the very complexity of their law made their survival possible: a pious man could not live among the Gentiles and observe all his customs, the very number of which compelled Jews to live together and prevented them from dissolving in the Christian environment), they might have produced outstanding Talmudists and commentators, but their cultural life was necessarily self-contained. Geographically they lived for generations as expatriates, but they were by no means aliens in ghettos; they kept sheltering tenaciously in heart and mind the lost imaginary fatherland, more or less indifferent to the Gentile cultural world; to a pious Hassid it did not matter much, in cultural terms, whether he lived in Warsaw, Shanghai, or Buenos Aires; he carried the deposit of faith, and to be a guardian of this deposit was enough to sustain his mental life. Once the walls of ghettos began to crumble with the so-called emancipation (one needs to be aware of dubious aspects of this value-loaded word), the Jews invaded the spiritual space of Europe in an astonishingly rapid and powerful march. Some of them, like Marx, Freud, and Einstein, were to become real world-conquerors; thousands found their place in the élites of all realms of civilization—the sciences, arts, humanities, and politics. It was only by, as it were, exiling themselves from their collective exile that they became exiles in the modern sense. However hard they might have tried, they failed (at least most of them) to lose entirely their identity of old and to be unreservedly assimilated; they were looked upon as alien bodies by the indigenous tribes, and it was probably this uncertain status, the lack of a well-defined identity, which enabled them to see more and to question more than those who were satisfied with their inherited and natural sense of belonging. One is even tempted to say that it was the anti-Semites (as long as they did not express their ideas in terms of gas chambers) who were to a large extent responsible for the extraordinary achievements of the Jews, precisely because by barring to them the path to the moral and intellectual safety of the tribal life—whether French, Polish, Russian or German—they left them in the privileged position of outsiders.

That the position of an outsider offers a cognitive privilege is well known and unquestionable. A tourist often sees things which a native does not notice, as they have become a natural part of his life (one thinks of a tourist in America named Alexis de Tocqueville). For the peoples of the Book, both Jews and Christians, exile is, of course, the normal and inescapable lot of mankind on earth. One can go further and say that the myth of exile, in one form or another, lies at the core of all religions, of any genuine religious experience. The fundamental message embedded in religious worship is: our home is elsewhere. We know, however, at least two radically different practical interpretations of this message. There is the contempt of earthly realities and eventually of life itself, which can offer nothing but misery and suffering—this is the conclusion which Buddhist wisdom often endorses. And there is also the notion that exile provides the human race with a great opportunity to be exploited on its way back to the Father—this interpretation prevails in the mainstream of Judaeo-Christian civilization. A global scorn for matter, for the body, for terrestrial values, was a marginal phenomenon in Christian history. The kernel of the concept of Christian life may be summed up thus: we live in exile and we must never forget it; therefore all the temporal goods and goals have to be seen as relative and subordinate; they are real all the same, and our natural duty is to use them; Nature is an adversary to be conquered, not to be denied.

Suppose that the theologians are right and that our progenitors in Eden would have acquired the knowledge of carnal love and produced offspring even if they had resisted temptation and remained blissfully unaware of Good and Evil. They would nonetheless never have originated mankind as we know it—a race capable of creating. It was the *felix culpa* and the subsequent exile, including its miseries and risks, that tore them out of their celestial safety, exposed them to evil, danger, struggles, and suffering and thus laid the necessary condition of human existence. Creativity arose from insecurity, from an exile of a sort, from the experience of homelessness.

Philosophy can simply deny the fact of exile or rather, as Christians would contend, conceal it from us—this is what the adherents of empiricism, naturalism, materialism, and scientism used to do. It can accept the fact and try to show a path of return to an ultimate reconciliation of man with Being—this is the Hegelian approach. Or it can accept the fact but deny that our condition is curable, thereby condemning us to a never-ending nostalgia for the nonexistent paradise; the existential philosophy of our century was most successful in expressing this gloomy insight, thus exposing the bitter harvest of the Enlightenment.

The Christian notion of the first exile can be enlarged and applied to the second one—that is, the exile from exile—and the third, and the fourth. (It is arguable, for instance, that Spinoza was a quadruple exile, being excommunicated from the Jewish community which established itself in Amsterdam after the expulsion from Portugal, where they had lived as exiles from the Eretz given them by God as a place of exile from Eden.) Any exile can be seen either as a misfortune or as a challenge; it can become no more than a reason for despondency and sorrow or a source of a painful encouragement. We can use a foreign tongue simply because we have to, or try to discover in it linguistic treasures which are unique to it, untranslatable, and which therefore enrich our mind, not only our technical ability to communicate. We can confront the perspective of an alien with that of a native and thus sow an alarming mental discomfort which frequently turns out to be productive and mutually beneficial. The examples abound throughout modern history. I am not aware of any study specifically examining the cultural role of various forms of exile, individual and collective, in the history of Europe. There is no doubt, however, that without so many religiously or politically motivated expulsions and self-expulsions, without all those wanderers and refugees, European intellectual and artistic life would be much different from what it is. One thinks of Huguenots in England and Holland; of Italian Christian radicals and Unitarians looking for shelter in the (then very tolerant) Poland of the second half of the sixteenth century; of Polish Unitarians in Western Europe in the second half of the seventeenth century, promoters of the early Enlightenment; of Jews expelled from Iberic countries; of refugees from communist-ruled Central and Eastern Europe. All of them contributed, sometimes dramatically, to the civilizations of the host lands, much as they might have been occasionally less than welcome and greeted with suspicion. Emigrés from the Third Reich made an enormous impact on American intellectual life (some say it was a nefarious impact, but who knows the ultimate balance?).

We have to accept, however reluctantly, the simple fact that we live in an age of refugees, of migrants, vagrants, nomads roaming about the continents and warming their souls with the memory of their—spiritual or ethnic, divine or geographical, real or imaginary—homes. A total homelessness is unbearable; it would amount to a complete break with human existence. Is a perfect cosmopolitanism possible? Diogenes Laertius reports that Anaxagoras, when asked if he did not care about his motherland, replied that he did care very much indeed and pointed at the sky. Some people today make similar claims, denying any partial interest in, or special loyalty to, their original tribal community; to what extent this claim may be made in good faith is debatable.

Aside from individuals who have either escaped tyranny or been driven away from their land, there are entire nations whose people, without moving from native soil, have been robbed of their right to be citizens of their motherland, while being citizens of the State, because their country itself is under foreign rule; this is the destiny—temporary, let us hope—of Central and East European nations. The split between the State, which people feel is not theirs, though it claims to be their owner, and the motherland, of which they are guardians, has reduced them to an ambiguous status of half-exiles. The ambition of the unsovereign State is to rob its subjects of their historical memory by distorting and falsifying it according to actual political requirements. And the collective memory is ultimately the motherland. One half of Europe having been thus uprooted, what can the other half expect? Is the entire world going to be driven into an internal half-exile? Does God try to remind us, somewhat brutally, that exile is the permanent human condition? A ruthless reminder, indeed, even if deserved.

One True Sentence

Fernando Alegría

WHEN I LEFT MY homeland on September 23, 1973, there was no time to go out on the balcony and look at the white mountain range, the dove-like image of the Virgin on the San Cristobal hill, the dusty treetops of the Parque Forestal; to sigh and silently wonder what fate held in store for me. One had to leave quickly, quietly, without looking back, wrapped in a scarf, if possible without showing one's face. A few days later I wrote an article for the magazine *Ramparts*: "The Battle of Santiago." I told what I had witnessed.

The truth is that for me, an ordinary man, an exile was beginning which is characteristic of our time—that expatriate existence no longer associated with any single country, time or place: a condition of homelessness among other homeless people. An exile without peace, charged like a dark storm, set in no-man's-land.

So I did what everybody does: I told my story, avoiding exaggeration, muting it in the somewhat musical and poetic language I brought with me from Chile, using the minor keys and matter-of-fact tone of the man who, having survived an earthquake, sips his tea, neither complaining nor protesting very much, just talking. The first months of numbness, pain and depression passed. So did the undeniably moving, useful and yet destructive period of bearing witness before the world. I realized that a new phase of exile was beginning, that from now on there would be other periods, all different, each with its own anxieties, all shattering and overwhelming, and that I would be changing too, passing from one crisis to the next until I reached the moment of truth, unique and definitive—the day on which I would either stop being an exile and return home, or unavoidably, with sadness and resignation, become an immigrant.

As a result of my article for *Ramparts*, I received a letter from a New York publisher asking me if I would be interested in writing a book elaborating on the experiences I described in "The Battle of Santiago." Interested! Of course I was interested. But, and this fell on me like a bucket of cold water, I would have to give him the manuscript within two months. As a matter of fact, I did write that book—not for him, of course: it took me two years, plus another year looking for a publisher. How many Chilean writers must have been faced with the same problem? Exile offers opportunities that are great but fleeting. In Chile, our writers generally did not lack the support of publishers. Nascimento, Editorial Universitaria, and Zig-Zag kept their doors open to established writers, and occasionally dared to publish the work of novices. The university presses of Valparaíso, Concepción, Valdivia and Antofagosta encouraged new talent. With the help of literary circles and prizes, an unpublished writer could get started. Quimantú, the press of the Unidad Popular government, published Chilean writers in huge printings. This beneficial policy resulted in a dangerous inbreeding. The Chilean writer, profusely published in his own country, was condemned to purely local distribution. Abroad, he was unknown. Now in exile, this same author approaches Mexican, Spanish or Venezuelan publishers—Argentina doesn't count because of the political situation—and if they don't slam the door in his face they nearly smash his fingers in it. There are some Chilean writers who have spent most of their seven years of exile warming over unpublished manuscripts. The more fortunate succeed in getting their novels or poems back-logged by an important publisher, waiting their turn, which will come sometime after the turn of the century. How can they get by? By publishing in magazines? It's not enough. Some, enterprising and spirited, join forces and launch their own publishing houses: in Ottawa, Winnipeg, Los Angeles, Madrid, Paris and Mexico City. Heroic presses-in-exile, they bring out their books, like poor relatives, a modest coarseness showing in their basic colors, rough paper and artless binding. The distribution is minimal, but it counts. These are books with an assured destination: libraries and universities take them; they race toward Chile, enter with false covers, and pass from hand to hand. They are read and hoarded. They fulfill their purpose. The exiled author who has found a refuge in prestigious international universities and institutes can, of course, count on a certain distribution. Nevertheless, some enterprises born of difficult circumstances eventually become established, living on to flourish later in times of peace; it might be worthwhile for us, Latin American writers scattered throughout the world, to consider a Press-in-Exile, a joint, combative effort in which all of us, young and old, without exception, could take part, for the duration of our wait, which may be long.

In a contradictory way, the first phase of exile equalizes us; we all fall into the same pattern of criticizing, yearning, wandering in anguish: we all wish we could miraculously shed some light on what our particular nation means to each of us. But it happens that, unlike the "elitist" expatriates of times gone by, we share our exile with thousands of laborers and peasants, office workers and professionals, Chileans who show us with their presence and the depth and complexity of their experience, that we, as writers and artists, are in reality nothing special, nothing out of the ordinary; on the contrary, we are part of the common run of humanity—helpless, useless, subject to all kinds of depression from metaphysical to economic, as well as to wishful-thinking and militant or extremist euphoria. Beings who have been living on dreams, where dreams were not enough, we are now confronted by people who firmly put us in our place. And rightly so.

It seems to me that only an exile who intends to return has a true exile's consciousness. There is no exile without the intention to go back. For this reason, those who feel most keenly the uprootedness of exile are the workers who will never "adapt" to their situation, those laborers and their families who will live for years, perhaps all their lives, with their bags packed, awaiting the moment of return. The Latin American intellectual grows in his profession, opposing and fighting the system, but also using it to gain respectability in his protest. Wherever he goes there will always be an establishment to rebel against and in which to succeed, or seem to succeed—to be celebrated, admired and rewarded to the extent that he excels in making his protest and uses his alienation effectively and imaginatively. It is among intellectuals, naturally, that the complete break and permanent exile most frequently occur. The boundaries have fallen, the frontiers vanished, says the man who believes himself a citizen of the world as he recognizes in exile the same alienation he brought from home. For our workers and professionals the struggle is not metaphorical—it takes its toll in the physical and moral wear and tear of expatriate life: their only hope is the road that leads directly back to Chile, to confrontation or resistance. They have been exiled as families, and with their families they will sink or swim. It's true that the children will learn a new language and forget the old one. The adults are forgetting too, but they will never learn the art of replacing what they forget with something else.

It is possible to become a professional exile. I can understand this now. And I don't necessarily mean an immigrant. Such a man or woman would have learned a difficult formula for constantly taking leave, and would offend those who want to make themselves personally responsible for the so-called social ills. It probably isn't exile that they get used to so much as a daily, individual, untransferable delirium. For them, the boundaries that people normally use to differentiate between specific and general realities disappear. That is, they would make no effort to recognize individual cases; though they would continue dealing with others, it would be done according to their own standards, not to control the delirium or the delirious, just to give them substance with no particular significance.

Nevertheless, I believe that all of us, intellectuals as well as workers, have learned to recognize during these years one thing that should be emphasized: the true extent of international solidarity. For those of us who are not professional politicians this means that living in a genuine revolutionary internationalism we have learned to make some concessions to reality within the exaggerated dreams of our poor, small and suffering land, to see the ephemeral, and therefore hollow and false, adornments of our literary pretensions, to accept the lessons of exile as a stage in our intellectual and professional growth which will enrich the experience of our return.

We lived through a time, those years of militant though disorderly politics when we were students, during which a form of exile could have attracted us. Without bitterness, on the contrary, with enterprising enthusiasm, we could have said then, along with Santayana:

> The times also were moving, rapidly and exultingly, towards what for me was chaos and universal triviality. At first these discords sounded like distant thunder. Externally they were not yet violent; the world smiled in my eyes as I came to manhood, and the beauties and dignity of the past made the present unimportant. And as the feeling of being a stranger and an exile by nature as well as by accident grew upon me in time, it came to be almost a point of pride.

For us, as novice writers, the euphoria of the popular triumph of 1938 came to heal the wounds left by the defeat of the Spanish Republic. We had a free rein and could begin with a mandate, carried along by the strength of that emancipating movement, both in acts of collective creativity—such as the Teatro Experimental de la Universidad de Chile—and in individual ventures: our first books. The 1970 victory of the Unidad Popular found us in a similar situation. It is important to point out that in that Chile, divided almost equally in half, the writers who identified with Allende immediately entered government service, either at home or abroad. We all know that the 1000 days of Allende produced no distinct literature. There was singing, of course, as well as film and theater, but there was no substantial narrative between 1970 and 1973. It was not until after the military coup that Chilean literature let loose, with its batteries overcharged; it came out angry, tormented, looking anxiously, too anxiously perhaps, for a way to confer aesthetic dignity on something which could, if one were not careful, be reduced to a mere explosion of sentimentality.

The testimonial unleashing of those days produced at least three works of great merit: *Cerco de Púas* (Barbed Wire Fence) by Aníbal Quijada Cerda, *Tejas Verdes* (Green Tiles) by Hernán Valdés, and *Reportaje en el Frente Chileno* (Report from the Chilean Front) by Ilario Da, as well as some four or five novels which, wisely keeping their distance, from an angle that allows them to absorb the blow and at the same time judge its consequences, took the first step toward a literature of resistance rather than a mere catharsis.

How could people like Guillermo Atías, for instance, write and publish novels? I know that Atías had to struggle to earn a living in his exile in Paris, and I mention his case because it is typical. Chilean writers have had to accept positions at unrelated jobs and obscure universities, make up scripts for television, radio, film and musical comedies, translate for international publishers or organizations and, at the same time, contribute enthusiastically and with a clear sense of self-criticism to the cause of solidarity with the Chilean people. All this can be described with a splendid word I have already used: resistance.

No one that I know of has broken. Some of our finest have died—Enrique Bello, Lira Massi, Guillermo Atías, Hernán Ramírez Necochea—but they did not give in: they resisted magnificently to the end.

This literary movement has achieved quality and historical status in theatrical groups in Caracas, Costa Rica and Madrid; in journals from France, Spain, Canada and California; in publishing enterprises, centers and groups in Berkeley, Ottawa, Toronto, New York, Paris and Mexico City. At this moment, I know of five works in preparation on the history of the Chilean literature of exile.

The moment of truth seems to have arrived. What is our writer to do when the anecdotal quality of the military coup runs out? When the emotional charge of the defeat doesn't work any more and diatribe no longer finds an echo? Learn the lesson? We will not forget it: making our individual, parochial voices heard and understood in exile almost always means suppressing sentimentality and wise-cracking, editing out the easy lament and beginning to speak firmly. Hemingway tells in the memoirs of exile of his lost generation that when he didn't know how to start the daily routine of his task as a writer, lacking words but full of some formless thing that needed expression, he would write "one true sentence" and after that the rest would flow like a river. One true sentence. Yes. Never a filler, nor a rhetorical flourish, no matter how successful they might be with our friends: simply a sentence that plainly tells the situation that at this moment keeps us going, or not; the recognition of our distance as well as of the solidarity that renews us at each step; the memory of some defeat that is becoming blurred; and the vision of a morning, not far off, that will surprise us at the day's task, finally writing something else, something true. For example: "the return has begun" or "the dictatorship has fallen."

Translated by Kathleen McNerney

To a Young Exile

Plutarch

ASSUME THAT EXILE is a calamity, as the multitude declare in speech and song. So too, many foods are bitter and pungent and irritate the taste; but by combining with them certain sweet and pleasant ingredients we get rid of the disagreeable savour. There are colours too, painful to the sight, and when confronted with them our vision is blurred and dazzled by their harshness and unrelieved intensity. Now if we have found that we could remedy this inconvenience by mingling shadow with them or turning our eyes aside and resting them upon something of a greenish and pleasant shade, the same can be done with misfortunes as well: they can be blended with whatever is useful and comforting in your present circumstances: wealth, friends, freedom from politics, and lack of none of the necessities of life. For I fancy that there are not many Sardians who would not prefer your circumstances, even with exile thrown in, and be content to live on such terms in a foreign land, rather than, like snails, which are of a piece with their shells but enjoy no other blessing, maintain a painless connexion with their homes.

As, then, in the comedy a character who is urging an unfortunate friend to take heart and make a stand against Fortune, when asked, "How?" replies, "like a philosopher," so let us too make a stand against her by playing the philosopher worthily. But how are we to face "Zeus when he pours down rain? And how the North Wind?" Why, we look for a fire, a bath-house, a cloak, a roof: in a rainstorm we do not sit idle or lament. You too, then, are as able as any man to revive this chilled portion of your life and restore it to warmth: you need no further resources; it is enough to use wisely those you have. For whereas the cupping-glasses of physicians, by drawing out of the body its most worthless elements, relieve and preserve the rest, lovers of grief and fault-finding, by constantly collecting and counting up what is worst in their lot, and by getting absorbed in their troubles, make even the most useful things in it useless for themselves at the moment when these would naturally afford the greatest help.

If, therefore, we suffer some real and truly painful calamity, we must summon cheerfulness and peace of spirit by drawing upon the store of good still left us, using our own resources to smooth out the roughness of what comes from outside ourselves; but with things which have no evil in their nature, and whose painfulness is wholly and entirely a figment of unfounded opinion, we must act as we do with little children who are frightened by masks: by bringing the masks close and putting them into their hands and turning them about we accustom the child to make light of them; so, by coming to close quarters with these things and applying to them the firm pressure of reason, we must expose their unsoundness, their hollowness, and their theatrical imposture.

Such is your present removal from what you take to be your native land. For by nature there is no such thing as a native land, any more than there is by nature a house or farm or forge or surgery, as Ariston said; but in each case the thing becomes so, or rather is so named and called, with reference to the occupant and user. For man, as Plato says, is "no earthly" or immovable "plant," but a "celestial" one—the head, like a root, keeping the body erect—inverted to point to heaven. Thus Heracles spoke well when he said "an Argive I / or Theban, for I boast no single city; / There is no fort in Greece but is my country"; whereas the saying of Socrates is still better, that he was no Athenian or Greek, but a "Cosmian" (as one might say "Rhodian" or "Corinthian"), because he did not shut himself up within Sunium and Taenarus and Ceraunian mountains. "Seest thou yon boundless aether overhead / That holds the earth within its soft embrace?"

This is the boundary of our native land, and here no one is either exile or foreigner or alien; here are the same fire, water, and air; the same magistrates and procurators and councillors—Sun, Moon, and Morning Star; the same laws for all, decreed by one commandment and one sovereignty—the summer solstice, the winter solstice, the equinox, the Pleiades, Arcturus, the seasons of sowing, the seasons of planting; here one king and ruler, "God, holding the beginning, middle, and end of the universe, proceeds directly, as is his nature, in his circuit; upon him follows Justice, who visits with punishment those that fall short of the divine law," the justice which all of us by nature observe toward all men as our fellow-citizens.

That you do not live in Sardis is nothing; neither do all Athenians live in Collytus, all Corinthians in Craneion, all Laconians in Pitanê. Are those Athenians foreigners and men without a country who removed from Melitê to the region of Diomeia, where they observe both the month Metageitnion and a festival, "the Metageitnia," named for their migration, accepting this change of neighbours in a serene and joyful spirit, and remaining content with their condition? You would not say so. What part, then, of the inhabited world, or of the whole earth, is remote from another, when astronomers teach that in comparison to the universe the earth is a mere point, without extension? But we, when like ants or bees we have been driven out of one anthill or beehive, are dismayed and feel strange, possessing neither the knowledge nor the instruction that would teach us to take and consider the whole world to be our own, as indeed it is. Yet we laugh at the stupidity of the man who asserts that at Athens there is a better moon than at Corinth, although we are in a sense in the same case as he, when, on coming to a foreign land, we fail to recognize the earth, the sea, the air, the sky, as though they were distinct and different from those familiar to us. For nature leaves us free and untrammelled; it is we who bind ourselves, confine ourselves, immure ourselves, herd ourselves into cramped and sordid quarters. And then we scoff at the Persian kings, if in truth, by drinking no water but that of the Choaspes, they turn the rest of the inhabited world for themselves into a waterless waste; but when we move to other lands, in our attachment to the Cephisus and our longing for the Eurotas or Taÿgetus or Parnassus, we make the inhabited world empty of cities for ourselves and unfit for habitation.

The Egyptians indeed, who because of some outburst of anger and severity on the part of their king, were migrating to Ethiopia, replied to those who entreated them to return to their children and wives by pointing with Cynic licence to their private parts and remarking that they would be at no loss for either marriage or children so long as they had these with them. One can, however, with greater decency and decorum, say that wherever a man happens to find a moderate provision for his livelihood, there that man lacks neither city nor hearth nor is an alien. Only he must also have good sense and reason, as a skipper needs an anchor that he may moor in any haven and make use of it. For while loss of wealth cannot easily and quickly be repaired, every city at once becomes a native city to the man who has learned to make use of it and has roots which can live and thrive everywhere and take hold in any region.

Indeed, if you lay aside unfounded opinion and consider the truth, the man who has a single city is a stranger and an alien to all the rest; for it is felt he can neither in decency nor in justice forsake his own city to inhabit another, whether it be obscure, or unhealthy, or a prey to faction and turbulence. But Fortune grants possession of what city he pleases to the man she has deprived of his own. For that excellent precept of the Pythagoreans, "choose the best life, and familiarity will make it pleasant," is here also wise and useful: "choose the best and most pleasant city, and time will make of it your native land"—a native land that does not distract you, is not importunate, does not command: "pay a special levy," "go on an embassy to Rome," "entertain the governor," "undertake a public service at your own expense." For if a person in his senses and not utterly infatuated bears this in mind, he will choose, if exiled, to live even on an island, Gyaros or Cinaros, "rocky, unfit for corn or vine or tree," not downcast or lamenting or uttering the words of the women in Simonides—"The clamour of the blue salt sea / Tossing about me, hems me in"—but he will rather reason as Philip did, who said, on being thrown in wrestling, as he turned about and saw the imprint of his body: "Good God! How small a portion of the earth we hold by nature, yet we covet the whole world!"

You have, I think, seen Naxos, if not, Hyria, which is not far from here; yet Naxos had room for Ephialtes and Otus; Hyria was the habitation of Orion. When Alcmaeon was fleeing before the Eumenides, he settled, as poets tell, on newly hardened silt built up by the Acheloüs; but my conjecture is that he too, fleeing from the tumults, factions, and fiendish legal blackmail of his countrymen, chose to dwell on a small plot unharassed and in peace. Tiberius Caesar passed the last seven years of his life at Capri; and the ruling part of the inhabited world, as if gathered up into a heart, made not the slightest change in its abode for all that time. Yet in his case the cares of state, pouring in upon him and brought in from everywhere, made the island repose not unmixed and not free from storms; whereas the man who finds that by disembarking on a small island he can be rid of no small troubles, is pitiful indeed if he does not recite to himself the words of Pindar and often repeat them as a spell:

> Forgo, my heart, the cypress;
> Forgo the contested land;
> To me but little earth is given, where grows the oak;
> But to my lot has fallen no sorrow, no discord.

Zeno, when he learned that his only remaining ship had been engulfed with its cargo by the sea, exclaimed: "Well done, Fortune! thus to confine me to a threadbare cloak" and a philosopher's life; while a man not wholly infatuated or mad for the mob would not, I think, on being confined to an island, reproach Fortune, but would commend her for taking away from him all his restlessness and aimless roving, wanderings in foreign lands and perils at sea and tumults in the market place, and giving him a life that was settled, leisurely, undistracted, and truly his own, describing with centre and radius a circle containing the necessities that meet his needs.

For what island is there that does not afford a house, a walk, a bath, fish and hares for those who wish to indulge in hunting and sport? And best of all, the quiet for which others thirst, you can repeatedly enjoy. But at home, as men play at draughts and retire from the public eye, informers and busybodies track them down and hunt them out of their suburban estates and parks and bring them back by force to the market place and court; whereas it is not the persons who plague us, who come to beg or borrow money, to entreat us to go surety for them or help in canvassing an election, that sail to an island, it is the best of our connexions and intimates that do so out of friendship and affection, while the rest of life, if one desires leisure and has learned to use it, is left inviolate and sacred. He that calls those persons happy who run about in the world outside and use up most of their lives at inns and ferry-stations is like the man who fancies that the planets enjoy greater felicity than the fixed stars. And yet each planet, revolving in a single sphere, as on an island, preserves its station; for "the Sun will not transgress his bounds," says Heracleitus; "else the Erinyes, ministers of Justice, will find him out."

But, my dear friend, let us address the preceding remarks and the like and repeat them as a spell to those others who have been banished to an island and are cut off from the rest of the world by "the grey salt sea, that bars the way to many / Against their will." For you, to whom one solitary spot is not appointed, but forbidden, the exclusion from one city is the freedom to choose from all. Further, set off against the consideration "I do not hold office or sit in the council or preside at games" the other consideration: "I am not involved in faction; I am not exhausting my fortune; I wait upon no governor; I care not now who has obtained the province, whether he is quick to anger or in other ways oppressive." Intent upon one part of exile, lack of fame, we overlook its lack of politics, its leisure, and its freedom. Yet the kings of the Persians were called happy for spending the winter in Babylon, the summer in Media, and the most pleasant part of spring in Susa. Surely the exile too is free to sojourn in Eleusis during the Mysteries, to keep holiday in the city at the Dionysia, and to visit Delphi for the Pythian and Corinth for the Isthmian games, if he is fond of spectacles; if not, he has at his command leisure, walking, reading, undisturbed sleep, and what Diogenes expressed when he said: "Aristotle lunches at Philip's pleasure, Diogenes at his own," since no politics or magistrate or governor disrupts the customary tenor of his life.

On this account you will find that few men of the greatest good sense and wisdom have been buried in their own country, and that most of them, under compulsion from no one, weighed anchor of their own accord and found a new haven for their lives, removing some to Athens, some from Athens. For who has pronounced such an encomium on his native land as Euripides?

Where, first, the people are no immigrants
But native to the soil; all other cities,
Disrupted once, as in the game, have been
Pieced out by importation from abroad.
If, madam, you permit a passing boast,
The sky above our land is temperate,
Where neither comes excess of heat nor cold,
And all the fairest fruits of Greece and Asia
With Attica as bait entice we hither.

Yet the writer of these lines went off to Macedonia and spent his remaining years at the court of Archelaüs. Take that spirit of poetry, holy and inspired, "who glorified the Phrygian fray": Homer. What else has made many cities contend for him, but the fact the he eulogizes no single one?

If it is objected that these men went in quest of fame and honours, go to the wise men and to the schools and resorts of wisdom at Athens; pass in review those in the Lyceum, in the Academy; the Porch, the Palladium, the Odeum. If it is the Peripatetic school you favour and admire most, Aristotle was from Stageira, Theophrastus from Eresus, Straton from Lampsacus, Glycon from the Troad, Ariston from Ceos, Critolaüs from Phaselis; if the Stoic, Zeno was from Citium, Cleanthes from Assos, Chrysippus from Soli, Diogenes from Babylon, Antipater from Tarsus, and the Athenian Archedemus removed to the country of the Parthians and left a Stoic succession at Babylon.

Who, then, pursued these men? No one; it was they who pursued peace, which at home is hardly the portion of those who have any fame or power, and thus, while teaching the rest of their doctrines by what they said, teach us this lesson by what they did. So too at present those men who are of most approved and surpassing merit live abroad, not forced to depart, but departing of themselves, and not put to flight, but themselves fleeing the cares, distractions, and press of business that are the product of their native lands. Indeed the Muses, it appears, called exile to their aid in perfecting for the ancients the finest and most esteemed of their writings. When driven from their country, they did not despair or lie prostrate in grief, but put their native abilities to use, accepting their exile as a provision granted by Fortune for this end, an exile that has made them everywhere remembered even in death; while, of those who banished them and triumphed over them in the struggle of factions, not one enjoys at present the slightest recognition.

He, therefore, who thinks that loss of fame is attendant upon exile is ridiculous. What nonsense! Is Diogenes lacking in fame? Why, Alexander, seeing him sitting in the sun, stopped to ask whether he wanted anything; and when Diogenes merely requested him to stand a bit out of his light, the king, struck with such high spirit, said to his friends: "Were I not Alexander, I should be Diogenes." Was Camillus deprived of fame when he was banished from Rome, of which he is now acclaimed the second founder? Indeed, Themistocles after his banishment did not lose his fame among the Greeks, but won new fame among the barbarians; and no one is so indifferent to fame or so ignoble that he would rather have been Leobotes, who brought the indictment, than Themistocles, who was condemned to exile, Clodius the banisher than Cicero the banished, or Aristophon, who made the accusation, than Timotheüs, who withdrew from his native land.

But since many are stirred by the words of Euripides, who is thought to arraign exile very forcibly, let us see what he has to say on the several counts of his indictment, as he presents them in the form of question and answer:

> Jocasta: What is the loss of country? A great ill?
> Polyneices: Surpassing great; no words can do it justice.
> Jocasta: What is it like? What ills beset the banished?
> Polyneices: One greater than the rest: speech is not free.
> Jocasta: That is a slave's part—not to speak one's mind.
> Polyneices: The folly of the mighty must be borne.

These initial assumptions are wrong and untrue. In the first place it is not a slave's part "not to speak one's mind," but that of a man of sense on occasions and in matters that demand silence and restraint of speech, as Euripides himself has elsewhere put it better: "Silence in season, speech where speech is safe."

In the next place we are compelled to bear "the folly of the mighty" no less at home than in exile; indeed, those who remain behind are often in even greater terror of men who wield unjust power in cities through chicanery or violence than those who have taken their departure. But the last and greatest absurdity is that banishment should deprive the exile of free speech: Did Diogenes lack freedom of speech? Did Hannibal the Carthaginian mince his words to Antiochus, an exile to a king, on that occasion when he urged him to seize a favourable chance to attack the enemy? Nay, exile does not even destroy freedom of speech in geometers and grammarians, when they converse about the subjects they know and have been taught; how, then, could exile destroy it in good and worthy men? It is meanness of spirit that everywhere "stops up the voice, ties the tongue, chokes, imposes silence."

What are we to say of the next words of Euripides?

> Jocasta: 'Tis said that exiles live upon their hopes.
> Polyneices: Their eyes hold promise, but they tarry ever.

This too is rather a charge against stupidity than against exile. For it is not those who have learned and know how to put the present to good use, but those who are ever hanging upon the future and longing for what they do not have, that are tossed about on hope as on a raft, though they never go beyond the city wall.

But "exile" is a term of reproach. Yes, among fools, who make terms of abuse out of "pauper," "bald," "short," and indeed "foreigner" and "immigrant." But those who are not carried away by such considerations admire good men, even if they are poor or foreigners or exiles. Nay, do we not observe that, like the Parthenon and the Eleusinium, so the Theseum is saluted with reverence by all? Yet Theseus was banished from Athens, though it is because of him that Athens is now inhabited. Do you not commend Antisthenes' retort to the man who remarked, "Your mother is a Phrygian:" "So too is the Mother of the Gods"? Why then do not you, when "exile" is cast in your teeth, make a similar reply: "So too the father of Heracles the victorious was an exile, so too the grandsire of Dionysus, when sent out to find Europa, like her, did not return."

Now as to the matters at which Aeschylus hinted darkly when he said, "And pure Apollo, god exiled from heaven"—"let my lips," in the words of Herodotus, "be sealed." Empedocles, however, calls himself a "wanderer and exile from heaven." He indicates that not he himself merely, but all of us, beginning with himself, are sojourners here and strangers and exiles. "For," he says, "no commingling of blood or breath, O mortals, gave our souls their being and beginning; it is the body, earth-born and mortal, that has been fashioned out of these," and as the soul has come hither from elsewhere, he euphemistically calls birth a "journey," using the mildest of terms.

But it is truest to say that the soul is an exile and a wanderer, driven forth by divine decrees and laws; and then, as on an island buffeted by the seas, imprisoned within the body "like an oyster in its shell," as Plato says, because it does not remember or recall "what honour and what high felicity" it has left, not leaving Sardis for Athens or Corinth for Lemnos or Scyros, but Heaven and the Moon for earth and life on earth. If it shifts but a short distance here from one spot to another, it is resentful and feels strange, drooping like a base-born plant.

And yet for a plant one region is more favourable than another for thriving and growth, but from a man no place can take away happiness, as none can take away virtue or wisdom. Nay, Anaxagoras in prison was busied with squaring the circle, and Socrates, when he drank the hemlock, engaged in philosophy and invited his companions to do the same, and was by them deemed happy; whereas Phaëthon and Tantalus, as poets tell, when they had ascended to heaven, met with the most grievous disasters through their folly.

Translated by Phillip H. DeLacy and Benedict Einarson

Why Do Americans Live in Europe?

Harry Crosby

Why do you prefer to live outside America?

I prefer to live outside America

1. because in America the *stars* were all suffocated inside
2. because I do not wish to devote myself to perpetual hypocrisy
3. because outside America there is nothing to remind me of my childhood
4. because I prefer perihelion to aphelion
5. because I love flagons of wine
6. because I am an enemy of society and here I can hunt with other enemies of society
7. because I want to be in at the death (of Europe)
8. because I like tumults and chances better than security
9. because I prefer transitional orgasms to atlantic monthlies
10. because I am not coprophagous
11. because I would rather be an eagle gathering sun than a spider gathering poison
12. because by living outside of America New York can still remain for me the City of a Thousand and One Nights
13. because the Rivers of Suicide are more inviting than the Prairies of Prosperity
14. because I prefer explosions to whimperings.

IV
Speaking and Writing

Writers have to have two countries, the one where they belong and the one in which they live really.

—Gertrude Stein
Paris France

Exile

William H. Gass

for Heide Ziegler

LET US BEGIN where we began—in darkness: a darkness in which there was yet no color to the skin, no distinction between thine and mine, no tangle of tongues, no falsely alluring ideas, no worries which might spread like an oil slick over our amniotic ocean; hence no hither and thithering either, no mean emotions, treacheries, promises, prohibitions, no life-long let-downs. We began in a place where darkness really did cover the face of things, and not because the shades were drawn and the lights were out, but because darkness was our ether, and let us sleep. It was a world where *que pasa?* could be honestly answered, *nada.*

What colored this darkness with calamity? We soon grew too big for our boots, our britches, and our own good. So the walls of our world moved against us like a wrestler's hold, squeezing us out as though we were a stool: what a relief for the old walls, loose at last, lax as a popped balloon; but what confusion for us, now overcome by sensation, seared by the light. Some still call it a trauma—birth—and the earliest Greek poets bewailed the day just as the babies themselves bewailed it, explaining that we cried out at the cruelty of being cast into the harsh bright air where perceptions and pain were one, where screaming was breathing.

Before, we had been in nurture and in nature's care, and although poisons may have seeped into us, or our genetic codes been badly garbled, all our exchanges had been innocent and automatic and regular as was our pulse. Now, suddenly, we were in the hands of Man; that is, in the hands of Mom and Dad, proud in their new possession, proud because they have fulfilled their function, happy because they are supposed to be happy, cooing their first coos, which will be our first words—*coup de coude, coup de bec, coup de tete, coup de main, coup d'etat; coup de grace*—while we wonder why we are wet and where the next suck is coming from, or why there is so much noise when we bawl, why we are slapped and shaken, why we are expected to run on empty, and not scream when stuck or cry when chafed, not shit so much, and not want what we want when we want it.

Life is itself exile, and its inevitability does not lessen our grief or alter the fact. It is a blow from which only death will recover us, and when we are told, as we lie dying, that we are going home, we may even be ready to welcome the familiar darkness, the comforting *nada* of the grand old days when days were nothing but nights. Perhaps that is the last lie we shall be told, however, for the advancing darkness is a darkness we shall never even dream in. It will not be the sincere zero of a release after long suffering—a quilt covered quiet, the past recaptured, a womb reoccupied—but the zero with the zero in it. It will not be the Nothing from which nothing comes, but the Nothing that is nothing but its no—and a no, in addition, that is nothing but the pure brief round of its 'o'.

When Adam and Eve were expelled from Paradise, according to the Christian story, death, pain, and labor followed them to serve as punishments for their transgressions—for falling for the first apple that fell in their lap. With an orchard of pears, plums, and cherries to choose from—the Tree of High Times, the vine of Accomplishment, the Hedge of Military Hardware, and the dense Bush of Indecision—what must they do but pick a piece of fruit a worm has recommended. For the Greeks, far wiser in my opinion, life was a sentence, the Denmark that made our world a prison, and the body was the coffin of the soul. That attitude became a poetic tradition, so that centuries after the Greek poets had grumbled that the worst thing that could happen to a man was to be born, while the best was to get to the end as quickly and painlessly as possible, Guillaume Du Bartas was writing:

> You little think that all our life and Age
> Is but an *Exile* and a Pilgrimage.

That things were better for us once upon a time—before the revolt of the Angels (all those puissant legions, Milton wrote, whose exile hath emptied heaven), before the Fall, back in the Golden Age, prior to the Flood, the destruction of the Tower of Babel, when giants walked the earth, when there were real heroes, honest kings, and actual dragons, in any case before we were brought, through birth, into this brutality—is a belief which constantly accompanies us and somehow gives us comfort. The comfort, of course, is in the note of grace it lets us sound: that wretched things will one day be put right, and the wrongs of our distant forefathers finally paid for in full, and death will release us from present pain, and we can go home again to paradise.

We continue to mimic these mythological banishments with ones of our own. The Greeks punished people by driving them out of their cities, by sending them into exile the way unwed former maidens were sent away from the door of their family home—with babe and blanket and much weeping—into the cold and falling snow. Even Hades was considered just another foreign country, a lot like Persia, where the barbarians bowed down to their superiors, sniffing the dust of their lordling's feet.

As we invariably exclaim: how things have changed! A vast reversal of value has taken place. Children wish to leave home and home town, the sooner the better. Down-on-the-farm has been replaced by up-on-the-town. High on the hog is not where we choose to feed but on the shrimp and the sole and the slaw, in our low-cal life, a life through which—in lieu of jig—we jog. Money is our country now. We go where it goes—we followers of the cash flow. There is nothing more seductive than the bottom line. Money makes the world go around, the song says, but the word keeps the wheel of fortune spinning, and that's as warming as the Gulf Stream to us all.

Money. The Japanese make it, Hong Kong smuggles it, Singapore launders it, the Swiss horde it for everybody, the Italians style it, the French flavor it, the Germans mark it, Americans lose it, the English pout, the Russians long, the Chinese make change.

Increasingly, to be exiled means to be sent to a place where you can't conduct any business.

In our brave new world, there isn't a single exciting word that won't fit upon a billboard. Pictures contain our immediate information. We go blank when the screen does. Our previous definition of the human—that we reason; that we reflect upon ourselves; that we make tools; we speak—is in the shop for micro-chip repairs. We are really, when you count performance and tabulate behavior, not super-computers, but a lot like locusts, little chafing dishes maybe, small woks, modest ovens, simple furnaces, barbecue pits and picnic grills: we consume. A universe is burning—a forest for our flame.

We number ourselves now in billions, a profusion so dangerous that were we, all told, to fart in unison, we would windsweep and poison the world; and were one to strike a match to such a methane-colored cloud . . . boom would not be the half of it.

We also live in an age of migration and displacement. Driven by war, disease, or famine, out of fear of genocide or starvation, millions are on the move, by boat, mostly, as it has always been. Not every foot of ocean is under someone's boot. But boot people don't let boat people land. And, as if to balance those who have been thrust out of their country like a dog to do its business, there are an equal number who have been shut up inside it;

who would leave, if they could, in search of freedom, a better living, compatible ideals.

So we have learned to punish people by keeping them home as well as by kicking them out. Yes. Stay home at the range, with mom and dad and their ideas, stay home by the monitored telephone, out of the shops and markets, behind the bamboo, lace, or iron curtain, stay home where home rules rule, and the roost has already got its rooster.

Then, when the walls come tumbling down (as, eventually, they always do), the confined will run away in search of freedom, unaware that they have been sent into exile by circumstances.

We should always allow the Greeks to instruct us. You may remember how the soothsayers came with their worry to the king when Oedipus was barely born and scarcely asleep in his cradle. They foretold what every father fears: your son will succeed you, and enjoy all you now enjoy, and possess the love of your wife in her role as a mother; her breasts will be no longer yours, nor her caresses, nor her looks of love; your son's youthful vigor shall shade you and stunt your growth; and he shall slowly edge you into your grave with the negligent side of his shoe. In heed of these warnings, the babe was taken to the mountains during the night, his ankles pinned the way a skinned kid is trussed for the spit, and there he was abandoned in the belief that the cold wind would freeze his heart, and his lungs would expell his soul with their last outcry of breath; hence no human hand could be blamed by the gods for the child's demise.

Of course the infant is rescued and raised by a shepherd who finds him in among the rocks or under a bush, or by an animal who takes him to her den (the stories vary), and he grows up in increasing puzzlement about his nature, because he doesn't resemble a wolf or a bear, or the parents who adopted him. Twice an exile, first into life, as we all are exiled, then into another country, and now an alien among his so-called kin. Why wasn't he drowned in a butt of malsy, a method favored by the English kings? Or simply swallowed as Saturn swallowed his children, or the whale did Jonah, or Mt. Etna vain Empedocles?

This becomes an important theme. The dead have relatives, sons have mothers, few expungements are really complete. Six million erasures were realized, yet there remained still more Jewish names. The mother arms the swallowed son with a dagger, and there in the darkness of his father's belly, center of his father's powers, he slits his way out while the Titan is asleep, or (the stories vary) the Titan is given an emetic and vomits the gastrically scalded boy, or a stone is substituted for the baby's body (stories vary), and a gluttonous Saturn swallows that. In any case, the saved child seizes a sickle and cuts his father's cock, his father's balls off, and heaves them out an embrasure, over a parapet, across a cliff edge, into the sea. It is an instructive story. More morals than an evangelist's sermon. The Greeks were great educators. Aphrodite, the goddess of love, rose from the ocean in the splash, and, blood borne, rode to shore on a shell formed from the foam of what had fallen. We could go on—it is tempting—but the tale would take us toward another lesson, rather than the one we are intent on now.

Let us move, for a moment, from myth to history. You recall how the friends of Socrates had arranged his escape. Athens had no desire to make a martyr of a man who had practically pushed them into voting his execution. His enemies would be well-satisfied if the troublesome sage would go into exile like his protegé, Alcibiades, and encourage the decay of some other city. Let the gadfly bite another rump. Here was one horse, at least, who was weary of being kept awake. But Socrates declined, nettlesome to the last, claiming, among other things, to be a son of the State, and unable to renounce his parentage. His arguments are interesting, although their reasons are hidden, and one of them can tell us something of what exile is. He claims, of course, to have gotten fair treatment at his trial. All he, or you or I, can correctly ask of the judicial system is that it give us our due, and Socrates felt that he had received it. If the umpire's call goes against him, he can't, then, take himself out of the game in a snit, a game of rules he has accepted, and whose advantages he has enjoyed. Above all, exile is amputation, a mutilation of the self, because the society Socrates lives in is an essential part of his nature, a nature he cannot, now, divide.

In short, Socrates invokes three principles, none precisely put, but each profound: he affirms the importance of due process (which means he places a sound method above any result, however right it might chance to be, if it remains unsubstantiated); he believes in the co-relativity of rights and duties (which means that none is inalienable, but that each right is earned through the discharge of a corresponding and defining obligation); he takes for granted a kind of anatomical connection between individuals and their society (which means that our community is to each of us like a shared arm, and is thus a vital increase of the local self).

We are generally related to other things and persons in one of three ways: instrumentally, as Locke saw us connected, in terms of our interests, so that the State, for example, is seen as a means to the individual happiness of each of its citizens; collectively, as Hegel saw us constituted, in which we are all functional elements contributing to the health of the whole; and, as I shall call it, Socratically, where the community is an essential organ of the self, but not the sum of that self.

Families, societies, governments, are properly dissolved, on the instrumental view, when they fail to serve the interests of their members, just as we would replace a broken drill bit with another, or an incompetent business associate with a go-getter, or a losing football coach with one who will win. Let us suppose I am a bachelor troubled by nerves, acne, and anorexia. Life seems pointless, i.e., without sexual direction. My doctor advises me to marry. "Marriage will clear your complexion, calm your nerves, fatten you up." So I decide to say, "I do," and await the benevolent consequences. After several years, however, my zits return, my nerves refrazz, once again I can't keep my pasta down. Clearly, divorce is indicated.

Under the concept of the collective, on the other hand, individuals can be substituted for others when they fail to perform their function, the way a pitcher is replaced on the mound, because it is the team which will continue (doesn't our Alma Mater?), even though the coach, and those who played for him, have passed into history. The bachelor who happened to have bad skin was admitted to the Family in order to perform his function there, as husband and father, even grandfather eventually. If, however, his performance is poor, then he may be removed for a better breadwinner, or for one whose social standing is on steadier stilts. Families, in this ruthless fashion, sometimes survive centuries of misfortune and calamity. We have seen teams limp through losing season after losing season, with coaching staffs dismissed and players continually shuffled.

This example allows us to observe that, although the team itself may be collectively constituted, the owner's relation to it may be completely instrumental. If the club not only loses games, but also loses money, he may sell it and establish, instead, a line of ladies' hosiery. Money, of course, is the pure and perfect emblem of instrumentality, and that is why, though so universally desired, it has always been, by the better sort, despised. The true fan, of course, thinks of the team as a mutuality, and, through it, the community participates in its varied fortunes, and maintains a common temperature, as if its members shared the same heart.

A common blood is the common bond in the case where the community is defined as the shared self, like a public park or a library, belonging to all but owned by none. If my arm is injured, I feel sorry for it; I worry for it; I tend it, heal it; and even if it has offended me, I do not cut it off. Only when the whole self is threatened would that remedy be recommended. The loss would be mourned, and considered irrevocable. So if the bachelor's skin breaks out again, or if the family's fortunes decline because of him, he is not to be turned out of doors. Rather, the reasons for his earlier happiness must be discovered, the healthy state-of-affairs restored, and the family's welfare, in that way, sustained.

Exile, as I am trying to define it, is not a condition which can arise for the instrumentalist. I can, of course, be separated from my rod and reel, my hamburger franchise, my seventh wife, and that separation might be costly, especially if the fish are biting, or my wife is wealthy, or especially litigious; but exile would always be far too strong a word for what really would be an inconvenience and a disappointment, even if these were severe.

Under the collective conception, exile is an unmitigated catastrophe for the person expelled, since the entire self would depend upon the definition given to it by the State. On the other hand, the State which has cast that person out need suffer nothing, nor the other citizens sense a loss, so long as the job which was once done continues to be done obediently and well.

Athens may wish him out of the way, but Socrates will be missed, because his contribution, and the contribution of every citizen to the State, has to be regarded as unique, so long as we are speaking of society as a shared self. Only here does each man's death truly diminish me, in Donne's famous phrase, because only here is each individual, without any sacrifice of self or its sovereignty, a part of the whole.

City states were small, both in population and in territory, so that when the city felt it had a dangerous element in its midst—a cell which was becoming cancerous—expulsion was the reasonable recourse. But a body beset by enemies may not only attack and kill them, or send them away with a violent sneeze, it may seal them off inside itself, forming a sort of Siberian cyst. Countries with colonies can penalize one of them by shipping it idealists, convicts, and religious zealots. Individual malcontents, if simple disappearance isn't feasible, can be tossed overboard, marooned, or left to the mercies of the wilderness as Oedipus was. For its victim, exile has two halves like a loaf cut by a knife. Heart, home, and hearth fill one side—the land the exile loses; while foreignness, strangeness, the condition of the alien occupy the other—the strand on which the castaway is washed.

Despite the grim character which the Greeks gave it, the term nowadays has many honorific, romantic, even poetical, applications. Paris is clearly the most favored modern island of exile, but it is difficult to take seriously the punishment which sends you there. American writers who took extended vacations along Saint Germain because Paris was Paris and because of the favorable rate of exchange, liked to think of themselves as exiles, although they readily went home when their money gave out, or to further their careers.

Henry James and T.S. Eliot became expatriates out of sympathy and convenience, and from a vague distaste for their place of birth. In a way, they had been English all along, and the move merely confirmed their identity. Only Ezra Pound was ever a real exile, and that didn't occur until his incarceration in St. Elizabeth's. Shut away in an asylum for the insane (a common resort), he achieved, after those many years in Europe, exile's dubious status among the discomforts of home. These days there are a lot of things you can become besides an exile: you can be an immigrant, an undesirable alien, a displaced or stateless person, a dissident, an expatriate, a deportee, a wet-back, a criminal, a colonist, a tourist, a Flying Dutchman, a Robinson Crusoe, a Wandering Jew.

To be exiled is not to be flung out of any door, but out of your own door; it is to lose your home where home suggests close emotional belonging and the gnarled roots of one's identity. I cannot be exiled from Cafe Society because I never had a home there. I can be blackballed from my club or cashiered from the army, expelled from school or ejected from the game, but I cannot be exiled from any of them. However, those black people who were enslaved and carried out of Africa: they were being exiled from the human race, and reduced to instrumentalities, to machines, to money. Black people have not yet been let into America. They are the dark artery that is denied.

I can be forced from my homeland by a usurper, or by a conquering army, but so long as I cannot feel I have been excluded by the country itself, I am not really an exile. Exile involves rejection by a loved one, as if the face in your mirror grimaced when it looked out and saw you looking in. It is a narcissistic wound.

Our species cannot regenerate a limb. Only in rare cases, and immediately, can any severed member be reattached, sewn back like the finger of a glove. Perhaps one can pretend to be a tourist for thirty years as Gertrude Stein did, and never be an exile, just a Yank on an extended trip abroad. Perhaps one can write in Trieste, Zurich, and Paris, while becoming more Irish than ever, a Dubliner of dreams. Perhaps.

A friend has told me how it felt to leave East Germany as a child of ten, and to leave behind the real companions of her heart. She had a number of dolls which she cared for in a most motherly way, and she told them everything that happened to her, and shared with them what she read, and explained to them how she felt, and what she thought. Above all, she invented stories for each one, since each was an individual and had personal preferences. It was natural that the stories would begin to intertwine, creating a single enriched narrative, one part of which she would then relate to the doll most deserving of it, while another part she would tell to the doll desiring that. So she had a special listener for each part of her life, a listener who listened as she listened, and sympathized, and supported, and forgave perhaps more perfectly than she could. She was told that when she left she could take only one doll. The family's exit would be illegal, and they would travel light. But to choose? And to leave the others to take their chances, to be neglected, to be abused? To leave one thread intact and snap the others as if you were your own malignant fate? She never played with dolls again, and never invented another story. She says that for a time she closed down her soul like a shop.

She could return now to "her native haunts," of course. But her doll days are over. When you are exiled from a space, you are also exiled from a time—in my friend's case, a childhood. The hurt heart heals, but the healed heart still hurts.

What exactly is the crime for which exile seems such an appropriate punishment? There are scoundrels aplenty in our midst: murderers, muggers, robbers, rapists, vandals, addicts, extortionists, kidnappers, car thieves, safe crackers, embezzlers, arsonists, pickpockets, purse snatchers, drug dealers, skimmers, usurers (so many scoundrels we may be in their midst); those who make obscene phone calls, beat babies, steal from the poor box, drink or gamble away somebody else's savings, adulterate and poison, forge and deceive, or are guilty of cheating at parchesi, counterfeiting, bribery, kickbacks, pollution, jury rigging, tax evasion, libel, misrepresentation, plagiarism, peeping, high crimes and misdemeanors, including terrorism and treason; and all of these, and all those I haven't listed who nevertheless belong there, like those whose dogs foul the walkways and who litter our alleys and deface our walls, who chop down old trees and old buildings, who poison the air and offend the eye and din their dins in our ears; they are simply put in the pokey, and kept securely penned for varying periods of unpleasant time; but none of them, including those who threaten the welfare of the State by running from the enemy, selling secrets, disobeying their superiors, or abusing their high office, are sent into exile.

Rulers frequently suffer this demeaning fate, often as a simple consequence of usurpation; but we must remember that in any game of King-of-the-Hill, it is the hill which must send you spinning, if you are to taste true exile, not a knock on the head by some kid who wants your job. And if a kid anyway, then only by your son (the classic configuration, although nowadays a daughter will also do), who has to have the people behind him, as well as an army and a couple of International Cartels. Then it will be the Hill, indeed, that gives you the heave and the humiliation. At other times, the rulers we lose are simply scoundrels who would have a place or two reserved for them on my list if they didn't happen to be playing Big Daddy behind some polished desk, and, like Ferdinand Marcos, probably ought to be jailed for bad taste, murder, and theft, but, for many reasons, most of them morally obnoxious, escape this result through exile.

Who else? People of the wrong race sometimes. Yes. However, the ghetto is not a place of exile, or even a sealed-off area of infection. It is a convenient circle of moral and religious confinement which has the further advantage for the State of being economically useful. Like the slums in which black people are put, the occupants are encouraged to go out to do the Turk's work, the Mexican's, the Yugoslav's labor, to dig holes and touch caps, to fare forth upon a bus to ma'am the ma'ams and wipe cracks.

Who else? Artists. And among artists, it is only occasionally painters, sculptors, architects, who may have their shows closed, their buildings reviled, their casts smashed; but who are rarely banished for the reason of their work. Nor are musicians—who may have performances disrupted, who may find that the concert halls are closed to them, who will receive excoriating reviews, and then an ornately orchestrated silence—ordinarily ushered out of the country on account of a run of seditious notes.

The case of Socrates continues to be instructive. It was Socrates who felt, and taught, that the soul was the only true mover of the body, and that therefore it behooved us to learn its makeup, and something of the way it went about its business. Like plants, we had appetites, and these impelled us; in league with the animals, we had feelings and perceptions as well, and these sent us in search of satisfactions; but, in addition, and unlike any other creature, we could direct ourselves by means of reason to responsible ends. Speech was the principle organ of influence. Through speech we made our thoughts known to others, and through speech each aspect of ourselves endeavored to persuade our differing desires, by reasoning, flattery, or shouts, to fall silent. More often than not, the exiled are novelists and poets, journalists and playwrights, or any others, whatever their occupation, who speak out or up. Put generally, though I think centrally, what is exiled is nearly always someone's word.

And when a musician is sent away in disgrace, it is what his music is said to say that is the cause; and when the painter is put out like a wild fire, it is because of what his paintings are supposed to mean; it is the words which can be pulled from them, the ideas they then can be alleged to support, for which they are excluded. Socrates did not corrupt the youth by laying his lustful hands on them; he did not corrupt them by omitting to pay ritual homage to the gods; he corrupted them by teaching them intelligent talk; he taught them to quiz the wizards of the market place and the heavies of the politburo and the swifties of the courts, and to confront them in their places of power where their walk would be most swaggery and their talk most confident, and there, in that advantageous atmosphere, were there words to be examined, weighed in a just debate with other words.

The pimps and prostitutes, card sharps, bid riggers, and legal liars, on my list: why should we suffer the expense of their long stays in our iron-bar hotels, and the pay of the guards who must guard them, and the cost of the high walls which hedge them in? why should death row be crowded with criminals who have grown old on appeals and three square meals a day? why not wrap up our undesirables and ship them to Cuba? goons and contract killers and burglers by the boatload.

Couldn't we pay some country to be our penal colony? Like radioactive waste, nobody wants wife beaters, bad check artists, and confidence men. And so I wonder: why are writers always able to find a welcome in some country, when other kinds of bad guys are turned away at the border? Well, why are miserable and misunderstood wives so valued by the husbands of their neighbors? Over and over again, one nation's persecuted artists have become another's national treasure. The word which sounded foul in one ear may ring sweetly in someone else's. It was brave of Solzhenitzyn to tell the truth we wanted to hear about the USSR, and we were glad to give him a mountain top from which to broadcast, so long as he set off his charges in the right direction.

Rarely is an exile lucky enough to be kicked out of New Jersey only to fall on his feet in Devon. Normally he is taken from his family and friends, deprived of his livelihood, his habits, his haunts; his ordinary avenues of expression are closed, his countryside is altered utterly, snow begins to fall in a world which had heretofore held an Hawaiian heart, the birds no longer sing the right songs, the flowers wear the wrong colors, nor are the car horns happy; the winds blow in the different directions, the cities smell of fish or beer or paper, clothing is uncomfortably odd, and the words which once came to your tongue like your own soul freely, unashamed, naked to a wife or husband, now have to hide in your head, for there is no one to speak to, no one to read what you've written, no one to know about and protest your case, or understand the conditions of virtue which were called your crime.

You are no longer you when even your present daily life is as remote as a memory. You are no longer you, if—especially—you were defined by your way of life, the things you loved, the ideals you esteemed, your language.

Against this, celebrity exiles have often reported improved conditions: they got better jobs, were lionized, given opportunities to express themselves—in dance, in painting, in design—in directions they could scarcely have foreseen. They were put on TV, asked their opinion, smiled at by strangers in the street, by the CIA debriefed. And there was tea on the terrace following the replay of their defection. Universities paid them to speak, and offered them even more to teach. They had assumed, in effect, the mantle of a new profession: Herr Doktor Dissident, Professor of Exilese. And ease it is for some, and easy for some to shift tongues, to pick up this word and that and grammarize themselves, to adapt to a new far richer life than they, earlier, could have dreamed.

They might remarry, adopt a team (the Washington Redskins, most likely), disco around a lot, acquire a taste for scotch, begin to forget the wretched whom they once resembled and who lay in prison still or slid still in fear down gray streets or slept lightly as the cat sleeps when in the pound. It became equally easy to discount or forget their exiles, who hadn't landed in swimming pools with surrounding lawns, but who found themselves taken down every peg possible, driving a taxi through streets they couldn't recognize or pronounce, selling bruised fruit, cleaning house when before they had owned one, patronized or ignored, handed a visored cap or a broom, and cast adrift where there was neither water nor a boat.

To enjoy such success, cold wars need to be kept hot. To enjoy such success, other exiles are unwanted competition: for limelight, available sympathies, restricted access to the goodies of the new life. Back in the old country, they had often cultivated a fine hatred for one another, so why should they change this comforting relation just because both were in a new place? Besides only they, of this country or that, region or that, race or that, language or that, this or that kind of cruel repression, grim persecution, special pain and particular rage, only they, that is, were exiles really, exiles in extremis, with an island in their name, exiles in essence. Others were carbons, copies, no-accounts, unable to muster up the misery, the enmity, the enemies who might give them an honest exile's status, and an entry into the aristocracy of the properly deposed.

Who are those who make this transition most easily? those for whom exile almost turns out not to be? The lucky ones scarcely cared about their native soil, were into making it one way or in one place or other, were cosmopolitan in their dress and tones and taste and bones, and had early on freed themselves from clan and family, from countryside and climate—perhaps they lived in an apartment complex on a city block amidst a lot of similarly anonymous buildings, and saw only the sky through a sooty window, and wrote on mimeograph paper. Coca-cola and corn dogs comfort them now; their microwave knows how much better off they are—with clean sheets and a car, some good dope and their own towel. The region they had always cared about remained a region of the mind, and the mind was mainly a midden made of texts, of pages of reportage and consignment, and drama, of course, sentiment, sob-stuff, high-minded alignments of rhymes recited in a Racinean hurry before being shot or having a head cut off; and they understood geography as a text, history as a text, texts as texts, and were able then to transfer themselves as on library loan from one book depository to another, suffering only the ordinary wear and tear of careless usage.

In particular, those who did well in their adoptive country were those who learned the new language quickly, and who stepped smartly into the idioms and lingo of the times, who wrote in their new home as they had written when in the old one: rapidly, breezily, glibly, satirically. For them, the forced switch from one language to another put both the new one and the old one in a revelatory light. They saw their mother tongue no longer as a daughter might see her mother, but as mother's seducer might, or the baker whom she owed for last week's rolls. And they saw their adopted tongue as an entirely new, wholly free, wonderfully energized way of thinking, because nothing of their rejected history clung to it, the lint of a past life didn't remain; it was as clean of guilt and memory and old emotion as algebra is (one reason why algebra has always been a haven for the haunted).

There was guilt enough. The old days had gathered it like cloud. That was one more factor in favor of another language, another country; because every difference was desirable, and every distance; because no matter what wrong your Motherland had done you, or how clearly mistaken in you it had been, or how unjustly you had been treated, how severely you had suffered, how bitterly you had been made to play Job; you were nevertheless still haunted by your Father Figures, your idols of the Family; you were bitten by your conscience regardless; you called yourself an ungrateful whelp, disgraceful offspring, rotten kid—all the regular stuff—while knowing that your voice, at such times, was only the flavored echo of your enemies, that it was your own arm they were using to bring the gavel down, and *your* mouth which dolefully pronounced *their* sentence. That was another unfairness. Perhaps the final one.

Well, it is certainly sensible, under such circumstances, to make yourself over in the image of another culture, if you can, because you are going to want to call cabs and order croissants, and you may want to blow the whistle on the bastards who drive you from your homeland—a vigorous article in the local language might do that—or cash in on your new celebrity. It may be, however, as I've already suggested, that you used your first language as superficially as you will use every other, just to request cold toast and tea, or to kiss off an unwanted lover, get a good lie going; and it may also be that you know no other way to use it but badly, as if it were a laundry basket or a paper cup you could crush and throw away after use.

The scientist, for example, is presumed to be working at a level of concept which escapes the parochial, so that, although the summaries of his experiments are in German or French, they are not in French and German, but in perception records and logarithms. Suppose our words spilled from our mouths as palpably as spit; suppose some were encased in soft pink clouds like cotton candy or encircled like comic strip balloons, or came out in Gothic; suppose they filled up small rooms, and we waded through them to reach the phone or the door, and little language ladies spent the night collecting them in nets, hosing them into vats, and at earliest dawn trucks laden with the *logos* slunk through the streets to great dictionary shaped dumps. I suppose it only to indicate how well rid of our words we are. No sooner spoken than absorbed by the wide, though increasingly worried, sea of air around us. As for the similarly useless written word . . . well, we may die of our records; bad writing is more contagious than a cold; and if it isn't pieces of plastic and those wormy twist-ties that get us, it will be vast memo slides, best seller blow-ups or stock certificate subsidence.

But if your language is supposed to be the medium of an art; if you, its user, are an artist and not a reporter, a persuader, a raconteur; if you aren't writing principally to get praise or pay, but wish to avoid the busy avenues of entertainment, to traffic in the tragic maybe, dig down to the deeply serious; then (although there are a few exceptional and contrary cases) you will understand right away how blessed you are by the language you were born with, the language you began to master in the moment you also started to learn about life, to read the lines on faces, the light in the window which meant milk, the door which deprived you of mother, the half-songs sung by that someone who loaned you the breast you suckled—the breast you claimed as more than kin.

Only if you spring fully grown from the brow of Zeus can you escape being born, and learning a language before you get big, and losing that language along with growing old. It is like living under a certain sort of sun, except that the word begins as merely the wind and weather of the spirit, because what occurs in the outside world initially as a kind of din is slowly made sense of and assimilated. Gradually, too, is a style formed, like the hardening of your bones and physiognomy, by degrees, the way your character comes into being—assertive and tough, mild and weak. That you will learn a language, then, is likely; that you will learn it well is unlikely; that you will live well is unlikely; that you will have a shape is certain; that your soul—that old ghost—will be the source of your speech and the words you write is a Socratic conjecture I support; the word is all the soul is.

So what is sent away when we are forced out of our homeland? Words. It is to get rid of our words that we are gotten rid of, since speech is not a piece of property which can be confiscated, bought or sold, and therefore left behind on the lot like a car you have traded, but is the center of the self itself. The excruciation of exile lies in this: that although the body is being sent into the world as Adam and Eve were sent by the Angel, the soul is being cast into a cell of the self where it may mark the days with scratches on the wall called writing, but where it will lose all companions, and survive alone.

This claim of mine concerning the centrality of the spoken word, is, of course, not believed. In our picture perfect time, who should believe it? So on your next date, draw a picture of your passion. Thus explain your needs. How far into real feeling will it take you? Will it not inadvertently possess a certain lavatory style? When next you are alone, and pondering some problem (should you call him? will she or won't she? does he like the amplified guitar better than the cradled bass? in what will she prefer that I express myself, chalk or crayon?), try posing your questions in terms of the flickering image so many say they love and is the future's salutary wave. Think through anything. Start small. Continue simple. But doodle the solution into being.

If we can read, it is expected that we also ought to be able to write, or, anyway, type. How many of us, in our camera crafted age, can take a really good photograph, or copy a pictured face, or form an interesting image in any medium, or read a blueprint, understand a map or set of architectural plans, or even follow the right arrows when trying to catch a suburban train? If this is a visual age, why is our visual literacy next to nil? We can't even doodle with any skill.

We could say, of Saturn swallowing his children, that he had sent them to hell inside himself. For quite a few of its sufferers, exile is a spiritual condition, not merely a geographical one. This is what many of our American writers of the teens and twenties meant when they described themselves as exiles, and when they weren't just putting on airs. Gertrude Stein said that when American expansion had reached the Pacific, there was no where else to go but "west in the head." And into the head we went. Then sent our luggage east of us to Paris. Where we spent our exile wasn't the real issue. James Baldwin wasn't sent into exile in France. His exile began before he was born, when the darkness of all our beginnings darkened his skin.

The expression "spiritual exile" is a metaphor, of course, but a significant one, since there is a large number for whom exile is only a *pro forma* punishment: they are doing well and have found a happy home in their adoptive country. "Alienation" pretty well describes the condition of heart and mind which constitutes the inner content of actual, of effective, exile. While alienation can be mutual, as it often is with married pairs, it is often as solitary as masturbation. Citizens can become alienated from their government without the nation noticing. That failure to notice is often part of it. Still, being indifferent to someone or something does not imply that you once upon a time felt otherwise, or that you must continue to mourn your separation.

"Alienation," as a philosophical term, is no longer in vogue, so perhaps it is safe to pick it up again, if only for a moment. What is more familiar than your own face—the one there in the mirror, the face you are shaving. But what is that behind the head? It is a wall you've never seen, a wall the mirror has invented, and the head, too, wobbles on its neck now, as if it were under water. Remember how it felt to return after many years to the High School of your youth: how small the halls were; how tattered the blinds; how grim the lockers—a greasy green, and dented without design. Reality and memory were out of tune then, and now they are again.

The movement of the razor over the face, the scrape of the blade, the cream being pushed here and there like suds across a floor, have all leaped over oddity and reached the surreal. The operation of doorknobs is inexplicable. Doorknobs ought to be easy. We only expect bidets to be mysterious. But as alienation settles over our souls like a fog, features, operations, relations, without actually altering, offer us different points of reference, their aims shift, their essences dissolve. An inner weariness wells up, everything is an obstacle, asking us questions we do not understand. We issue the same old orders to our will, but after that our limbs flail awkwardly; walking cautiously straight ahead we still back into things as though blind; we forget how to sneeze.

At the same time, of course, how vividly, how accurately, how freshly, we see; for everything we had known well, we had long since ceased to know: the flag was noble, the flag always waved, priests, presidents, and poets were worthy of respect. And now the bathroom wall surprises us; so does the tone in our wife's voice when she says "no" once again—a sound which suddenly seems the same as the scrape of our razor. We really hear, perhaps for the first time, the guggle of water down the drain—down the drain like the departure of all hope. In the blink of an eye, we've placed a Duchamp here, another there, until we have a world full of the familiar made strange.

We have spent a lifetime making things a part of ourselves, constructing, as they say, a second nature: learning to walk, to speak, to ride a bike, pick a lock, spoil a party, dance the fandango, wash dishes, shovel snow, swim, do our job, turn on, turn off, go to the bathroom, stoop to conquer. We had felt at home in our neighborhood, safe and sound, until houses were looted, purses snatched, and Pakistanis moved in. So now we walk a fierce dog. We had felt at home in our yard with its swimming pool until someone threw an open can of paint in it, until adolescents made a habit of swimming nude there in the middle of the night, until a squirrel drowned. We had felt at home in our home, freshly done in chintz and lacquer, until the kids brought their noisy punk friends in the den, the dog began pooping in a corner, robbers ripped us off, and the wife stopped making the bed. We had felt at home in our flesh until our flesh grew old, grew flabby, went fat, and then there was that stranger in the mirror with his red-rimmed eyes, and the stubble, every morning, like an early field gray with frost.

Then strangers invaded our private hunk of public space with their hands out and their staring eyes. Then strangers came too close to us in the subway, and sat down beside us with empty seats on every side. So now we come warily up to the ports of our eyes, and go about, even when alone, hidden deep within like a pip in a pumpkin, and protected from the actuality of everything, especially every touch, as we always did at rush hour, so as not to feel felt when packed in the train like a tin.

Alienation is the exile of the emotions—of hope, of trust—sent away somewhere so they won't betray us.

The exile that I personally know about is an exile far less gruesome than the fate which befell Saturn's children; it is not at all dramatic like the epic of Oedipus, not a bit lyric, either, like a ballad bemoaning the old days from the lute of a Slavic poet. It does not even concern the exile of a person whose speech was found to be offensive, and who was sent away where his message could be heard no more. I am talking about the loss of a use of language, in my opinion its fundamental employment—the poetic in the broadest sense—and how that limb of our language has been cut off and callously discarded.

This has been, of course, my subject all along. And someone may ask, so complete has been its disappearance, what is this special use of language, and what makes it so special? Alas, to answer would require another essay and an honesty absent from most hearts. It is, first of all, a use of language which refuses to be a use. Use is abuse. That should be the motto of every decent life. So it treats every word as a wonder, and a world in itself. And it walks between them, even over dizzy heights, as confidently as a worker on beams of steel. And it does not care to get on, but it dwells; it makes itself, as Rilke wrote, into a thing, mute as the statue of an orator. It reaches back into the general darkness we—crying—came from, retouches the terrors and comforts of childhood, but returns with a magician's skills to make the walls of the world dance.

Paul Valery divided buildings thus: into those that were dumb, and therefore would be, on my account, soul-less, dead; those that spoke, and would be, on my account, solid citizens and a worthy norm, provided their speech was clear and honest and unaffected; and those that sang, for these found in themselves their own true end, and rose like Shelley's lark, through the heaviest atmosphere.

We have grown accustomed to silence from this sort of singing. We make other noises. Yet it is an old rule of history that exiles return, that they return wrathfully, whether a banished people, a forbidden idea, or a barricaded way, to reclaim what should have been their heritage. They return wrathfully, not only because they remember and mourn the life they were taken from, but because the past can never be recovered, not even by a Proust, not if you wish to take up residence in it again. To listen to our stories other selves have been invented to replace the dolls, who, if any remain, are alive somewhere in other arms. But of course poetry, if it returns, will never make us pay. No. It will not put us to death or in prison or send us, as it was sent, so sadly away. It will simply put us to shame.

Obsessed with Words

Eva Hoffman

I'VE BECOME OBSESSED with words. I gather them, put them away like a squirrel saving nuts for winter, swallow them and hunger for more. If I take in enough, then maybe I can incorporate the language, make it part of my psyche and my body. I will not leave an image unworded, will not let anything cross my mind till I find the right phrase to pin the shadow down. Each week, as I drive a route of leafy New England roads to teach a class at the University of New Hampshire, my head heats up as if the circuitry were overloaded. "Beveled, chiseled, sculpted, ribbed," I think as a wooden lampstand I liked flashes through my mind. I see myself, speeding in my orange VW, a comical figure, mouthing a litany of adjectives like some overeager freshman. But this stream of hypertrophied consciousness is not something I can stop. I search for the right shade of a pearly pinkish shell I found on the beach as if my life depended on it, and to some extent it does. I can't live forever in a windy, unfurnished imagination; I have to make a comfortable habitation there, fill it with a few household things, some comfy, everyday objects, maybe a beveled lamp. I have to add a bottom to the language that I learned from the top.

The thought that there are parts of the language I'm missing can induce a small panic in me, as if such gaps were missing parts of the world or my mind—as if the totality of the world and mind were coeval with the totality of language. Or rather, as if language were an enormous, fine net in which reality is contained—and if there are holes in it, then a bit of reality can escape, cease to exist. When I write, I want to use every word in the lexicon, to accumulate a thickness and weight of words so that they yield the specific gravity of things. I want to re-create, from the discrete particles of words, that wholeness of a childhood language that had no words.

I pounce on bits of colloquial idiom, those slivers of Americana in which the cultural sensibility is most vivid, as if they could give me America itself. "Hair of the dog that bit me," I repeat to myself with relish; "pork-barreling"; "I'm from Missouri, show me"; "He swallowed it hook, line, and sinker." When I speak, I'm awkward in using such homely familiarities; I still feel the presumption in it. But in writing, I claim every territorial prerogative. Perhaps if I cast my net wide enough, it will cover the whole continent.

My voice is still a highly unreliable instrument. At the oddest moments, it betrays me, buckles, rasps, refuses to go on. It plays only in flat, shallow registers, and sometimes I literally cannot find it. Sometimes it seems to be lost in an echoing well; or else it shifts location to someplace high within my throat, from where it emerges tight and choked. In a Cambridge coffeehouse, where I sit at my ease, gossiping or listening to a friend, it begins to do its tricks.

"So there I was"—Tom launches into one of his stories—"in this Indian village in the middle of the Punjab, I mean I hardly know how I got there except there was this guru-type I was following, an American, but he had been there for a while so he set himself up as a guide to us eager beavers, so there I am, early in the morning, nothing is moving, nothing I tell you, except this mangy mutt comes out, this was no Brahman mutt, I mean the animal can't even make a sound it's so famished, and there's this dusty road through the middle of the village, and it's so quiet you think maybe it's time for Krishna to put in an appearance, I mean he has this tendency to show up in unlikely places—and then all of a sudden, I tell you, I don't know why, but it was significant, it was a eutectic point, I realized, it just came to me, bingo, just like that: this wasn't on television! This was the real thing! Then this woman comes out of a clay hut, I think it was made of clay, and she's wearing this gorgeous sari, you know how lush they look, you can hardly believe they're not in *Semiramide* or something, but she rubbed her eyes because she'd just woken up, and she looked sort of pissed off, and she was real too! So then I knew something had happened, and that's the end of the story, kid, but nothing since has been the same, I mean, even my parents' goddamn house in Westchester, I mean how much more unreal can you get—even that's real, well, sort of . . ."

This is one of Tom's solos, his riff—that all-American form, the shape that language takes when it's not held down by codes of class, or rules of mannerliness, or a common repertory of inherited phrases. A riff is a story that spins itself out of itself, propelled by nothing but the imagination—a story that can go anyplace and take off into the stratosphere without anyone minding . . . Tom invents himself with every phrase, for every phrase is a surprise to himself; he swerves into digressions that go on forever, conducts whole jam sessions with himself, sparks off metaphors as if they were encoded in his chromosomes. Language takes off like a sudden gust of swallows, observations collide unexpectedly and procreate a joke, words jump around like fireflies, so that there's no telling what's up or down, what ground and what outer space, no telling where the always frail connection between words and reality breaks off and pure performance takes over. It makes me dizzy, this hurling of antic verbal balls in the pure air; with my earthbound sensibility, I want to touch ground, want to know what, where is the real thing. But who can tell and who cares: this is America, where anything is possible, and this slip-and-slide speech, like jazz, or action painting, is the insertion of the self into the space of borderless possibility.

I listen breathlessly as Tom talks, catching his every syncopation, every stress, every maverick rush over a mental hurdle. Then, as I try to respond with equal spontaneity, I reach frantically for the requisite tone, the requisite accent. A Texas drawl crosses a New England clip, a groovy half-sentence competes with an elegantly satirical comment. I want to speak some kind of American, but which kind to hit? "Gee," I say, "what a trip, in every sense of the word."

Tom is perfectly satisfied with this response. I sound natural enough, I sound like anybody else. But I can hear the artifice, and for a moment, I clutch. My throat tightens. Paralysis threatens. Speechlessness used to be one of the common symptoms of classic hysteria. I feel as though in me, hysteria is brought on by tongue-tied speechlessness.

When I fall in love, I am seduced by language. When I get married, I am seduced by language. My husband too is a master of the riff, and when I listen to him improvise about Whitman's poetry, or his Jewish aunts and uncles, or a Wasp Connecticut wedding, I think, maybe this bebop speech can carry me right into the heart of America. . . . It's a tricky contract, and I get confused between my husband and his eloquence, distracted as by shadows and shimmers thrown on a white screen by a camera obscura, but I want to catch the wordplay, ride the energy of the nervy bounds and rebounds, give myself over to the insouciant leaps. . . . .

All around me, the Babel of American voices, hardy midwestern voices, sassy New York voices, quick youthful voices, voices arching under the pressure of various crosscurrents. I've become a skilled diagnostician of voices, and of their neuroses. I know how people feel, how they are, not from what they say but from how they sound. I can hear the snags and broken rhythms of nervousness, the jumps of pitch that happen when someone is uncomfortable, the tensing of the vocal cords in disapproval. I can also hear the sounds of good health—the even tones of self-assurance, the deepening melodiousness in consent to deep feeling, the canter of clean enthusiasm.

Since I lack a voice of my own, the voices of others invade me as if I were a silent ventriloquist. They ricochet within me, carrying on conversations, lending me their modulations, intonations, rhythms. I do not yet possess them; they possess me. But some of them satisfy a need; some of them stick to my ribs. I could take on that stylish, ironic elongation which is X's mark of perpetual amusement; it fits something in my temperament, I could learn to speak a part of myself through it. And that curtailed, deliberate dryness that Y uses as an antidote to sentiment opens a door into a certain New England sensibility whose richness I would never otherwise understand. Eventually, the voices enter me; by assuming them, I gradually make them mine. I am being remade, fragment by fragment, like a patchwork quilt; there are more colors in the world than I ever knew.

Like a tourist in a new city, who has no particular neighborhood and who therefore is always confronting "the city" as a whole, I, an incompletely assimilated immigrant, am always confronting "the Culture." In this too it turns out that I am like my American friends, though perhaps a little more so. "The Culture," in America, has become a curious monster, a thing that throbs and vibrates out there and bellows. Everyone I know measures the Culture, gauges it, diagnoses it all the time, because, after all, the monster might enter the living room, and so it's important to be on the lookout. The Culture is becoming more conservative, more progressive, more celebrity obsessed, more materialistic, more sentimental. Each shift is carefully observed; the beast may, after all, lurch or bite, or co-opt us, make us more like itself, a graceless, lumpish, philistine thing. The Culture is a dangerous seducer; one must resist its pull.

I'm a vigilant Culture watcher, like everyone else. And undoubtedly, like everyone else, I've ingested parts of the Culture even while I've prudishly pulled my skirts around me. I see this paradox in my friends clearly enough, culture turning into counterculture and counterculture into culture despite everyone's best intentions, the organization man giving way to the dropout and the dropout to a new technocrat, loneliness to love-ins and then loneliness again, as if any set of cultural terms necessarily determines the terms of the subsequent rebellion, and the rejections carry in them the seeds of what is rejected. It is always difficult to know how a culture flows through our veins, and by now I've lost track of how much America flows through mine. Fragments of Janis Joplin songs and the Rolling Stones surface in my mind as I walk down the street; the landscape of Amagansett, where I've spent several summers, is just under my retina, to be retrieved whenever I think vacation, time off; films about New York are films about my hometown; "Gimme a break," I say, when a street vendor gets pushy, and the issues I debate—how to conduct one's career without losing one's sanity, what to eat without becoming contaminated, how to deal with passive-aggressive lovers—are American conversations, dictated by "the Culture" as much as this season's fashions. And I never, never say "It's only psychological" anymore. Maybe, behind my back and while I wasn't looking, I've acquired a second unconscious, an American one, made up of diverse cultural matter. Like any unconscious, this one is hard to pin down. I only know that the hybrid creature I've become is made up of two parts Americana, that the pastiche has lots of local color. Despite my resistance, or perhaps through its very act, I've become a partial American, a sort of resident alien.

Lungs and Gills

Vassily Aksyonov

TAKING PART IN THE conference "The Third Wave: Russian Literature in Emigration," the American playwright Edward Albee said: "I've tried to imagine what it must be like to be a writer in exile. I've almost wished it in the same way that Wystan Auden is reputed to have day-dreamed about his lover's death so that he could experience ultimate grief . . . What must it be like to have to create one's private world in a totally different world? I don't know."

His fellow participants at that conference, fourteen Russian writers from the USA, Canada, France, Germany and Israel, did not know either. The conference took place some years ago, and most of those people just started creating as if from scratch.

One of their great predecessors, Nikolai Gogol, in spite of eighteen years of self-imposed European exile from Russia, also failed to make it out. Desperately changing stage coaches on Italian, French and German roads, he didn't make any attempt to come closer to the life of the European nations. Vexed by the sounds of foreign speech, he was always making fun of foreign languages, customs, fashions, etc. He cherished his "Russianness" as if he had a stock of Russian air on his back like an astronaut on the moon. Everybody knows that the results of such a way of life turned out to be rather lamentable.

In order to survive as a working writer, one shouldn't count on the steadily leaking container on his back. Being a working writer surrounded by a foreign culture, one might (and should) experience certain psychological departures from one element to another many times on any given day.

Still, one's first preoccupation must be language, even if in exile. The mother tongue has undergone a process of shrinking: from a bubbling ocean, it may turn into a placid pond or, to the contrary, a language which used to be perceived as the fancy amenity of a certain elite may become a gigantic mixture containing all sorts of things.

In exile you dive and emerge from one language to another all day long. Inside your car you talk with your wife in Russian; getting gas or looking for a parking space you switch to English. Sitting at your desk you plunge into the language of Pushkin, but you can hardly manage not being interrupted by your plumber, the delivery man, solicitors of all kinds, or some lovely wrong-number caller—in other words, by bearers of the King's English. Elbowed by this friendly crowd you retreat, sometimes not without losses, as when you use inappropriate Russian constructions in order to approximate ordinary English idioms like "small world" and "I can't wait." Or you might find yourself saying an English word in place of a familiar Russian word in conversation with your compatriots. This is emigration.

On the other hand, all of a sudden you realize how intensely tangible Russian words have become to you and how you do appreciate the very sound of your native speech.

Literary exile has something to do with amphibious existence. In order to survive, one should develop a certain type of gills in addition to his lungs. From my angle of view, the exiled writer is none other than an amphibian, and even more importantly, he should stay this way, maintaining a delicate balance between his "lungs" and his "gills."

This concerns not only such a great and obvious problem as language but also some subtler matters. Consider what we call cityscape. When we went overseas we found ourselves totally alienated from American urban nostalgia. But we have found that American cities aren't clusters of glaring skyscrapers, but more likely red brick walls with fire escapes, back alleys with lampposts, rows of townhouses with porches. All these things spoke neither to our memory nor to our literary reminiscences. We missed the European eclecticism of Moscow and Leningrad. Roaming about the United States during the first year of my American life, I didn't realize that I was looking for urban eclecticism. When we ran into it in Washington, we decided to settle there for good. It took five years before American nostalgia ceased to be foreign to me.

Besides the cultural, historical and geographical notions of homesickness, there is also a certain biochemical nostalgia which includes of course a great number of gastronomical and olfactory matters. Our "Russianness" or, if you wish, "Sovietness," has a lot to do with the most subtle structure of our bodies' cells. With a limited amount of the authentic Russian air in your shoulder cylinders, those batteries cannot be recharged whenever you want. Thus your Russianness must undergo a process of change along with the inevitable biochemical restructuring.

Everything I have talked about thus far is none other than the fight of a writer to keep his imagination alive. The expulsion of a writer is the imagination of the State in action. In its wildest dream, the Empire identifies itself with the Motherland. By having an undesired writer expelled, the

Empire imagines him as deprived not only of his legal status and police registration papers, but also of his home, his culture, language, sentiments—in other words, deprived of his imagination. Under these circumstances of the ultimate clash between two types of imagination, we talk about the threatened existence of the writer's imagination rather than of its competing with an omnipotent state.

After each publication of his stirring prose or the staging of his troublemaking plays, Gogol fled Russia like a naughty boy. He spent most of his creative time outside his beloved Fatherland, although he, unlike the exiled authors of our time, could come back whenever he wanted. The emperor, Nicholas the First, "The Stick," was a "rotten liberal" compared to the Politburo. Gogol simply could not stand seeing those, as he put it, "mug faces." In our time, it's exactly the other way around: the "mug faces" can't stand seeing writers.

When he was abroad for extended periods, Gogol's imagination suffered from a lack of authenticity. In his numerous letters, he urged his friends to send to him in Europe as much Russian authenticity as possible—anecdotes, quips, rumors, diaries, notes on politics, culture, agriculture, religion, etc. His quest for Russian authenticity was a part of his desperate attempt to remain a Russian writer without physically being on Russian soil. All those attempts turned out to be in vain. Having robbed himself of any real impressions, he didn't succeed in getting artificial authenticity. *Dead Souls* Part II was not written by the author who wrote Part I.

This is only one classic example of lost authenticity, and so what? To the alienated writer I say, Don't cry for your authenticity and don't keep chasing it. If it is impossible to remain a genuine Russian writer, don't keep insisting on that. Be an emigre Russian writer and stand tall.

In order to survive as a working writer, one should not maintain the perspective of a polar explorer. Look for other sources of inspiration around you and try to take advantage of your unexpected cosmopolitanism. You cannot vouch that this is not exactly what your native culture wants from you at the moment.

What the vagabond Gogol truly succeeded in was a steady current of correspondence with his friends in Russia. He successfully used the already decently developed network of stagecoaches and seamail, whereas we, the contemporary exiled writers, cannot count on the postal service, except for homing pigeons or some rare occasions akin to the Marco Polo expedition to medieval China. On the other hand, we can enjoy the achievements of modern technology which are rather helpful in allowing us to maintain links with the metropolis.

Vladimir Nabokov was once told that his books were reaching Russian shores by means of balloons that were launched by some enthusiastic boys over the North Pole. Well, he responded, I can imagine Lolita's impact on polar bears. Balloons would seem to be a totally obsolete means of transporting books in the coming age when, as Kurt Vonnegut put it, we'll be able to hide the complete works of Shakespeare in a hollow tooth. Anyway, thanks to the growing porousness of a notorious Curtain, Nabokov's books, as well as the books of the ousted Russian religious philosophers, did reach Russian shores and significantly influenced the bears, wolves and foxes of our literary generation some twenty years ago. So in a way, we can regard literary emigration as a sort of "time capsule."

In conclusion of this presentation, I would love to cite another classic example.

The young hero of Ivan Bunin's novel *Lika,* while strolling down the street, spots a tramp. The well-groomed young man is shocked by the appearance of the beggar who is sitting in a snow bank in a state of semi-undress—specifically, without pants on.

"How can you sit on snow with your backside naked?!" exclaims our hero. "How terrible your life conditions are!"

Responding to this burst of empathy the pantless tramp just smiles defiantly: "By and large, sir, I see nothing terrible in this!"

Writing: A Metaphor of Exile

Augusto Roa Bastos

THE POLITICAL, SOCIAL and cultural panorama in Paraguay today, under the longest dictatorship on the Latin American continent, provides a striking picture of the devastation such oppression causes to the whole range of its sources of creativity. The phenomenon of exile in this backward country seemingly forever saddled with the 'continuing hallucination of its history' that is the culmination of a century of those recurring, endemic dictatorships which beset the land like tropical fevers, has become an integral part of its nature and destiny.

The exile, first and foremost, of the country itself, in its landlocked inaccessibility, characterized by territorial segregation, internal migrations, emigration, and mass exoduses: with, among the latter, that of its indigenous people, the first to take place after the expulsion of the Jesuits in 1767 which, in turn, was the first example of the forced exile of foreigners seen in colonial Paraguay. Once it had won independence from Spain, however, it managed, despite the isolation, to become the most materially and culturally developed nation in Spanish America. Under the rule of the famous Doctor Francia, who founded the Republic and built the nation state according to the principles of the Englightenment and the French Revolution, Paraguay conducted the first experiment in real autonomy and independence ever seen in the history of Latin America, something not even the liberators had been able to achieve in the battles for liberation. Economic interests, chiefly the penetration and dominance of the British empire in the region, could not permit this dangerous precedent of self-determination to set a bad example in this tiny, out-of-the-way, landlocked country. At Britain's instigation and with its support, the financial centres of the Brazilian empire, together with the Río de la Plata oligarchies who depended on Britain, concocted what became known as the War of the Triple Alliance (1865–70). Paraguay was destroyed. Two-thirds of its inhabitants were killed, half its territory lost. Nothing was left but ruins. All that survived of the unfortunate nation was a 'vast catastrophe of memories' with at its centre a delirious reality that flung handfuls of its history into the faces of the survivors, as the Spaniard Rafael Barret wrote at the beginning of this century.

This emptying of its past, combined with its isolation and the lack of contact with the outside world and the pressure of neo-colonial interests, to prevent this island surrounded by land, turned inwards on its own disasters, from receiving so much as the echoes of the cultural innovations that were transforming the ideas, arts, and literature of the rest of Latin America. Moreover, the double seclusion of its bilingual culture also has to be taken into account. Paraguay is the only entirely bilingual country in Latin America: Guaraní, the autochthonous spoken language, is the true language of its people. It provides the *mestizo* cultural space in which for over four centuries orality has converted the written language into an absent text: the root metaphor of exile.

This cultural and linguistic exile compounds from within the other forms of alienation created by internal exile, since it implies the destruction of the final freedom, consumed by fear, fear enthroned as a public duty in a country crushed by the system of totalitarian repression which constantly mocks its possibilities.

This fragmentation of Paraguayan culture, together with the imbalance of its forces of production and this paralysing fear which has taken on the characteristics of both a public and a private, an individual and a collective conscience, has had a profound effect on the creative forces of a society which, to add insult to injury, is situated on the banks of one of the world's most beautiful rivers, a river which gave the country its mythical name: *Paragua'y*, 'plumed water' or 'river of the crowns'.

Brutality and terror have dried up the sources which feed those works of writers and artists that illustrate the originality of a people. It is clear that the latter can only happen when these works are produced at the centre of a community's social energy and are drawn from the essence of its life, reality, history, and those social and national myths which fertilize the creative subjectivity of poets, novelists, and artists. Their greatest alienation is having to live torn between reality as it should be and the actual reality—between the fullness of the life they have been robbed of and the monstrosity of the vegetative life forced on them by causes foreign to their country's historic and social nature.

The writer cannot pretend he is an ethnologist. Passivity and distance are not his strong points. Paraguayan writers, narrators, storytellers and poets belong to a culture whose internal structure is still oral and resists the signs of educated writing, seen as signs of artificiality and domination. So, the imagination becomes trapped in this double alienation: from language, as it struggles to express an overwhelming reality, and from reality itself, which is polyphonic sound, and which shows itself only in orality, in the inflections and modulations of verbal expression. It is well known that a piece of literature owes its value not to its good intentions but to the resonance of its internal structure and the instinctive force it generates through the workings of 'an art which while being conscience is in search of a form that is not conscious of itself', something which, though not itself ideology, cannot escape ideology.

In this account of the kinds of exile the Paraguayan writer faces (external, internal, the loss of unlived life, the alienation of the still-unformed work, the split from reality, the impossibility those forced to live abroad have of making contact with their national public, and conversely the lack of communication with these writers which those suffering internal exile feel) linguistic exile represents the paradigm, the basic metaphor of this reality become unreal.

The dilemma of the bi-polarity between Spanish and Guaraní is at the heart of this sort of linguistic schizophrenia. Which of these two languages is a Paraguayan writer to choose? If at bottom literature is a linguistic act, and as such an act of communication, then the choice would seem obvious: Spanish. But when he uses Spanish, the Paraguayan writer, and above all the writer of fiction, experiences his most heartfelt alienation, that of linguistic exile. Can he ever limit this distancing from that part of his reality and the life of his community which finds expression in Guaraní, from Paraguayan culture as a whole, since it is so indelibly marked by the sign of orality, by its original mythical thinking? As soon as he starts to write in Spanish, the writer feels he is carrying out a partial translation from the severed linguistic context. In so doing, he is splitting himself. There will always be something he cannot express. This creates a need for the Paraguayan writer to construct a literature which goes beyond literature, to speak against words, write against writing, invent (his)stories which counter the official history, to undermine in his subversive, demythifying writing the language built on the ideology of domination. It is in this sense that the new generations of storytellers and poets are dedicating themselves to the task of forging a *literature without a past*, born of a past without literature, of bringing it to expression in their own language.

According to Guaraní cosmogony, human language was seen as the foundation of the cosmos, man's original state. At the heart of this basic myth is the esoteric, untranslatable *ayvú rapytá o ñe'eng mybte rá*, the kernel of the word-soul: the *ayvú* of the dawn of time. It is a noise or sound imbued with all the wisdom of nature and the cosmos, brought into existence by the austere, melodious Father of the beginning and end, inspirer of the founding word. A secret word, never uttered in the presence of strangers, which together with *tataendy* (flame of the sacred fire) and *tat-achiná* (mist of the creative power) makes up the three original elements of the ancient Guaraní cosmology. Their founding divinities did not decree laws of retribution against anyone who aspired to knowledge. Instead, they agreed on the communion between knowing and doing, between oneness and plurality, between life and death. Every human being was God on the path towards purification, and God—or rather the many gods of their theogony—was the first and the last man. They did not cast anyone out, but spoke of the peregrination of the person-multitude in search of *land-without-evil* which everyone both carried with themselves and shared with everyone else.

In today's Paraguay, distorted by oppression, even this ancestral voice has been silenced, this final language in which a threatened, persecuted people could find refuge. This language without writing, which in earlier times encapsulated the essence of the word-soul, the seed of all that is human and sacred, is now obliged to seek a space for its message, for the illumination of reality through the unreality of signs.

Contemporary Paraguayan writers are aware of finding themselves at one extreme of the historical process. This makes them enormously sensitive to the problems not only of their society but of their own artistic labours. Those writers forced to live in internal exile share with those living outside the country a sense that the task of literature is once again to embody a destiny; their task to plunge themselves into the living reality of a community—their own—to draw sustenance from its deepest essences and hopes, in a way that will also embrace the universality of man.

These tellers of stories understand that, by their very nature, such feats can only be achieved on the aesthetic level, on the level of language and writing, in the idea of narration itself, which is not, as is commonly thought, the art of describing reality in words, but the art of making the word itself real.

The writer's task is to penetrate as deeply as possible beneath the surface of human destiny, to create the most complete picture possible of both individual and society, one that is most closely linked to the vital and spiritual experience of present-day mankind. Thus it is that, by allying personal subjectivity to a historical and social awareness, creative imagination to moral passion, Paraguayan writers can overcome their tragic confinement and isolation and play a full part in literature in the Spanish language.

Translated by Nick Caistor

Tongue-Tied Eloquence: Notes on Language, Exile, and Writing

Stanislaw Baranczak

AMONG MANY HILARIOUS, outrageous, sublime, crazy, profound, or otherwise memorable scenes that fill the pages of Josef Skvorecky's unparalleled *The Engineer of Human Souls*, one brief episode seems to me particularly pregnant with meaning. One of the novel's minor characters, Milan, a recent Czech defector granted asylum in Canada, is throwing a housewarming party. Except for his Canadian girlfriend, all the guests are, not unexpectedly, Czech émigrés:

> Someone is telling a joke about the Prague policeman who drowned trying to stamp out a cigarette a passer-by had tossed in the river. There is loud laughter.
>
> Barbara hands Milan his glass.
>
> "I suppose he's telling jokes?"
>
> "That's right."
>
> "Well," says Barbara deliberately, "couldn't you translate them for me?"
>
> "They're only word games. My English isn't good enough."
>
> "Then how about making an effort? Your English is good enough for some things."
>
> But Milan ignores her . . .

. . . and, bad conversationalist though he might seem, he is right to do so. On the list of things that are the hardest to translate into another language, jokes come a close second after rhymed poetry (whereas love entreaties, as Barbara pretends not to realize, are among the easiest, if they require any translation at all). This is particularly true when the jokes are Eastern European, and told anywhere west of the Iron Curtain. Though no intellectual giant, Skvorecky's Milan understands this instinctively and immediately.

More sophisticated minds sometimes need a dozen years to grasp this simple truth. I have in mind the example of a famous Eastern European wit, the poet Antoni Slonimski, who in pre-1939 Poland had been nearly idolized by the readers of his side-splitting feuilletons published in every issue of the most popular literary weekly. When war broke out, he took refuge in the West and spent the next twelve years in London, but in 1951, of all moments, he decided to come back to Poland for good. Asked many years later why he had chosen to do so, he gave a disarmingly frank answer: in England, he was unable to tell a joke. No, he had no qualms about living under capitalism, especially since Stalinism anno 1951 was hardly a more attractive option. No, he had nothing against the English and their ways either (in fact, he was a declared Anglophile all his life). And no, he did not really feel lonely, or materially underprivileged, or socially degraded. What he could not stand was that whenever he tried to tell a joke to an English friend, he somehow was not funny.

For a while, he was determined to do anything in his power to succeed. He worked doggedly on his English and prepared all his jokes beforehand, endlessly chiseling their fine points and rehearsing for hours on end; once, before meeting some natives he particularly wished to impress, he stooped so low as to jot down a witticism on his cuff. All in vain; every joke of his was a flop. This would have been unbearable enough for a mere mortal. For Slonimski, who had spent twenty years building up his reputation as the wittiest man in Poland, this was sufficient reason to go back to the lion's den. There, hardships or no hardships, censorship or no censorship, he could at least sit down at his regular table in his favorite café, crack a joke, and hear his admirers laugh.

As told by Slonimski, this story of the return of the prodigal joker may well have been a joke in itself—the motives behind his decision were certainly more complex than that—but it says something about the expatriate's experience that usually escapes definition. And it says even more about the experience of the expatriate writer. After all, works of literature, just like jokes, are essentially "word games," as Skvorecky's Milan would have it. Easy for Robert Frost to say that poetry is what's lost in translation! Squarely settled in his homeland, he wrote for an audience that shared both his experience and his language, and it was of secondary concern to him just how much of what he intended to say was lost on some distant Chinese or Chilean reader. A writer who lives in exile has to care much more about what is "lost in translation." His foreign readers are within earshot, since he lives among them: if they don't laugh at his translated "word games," it hurts.

Of course, he may choose to stay forever on the safe side—that is, to lock himself up in the comfortable cell of his native language and write exclusively for the audience formed of his compatriots, either at home, or in the diaspora, or both. (Needless to say, this solution is only relatively safer: literature that deserves its name is always a risky business, and the fact that you share a language, literary tradition, experience, and whatever else with your readers does not necessarily mean that they give a damn.) But once the writer decides to reach beyond his native language and familiar audience, once he lets the very problem of "translation" cross his mind (regardless of whether he is to be translated by someone else, translate his works himself, or write originally in the language of his adopted country), the balance sheet of gains and losses will always loom in his consciousness ominously and inexorably.

What makes things even more bothersome is that the whole process of balancing the necessary losses against the uncertain gains is a two-way street. Trying to adapt his work to a foreign culture, the writer living in exile has no choice but to let this work lose some of its original flavor—that seems an obvious price to pay. Less obvious is the fact that this loss has its reverse side: being, after all, an outsider in the culture he is trying to conquer, the writer sooner or later realizes that some of this culture's qualities are lost on him as well. While attempting to hammer the peg of his work into the hard, resisting log of a foreign culture, he cannot help damaging both pieces of timber—that is, simplifying to some extent both the work and the culture as he sees it.

Again, the telling housewarming-party episode in Skvorecky's novel illustrates this double point in a neatly symmetrical way. Barbara's failure to comprehend an Eastern European joke is paralleled by Milan's failure to appreciate an allusion to American cultural lore. Her playing with a jigsaw puzzle (to which she, left out of the Czech conversation, has resorted) is for him just "a Canadian habit"; for her, it's an echo of a mythical Hollywood shot, one heavy with the symbolism of rejection, loneliness, and disenchanted love: "How could he know it? When *Citizen Kane* last played in Prague, Milan was not yet in this world. 'You never give me anything I really care about,' says Barbara, waiting against hope for Milan to understand."

But the line is lost on Milan, as well as the message that Barbara's quote was supposed to convey. An exiled writer similarly loses a considerable part of the intricate meaning of the culture he attempts to enter. He may try, for instance, to tell a typically absurd Eastern European story; yet in order to believe in the validity of such an undertaking at all, he must block out his awareness of the fact that his American audience has been brought up in a tradition whose pragmatism excludes the very notion of the absurd. Thus, in trying to impose his own vision, his own set of values, his own symbolism upon the foreign culture, he unavoidably distorts it: not only by enriching it but also by ignoring some of its intrinsic laws. And the only difference between him and Milan is that he is more or less aware of his ignorance.

Natural human egotism being a factor, however, it is understandable that what strikes the exiled writer first and foremost is how much of his own message is "lost in translation" or untranslatable altogether. A short poem by my coeval and compatriot, the Polish author Ewa Lipska, expresses it better than any semantic analysis. The poem is entitled "To Marianne Büttrich"; we are not told who Marianne Büttrich is, but it is clear that she lives on the other side of the European Great Divide, presumably in West Germany:

> For a year now I've been trying
> to write you a letter.
> But
> the locusts of my thoughts
> are untranslatable.
>
> Untranslatable are the people on duty
> guarding my words and grammar.
>
> My hours are untranslatable
> into yours.
> The black lilacs behind the window.
> The unbuttoned gates. The yellowed cigarette end of a day.
> The dead eye in the peephole
> at six a.m.
>
> *Rilke is untranslatable too.*
> *Die Blätter fallen, fallen . . .*
> *Wir alle fallen . . .*
>
> I've got so much to tell you
> but
> a tunnel is approaching
> my delayed train.
>
> A long whistle sounds.
>
> *I'm tired, Marianne,*
> *I'm leaving for the Bermuda Triangle*
> *to take a rest.*

Mind you, Lipska is not an exile (though she has visited the West), and she wrote this poem from the perspective of someone living in Poland in the

1980s. Still, there is no significant difference between her and the exiled writer, so far as the notion of the fundamental untranslatability of Eastern European experience is concerned. If anything, the feeling of tongue-tied helplessness is stronger in the latter case. It is exacerbated by an inevitable clash of two facts. On the one hand, any writer who moves—either voluntarily or under pressure—from behind the Elbe line to the West is convinced that he has a special mission to carry out. His task, as he sees it, is to open Westerners' eyes to what is going on "over there" and what threatens to engulf their free and well-to-do world. But on the other hand, precisely because he is now in direct touch with his new audience, he soon finds out, to his utter astonishment and horror, that Westerners do not exactly desire to have their eyes pried open. Czeslaw Milosz is a writer who should know about this: he came forward with one of the first such eye-openers when he defected in 1951 and soon afterward published *The Captive Mind*, to the boos of the largely pro-Stalinist Western European intellectual community. In his brief essay, "Notes on Exile," written much later in America, he describes this sort of clash as a classic paradox: in his homeland, the writer's voice was listened to but he was not allowed to speak; in exile, he is free to say whatever he wishes but nobody cares to listen (and moreover, Milosz adds, the writer himself may have forgotten what he had to say).

Granted, in real life the stable symmetry of this paradox sometimes wobbles. There are areas and periods of suddenly awakened or slowly growing interest in the part of the world the exiled writer came from, and his voice may come through with unexpected force. But even then his experience is hardly translatable in its entirety. Consider two skimpy lines from Lipska's poem: "The dead eye in the peephole / at six a.m." The Western reader's gaze will slide over this phrase as just another metaphor, perhaps a slightly macabre one: it may remind him of, say, a scene from "The Return of the Living Dead." For the Polish, or Czech, or Russian, or Rumanian reader, the phrase's impact is much more direct and its meaning is much more specific. In the "dead eye" he will recognize the blank stare of a secret policeman he may have seen more than once through the peephole in his own door, and "six a.m.," the typical time for police raids, will refer him unequivocally to the notion of a home search and arrest. If fear is the common semantic denominator of these two readings, it is fear of two distinctly different sorts: the enjoyable and leisurely fear of a horror-movie goer versus the ugly, shabby, completely unalluring yet very genuine fear of a citizen of a police state. The former smells of popcorn; the latter reeks of cold sweat.

"Wer den Dichter will verstehen, muss ins Dichters Lande gehen" (Whoever wants to understand the poet must go to the poet's homeland): old Goethe's noble adage sounded perfectly empirical in his enlightened time, but we, in our posttotalitarian epoch, should know better. Our century has known too many pilgrims who went "to the poet's homeland" only to be given red-carpet treatment, courtesy of Intourist, and a watchful guide, courtesy of the KGB. As the well-known book by Paul Hollander has documented, under certain circumstances there is nothing more false than the so-called eyewitness account. If the eyewitness comes from a nation or system with no experience in matters of all-out deceit and especially if he is willing to be duped, it is enough to hand him a skillfully packaged reality, and *voilà*—in his account all the barbed wire miraculously disappears and citizens' happy faces shine all around. Attempts to penetrate the inscrutable East from outside usually stop at the first banquet table with a generous supply of caviar. It speaks volumes for the futility of such pilgrimages that caviar was indeed the most vivid memory Billy Graham brought home from his preaching tour of the Soviet Union a couple of years ago. During the same tour, the sharp-eyed evangelist did not notice a ten-foot-long banner with precise data about the scope of religious persecution, nearly thrust into his face by some naïve dissident.

Would the West, then, ironically be better off if it believed so-called literary fiction rather than the sort of facts that the conveniently myopic eyewitnesses provide? Have things perhaps gone so far that the Westerner thirsting for first-hand knowledge of the Eastern bloc is much less likely to obtain it by visiting one of the bloc's countries than by reading a poem by Czeslaw Milosz, a novel by Josef Skvorecky, or an essay by Joseph Brodsky?

What I am saying amounts to praise of the cognitive potential of literature, which here, in this hemisphere swarming with deconstructionists, is a rather contemptible opinion to hold. Yet at the risk of sounding hopelessly backward, I hereby admit that I indeed believe in literature's power in naming reality—or, to put it differently, in letting us hear and comprehend reality's many-voiced hubbub more subtly and fully than any other kind of account. In this sense, the testimony supplied by the literary imagination may carry more weight on the witness stand than the evidence of our senses, especially when the evidence has been fabricated in order to fool us; and the imagination may be a more efficient interpretive tool than abstract reasoning, especially when we face a reality whose absurdity transcends rationalistic thinking. As witnesses go, literary fiction nearly always beats both being on the safe ground of supposedly hard facts and being in the clouds of ideological dogmas.

This also—perhaps above all—applies to the works of exiled writers. Their evidence has a special value despite the fact that their precarious balancing between two worlds, two cultures, two value systems, and two languages puts them, in more ways than one, at special risk. For one thing, there is the aforementioned barrier of different experiences: the audience in the exiled writer's adopted country, even if not entirely indifferent, is often unable to understand not merely his interpretation of reality but simply what he is speaking about. And quite naturally so, since neither the material of the readers' own experiences nor their inherited way of viewing reality has prepared them to accept this sort of a literary world. A world in which, for instance (to draw once again on Skvorecky's *The Engineer of Human Souls*), it is perfectly possible that one day workers in a factory are called to a meeting, aligned in single file, and ordered to sign, one by one and with no exception, a petition demanding the execution of the nation's political leader, whom they were told to worship only yesterday. For an American reader, this is an Orwellian fantasy; for a Czech writer, this is what in fact happened in his country and what he could have seen with his own eyes.

Yet different experiences, heterogeneous though they may be, can be forcibly brought together by the writer to reveal some common human denominator; they can be juxtaposed and compared, and their mutual differences can be defined, explained, and reflected upon. The annoying thing about literature is that all this has to be done in this or that ethnic language, which naturally limits the defining, explaining, and reflecting to the writer's native audience. (Classical dancers are, obviously, better off in this respect: the language of their art is international. But then, I somehow cannot picture myself pirouetting in public. Toiling at my untranslatable manuscripts poses, I should think, a relatively smaller risk of making a fool of myself.)

The problem of translation rears its ugly head once again. Once someone has tried to translate a literary text, his own or someone else's, he knows well that the chief difficulty of this endeavor lies not in the mere tedium of rummaging through dictionaries and laboriously substituting one word for another. The chief difficulty is that two different languages are never a mirror reflection of each other; their seemingly corresponding parts never exactly match. The semantic ranges of supposedly equivalent words in fact only partially overlap; or a meaning may be expressed by three different synonyms in one language and five in the other; or a word may have no counterpart in the other language at all; or the emotional tinge of a word may disappear in its foreign equivalent . . . And we are still on the level of separate words. What about phrases, sentences, verse lines, stanzas, paragraphs? What about the nation's accumulated historical experience, which is reflected in words' and expressions' elusive connotations, not to be found in any dictionary? What about complications of a literary and poetic nature that raise the elementary incompatibility of two language systems to the second and third power? There is no end to the translator's woe, and his most brilliant effort may result at best in an approximation that is more ingenious than other approximations.

But the author—particularly the author who lives in exile and harbors the ambition to conquer the minds of his foreign-tongued hosts—is not interested in approximations. He wants his one-of-a-kind message to come across in unaltered and unbent shape, just as he intended it to look and sound. In this situation, the translator is the author's adversary rather than his ally, a spoiler rather than helper, a necessary evil. Even if the translator is the author himself.

A glance at the contemporary literary scene make one realize that the panorama of ways of dealing with this problem stretches between two extremes. One extreme solution, represented, I believe, by Milan Kundera, consists in minimizing the translator's potential interference. The author is to make his original work as translatable as possible—in fact, he makes himself write in a deliberately translatable, clear, and unequivocal style, so that the translator will not be prodded into too many deviations from the intended meaning.

The other extreme, best illustrated by Kundera's opponent in other matters, Joseph Brodsky, consists in skipping translation altogether. Brodsky's literary evolution in exile—as an essayist but also a poet—has aimed at achieving linguistic self-sufficiency, becoming capable of writing the most artistically complex works directly in the language of his adopted country, so that a translator's services would no longer be called for.

Both extreme solutions may be admired for their radical boldness, and in fact it is very rare that a writer dares adopt either of them in their pure form. The more common solutions can be located somewhere in between: these are the fairly usual cases of authors who, for instance, are capable of writing a decent essay or article in their second language, but wisely refrain from writing poems or novels in it, and instead rely on translators (at best trying to keep the translators' arbitrariness in check by cooperating with them). Even though the Kundera and Brodsky solutions have their respective advantages, the risk involved in either is indeed great. In the first case, the writer constantly faces the danger of losing his unique voice, slipping into some bland, abstract, international style, sounding like translationese even before the translation as such has been undertaken. In the other, the writer is constantly engaged in a high-wire act of imposture, usurping a language that will never be genuinely his own; and the more breathtaking the heights of stylistic bravado he manages to reach, the more painful may be the fall. Of course, both Kundera and Brodsky are artists masterful enough to dodge these dangers. Yet even they are not shielded from criticisms by those whose opinions matter the most—the readers for whom the French or English of these authors' works is a native language.

This is also true of anybody who attempts to bypass the translation problem on a more limited scale, for instance by trying to write—like the author of these words—some relatively plain essayistic prose directly in his second language. Perfect bilingualism is not a very common ability, even when it comes to you naturally (for instance, by virtue of having been raised by an ethnically mixed pair of parents), much less when you try to attain it by learning. As a practical consequence, the exiled author who writes in his adopted language can do pretty well without a translator but, as a rule, he cannot do without an editor. No matter how hard he tries, and no matter how linguistically proficient he is, there will always be some wrongly used the's or a's, some misshaped syntactic patterns, some ill-fitting idioms that will expose his hopeless position as an eternal outsider. After all, even in Joseph Conrad's English, some Polish turns of phrase occasionally occur. Or so I'm told by native speakers of English.

This, obviously, teaches you humility. The chief reason the exiled writer tries to write in the language of his adopted country is his desire to accomplish his mission—that is, to get his message across to a broader audience. But, ironically, exactly by accomplishing his mission in this way he fails to accomplish it in another, arguably more important sense. For his mission as a writer is not merely to get his message across but also to leave his individual imprint on this message; literature's essence is not so much the message itself as the endless spectrum of "word games" (to quote Skvorecky's Milan once more) in which the writer's uniqueness may be revealed. This is extremely hard, in fact almost impossible to achieve if you write in a language that is not yours by birth.

True, even though the absolutely perfect command of a language is something an outsider cannot really acquire, he can, through a lot of effort, finally attain a fluency and glibness that make him sound almost like a native writer. But literature is something more than glib writing. It also includes the right—and necessity—to violate glibness, to make light of rules, to speak in a novel way without bothering to be correct. In literature, a new thought cannot emerge except from a new way of speaking: in order to say anything relevant, you must break a norm. And this is precisely what an outsider cannot afford, since if breaking is to make any sense at all, you may break only the norms that bind you, not those that bind someone else. If a native writer purposely violates language, it's called progress; if an outsider does it, it's called malapropism.

The exiled writer is someone who has left the cage of an oppressive political system; but if he is to remain a writer at all, he must never really leave another cage—that of his native language. There, he was gagged; here, he is tongue-tied. The ultimate irony: those who are the most tongue-tied may have the most to say.

A Woman and Her Poems

Belkis Cuza Malé

THERE IS AN IMPERCEPTIBLE sensation of unreality that, in spite of our wishing otherwise, will not abandon us and makes it difficult for us to imagine if we have not had the same experience: that of one who flees. Flees from what, from whom? From an endless mystery? From a certainty which, being less than immediate, has traces of the irrational? From an unhealthy phobia? From a contagious sickness? From nothingness.

I escaped from nothingness, having lived in a vacuum surrounded by mountains and snakes. Someone—I don't know who—opened the door and I escaped. I was a caged animal. I couldn't look to either side of me, nor did I know the color of the world in which I hadn't lived but which I had dreamed of knowing.

And when one escapes inward, when one goes through and slams shut that interior door, and in so doing, shatters with body and soul that thick glass that separates us from our true nature, the harm can, at times, be irreparable.

That happened to me. Born in the easternmost part of the island of Cuba, having felt and suffered the thousand and one nights of my life, I now find myself opening like a fan in the midst of a horizon which, if not unknown, is at least different enough to affect one's cardiac rhythm.

What is a woman like me, a writer from the "third world" who has known and endured the experience of living in a socialist country—I already know the answer—doing in a democratic community like this, surrounded by cordial strangers whose apparent interests are limited to avoiding overweight and insomnia and to playing tennis on Saturday afternoons? I—who know what it's like in a country of shortages where everything is rationed—can only and always cite my two reference points: the earth and the sky.

If the one who left the cage had been a woman with normal concerns, surely everything would be easier: have a family, bring up children, combine the housework with that of an office or factory—routine undertakings common to all women of the world. But in my case—and I can only speak for myself—the woman who went out that door carried a bundle of papers under her arm. When the x-ray machine examined my luggage, I feared for no object of material value. I trembled inside for my poems, clumsily camouflaged. And who in today's world cares about a poem? Only and exclusively a customs official in a communist country. Only they believe in the efficacy of poetry. Although unwholesome as readers, they find it stimulating to think that one writes for someone: to play a dirty trick on a bureaucrat.

Here in the United States, in the midst of what I'd dreamed of, life vibrates differently: a poem doesn't upset anyone, in fact it has ceased to function on an ideological level and must succeed on its own.

The woman and her poems are a part of that unreality familiar to those of us who, in paper boats or perhaps flying, left our countries to begin a new life. Once here, one lives—the woman and her poems, I mean—at loose ends, or rather, walking life's line a bit terrified of whatever steps on our heels. To change one's town, one's city, one's country, only brings us face to face again with our defenselessness: meeting people, opening up new paths, sitting at a typewriter and writing. But writing about what, about whom, and above all, for whom?

First of all, I write about what I see, about what I am learning. I allow myself the exercise of looking at a distance, over my shoulder, at the world I left behind, the one I looked at in a special way. I must clarify that my unhappiness had another tone, not that of bitterness but that of the profoundest sadness: disillusionment. Because I really took advantage of my captivity in many ways: by painting, by cooking sophisticated meals (casseroles with unfamiliar flavors, rice dishes I invented depending on available ingredients), by growing plants, by learning tropical botany, by delving into the moth-eaten papers of the National Archives, by getting to know Old Havana, by writing about nineteenth-century Cuban literature, by writing a novel and stirring up among the women of my country a story of struggle and repentance. And if that wasn't enough, I was the friend of unforgettable individuals who taught me theosophy and esoteric religions. I was also the friend of a most incredible woman, Mercedes Borrero, for whom Rubén Darío wrote a special poem, who revealed to me many of the secrets of her marvelous family. And I survived thanks to the prayer of the eternal Joseíto, a powerful mind capable of traversing space, who knew better than anyone the art of spirituality.

When one has made a drive lever of adversity, nothing is easier than to keep acting by reflex. Thus, the woman and her poems find a certain satisfaction in knowing that, outside of the context of suffering, one still suffers. I have opened my bags like a tourist in a hotel room, and I have looked out the window to see the sky and really compare it with the other one, the one I left behind which they say is always so blue.

But I also like velvety skies, sophisticated moons, frosts, and snow. I am atypical, for I think my nostalgia is composed of the bygone minute, the one that vanished with my friends and their death, the one that will never come again even though I might return to the island. And since it is nostalgia (not because I am here, but because I am different), it has no remedy nor am I interested in ending it. I live from my nostalgia, from this very special nostalgia which prevents bitterness and false ideas.

Speaking of the future, I said that I arrived, opened my bags and told myself that I would only have to go out to the street to find everything that interested me, because, like me, thousands and thousands of hopeless nostalgics (in their own way) are crowded at their windows waiting for me to go by. I am the one they secretly wait for: they speak my language, they suffer, they live, they are here like me, and their past and their future are one puzzling drama. Now my world has become vast, something like that of an amnesiac who suddenly assumes the memory of others—of Colombians, Venezuelans, Dominicans, Puerto Ricans—of infinite nationalities like and unlike my interior world. Between them and me there exists the unsuspected link of a tragedy which we have not only attended as spectators but as participants: the world of those who venture into the voluntary exile of their sensitivity.

Nevertheless, it won't be easy for us to realize that in the tomorrow we are living today, there won't be a glance that isn't invariably thirsty for the past, that is, for roots. This happens, like it or not, to all writers who detach themselves from their vital center in order to conquer a neighbor's terrain; but neither Shakespeare, for example, nor the other great classic writers worried too much about sticking to characters of their own area or nationality. They simply felt themselves universal, and every person, with his individual tragedy, awakened in them the same interest.

If the classics weren't the best example, suffice it to say that, as a Cuban woman, I also feel Spanish, Haitian, Mexican, and each one of the nationalities that pass by my side. My tragedy as a social being is minimized to the extent that I am the Jewess who managed to survive the atrocities of the concentration camp, the Hindu or Pakistani woman who contemplates with resignation the ceaseless waters of the sacred river in which her youth rots, the child who learned her ABCs in an African village, and I know I have lived the life of any Chinese girl. That's how I see myself, detached from the sun, fluttering like a butterfly, warbling among the leafy trees of Virginia.

Perhaps it's because, as those who know say, I have lived all this already and I am in my fifth or sixth reincarnation. But if that's not the case, if my defenses were reduced to the historical present, I would throw my cards on the table and shout that I will invent a future for myself. Fortunately or unfortunately, I have "lived" too much to begin again at zero. The eloquence of sarcasm will suppose that I possess all the magic arts needed to change me into a "civilized" writer. I forgot to say that categories interest me very little. I am the child of another era and I do not renounce any part of what I have lived and learned with blood.

Translated by Doris Meyer

The Working Problems of the Writer in Exile

Lion Feuchtwanger

I

WHEN I WAS A STUDENT in Munich I participated in a seminar which dealt with the subject "Experience and Fiction." That was in the period of deep peace before the first World War; the ivory tower was the literary fashion, and the professor in charge of the seminar drew a neat dividing line between external and internal experience. To him the writer's inner form seemed predetermined from birth, and he refused to admit that an author's work could be in any way influenced by the spot where his desk stood.

There was much talk in that seminar of the many authors of all nations and all times who had had to spend a large span of their lives in exile, and of the many works of highest literary merit that were composed in exile. The professor declared that these years of exile might have influenced the authors' choice of material but not their inner landscape. I confess that even as a callow student I looked upon this thesis with suspicion. I could not bring myself to believe that the exile of Ovid, Li-Tai-Po, Dante, Heinrich Heine, and Victor Hugo had influenced only the subject materials of these poets. It seemed to me that the innermost character of the works which these authors wrote in the period of their exile was conditioned by their external circumstances, by their exile. The infernal malice of certain of Dante's terza rima, the flashing sharpness of Victor Hugo's polemics, the sadly cheerful, sweet and deep nostalgia of Li-Tai-Po's verse, the elegantly poisonous sarcasm of Heine's poems—all these are unthinkable without the exile of the authors. Their exile is not a fortuitous coincident, it is the very source of their works. Not the subject matter but the character of these writers was changed by exile.

Now, at the outset of the second decade of my life and writing in exile, this belief of mine has become far more than a mere opinion. It has become one of the foundations of my inner being; and when I now speak to you on the external and internal problems which confront the author in exile, I hope that my remarks will not be too markedly tinted with the colors of painful personal experiences.

II

I will not dwell too long on the bitter theme of the many purely external difficulties with which the writer in exile must contend. I hope that those who have not experienced these difficulties will be spared them.

The author who has lost the reading public of his own land frequently loses at the same time the core of his economic existence. Very many writers of the highest talent, whose products were in great demand in their own countries, find no markets in foreign lands, either because their chief merit lies in the stylistic qualities of their language, and these qualities cannot be translated, or because their choice of subjects does not interest the foreign reader. Many exiled writers cannot or will not comply with the well-meant suggestions of their publishers to make concessions to the taste of the foreign public. It is surprising how many authors whose accomplishments the entire world has acclaimed, in spite of their most earnest efforts, now stand helpless and without means in the face of this situation.

Add to this the fact that many writers suffer far more than other emigrants from the trivial little annoyances that make up the daily life in exile. It is no great inconvenience to be forced to live in a hotel room and to be constantly subject to bureaucratic regulations. But not every writer is capable of composing a comprehensive novel in a hotel room; it tears down his nerves. And it tears them down doubly when he does not know whether he will be able to pay his hotel bill tomorrow, when his children beg for food, and when the police inform him that his residence permit will expire in three days.

The sufferings of banishment have only rare heroic moments; they generally consist of little, silly annoyances that often have a tinge of the ludicrous. But at best it costs much time and money to overcome these little external difficulties. In various countries, for example, I was expected to produce papers which I, as a refugee, could not possibly have; I was expected to prove by means of documents from my home that I am I, that I had been born, that I am an author. It is no exaggeration to state that the efforts to produce such evidence cost me as much time as the writing of a novel.

The economic difficulties and the enervating struggle with endless trivialities characterize life in exile. Many writers have been crushed by this life. Many preferred suicide to the tragicomedy of such an existence.

III

The fortunate writer who survives all that, finds his work beset with inner difficulties undreamt of in his homeland. There is, first of all, the bitter experience of being cut off from the living stream of his mother tongue. Language changes from year to year. In the ten or eleven years of our exile, life has moved on very rapidly and has invented a thousand new words and sounds for a thousand new concepts. We first hear the new words for these new concepts in the foreign tongue. Always and everywhere the sounds of foreign speech din in our ears, its symbols press in upon us daily and hourly, they gnaw away at our own powers of expression. Everyone of us has had the experience that the foreign word, the foreign construction sometimes usurps a dominant place in our thinking.

Some of us have tried, with reasonably acceptable results, to write in the foreign language; none of us has really succeeded. None of us can succeed. To be sure, one can learn to express oneself in a foreign language, but the ultimate emotional values of the foreign idiom can never be learned. It is impossible to create in a strange tongue. The Greeks and Romans called him a barbarian who could not speak their language. The poet Ovid, banished among such barbarians, wrote in their barbarous tongue and was highly honored by them. And yet he complained: "Here I am the barbarian, for no one understands me."

It is a strange experience to observe how the effect of our work does not emanate from the form in which we wrote it, but from a translation. The echo which we hear is not the echo of our own word. For even the best translation remains somehow foreign. We have perhaps wrestled with a sentence, with a word, and after a long search we have found the sentence, the word, the happy phrase which is completely molded to our thought and feeling. And then we see the translated word, the translated sentence. It is quite correct in all details, but the aroma is gone, the life is gone.

IV

Gradually, willy-nilly, we ourselves change in the new environment, and with us changes all that we create. The only road to the inner vision is through the outer. The new land in which we live affects the choice of our subjects and also affects the form. The landscape which surrounds the writer changes the landscape within him.

Many of us are inwardly so bound to the content and form of our youth and home that we cannot free ourselves from them and strive with might and main against the new environment. This introversion into a dead past, this estrangement from real life, this proud seclusion reduces the strength of writers, makes them sere and sterile. The exiled writers who take this attitude—and there are many such, among them authors of the highest merit—these have drawn the hardest lot and they are most deeply embittered.

I am making an effort, as I said at the outset, not to show too much resentment in speaking of the sufferings of the writer in exile. That makes my exposition colorless, and I feel that everything I have said is understated and much too dry. But everything that I might say on the subject of the writer in exile has been much better expressed in my novel *Paris Gazette.* This novel, incidentally, in its original form is by no means entitled *Paris Gazette.* This title is a concession to foreign readers. In the original the title is simply, truthfully, and boldly—or if you prefer—impudently, *Exile.*

Incorporated in this novel *Exile* is a chapter which deals with the effects of banishment, written during one of the gloomiest interludes of my exile, a pause between internment in two different French concentration camps. Today I am glad that, even in those sad days, I placed the emphasis not upon the sufferings of the exiled artist but upon the fact that the true writer, the one deserving of this name, grows in strength in exile.

For although banishment is destructive and makes the victim small and miserable, it also hardens him and adds to his stature. A vast abundance of new material and new ideas pours in upon him, he is confronted with a variety of impressions he would never have known at home.

If we make an effort to take a historical view of our life in exile, it becomes evident even now that almost everything that seemed to hamper our work finally contributed to its welfare. In this connection I must not conceal the fact that, for example, even the constant, enforced contact with a foreign language, which I loudly deplored a few paragraphs earlier, finally results in an enrichment. The author who lives in a foreign speech environment almost automatically and constantly checks his own against the foreign word. He frequently finds that the foreign language has a more striking word for that which he wishes to express. He is therefore not satisfied with that which his own tongue has to offer, but sharpens, files and polishes the existent expression until it has become something new, until he has wrested the new, the more striking word from his own language. Everyone of us has adapted fortunate turns of phrase from the foreign language to his own.

V

It can be said that suffering makes the weak weaker, but the strong stronger. Banishment has constricted some of us, but to the stronger, the more able, it gave breadth and elasticity, it opened their eyes more fully to the great and essential things, and taught them not to cling to nonessentials.

> And till thine this deep behest:
> Die to win thy being!
> Art thou but a sullen guest
> Upon earth unseeing,

says Goethe. Banishment is a hard school that sternly teaches the meaning of the behest: Die to win thy being. A number of exiled writers have become inwardly more mature, have been renewed and rejuvenated. They have not only become more bitter, but also more wise and more just toward their new world, more grateful and more conscious of their own mission. "Die to win thy being" has become their experience and their possession.

All in all, literature in exile has stood the test fairly well. When the tide has passed and when we can again weigh with accurate balance what is good and what is not, posterity will find that, among the works of this period, those composed in exile will not be light in the scales.

The Typewriter Made Me Do It

Jan Novak

IN 1967, I DECIDED TO become a poet. I was then living in Kolin, a small town in Czechoslovakia, so I was going to become a Czech poet. I was 14 years of age, so I was going to be a *major* Czech poet.

To the time and the place, a poet appeared to be a kind of instrument, a medium of the Czech language. Poetry seemed mostly a matter of words: you used obscure, shocking or archaic words; you juxtaposed them in unexpected ways, and the meaning took care of itself. You got published; you became famous; and finally, love-starved women began to call you from noisy bars to slur propositions.

Poetry had not been a vocation of choice for me, but I had had to admit to myself that I did not have it in me to make the national team in hockey. However, I managed to be big about my existential adjustment and I set out to learn the business of poetry without bitterness.

Two years later, before I had published a single line, I was severed from the Czech language forever. One humid summer morning, I landed in Traiskirchen, a massive transit camp of bedbugs and knife fights about 25 kilometers south of Vienna, where most Eastern European refugees get stuck waiting for visas to the country of their particular dream. It had been my father's decision that put me there. I did not like it and I fought with him about it, but I was under age and there was nothing I could do about it: we were stateless and we were not going back.

My transformation into the phantom of my provincial anxieties had begun.

The Czech language was then clearly and indisputably the most precise, expressive and graceful tool of communication ever breathed by man, and I became consumed with the fear of losing it. I would toss and twist on the squeaking bunk bed deep into the night, squeezing my memory for poetic Czech words and expressions. I dreaded the inevitable linguistic debilitation of exile, and I fought against it by making fervent resolutions: I was never going to perceive and feel the world through another language; I was going to keep up my Czech at any cost. And if, in 30 years, this were to reduce me to the mental dimensions of a Beckett character, so be it.

Our classroom-sized dormitory in Traiskirchen housed about 60 people, and in the morning the squeaking of my bed rated as the gossip event of the night: the mothers of adolescent daughters slew me with their eyes; their daughters giggled; older gentlemen grinned at me and winked. . . . I did not care. I had work to do, and I kept hoarding my poetic capital. The daily encounters with another vigorous language, German, had been too menacing.

My family was hoping to settle in an English-speaking country, but it seemed peculiar to study English while we were hanging on to the edge of Austria, so I spent my year in Traiskirchen learning German. Toward the end of our sojourn, my German became good enough to get me the coveted camp position of the translator in the infirmary. I held the gravy job for two days, then got fired because gonorrhea was starting to spread in the camp and the female patients could not bring themselves to confide their symptoms to a longhaired kid with disdainful, know-it-all airs. The camp administration quickly hired an older matron to replace me, and I moved on to cut linoleum in a nearby factory.

I had been able to surrender myself to the German vibrations of Traiskirchen while knowing that in my future life somewhere overseas, I was going to need English only because I saw myself as a Czech poet. In fact, I was rather worried about becoming *too* proficient in another language. I thought I had to steep my entire consciousness in the chosen linguistic medium; I had to be careful not to scramble my vital Czech with the static of irrelevant verbal rhythms.

In June 1970, my family finally crossed the Atlantic and settled in Chicago, where, among other languages, English is spoken. This I had been prepared for, but what had blindsided me was the surreal Czech dialect used in the local émigré community.

The Chicago Czech is a fascinating hybrid: its singsong rhythms come from American English; its lexicon sports many English words modified with Czech prefixes and suffixes; its syntax frequently retraces American phrases word for word; some of its locutions have a sharply archaic flavor. Furthermore, the psychology of its usage is no less captivating because people often try to camouflage their ignorance of English with an ostentatious display of Czechagoese. (In general, the more Anglicisms a speaker lobs at you, the shakier his English.)

I of course raged at this immensely interesting vernacular. I swore myself to sleep once again, vowing that I would cut out my tongue before uttering a word of this stillborn, sterile monstrosity, this lazy brainless perversion of my supple poetic tool. English no longer seemed as threatening to my vocation as the American Czech, and I stopped thinking about protecting my unconscious from its creeping invasion.

For the next few years, I lived in my parents' house, where I spoke, read and wrote mostly in Czech and where I dreamed the habitual émigré dreams of returns and entrapments. English was the language of daylight, of school, of the immigration office, of the back seat of police cars and rusted gas guzzlers. I saw no reason to study this means of everyday misunderstandings in a purposeful way; I was sure to get it by osmosis. (This backward-looking mentality, typical for an off-the-boat immigrant, has profoundly shaped the pared-down, raw, punchy idiom of Chicago English, which suffers few stylistic anxieties: if you've got something to say in the city of broad shoulders, don't sweat how it sounds—just spit it out.)

Years passed; I put in my osmosis time in American schools, and girls began to ask me to talk to them in Czech. At first I stammered tentative banalities. Later I worked out a more elegant solution. I would stab my eyes into theirs and whisper theatrically, giving them all the Slavic passion they thought they had coming:

> Whether you make it far or near
> as this wide world turns on,
> be sure to be a good Pioneer!
> Be sure to be a good Person!

The jabberwocky I had had to memorize in the citizens' education classes of Kolin usually put these young women where I had once aspired to have the entire Czech reading public—they listened with half-closed eyes, their breaths bated. They were clearly in poetic transport. They had no idea that my Czech had begun to deteriorate.

There were times now when I could not recall an everyday word, such as "carrot," "filer," or "sloth." I would waste the day probing the labyrinthine recesses of my memory because to get help from the dictionary seemed only to legitimize the loss. At other times, I caught myself slipping into the despised Czechagoese. Computers, graft, football and other things were becoming easier to talk about in English. Most disturbingly, however, now and then a straightforward Czech phrase would suddenly turn opaque and abstract on me. To comprehend it, I would have to replay it in my mind as if it had reached me wrapped in a thick, unfamiliar accent. I would not be sure whether it was correctly put; there was a sense that something was wrong with it, but I could not say what.

The fleeting glimpses of Czech as a foreign language unnerved and depressed me, but I refused to think about the implications. A few of my poems found their way into émigré publications whose apparent obscurity only obscured their real obscurity. I was a published poet at last, but my verses smeared the fingers; the paper quickly turned yellow and brittle; no one called. What is a writer without adulation?

I had always written primarily to please myself, but I never thought of myself as a diarist, so in the mid-70s in Chicago I proceeded to translate my texts into English. At first I merely wanted to enter my poems in literary competitions, but gradually I realized that when drafting them I was now explaining things that a Czech reader would know. I had started to write for Americans; my linguistic transformation was under way. It was to happen in three delicately unburdening stages, as I moved from writing in Czech about Czechs for Czechs to writing for Americans in English about Americans.

Faulkner once accurately observed that we all start writing poems and, failing at that, go on to write short stories and, failing at that, become novelists. By the late 70s, I had failed my way up to the short stories that would become my first and only book written in Czech, *Striptease Chicago.* As I worked on longer and longer pieces, however, as the pages began to stack up, I started getting impatient with the tedious job of translating. My head was full of ideas for new literary projects, and I was compelled to lose time by doubling over things that I thought I had put behind me. The first drafts in Czech now gave me the feeling of driving with the hand brake stuck permanently on.

It also suddenly mattered that I had never obtained a Czech typewriter. Czech text crawls with accent marks, whimsical circles and check-mark hooks that soften the sound of certain consonants. On a Czech typewriter, the top row of keys is reserved for these specialized letters. If you do not happen to own the customized machine, you hand-print the phonetic marks onto a typed page. While composing sonnets, I never minded this detail work, but the maddening blizzard of hooks, slashes and circles began to strain my temper when I had to tattoo a novella with them.

In my dreams of that time, people were as likely to speak English as not, and I rarely returned to Kolin anymore. I was also now committing the various unthinkable transgressions I had lost so much sleep about: I used Czechagoese in sections of *Striptease Chicago* because the book dealt with the émigré community I was still living in. Whenever something became easier to express in English, I no longer twisted my Czech to fit it in. When I could not remember a word, I simply reached for a dictionary. I would never become a Czech poet; I did not care.

In 1983, I decided to write a novel. The story was going to come from my father's life: his embezzlements, his gambling, our immigration experience. I could feel that the book would take hundreds of pages, but it had not even occurred to me to draft it in English till I rolled a blank sheet of paper into my American electric typewriter—suddenly, I was struck by the size of the tattooing job that I was setting myself up for. Then I thought of the boring days and wasted weeks of translating that lay ahead, and I switched off the machine. I agonized over the problem for as long as it took to brew a pot of tea, then sat back down and started writing in English. I sensed immediately that the hand brake was off.

The Willys Dream Kit practically poured out of me. It came so easily that it was clear I had been ready to trade languages. For some time, when translating from Czech to English, I had been soaring through sentences while, in the opposite direction, I had to slog my way through. And English had become the official language of my subconscious—the Czechs too now spoke unaccented English in my dreams. (Some nights, however, a kangaroo, my Irish-American boss, a black woman or an assassinated President may still address me in colloquial Czech. . . .)

My second novel, *The Grand Life*, recycles my experience in the working world of corporate America. It is about overworked corpo lifers and dynamos whose dizzying days revolve around coffee carts, office furniture and departmental imperialism. They speak the computer bureaucratese that I hear around me every day, and there is not a single Czech character in the book: *The Grand Life* completed my linguistic transformation.

I have now spent less than half my life in the country of origin and more than half in what I take to be the country of terminus. Though I consider myself a Chicago writer, I often wake up with the distant echo of Czech rhymes in my ears. I write in a language that I will never stop learning, but I teach my children Czech. On occasion I use words that I cannot pronounce because I have lost the words that have shaped my larynx. In public, my Czech self still surfaces in sudden flashes—in the heat of a hockey game I yell at the referee, get a blank stare in reply, realize that I had shouted in Czech, and scramble to transfer my protestations into English, only to see them dismissed because their emotional load has dissipated. (This process encapsulates the entire problem of translation.)

There have been times when my linguistic schizophrenia has brought me eerie and delirious experiences. I have recently read *The Willys Dream Kit* in Czech. I had almost written the book in the language and now it has been translated into it. The translation had been arranged by Josef Skvorecky (whose Sixty-Eight Publishers will publish the book in Toronto), and it was done in Prague and done expertly. The manuscript came to me misty with cold-war romance of diplomatic pouches, cryptic postcards, acts of faith. I started reading it and it was my novel all right, my stories, my characters, my long breathless rhythms, my words that said everything I had wanted to say—and yet I could never have written this book. Had it been composed in Czech, the novel would have been a totally different work.

As I read this book that is and is not mine, I got an alarming glimpse of my self as another (who, however, is no less myself). I was startled to hear how American my voice sounded, how arrested my development in Czech was, how focusing the limitations had been. It felt as if the last time I had looked into a mirror was in Kolin 18 years before, and now I was suddenly facing a dimly remembered reflection; as if my childhood now belonged to someone else, someone who has never grown up, while my puberty belonged to a budding Czech poet who may have lost his lyrical gift. Perhaps this poet never had much talent to begin with. He has remained in Kolin and probably became an alcoholic in his job of production clerk at the local power plant. He spends his mornings staring out of his office window at the rusted railroad bridge that spans the foamy brown water of the River Elbe as it flows toward the North Sea. Several times he and I had lain face down between the tracks of the bridge and listened to a freight train thunder louder and louder, dreading and longing for a hard slap of air the way he now waits only for his first shot of vodka at lunchtime. He remembers how his muscles stiffened, how goose bumps covered the back of his neck, how his ears rang with the deafening roar, how the bridge swayed as, inches away, tons of steel flew past him. He wants to write a poem about it, but the words keep eluding him and then it is nearly noon and, at the bar of the cafeteria, a line is starting to form and he has to hurry before it gets too long.

An Emigré from Immortality

Marina Tsvetaeva

IF ONLY NO POLITICIANS stood between poet and people!

Despite my isolation, my Russian works—by their will, not mine—are designed for multitudes. Over here, as a physical fact, there are no multitudes, only groups. Just as, instead of the arenas and terraces of Russia, there are little salons, instead of the ethical event of a public performance—though it be an assault!—there are literary evenings, instead of the irreplaceable anonymous listener in Russia, there's a listener with a name, even with a distinguished one. All this belongs to literature, not to the current of life. The wrong scale, the wrong response. In Russia, as in the steppes and on the sea, there is room to speak from and into. If they'd let people speak.

The whole thing is simple: over here is—*that* Russia; over there is—all Russia. To people here, in art it's the past that's contemporary. Russia (I mean Russia, not the authorities), Russia, the land of those who are in the lead, requires of art that it should lead; the emigration, land of those who have remained behind, requires that art should remain behind too, which means—roll uncontrollably backwards. In the order of things here, I am a disorder of things. There, I wouldn't be published, but I would be read; here, I'm published—and not read. (Incidentally, they've stopped publishing me now as well.) The chief thing in a writer's life (its second half) is writing. Not: to get ahead, but: get it said. Over here, I'm not hindered from writing—doubly not hindered, for it isn't only persecution that hinders, fame (love) does too.

Everything is point of view. In Russia I'll be understood better. But in the next world I'll be understood even better than in Russia. Understood completely. I'll be taught to understand myself completely. Russia is merely the limit of earthly understandability, beyond the limit of earthly understandability in Russia is unlimited understandability in the not-earthly. "There is a land which is God, Russia borders *with it*," said Rilke, who himself yearned for Russia all his life, everywhere outside Russia. With that land which is God, Russia borders to this day. A *natural frontier*, which politicians can't displace, since it isn't churches that mark it out.

Not only now, after all that has come to pass, but always Russia has been the other world to everything that is not-Russia, whether with white bears or with Bolsheviks makes no difference: other. Something like a threat of salvation—of souls—through the perdition of bodies.

And it was not much easier, then, to take the decision to go there—with all the pre-war blandishments—than it is now, through all the prohibitions. Russia was never a country on the earthly map. And those who went there from here really went over the frontier: of the visible.

It's on *that* Russia that poets stake their bets. On Russia-entire, Russia of all time.

But even Russia isn't enough. Every poet is essentially an *émigré*, even in Russia. *Emigré* from the Kingdom of Heaven and from the earthly paradise of nature. Upon the poet—upon all who belong to art, but most especially upon the poet—there's a particular mark of discomfort, by which you'll know him even in his own home. An *émigré* from immortality in time, a non-returner to *his own* heaven. Take the most various of them, line them up in your mind: whose face shows presentness? All of them are—over there. Kinship with soil or people, nationality, race, class, and that contemporality which they create—all this is only surface, the first or the seventh layer of skin, which the poet does nothing but try his utmost to shed. "'What time is it?' they asked him here, and he answered the curious: 'It's eternity'"—Mandelstam on Batyushkov; and "What millennium is it, my dears, out there?"—Boris Pasternak on himself. All poets of all times say essentially one thing only. And that one thing remains on the surface of the world's skin in the same way as the visible world itself remains on the surface of the poet's skin. Next to that emigration, what is ours?

> And long she languished upon earth
> filled with a strange desire,
> And could not replace the songs of heaven
> with the tedious songs of earth!

—no less tedious for being one's own.

Translated by Angela Livingstone

A Hero of Labor

Marina Tsvetaeva

I HAVE NO READER in the emigration. I have, at best, a hundred admirers. (Note! There are more, but: 1) I neither know nor see them, and 2) even if there are thousands of them, they can do nothing for me, because in the emigration the reader has no voice. To be fair, I will say that my regular "evenings"—which are not evenings, but *readings*: with no attractions! I just walk out and read—were attended for years on end by the same roughly 80 to 100 people. I knew my audience by face. Some of these faces disappeared from time to time: They died.)

The times would wear away at me like a physical force in any country (except for one immense or several, many—there are still many!—small countries). I don't suit it intellectually, nor does it suit me. "We cannot meet / We are of different tribes." I belong in the loner's camp, while the times are a desert with fewer and fewer outposts (soon only bushes, bare ones). What's more, they have made me loud and hostile; I've often had to speak (to bellow) in *its* language, in *its* voice, a stranger's voice, to which I prefer—my own; to which I prefer—silence.

I have failed in the emigration because I am by nature a non-emigré, that is, by my height and sweep—I am there, to there, from there. The emigration has not recognized my themes, because of their Homeric dimensions. Here only discontinued lines sell—and how strange to expect otherwise!

And also because of the complete absence of those who love my verse, their absence from my daily life: There's no one to read to, no one to ask, no one to be happy with. *Everyone* is busy with something else. Because of my utter creative isolation. Everything on your own account. From the work's *theme* to a particular *syllable* (I am talking precisely about syllables). Despising literary circles, I would so much like to have—friends.

Because my circumstances are oppressive. Because they suffocate me.

I don't know how long I have left to live, I don't know if I'll ever be in Russia again, but I do know that until the last line I will write *powerfully*, that I will not render weak poems.

And I also know that by comparison, at least with my lyrical inundation in Prague (1922 to 1925), I have dried up, shriveled—become poor. But this withering, this exhaustion is spiritual and not writerly. Of the creative depths, and not of the notebook.

And I know that I have only to pick up the pen . . .

And I know that I pick it up less and less.

(Note! I'm talking about lyrics, that is, about separate lyric poems, that come and—unrealized—leave again . . .)

Lord, may I be a *hero of labor* until the final breath:

"And so, may God be with you."

Translated by Catherine Ciepiela

V

Solitudes

The exile's trade is: hoping.
—Bertolt Brecht

The New Lost Generation

James Baldwin

THIS IS AN EXTREMELY difficult record to assess. Perhaps it begins for me in 1946, when my best friend took his life. He was an incandescent Negro boy of twenty-four, whose future, it had seemed to all of us, would unfailingly be glorious. He and I were Socialists, as were most of our friends, and we dreamed of this utopia, and worked toward it. We may have evinced more conviction than intelligence or skill, and more youthful arrogance than either, but we, nevertheless, had carried petitions about together, fought landlords together, worked as laborers together, been fired together, and starved together.

But for some time before his death, troubles graver than these had laid hold of my friend. Not only did the world stubbornly refuse his vision; it despised him for his vision, and scourged him for his color. Of course, it despised and scourged me, too, but I was different from my friend in that it took me nearly no time to despise the world right back and decide that I would accomplish, in time, with patience and cunning and by becoming indestructible, what I might not, in the moment, achieve by force or persuasion. My friend did not despise anyone. He really thought that people were good, and that one had only to point out to them the right path in order to have them, at once, come flocking to it in loudly rejoicing droves.

Before his death, we had quarreled very bitterly over this. I had lost my faith in politics, in right paths; if there *were* a right path, one might be sure (I informed him with great venom) that whoever was on it was simply asking to be stoned to death—by all the world's good people. I didn't give a damn, besides, *what* happened to the miserable, the unspeakably petty world. There was probably not a handful of decent people in it. My friend looked very saddened by these original reflections. He said that it seemed to him that I had taken the road which ended in fascism, tyranny, and blood.

So, I told him, have you. One fine day, you'll realize that people don't *want* to be better. So you'll have to make them better. And how do you think you'll go about it?

He said nothing to this. He was sitting opposite me, in a booth, in a Greenwich Village diner.

What about love? he asked me.

His question threw me off guard, and frightened me. With the indescribable authority of twenty-two, I snarled: Love! You'd better forget about that, my friend. That train has *gone.*

The moment I said this, I regretted it, for I remembered that he *was* in love: with a young white girl, also a Socialist, whose family was threatening to have him put in prison. And the week before, a handful of sailors had come across them in the subway and beaten him very badly.

He looked at me and I wanted to unsay what I had said, to say something else. But I could not think of anything which would not sound, simply, like unmanly consolation, which would not sound as though I were humoring him.

You're a poet, he said, and you don't believe in love.

And he put his head down on the table and began to cry.

We had come through some grueling things together, and I had never seen him cry. In fact, he went into and came out of battles laughing. We were in a hostile, public place. New York was fearfully hostile in those days, as it still is. He was my best friend, and for the first time in our lives I could do nothing for him; and it had been my ill-considered rage which had hurt him. I wanted to take it back, but I did not know how. I *would* have known how if I had been being insincere. But, though I know now that I was wrong, I did not know it then. I had meant what I had said, and my unexamined life would not allow me to speak otherwise. I really did not, then, as far as I knew, believe that love existed, except as useless pain; and the time was far from me when I would begin to see the contradiction implicit in the fact that I was bending all my forces, or imagined I was, to protect myself against it.

He wept; I sat there; no one, for a wonder, bothered us. By and by we paid, and walked out into the streets. This was the last time, but one, that I ever saw him; it was the very last time that we really spoke. A very short time after this, his body was found in the Hudson River. He had jumped from the George Washington Bridge.

Why do I begin my sketch of Americans abroad with this memory? I suppose that there must be many reasons. I certainly cannot hope to tell or, for that matter, to face them all. One reason, of course, is that I thought for a very long time that I had hastened him to his death. *You're a poet, and you don't believe in love.* But, leaving aside now this hideous and useless speculation, it is from the time of my friend's death that I resolved to leave America. There were two reasons for this. One was that I was absolutely certain, from the moment I learned of his death, that I, too, if I stayed here, would come to a similar end. I felt then, and, to tell the truth, I feel now, that he would not have died in such a way and certainly not so soon, if he had not been black. (Legally speaking. Physically, he was almost, but not quite, light enough to pass.) And this meant that he was the grimmest, until then, of a series of losses for which I most bitterly blamed the American republic. From the time of this death, I began to be afraid of enduring any more. I was afraid that hatred, and the desire for revenge would reach unmanageable proportions in me, and that my end, even if I should not physically die, would be infinitely more horrible than my friend's suicide.

He was not the only casualty of those days. There were others, white, friends of mine, who, at just about the time his indescribably colored body was recovered from the river, were returning from the world's most hideous war. Some were boys with whom I had been to high school. One boy, Jewish, sat with me all night in my apartment on Orchard Street, telling me about the camps he had seen in Germany and the Germans he had blasted off the face of the earth. I will never forget his face. I had once known it very well—shortly before, when we had been children. It was not a child's face now. He had *seen* what people would do to him—because he was a Jew he knew what he had done to Germans; and not only could nothing be undone, it might very well be that this was all that the world could ever be, over and over again, forever. All political hopes and systems, then, seemed morally bankrupt: for, if Buchenwald was wrong, what, then, *really* made Hiroshima right? He shook his head, an old Jew already, an old man. If all visions of human nature are to be distrusted, and all hopes, what about love?

The people I knew found the most extraordinary ways of dealing with this question; but it was a real question. Girls who had been virgins when they married their husbands—and there were some, I knew them—sometimes had to have abortions before their husbands returned from overseas. The marriages almost never survived the returning pressures, and, very often, the mental equilibrium of the partners—or ex-partners—was lost, never to be regained. Men who had had homosexual adventures in CO camps, or in the service, could not accept what had happened to them, could not forget it, dared not discover if they desired to repeat it, and lapsed into a paralysis from which neither men nor women could rouse them. It was a time of the most terrifying personal anarchy. If one gave a party, it was virtually certain that someone, quite possibly oneself, would have a crying jag or have to be restrained from murder or suicide. It was a time of experimentation, with sex, with marijuana, and minor infringements of the law, such as "boosting" from the A & P and stealing electricity from Con Edison. I knew some people who had a stolen refrigerator for which they had no room and no use, and which they could not sell; it was finally shipped, I believe, of all places, to Cuba. But, finally, it seems to me that life was beginning to tell us who we are, and what life was—news no one has ever wanted to hear: and we fought back by clinging to our vision of ourselves as innocent, of love perhaps imperfect but reciprocal and enduring. And we did not know that the price of this was experience. We had been raised to believe in formulas.

In retrospect, the discovery of the orgasm—or, rather, of the orgone box—seems the least mad of the formulas that came to mind. It seemed to me—though I was, perhaps, already too bitterly inoculated against groups or panaceas—that people turned from the idea of the world being made better through politics to the idea of the world being made better through psychic and sexual health like sinners coming down the aisle at a revival meeting. And I doubted that their conversion was any more to be trusted than that. The converts, indeed, moved in a certain euphoric aura of well-being, which could not last. They had not become more generous, but less, not more open, but more closed. They ceased, totally, to listen and could only proselytize; nor did their private lives become discernibly less tangled. There are no formulas for the improvement of the private, or any other life—certainly not the formula of more and better orgasms. (Who decides?) The people I had been raised among had orgasms all the time, and still chopped each other up with razors on Saturday nights.

By this wild process, then, of failure, elimination, and rejection, I, certainly, and most of the people whom I knew got to Europe, and, roughly speaking, "settled there." Many of us have returned, but not all: it is important to remember that many expatriates vanish into the lives of their adopted country, to be flushed out only, and not always then, by grave international emergency. This applies especially, of course, to women, who, given the pressures of raising a family, rarely have time to be homesick, or guilty about "escaping" the problems of American life. Their first loyalties, thank heaven, are to the men they married and the children they must raise. But I know American couples, too, who have made their homes in Europe quite happily, and who have no intention of returning to this country. It is worth observing, too, that these people are nearly always marked by a lack of spite or uneasiness concerning this country which quite fails to characterize what I tend to think of as the "displaced" or "visible" expatriate. That is, remarkable as this may sound, it is not necessary to hate this country in order to have a good time somewhere else. In fact, the people who hate this country never manage, except physically, to leave it, and have a wretched life wherever they go.

And, of course, many of us have become, in effect, commuters; which is a less improbable state now than it was a decade ago. Many have neither returned nor stayed, but can be found in Village bars, talking about Europe, or in European bars, talking about America.

Apart from GIs who remained in Europe, thoughtfully using up all the cheap studios, and nearly all, as it turned out, of the available goodwill, we, who have been described (not very usefully) as the "new" expatriates, began arriving in Paris around '45, '46, '47, and '48. The character of the influx began to change very radically after that, if only because the newcomers had had the foresight to arm themselves with jobs: American government jobs, which also meant that they had housing allowances and didn't care how much rent they paid. Neither, of course, did the French landlords, with the result that rents rose astronomically and we who had considered ourselves forever installed in the Latin Quarter found ourselves living all over Paris. But this, at least for some of us, turned out to be very healthy and valuable. We were in Paris, after all, because we had presumably put down all formulas and all safety in favor of the chilling unpredictability of experience.

Voyagers discover that the world can never be larger than the person that is in the world; but it is impossible to foresee this, it is impossible to be warned. It is only when time has begun spilling through his fingers like water or sand—carrying away with it, forever, dreams, possibilities, challenges, and hopes—that the young man realizes that he will not be young forever. If he wishes to paint a picture, raise a family, write a book, design a building, start a war—well, he does not have forever in which to do it. He has only a certain amount of time, and half of that time is probably gone already. As long as his aspirations are in the realm of the dream, he is safe; when he must bring them back into the world, he is in danger.

Precisely for this reason, Paris was a devastating shock. It was easily recognizable as Paris from across the ocean: that was what the letters on the map spelled out. This was not the same thing as finding oneself in a large, inconvenient, indifferent city. Paris, from across the ocean, looked like a refuge from the American madness; now it was a city four thousand miles from home. It contained—in those days—no doughnuts, no milk shakes, no Coca-Cola, no dry martinis; nothing resembling, for people on our economic level, an American toilet; as for toilet paper, it was yesterday's newspaper. The concierge of the hotel did not appear to find your presence in France a reason for rejoicing; rather, she found your presence, and in particular your ability to pay the rent, a matter for the profoundest suspicion. The policemen, with their revolvers, clubs, and (as it turned out) weighted capes, appeared to be convinced of your legality only after the most vindictive scrutiny of your passport; and it became clear very soon that they were not kidding about the three-month period during which every foreigner had to buy a new visa or leave the country. Not a few astounded Americans, unable to call their embassy, spent the night in jail, and steady offenders were escorted to the border. After the first street riot, or its aftermath, one witnessed in Paris, one took a new attitude toward the Paris paving stones, and toward the café tables and chairs, and toward the Parisians, indeed, who showed no signs, at such moments, of being among the earth's most cerebral or civilized people. Paris hotels had never heard of central heating or hot baths or showers or clean towels and sheets or ham and eggs; their attitude toward electricity was demonic—once one had seen what they thought of as wiring one wondered why the city had not, long ago, vanished in flame; and it soon became clear that Paris hospitals had never heard of Pasteur. Once, in short, one found oneself divested of all the things that one had fled from, one wondered how people, meaning, above all, oneself, could possibly do without them.

And yet one did, of course, and in the beginning, and sporadically, thereafter, found these privations a subject for mirth. One soon ceased expecting to be warm in one's hotel room, and read and worked in the cafés. The French, at least insofar as student hotels are concerned, do not appear to understand the idea of a social visit. They expect one's callers to be vastly more intimate, if not utilitarian, than that, and much prefer that they register and spend the night. This aspect of Parisian life would seem vastly to simplify matters, but this, alas, is not the case. It merely makes it all but impossible to invite anyone to your hotel room. Americans do not cease to be Puritans when they have crossed the ocean; French girls, on the other hand, contrary to legend, tend, preponderantly, to be the marrying kind; thus, it was not long before we brave voyagers rather felt that we had been turned loose in a fair in which there was not a damn thing we could buy, and still less that we could sell.

And I think that when we began to be frightened in Paris, to feel baffled and betrayed, it was because we had failed, after all, somehow, and once again, to make the longed-for, magical human contact. It was on this connection with another human being that we had felt that our lives and our work depended. It had failed at home. We had thought we knew why. Everyone at home was too dry and too frightened, mercilessly pinned beneath the thumb of the Puritan God. Yet, here we were, surrounded by quite beautiful and sensual people, who did not, however, appear to find us beautiful or sensual. They said so. By the time we had been abroad two years, each of us, in one way or another, had received this message. It was one of the things that was meant when we were referred to as children. We had been perfectly willing to refer to all the other Americans as children—in the beginning; we had not known what it meant; we had not known that we were included.

By 1950 some of us had already left Paris for more promising ports of call. Tangiers for some, or Italy, or Spain; Sweden or Denmark or Germany for others. Some girls had got married and vanished; some had got married and vanished and reappeared—minus their husbands. Some people got jobs with the ECA and began a slow retreat back into the cocoon from which they had never quite succeeded in emerging. Some of us were going to pieces—spectacularly, as in my own case, quietly, in others. One boy, for example, had embarked on the career which I believe still engages him, that of laboriously writing extremely literary plays in English, translating them—laboriously—into French and Spanish, reading the trilingual results to a coterie of friends who were, even then, beginning to diminish, and then locking them in his trunk. Magazines were popping up like toadstools and vanishing like fog. Painters and poets of thin talent and no industry began to feel abused by the lack of attention their efforts elicited from the French, and made outrageously obvious—and successful—bids for the attention of visiting literary figures from the States, of whose industry, in any case, there could be no doubt. And a certain real malice now began to make itself felt in our attitudes toward the French, as well as a certain defensiveness concerning whatever it was we had come to Paris to do and clearly were not doing. We were edgy with each other, too. Going, going, going, gone—were the days when we walked through Les Halles, singing, loving every inch of France, and loving each other; gone were the jam sessions in Pigalle, and our stories about the whores there; gone were the nights spent smoking hashish in Arab cafés; gone were the mornings which found us telling dirty stories, true stories, sad and earnest stories, in gray, workingmen's cafés. It was all gone. We were secretive with each other. I no longer talked about my novel. We no longer talked about our love affairs, for either they had failed, were failing, or were serious. Above all, they were private—how can love be talked about? It is probably the most awful of all the revelations this little life affords. We no longer walked about, as a friend of mine once put it, in a not dissimilar context, in "friendly groups of five thousand." We were splitting up, and each of us was going for himself. Or, if not precisely for himself, his own way; some of us took to the needle, some returned to the family business, some made loveless marriages, some ceased fleeing and turned to face the demons that had been on the trail so long. The luckiest among us were these last, for they managed to go to pieces and then put themselves back together with whatever was left. This may take away one's dreams, but it delivers one to oneself. Without this coming together, the longed-for love is never possible, for the confused personality can neither give nor take.

In my case, I think my exile saved my life, for it inexorably confirmed something which Americans appear to have great difficulty accepting. Which is, simply, this: a man is not a man until he is able and willing to accept his own vision of the world, no matter how radically this vision departs from that of others. (When I say "vision," I do not mean "dream.") There are long moments when this country resembles nothing so much as the grimmest of popularity contests. The best thing that happened to the "new" expatriates was their liberation, finally, from any need to be smothered by what is really nothing more (though it may be something less) than mother love. It need scarcely, I hope, be said that I have no interest in hurling gratuitous insults at American mothers; they are certainly helpless, if not entirely blameless; and my point has nothing to do with them. My point is involved with the great emphasis placed on public approval here, and the resulting and quite insane system of penalties and rewards. It puts a premium on mediocrity and has all but slaughtered any concept of excellence. This corruption begins in the private life and unfailingly flowers in the public life. Europeans refer to Americans as children in the same way that American Negroes refer to them as children, and for the same reason: they mean that Americans have so little experience—experience referring not to *what* happens, but to *who*—that they have no key to the experience of others. Our current relations with the world forcibly suggest that there is more than a little truth to this. What Europe still gives an American—or gave us—is the sanction, if one can accept it, to become oneself. No artist can survive without this acceptance. But rare indeed is the American artist who achieved this without first becoming a wanderer, and then, upon his return to his own country, the loneliest and most blackly distrusted of men.

Fifth Walk

Jean-Jacques Rousseau

OF ALL THE PLACES I have lived (and I have lived in some charming ones), none has made me so truly happy nor left me such tender regrets as St. Peter's Island in the middle of Lake Bienne. This small island, which is called Hillock Island in Neuchâtel, is quite unknown, even in Switzerland. As far as I know, no traveler mentions it. However, it is very pleasant and singularly placed for the happiness of a man who likes to cut himself off; for although I am perhaps the only one in the world whose destiny has imposed this on him as a law, I cannot believe myself to be the only one who has so natural a taste—even though I have not found it in anyone else thus far.

The banks of Lake Bienne are wilder and more romantic than those of Lake Geneva, because the rocks and woods border the water more closely; but they are not less cheerful. If the fields and vineyards are less cultivated, and if there are fewer towns and houses, there is also more natural greenery, more meadows, grove-shaded retreats, more frequent contrasts, and more variety in the terrain. As there are no large thoroughfares suitable for coaches on these happy shores, the countryside is seldom frequented by travelers; but it is interesting for solitary contemplators who like to delight in the charms of nature at leisure and collect their thoughts in a silence troubled by no noise other than the cry of eagles, the intermittent chirping of a few birds, and the rushing of torrents as they fall from the mountain. This beautiful basin almost circular in form has two small islands in its center, one inhabited and cultivated, almost half a league around; the other smaller, uninhabited, and uncultivated, and which will ultimately be destroyed because earth is constantly taken away from it to repair the destruction waves and storms make to the large one. Thus it is that the substance of the weak is always used for the advantage of the powerful.

On the island there is only a single house, but a large, pleasant, and comfortable one which, like the island, belongs to Bern Hospital and in which a tax collector lives with his family and servants. He maintains a large farmyard, a pigeon house, and fish ponds. Despite its smallness, the island is so varied in its terrain and vistas that it offers all kinds of landscapes and permits all kinds of cultivation. You can find fields, vineyards, woods, orchards, and rich pastures shaded by thickets and bordered by every species of shrubbery, whose freshness is preserved by the adjacent water. A high terrace planted with two rows of trees runs the length of the island, and in the middle of this terrace a pretty reception hall has been built where the inhabitants of the neighboring banks gather and come to dance on Sundays during harvests.

This is the island on which I sought refuge after the stoning at Môtiers. I found the sojourn on it so charming, I led a life there so suitable to my temper that, resolved to end my days there, I had no worry other than their not letting me execute this project which did not fit in with the one of transporting me to England—a project whose first effects I was already feeling. Because of the forebodings that troubled me, I wanted them to make this refuge a perpetual prison for me, to confine me to it for life, and—removing every possibility and hope of getting off it—to forbid me any kind of communication with the mainland so that being unaware of all that went on in the world I might forget its existence and that it might also forget mine.

They let me spend scarcely two months on this island, but I would have spent two years there, two centuries, and the whole of eternity without being bored for a moment, even though besides my helpmate, I had no companionship there other than that of the tax collector, his wife, and his servants, who in truth were all very worthy people but nothing more; but that was precisely what I needed. I consider these two months the happiest time of my life, so happy that it would have contented me for my whole existence without the desire for another state arising for a single instant in my soul.

Now what was this happiness and in what did its enjoyment consist? From the description of the life I led there, I will let all the men of this century guess at it. The precious *far niente* was the first and the principal enjoyment I wanted to savor in all its sweetness, and all I did during my sojourn was in effect only the delicious and necessary pursuit of a man who has devoted himself to idleness.

The hope that they would ask for nothing better than to leave me in this isolated spot where I had ensnared myself on my own, which it was impossible for me to leave without help and surely without being noticed, and where I could have communication or correspondence only by the assistance of the people who surrounded me, this hope, I say, led me to hope I would end my days there more peacefully than I had spent them until then. And the idea that I would have time to adapt myself to it in complete leisure caused me to begin by not adapting at all. Transported there abruptly, alone and destitute, I had my housekeeper, my books, and my few furnishings brought over, one after the other. And I had the pleasure of unpacking nothing, leaving my boxes and my trunks as they had arrived and living in the abode in which I counted on finishing my days as in an inn I would have to leave on the following day. All things, such as they were, went along so well that to want to arrange them better would have been to spoil something. Above all, one of my greatest delights was to leave my books well packed up and to have no writing table. When wretched letters forced me to take up a pen to reply, I grudgingly borrowed the tax collector's writing table and then hastened to return it, in the vain hope of not needing to borrow it again. Instead of depressing papers and heaps of old books, I filled my room with flowers and dried plants; for I was then in my first botanical fervor for which Dr. d'Ivernois had given me an inclination and which soon became a passion. Wanting no more toilsome work, I needed something amusing which would please me and require only as much trouble as a lazy man likes to take. I set about doing the *Flora petrinsularis* and describing all the plants of the island, without omitting a single one, in sufficient detail to occupy myself for the rest of my days. It is said that a German did a book about a lemon peel; I would have done one about each stalk of hay of the meadows, each moss of the woods, each lichen that carpets the rocks; in short, I did not want to leave a blade of grass or a plant particle which was not amply described. As a result of this fine project, every morning after breakfast, which we all had together, I would go off, a magnifying glass in hand and my *Systema naturae* under my arm, to visit a district of the island, which I had divided into small squares for this purpose, with the intention of covering them one after the other in each season. Nothing is more singular than the raptures and ecstasies I felt with each observation I made on plant structure and organization, as well as on the role of the sexual parts in sporulation, which was then a completely new system for me. I was enchanted to discover generic features of which I previously had not the slightest idea and to verify them on common species, while waiting for rarer ones to offer themselves to me. The forking of the two long stamens of the self-heal, the spring of those of the nettle and the pellitory, the explosion of the fruit of the balsam and the pod of the boxwood, a thousand little games of sporulation which I observed for the first time, filled me with joy and I went around asking whether one had seen the horns of the self-heal plant like La Fontaine asking whether one had read Habakkuk. At the end of two or three hours I would come back laden with an ample harvest, a stock with which to amuse myself after lunch in the lodging in case of rain. I would use the rest of the morning to go with the tax collector, his wife, and Thérèse to visit their workers and their crops, quite often joining my hand with theirs in work; and often the residents of Bern who came to see me found me perched in large trees, girdled with a sack that I would fill with fruits and then lower to the ground with a rope. My morning exercise and the good temper which is inseparable from it made the pause for lunch very enjoyable. But when it took too long and good weather beckoned, I could not wait so long. While they were still at the table, I would slip away and go throw myself alone into a boat that I rowed to the middle of the lake when the water was calm; and there, stretching myself out full-length in the boat, my eyes turned to heaven, I let myself slowly drift back and forth with the water, sometimes for several hours, plunged in a thousand confused, but delightful, reveries which, even without having any well-determined or constant object, were in my opinion a hundred times preferable to the sweetest things I had found in what are called the pleasures of life. Often, warned by the setting of the sun that it was the hour of retreat, I would find myself so far from the island that I was forced to work with all my might to get back before nightfall. Other times, instead of heading out to open water, I took pleasure in gliding along the verdant banks of the island where the limpid waters and fresh shadows often induced me to bathe. But one of my most frequent sailings was from the large to the small island. There I would debark and spend the afternoon, sometimes in very limited promenades through great round-leaved sallow, alder-buckthorn, willow weed, shrubs of every sort, and sometimes setting myself on the summit of a sandy knoll covered with grass, common thyme, flowers, even cockscomb and clover that had most likely been sown there some time ago and were very suitable for housing rabbits which could multiply in peace there without fearing anything and without doing any harm. I passed this idea on to the tax collector who had male and female rabbits brought from Neuchâtel, and in great pomp his wife, one of his sisters, Thérèse, and I went to settle them on the small island where they began to breed before my departure and where they will undoubtedly have thrived, if they have been able to withstand the rigor of the winters. The founding of this little colony was a festival. The pilot of the Argonauts was no prouder than I, leading the company and the rabbits in triumph from the large island to the small. And I noted with pride that the tax collector's wife, who dreaded water excessively and always felt uncomfortable upon it, embarked under my leadership with confidence and showed no fear during the crossing.

When the lake was too rough for boating, I would spend my afternoon wandering over the island searching right and left for plants, sometimes sitting down in the most cheerful and solitary nooks to dream at my ease and sometimes on terraces and knolls to let my eyes wander over the superb and breathtaking view of the lake and its shores, crowned on one side by the nearby mountains and on the other spread out onto rich and fertile plains over which my sight extended all the way up to the more distant, bluish mountains which blocked it.

When evening approached, I would come down from the heights of the island and gladly go sit in some hidden nook along the beach at the edge of the lake. There, the noise of the waves and the tossing of the water, captivating my senses and chasing all other disturbance from my soul, plunged it into a delightful reverie in which night would often surprise me without my having noticed it. The ebb and flow of this water and its noise, continual but magnified at intervals, striking my ears and eyes without respite, took the place of the internal movements which reverie extinguished within me and was enough to make me feel my existence with pleasure and without taking the trouble to think. From time to time some weak and short reflection about the instability of things in this world arose, an image brought on by the surface of the water. But soon these weak impressions were erased by the uniformity of the continual movement which lulled me and which, without any active assistance from my soul, held me so fast that, called by the hour and agreed-upon signal, I could not tear myself away without effort.

After supper, when the evening was fine, we would all go for a little walk together on the terrace to breathe in the air and the freshness of the lake. We would relax in the pavilion, laugh, chat, sing some old song which was easily as good as the modern rigmarole, and finally go to bed content with our day desiring only a similar one the next day.

Leaving aside unexpected and importunate visits, this is the way I spent my time on this island during my sojourn there. Tell me now what is so alluring about it as to arouse such intense, tender, and lasting regrets in my heart that at the end of fifteen years it is impossible for me to think of that cherished abode without each time feeling myself carried away again by waves of desire.

In the vicissitudes of a long life, I have noticed that the periods of sweetest enjoyment and most intense pleasures are, nevertheless, not those whose recollection most attracts and touches me. Those short moments of delirium and passion, however intense they might be, are, even with their intensity, still only scattered points along the path of life. They are too rare and too rapid to constitute a state of being; and the happiness for which my heart longs is in no way made up of fleeting instants, but rather a simple and permanent state which has nothing intense in itself but whose duration increases its charm to the point that I finally find supreme felicity in it.

Everything is in continual flux on earth. Nothing on it retains a constant and static form, and our affections, which are attached to external things, necessarily pass away and change as they do. Always ahead of or behind us, they recall the past which is no longer or foretell the future which often is in no way to be: there is nothing solid there to which the heart might attach itself. Thus, here-below we have hardly anything but transitory pleasure. As for happiness which lasts, I doubt that it is known here. In our most intense enjoyments, there is hardly an instant when the heart can truly say to us: *I would like this instant to last forever.* And how can we call happiness a fleeting state which leaves our heart still worried and empty, which makes us long for something beforehand or desire something else afterward?

But if there is a state in which the soul finds a solid enough base to rest itself on entirely and to gather its whole being into, without needing to recall the past or encroach upon the future; in which time is nothing for it; in which the present lasts forever without, however, making its duration noticed and without any trace of time's passage; without any other sentiment of deprivation or of enjoyment, pleasure or pain, desire or fear, except that of our existence, and having this sentiment alone fill it completely; as long as this state lasts, he who finds himself in it can call himself happy, not with an imperfect, poor, and relative happiness such as one finds in the pleasures of life, but with a sufficient, perfect, and full happiness which leaves the soul no emptiness it might feel a need to fill. Such is the state in which I often found myself during my solitary reveries on St. Peter's Island, either lying in my boat as I let it drift with the water or seated on the banks of the tossing lake; or elsewhere, at the edge of a beautiful river or of a brook murmuring over pebbles.

What do we enjoy in such a situation? Nothing external to ourselves, nothing if not ourselves and our own existence. As long as this state lasts, we are sufficient unto ourselves, like God. The sentiment of existence, stripped of any other emotion, is in itself a precious sentiment of contentment and of peace which alone would suffice to make this existence dear and sweet to anyone able to spurn all the sensual and earthly impressions which incessantly come to distract us from it and to trouble its sweetness here-below. But most men, agitated by continual passions, are little acquainted with this state and, having tasted it only imperfectly for a few moments, preserve only an obscure and confused idea of it which does not let them feel its charm. It would not even be good in the present structure of things that, avid for these sweet ecstasies, they should become disgusted with the active life their ever recurring needs prescribe to them as a duty. But an unfortunate person who has been cut off from human society and who can no longer do anything here-below useful and good for another or for himself can find compensations for all the human felicities in this state, compensations which fortune and men could not take away from him.

It is true that these compensations cannot be felt by all souls nor in all situations. The heart must be at peace and no passion come to disturb its calm. The one who experiences them must be favorable to them, as must be the conjunction of the surrounding objects. What is needed is neither absolute rest nor too much agitation, but a uniform and moderated movement having neither jolts nor lapses. Without movement, life is only lethargy. If the movement is irregular or too strong, one is awakened. By reminding us of the surrounding objects, it destroys the charm of the reverie and tears us away from within ourselves, bringing us instantly back under the yoke of fortune and men and returning us to an awareness of our misfortunes. An absolute silence leads to sadness. It offers an image of death. Then the assistance of a cheerful imagination is necessary and comes naturally enough to those whom Heaven has favored. Movement which does not come from outside then occurs inside us. One rests less, it is true, but also more pleasurably, when light and sweet ideas only skim the surface of the soul, so to speak, without disturbing its depths. Only enough ideas are needed to remember our own self while forgetting all our troubles. This kind of reverie can be enjoyed wherever we can be quiet, and I have often thought that in the Bastille—even in a dungeon where no object would strike my sight—I would still have been able to dream pleasurably.

But admittedly that was done better and more pleasurably on a fertile and solitary island, naturally closed off and separated from the rest of the world, where nothing but cheerful images came to me; where nothing recalled depressing memories to me; where the society of the small number of inhabitants was gentle and sweet, without being so interesting as to occupy me continuously; where I could, in short, give myself up all day long to the preoccupations of my liking or to luxurious idleness, without hindrance and care. It was undoubtedly a perfect occasion for a dreamer who, knowing how to nourish himself with pleasurable fancies in the middle of the most unpleasant objects, could satiate himself with them at his ease by making everything which really struck his senses come together in them. Upon emerging from a long and sweet reverie, upon seeing myself surrounded by greenery, flowers, and birds, and letting my eyes wander in the distance on the romantic shores which bordered a vast stretch of crystal-clear water, I assimilated all these lovely objects to my fictions; and finally finding myself brought back by degrees to myself and to what surrounded me, I could not mark out the point separating the fictions from the realities; it was this thorough conjunction of everything which made the absorbed and solitary life I led during this beautiful sojourn so dear to me. If it could only occur again! If I could only go end my days on this beloved island without ever coming off it or ever seeing there any inhabitant of the continent to remind me of all the different calamities they have taken pleasure in heaping on me for so many years! They would soon be forever forgotten. Undoubtedly, they would not likewise forget me. But what would that matter to me, provided they had no way to come there to disturb my rest? Delivered from all the earthly passions the tumult of social life engenders, my soul would frequently soar up above this atmosphere and commune in advance with the celestial intelligences whose number it hopes to augment in a short while. I know men will be careful not to give me back such a sweet refuge when they did not want to leave me there. But at least they will not prevent me from transporting myself there each day on the wings of my imagination and from enjoying for a few hours the same pleasure as if I were still living there. The sweetest thing I would do would be to dream there at my ease. In dreaming that I am there, do I not do the same thing? I do even more: to the allure of an abstract and monotonous reverie, I join charming images which make it more intense. In my ecstasies, their objects often eluded my senses. Now the deeper my reverie is, the more intensely it depicts them to me. I am often more in the midst of them and even more pleasantly so than when I was really there. The misfortune is that to the extent that my imagination cools this comes with more labor and does not last as long. Alas! it is when we begin to leave our skin that it hinders us the most.

Translated by Charles E. Butterworth

Encounter with New York

Lewis Nkosi

I

ONE PEARLY-WHITE evening in January of 1961 we were winging down over New York. From the air all I saw were the endless blocks of skyscrapers, forming themselves into patterns of light and darkness, and roadways scarring the face of the land like huge streaks of paint thrown recklessly over a large piece of canvas.

At night cities have always held a strange fascination for me. They seem always to conceal a streak of ruthlessness, or of something terribly bitchy and seamy; and New York was no exception.

However, once we had deplaned I was conscious only of the cold which seemed to have teeth in it. My immediate reaction was to flinch from this strange cold place, to sheathe my body more securely within my warm African skin. Also, almost immediately, there went up to my throat an insane, childish cry which demanded of this land that it should enfold me, love me more dearly than all the others, as though I deserved an especial attention.

Wasn't I one of those who had been hurt worse than most people, and didn't I therefore deserve more affection than anyone else? But I had also assumed, automatically, a guarded stance. As always is the case with conceited people there was a desire to resist being taken in by the spurious; I certainly wasn't going to allow myself to be blinded by the gadgetary gloss of America; and because I thought America expected every visitor from the smaller countries to pay homage to all this gadgetry—certainly to its magnificent technology—it suddenly became important to refuse to oblige.

Jack Thompson, the executive director of Farfield Foundation, and the man most instrumental in my coming out to America, was waiting on the balcony of the airport lobby. I saw him almost instantly: tall, handsome, always seeming to carry his American self-assurance with a kind of ease which precludes gestures of arrogance. Jack Thompson seems to embody all the qualities of the younger generation of Americans, especially New York intellectuals, who, knowing that they are citizens of the greatest country on earth, find it almost obligatory to be self-effacing and wryly self-contemplating. They look as though they are uneasy about the power which their country possesses; but there is also about them a strange look of a ravaged innocence.

Jack and I waved briefly at each other, then he went on smoking his pipe. American intellectuals are carrying on an extraordinary love affair with pipes. They are always stuffing them with tobacco the same way they stuff their minds with facts; and while they suck on them they manage, somehow, to look apocalyptic!

Jack Thompson and I had our first drink at the airport bar. The last time we had had a drink together was at Western Native Township on one very hot summer night. We had 'kidnapped' Jack from the self-consuming monotony and boredom of the Parktown-Houghton white suburban parties where we had been suffered to come for dinner, I suspected, rather as showpieces of what 'natives' can achieve in South Africa though I forget now what we were supposed to have achieved. Avoiding the notoriously keen-nosed Johannesburg police we had consummated one of those ritualistic, nocturnal excursions into the bawdy, crowded black townships on the fringes of the city. The following morning Jack had carried with him into the plane to Ghana a man-sized hangover. Now we sat at the Idlewild Airport bar, sipping somewhat obscenely, it seemed to me, whiskey that might have been tossed down the throat in the social claustrophobia of the Johannesburg 'speakeasy'.

On arrival at New York Airport an African begins to look out for the Negro especially, hoping, no doubt, for a particular kind of 'family greeting' or some special welcome, waiting rather naïvely for the much storied Negro humour—an expectation cruelly engendered by scores of Hollywood films which depict the Negro as indefatigably joyous and gay. To meet from the Negro, therefore, not only a complete absence of brotherly recognition but the same brisk no-nonsense attitude as from white attendants can be startlingly disconcerting. For a special welcome it seems that an African must wait until he gets to 125th Street, Harlem.

Besides being decidedly Negro the customs official who inspected my luggage was the most annoyingly thorough and efficient customs official I have ever encountered in any country outside Nigeria, an African state whose airport administration seems encumbered by officious, brutally sincere men exulting in the exercise of power.

The Negro official poked painstakingly at my clothes, occasionally raising his stern brown face to check on some detail. 'Hey Jack, how long have you owned this typewriter?' Meanwhile his poking fingers were driving me almost insane with worry. Any moment now I expected him to reach down and produce for public exhibit a few dirty shirts which lay suitably ensconced at the bottom of my case.

What finally saved me from the agony of this final disgrace was the sudden appearance on this anxious scene of two beautiful Negro girls—airport stewardesses, I guessed—whose good looks and supple figures proved too much even for the sternest Negro customs official. Beneath the insupportable weight of this awesome female sexuality the official seemed to stagger most ignobly, his brow troubled, his brown sober eyes suddenly bright and frenzied with unimaginable hungers and hopeless enthusiasms. Seeming to sway a bit on his feet he let go of my case, proclaiming his admiration and willingness to surrender to Venus with a slow and appreciative smile and whistle.

By now sensing the havoc they were spreading through their dark and stormy bodies, the girls became subtly charged with a sly secret mood of danger, unmistakable in the swaying of hips—a mood as disturbingly familiar as the cautious approach of a black storm. Everybody watched. I watched too, longing for the confirmation of whatever special relationship may exist between the African male and the American Negro female. But I admired our Negro official immensely for being prepared to suffer publicly. 'Lawd mercy,' he cried unashamedly, 'the troubles I *have* seen!'

During the long drive by cab from the airport to the Thompson apartment I felt nothing but awe for the new land—and this in spite of myself. This awe, I know, had something to do with bigness which seemed to swallow everything and to reduce the dimensions of everything to an uncomfortable size. The houses and the river bridges seemed to stretch on endlessly, and the cars streaked along the broad driveways with a kind of urgency which made a stranger to America wonder just where the Americans were all hurrying to. It seemed as though everyone was on wheels; everybody was going somewhere. Certainly if there is any one thing that has revolutionised the social character of American life, it is this cheap availability of the automobile to all social classes. Everybody seems to have a compelling urge to get out on the road and go somewhere.

The first encounter with New York is nothing if not the encounter with the New York cab driver. If the impressions which we gather from sociological textbooks about foreign places sometimes fail to coincide with reality, almost anything ever said about New York cab drivers is partly, if not wholly, true. They are mean to other drivers on the road; they are loquacious; and their encyclopaedic knowledge on any conceivable subject, from wage-price parity to popular nuclear physics, probably garnered from

'Teach Yourself' paperbacks, is certainly unnerving. We had hardly finished telling our cab driver that I was from Johannesburg than he was displaying his familiarity with the entangled problems of Dr. Verwoerd's republic: 'Isn't that the place where they are hard on Negroes?' he asked rhetorically. I settled back in my seat and allowed myself to be lectured on American democracy, which is a speciality with taxi drivers encountering foreigners in New York. The only jarring note which might have escaped my tutor was that we were driving through a nauseating Puerto Rican and Negro slum; however, he continued his lecture, his enthusiasm showing no signs of abating.

To tell the truth, my first encounter with New York was none too pleasing for me. It was extremely cold and the city had hardly recovered from a snowstorm which had paralysed it all through Christmas. But apart from the weather, there was something chilling about New York—at least during my first two days there. Not even the long drives and walks around the city succeeded in dispelling my disquiet about New York. The city was hard and cold in the same way, I suppose, Johannesburg is, except that Johannesburg's cold is tempered by an irresistible African gaiety. Although New York has much of the same robustness, and perhaps more, it is much too big. It is exasperatingly chaotic, tough, brutal. It also can be the loneliest city in the world. The loneliness has nothing to do with the strangeness of the place. I began to wonder whether I was not, overnight, turning into a reactionary setting his teeth firmly against the sheer bravura of industrial progress. I certainly yearned for the warm intimacy of Europe, for the sheer presence of old age and the gentle politeness of London. Whereas in New York it seemed important that one should be with the kind of people one knew and liked, in London, as soon as I had known my way around, I had needed nobody as I drifted around the city in a continuous flirtation with its ageless streets and buildings.

It was in the next months that I began to develop a sneaking affection for New York. One falls in love with that city—at least I did—in much the same way that one falls in love with an incurably and hopelessly bitchy woman. One suffers in the process, and sometimes in an impossible kind of fury, one leaves her only to return days later, tail between one's legs and flowers in one's hands. Even at the end of a love affair with New York, just before one leaves her, there is the same kind of dissatisfied longing for one more encounter. New York is metaphorically, and really, an awful kind of grabbing, gold-digging bitch, yet capable of extravagant passions.

II

Rain! Snow! I wondered if it would ever stop snowing. Wondered in the yellow cab all the way to Harlem, wondered as I walked across Seventh Avenue, ready to make my first march into 125th Street, world-famous corner of Negro America. I watched the snow 'carefully descending'—thin flakes of powder flecking the rooftops with white and hallowing the grimy tenements with a freshly minted frosty colour. So this was Harlem! I stood there on 125th Street in Harlem and saw, with a mixture of emotions, the Negro ghetto which was for me a reflection of what Sophiatown in Johannesburg might have been had it been suddenly transplanted to New York. There was the same kind of sprawling, exuberantly rich life despite the many privations which people so obviously suffered; there were the same kind of weird funeral parlours standing cheek by jowl with storefront churches, and elderly citizens who sat at their windows, leaning out and watching the world with the same kind of philosophical resignation which was so familiar to me.

And I saw—and this is what seemed to set the younger generation apart—a young Negro walking down Lenox Avenue in a kind of rolling gait, which was later translated for me into a taunting, mischievously arrogant jazz phrasing by Miles Davis at the Village Vanguard. Miles and the younger jazz musicians seem to be expressing all the colour, subtleties, the mocking arrogance, and the defensive quality of the life of a people who lived on the fringes of a racist society. There was a painful, though touching irony, when I saw the sons and daughters of white middle-class families desperately trying to appropriate this style, while the Negro was forever moving further 'out'—way out—in order to elude definition.

This part of the city felt strange to me—this city within a city; a peculiar limbo into which thousands of black men and women seemed to have been pushed and forgotten; it seemed, in fact, like a place situated peculiarly between the dream and the reality. An incursion into a darkened bar along 125th Street, even in broad daylight, was like an adventure into Hades, which revealed several black men, two or three women sitting on bar stools and so motionless that it was often difficult to determine whether or not they were alive. Occasionally a brown hand lifted a coin, deposited it into the slot of the jukebox and the forlorn voice of Ray Charles moaned about the agony of his exile from the South: 'Georgia, Georgia, on my mind!' Sometimes it was the voice of Dinah Washington—urban, despairing and anguished: 'What a difference a day may make!' The voice of the sprawling urban Negro slum and ghetto bravely attempting to keep us warm in the snow.

'Cheer up, baby!' said a hoarse Negro voice to me. A wry black man with a pancake face swathed in assorted winter clothes of unmatching colours, swinging his legs together, occasionally rubbing one hand against another in a smug self-satisfied manner, though it was not clear what anybody could be satisfied about in a place like that. But suddenly I felt cheerful and ordered some more Scotch for myself and Pancake Face. I wondered what all these people did when they were not drinking in bars. After all you can't make love all day, even if you are a Negro, contrary to all received opinion.

'You live around here?' said the hoarse voice.

I sipped Scotch; we both sipped Scotch. A black man yawned, another sitting across from us yawned almost immediately. Someone had 'cut wind' and there was now a warm cheap odour slowly filling the bar. Men came, pausing near the door to knock the snow off their rubber covers, and they left a trickle of water from the melted snow. London—to say nothing of Africa—seemed suddenly very far away.

'You come from London! Shit, man!' My companion exulted. 'Ain't that a bitch!'

This seemed to me a peculiar rejoinder, to say the least. 'I was out there during the War,' said Pancake Face. 'Nice place, London. Nice English girls, not like these white crackers here! I bet you got one hugging her pillow right now. Eh, crazy, man!' And he punched me on the arm, grinning conspiratorially. However, his brow was soon clouded: 'Hey, man, I hear things ain't so different out there any more. Where you come from originally? West Indies?'

I told him Africa.

'Africa! You don't say! *Sheet!* Hey, Sam, come on over here. Guess where this cat come from?'

Sam was a tall brown man wearing a white apron. He looked me up and down with some interest. 'Africa?'

'Yeah, that's right. How you know that?'

'I can tell,' Sam boasted. 'He don't look like you bunch of do-nothing Negroes.' Sam turned to me: 'What do you do, son? Go to school over here?'

By now I was wishing they would stop being so interested in me and drawing all the attention I was anxious to avoid. The other faces in the bar were beginning to look animated. A woman, quite pretty, with a heart-shaped face and large soulful eyes, listened to the conversation without seeming to listen. I suspected her to be an old hand in the dangerous game of the street. For the third time that afternoon Dinah Washington was happily surprised: 'What a difference a day may make!'

'No kiddin? A writer? How about that!'

A thin dark man—darker than I am—leaned across the bar and said: 'Tell me somethin', buddy. Now if I go over there—what's this place—no, not Ghana, man . . . The other place . . . Tangany'ka! That's right . . . You think there's a fair chance to start business over there? I could build me a factory there. You guys need a few things like tractors, you know, to raise the standard of livin'. You got freedom but you ain't got the standard of livin' . . . What you need is technical know-how!'

'What you talkin' about man!' Sam objected. 'This cat is from South Africa. He don't need no standard of livin'. What he needs is guns to fix them white crackers real good. Isn't that right, brother!'

When everybody had seemed somewhat mellowed in the bar I brought up the subject of the Negro in America. What were they going to do with 'the man'? Sam snorted; they all began talking all at once, shouting to be heard above the din of the jukebox noise while the dainty 'soul sister' sitting on the bar stool nearby peered at all of them contemptuously from under heavy eyeshades. She muttered ominously: 'You niggers *talk* too much!'

The man with a pancake face who called himself Hill was now very excited: 'It's all a matter of sex, man! These white cats think if they give you a good job with good money you goin' to look so sharp in 'em clothes, lay up so much bread on the line, you're bound to steal their womens. That's what they think!'

There were mad giggles: 'Yeah, they knows it too! They ain't doin' nuthin' with them chicks. They jus' sittin' on it!' In the jukebox slot a coin slid down, tinkling, and after a couple of minutes a record slid into place and out of the organ Jimmy Smith ground out a thumping blues number.

'Shit, man, when it's time to get up and fight I'll be out there in the streets with the best of them. There's goin' to be hell in these U.S.A. You can put that down if you want. And you can tell them I said J. P. Hill will be out there in the streets with the best of them, raining shit!'

Sam looked pleased with himself and the lot of them. To show it he complained: 'All these Negroes do is come here and talk but they ain't goin' to do nothing!'

III

During my three months' vacation from Harvard University I went back to New York and took up an apartment at Greenwich Village, the fading bohemian quarter of New York which used to harbour most of the radicals of the thirties and provided a sort of haven for artists and writers seeking cheap rooming houses and a sense of community. As New Yorkers love to remind you, 'The Village is no longer what it used to be.' At the time there were still writers like E. E. Cummings, now late, still living there, but even he was fighting a last-ditch battle against the Department of Buildings which was then out to rase Patchin Place to the ground because, so the Department argued, it lacked 'adequate toilet facilities'. John V. Lindsay has mourned Mr. Cummings' plight in *The Village Voice*:

> He has through his poetry brought pleasure and insight to many of us and has certainly enhanced the cultural reputation of Greenwich Village and New York City. We will be losers if Mr. Cummings and his wife are forced to leave Greenwich Village.

However, at the time the Department of Buildings seemed to have made up its mind that superannuated buildings and poets must have adequate toilet facilities. Middle-class New Yorkers, with their towering skyscraping blocks of modern box structures, were creeping closer and closer to the Village.

What do I remember most about the Village? Certainly it is now hard to sift the conflicting impressions and images. Perhaps it is the strange look of looseness, the self-conscious decadence quite preposterous by any European standards, this nerve-racking effort on the part of some of its citizens to be different from Uptown New Yorkers. I remember tourist buses trundling through the narrow streets and the malevolent stares from Villagers; and I remember one sandalled citizen, in particular, yelling meanly at the intently peering faces: 'Tourists!' The simple fact of the matter is that the Village would be shabbier than it now is, perhaps would have long given way to better commerce, had it not been for the tourists who still go there in search of beatniks.

It is strange, though, how quickly one becomes part of the Village scene if one lives there; how quickly one begins to resent the intrusion of curiosity-seekers. There was, for instance, this inexpressibly naïve blond boy who approached me while walking down MacDougal Street and enquired: 'Say, bud, where's fun tonight?' My throat constricted with irritation. I knew he was looking for beatniks, for the mythical wild free love scenes.

Also I remember those very hot summer days, hotter than any I had known in South Africa, sitting at the Figaro with a half-finished script of my play and consuming endless cups of espresso coffee. One sat there peering though a haze of heat-induced stupor at the beautiful girls—gold-legged, stockingless, embrowned by the summer heat.

Most of the girls weren't beatniks at all, were going to New York University nearby or Columbia uptown, were actresses in-between productions, were young wives of Village young men grubbing for money on Madison Avenue, their wives sitting with stone-eyed babies or boy friends in the lethargic coffee-houses. And I have a vision of one summer afternoon during which my girl friend and I sat in a restaurant, watching through a huge glass window the perpetual motion of people passing by. And there was this girl, walking gracefully with bare feet, and seeing me watching her, she paused, her face cracking into a wide bewitching smile and she waved a slim hand. There was something awfully childish in the gesture, and yet a grace, a love, a tenderness almost too dear because it was so freely given to a stranger. It is something that one never encounters in London.

For instance there was the afternoon in which we walked down MacDougal Street. A white girl walking toward us with her Negro boy friend paused, and, I suppose, feeling a sense of camaraderie with another interracial couple, simply barred our way and compelled us to declare: 'Whose eyes are prettier, his or mine?' My girl friend thought the boy's were and I thought the girl's were. But those were the summer afternoons when one felt the natural warmth of the Village, the indefatigable candour of its loves and its brave struggles against the withering bigotry of racial hatred.

Also I remember the night-clubs and the crepuscular cellars, the sad cafés and the rain streaking down the soulless bars on the Avenue of the Americas. I remember the long-haired beatniks who hung outside a coffee-house on Bleecker Street, waiting—God knows for what—while inside the smoky dimly-lit coffee-house Tad Joans, the Negro poet, yelled obscenely to the elect: 'White America, my hand is on your thigh,' or whatever it was that he was reading.

But also the Village was for me a warm place, whose aging streets were full of bookshops peddling avant-garde paperbacks. Here you went in at about 11 p.m. and browsed until well after midnight, something one misses in London and in Africa. More often than not your bookseller played host; sometimes engaged you in a discursive scholarly conversation on the poetry of Ezra Pound or the sad obscurity of Beckett.

Beneath this surface of decay and decadence I referred to earlier, the

Village often conceals the dauntless temper of radicalism and rebellion. Architects and city-planners like Jane Jacobs (author of *The Death and Life of Great American Cities*) turned out to be social scientists who spent part of their time gathering signatures for petitions at the Village. Peace and protest movements against nuclear armaments proliferated, and usually had their nub at the Village.

I also remember, that summer, with a glint-eyed clarity, James Baldwin, the brilliant Negro writer, sitting on the floor of Vusi Make's apartment in New York, ferociously making a point and then his very dark face suddenly splitting into a wide mischievous grin which seemed to belie the intensity of his belligerent pontifical tone. Loften Mitchell, the Negro playwright, reading passages out of Peter Abraham's *Tell Freedom*, and suddenly breaking into genuine tears: 'Man, I tell you, this cat suffered!' Or Julian Mayfield, author of *The Grand Parade*, angry and bitter: 'I'm going to Ghana. I hope they can use me; because if they can't I sure can use them!' Or Margaret Beels, one sultry afternoon, heartlessly and ruthlessly pondering America's future, looking, therefore, terribly fragile and vulnerable, because, tough as she was, something like panic seemed to have crept into her eyes.

So for me New York was a collection of individuals whom I loved and some of the things they said—a single incautious word said passionately and burned for ever in the consciousness of my mind—and these individuals and what they said bound me more irrevocably to America than all the insulting propaganda about 'the democratic way of life'.

Eventually, everybody has his own particular New York—a New York of his own choice. For some people New York is Times Square and the insomniac glitter of Broadway by night; for others it is Fifth Avenue at the lunch hour and the enchanting lyricism of its humanity in motion; or it is the chic long-legged Madison Avenue girls questing for the heroic males to whom they might gladly surrender their costly independence. My own New York is terribly narrow and perversely chosen.

In my memory I am sitting again in the dumpy night-club in the Village, listening to a white girl—a wonderful girl and a wonderful singer—Sheila Jordan. Her eyes are closed and she is singing, *Willow, Weep for Me*. Halfway through, her face grows really incandescent, and she tries desperately to convey through some kind of superhuman effort, what even her personal lyricism so disastrously fails to convey. I seem to see her again walking down Seventh Avenue, at the Village, with her very dark daughter by her Negro husband; they both set patterns of black and white against the blazing summer heat!

A Letter from Exile

Proposal for a Long Stay in Vaucluse

Petrarch

YOU CAN LEARN from me, if you like, how unstable and variable are men's wishes, and how provisional are all our plans for the future—especially the plans of those lacking in wisdom. I was seized with a longing to see again my hills and caves and groves carpeted with green moss and the ever-resonant rocks by the Fountain of the Sorgue. Where I came as a boy, and then as a youth, and again as a grown man, I have now returned when near to old age, though, as you know, I had sworn never to come here again. The charm of the place and some inward spur compelled me; sober reason could not hold me back. No hopes drew me here, no necessity, no delights except rough rustic pleasures, not even love for my friends, the worthiest of all causes in this transitory world. What friends shall I have here, where no one even understands the meaning of friendship? This miserable people, intent only on their thin soil, their more flourishing vines, their olive trees, their lines and nets in the river, can have no community of life and converse with me. But I came here with my eyes open, not by some hazard of fate, since I could return to this my home of many years only with full knowledge and awareness of what I should gain and what I should sacrifice.

If there is any justification for my change of plan, it is my compelling love of solitude and quiet. Trying to escape the boredom of notoriety in my home city, I seek a place to lie hid, alone, inglorious, unknown. A strange desire, no doubt, when we see so many in hot pursuit of vainglory. But that's the way of it; that is what I seek and crave, nor am I led astray by fame's bright dazzle, which once so enticed me, nor am I tempted by the satisfactions of celebrity. Here it is quite the reverse; my simple world requires a rustic way of life.

Let me tell you how much I prize my leisure. I would not have it altered in any detail. As I have told you, I was invaded by a curiously sweet recollection of this secluded, silent spot where I had lived in younger days. I have the less reason to wonder that the exiled Camillus, that great man, could long for his fatherland and feel all the charm of Rome, as I, though born an Italian by the banks of the Arno, could dream of the sweetness of my transalpine home. Indeed long custom becomes a second nature; that explains why I have always so eagerly gone to fix my abode in these foreign parts. For by habit I have become an inhabitant of this country retreat, and in coming here I seem to have regained my native land. But nothing moved me more than my devout hope of terminating certain literary efforts of mine. As they were begun here with God's favor, so may they be finished by his continuing guidance.

If you want to know how long I expect to stay here, I must answer that it is uncertain, as the future must be. On the way here, indeed before I had left Italy, I wrote to inform my friends of my departure and of my projected return, and I said that I should be back next autumn. So I thought at the time; but one shouldn't make decisions too far in advance. That's a fine old phrase: "the gladiator should make up his mind in the arena." One must be on the spot to argue properly. Often the time, the aspect of the place, the advice of friends sway our decisions. But to judge the future by the past, two years will be enough for my projects. I usually shift my Italian and French residence at about that interval. Of course I know that a two-year plan is insecure, as is a plan for a single day. I always liked the remark of that old monk who, one evening, was asked by his king to dinner on the morrow, and who replied that there is no such thing as tomorrow. That was a fine, serious statement of a man without illusions, unlike most people, who let today escape in the hope of tomorrow. The words suggest that the old monk packed his bag daily and treated every day as his last; and they say that he died that very night, making his words correspond the better with the event. It is appointed to us to lose the present in expectation of the future. But I shall dismiss this almost universal subject of error and return to my own purpose.

If I seem to you to have acted contrary to our agreement, please overlook it. Let my excuse be the variability of the human mind, which is characteristic even of the most learned sages. It can be escaped only by the perfect, who have given themselves to the pursuit of the Supreme Good. Let my further excuse be the boredom of sameness, which one can divert by a change of scene. I have spoken of this at length. Let me, further, inspect my fruit trees, planted with my own hands, and my property, or what of it has survived mismanagement. (It is still more than I need.) Let me anyway revisit my hills and fountains and woodlands, so dear to my studies. Let me, finally, bring out into the light my books, considerable in number and so charming. I have long missed them, locked up in their chests. Let them open their eyes; and let my eyes dwell upon them. At least let me shake off the worms and dust from their ancient parchments. But something more will be granted me, I hope. As I have said, I think that two years will suffice to finish the works begun and pending. If I be allowed to finish them, another way of life will open before me, for which—except when weighed down by my burdens—I yearn and sigh with the greatest eagerness.

Farewell.

Translated by Morris Bishop

They Were Emigrants

Heinrich Heine

I WILL MAKE CONFESSIONS now. It was no vain desire of my heart that made me leave everything that was dear to me and fair and smiling, in the Fatherland—many loved me there: my mother, for instance—but I went without knowing why. I went because I had to. Afterwards I felt very weary. For so long before the July days I had fulfilled the prophet's office that the inner fire had all but consumed me; and my heart, by the mighty words gone forth from it, was lax as a woman's body in the hour of birth . . .

I thought: you need me no more; for once, I will live for myself and write lovely poems, comedies and novels, the tender and gay plays of thought stored up in my skull, and I will quietly slip back into the land of poetry, where I lived so happily as a boy.

And I could have picked no better place to execute this project. It was a little villa close to the sea, near Havre-de-Grâce in Normandy. A wonderfully beautiful view of the great North Sea, an ever-changing and yet simple sight; today a grim storm, tomorrow a pleasant calm, and above it the trailing clouds, gigantic, fantastic, as if they were the haunted shades of those Normans who once pursued their wild ways on these waters. Under my window grew the loveliest flowers and plants: roses that looked at me, lovelorn, red carnations with shyly pleading scents, and laurel climbing up the wall to me and growing almost into my room, like the fame that pursues me. Yes, once I timidly ran after Daphne; now Daphne runs after me like a harlot and pushes into my bedroom. What I once desired has become uncomfortable; I want peace and wish that nobody would mention me, at least not in Germany. And I would write quiet songs, for myself alone, or at most to read them to some hidden nightingale. And in the beginning it worked; my mind found peace again within the spirit of poesy, familiar noble and golden images dawned afresh in my memory; I grew again as dream-happy, as fairy-tale-drunk, as enchanted as of yore, and had only to write down with a calm pen what I just felt and thought. I began.

Now everybody knows that in such a mood one does not keep sitting quietly in his room but sometimes runs into the open fields with high heart and glowing cheeks, without paying heed to the road. So it happened to me, and without knowing how I suddenly was on the highway out of

Havre, and in front of me several big peasant carts were moving slowly, loaded with all sorts of beggarly chests and boxes, old-fashioned furniture, and women and children. The men were walking alongside, and great was my surprise when I heard them speak: they spoke German, with a Suabian accent.

I realized quickly that these people were emigrants, and when I looked closer a feeling flashed through me as I never felt it in my life. All my blood rushed suddenly into the chambers of my heart and knocked at the ribs as if it had to get out of my breast, as if it had to get out as fast as possible, and the breath stuck in my throat. Yes, it was the Fatherland itself that met me; on those carts sat fair-haired Germany with her grave, blue eyes, her homelike, all too thoughtful faces; in the corners of the mouths there was still that pinched narrowness which had once bored and angered me so but now touched me sadly—for if once, in the thriving lust of youth, I had often disparaged the native wrongs and philistinism, if once my happy, burgomasterly pompous, slow-as-a-snail Fatherland and I had had some small domestic squabbles as will occur in large families, all such memories had left my soul when I saw the Fatherland in need, in a strange land, in exile. Even her infirmities suddenly grew dear to me and of great value; I was reconciled even to her small-town pettiness and I shook her hand—I shook the hands of those German emigrants as if pledging a new bond of love to the Fatherland herself, and we talked in German.

They too were very glad to hear these sounds on a road in a strange land; the anxious shadows vanished from their faces and they almost smiled. And the women, some of whom were very pretty, called their pleasant "*Griesch di Gott!*" down from the carts, and the little boys greeted me, blushingly polite, and the very small children squealed at me with their dear toothless little mouths. "And why did you leave Germany?" I asked those poor people.

"The land is good and we'd have liked to stay there," they answered, "but we couldn't stand it any longer."

No, I am not one of the demagogues who only want to rouse passions, and I will not relate everything I heard on that country road near Havre, under the free sky, of the mischief done by high and noble—and even by the highest—houses at home. Besides, the greater indictment lay not in the words as such but in the plain and straightforward tone in which they were spoken, or rather sighed. Those poor people were no demagogues either; the final word of their complaints was always: "What should we have done? Should we have started a revolution?"

I swear by all the gods of heaven and earth, the tenth part of what those people had endured in Germany would have caused thirty-six revolutions in France and cost thirty-six kings their crowns and their heads as well.

"And yet we'd still have borne it and would not have gone away," said an eighty-year-old and accordingly twice-sensible Suabian; "but we did it on account of the children. They are not as used to Germany as we are, and maybe can find happiness abroad; but of course, in Africa they'll also have a few things to put up with."

For these people were going to Algiers, where they had been promised a stretch of land for colonization on favorable terms. "The land is supposed to be good," they said, "but we hear that a great many poisonous snakes are there. They're very dangerous. Also, the apes are very troublesome; they filch the crops from the fields, or they even steal the children and drag them off into the woods. That is cruel. But at home the bailiff is cruel too, if one cannot pay the taxes; and the fields are spoiled even more by the game and the hunt, and our children were taken away to be put into the army—what should we have done? Should we have started a revolution?"

In honor of humankind, I must here mention the sympathy which, according to those emigrants' testimony, was accorded them on the stations of their passion, throughout France. The French are not only the wittiest of nations but also the most compassionate. The very poorest of them sought to show some kindness to the unfortunate strangers, gave them a hand with packing and unloading, lent them their copper kettles for cooking, helped them with wood-chopping, water-carrying, and laundering. With my own eyes I saw a French beggarwoman give part of her piece of bread to one poor little Suabian—for which I, too, thanked her very heartily. Besides, it should be pointed out that the French know only the material distress of these people. They really cannot quite understand why the Germans left their country. For when the French find their troubles at their rulers' hands insufferable or even somewhat too vexatious—it would never occur to them to take to flight; rather, they dismiss their tormentors, throw them out of the country, and jolly well stay there themselves—in short, they start a revolution.

As for myself, I retained from this encounter a deep sorrow in my heart, a black gloom, a leaden despair the like of which I can never describe in words. I, who had just been swaggering along like a conqueror, walked limply and weakly now, like a broken man. It was really not the effect of a suddenly excited patriotism. I felt it was something nobler, something better. Besides, I have long disliked everything that bears the name of patriotism. Even the thing itself was spoiled for me to a degree when I observed the mummery of those black fools who used to make a regular trade of patriotism, donning an appropriate trade uniform and dividing themselves into masters, journeymen and apprentices, and who also had their guild salutes with which they went through the land, to live off it.

Fighting, with swords, was not one of their trade practices. It is well known that Father Jahn, the "Turnvater" Jahn, was as cowardly in war as he was silly. Like their master, most of the journeymen were merely low creatures, slimy hypocrites whose churlishness was not even genuine. They knew very well that simple-minded Germans still regard bad manners as a mark of courage and honesty, although a glance into our jails should make it sufficiently clear that there are ill-mannered villains too, and boorish cowards. In France, courage is well-bred and polite and honesty wears gloves and takes its hat off. In France, also, patriotism means love of a native country which is at the same time the home of civilization and human progress. The above-mentioned German patriotism, however, consisted of hate of the French, hate of civilization, and hate of liberalism. I am no patriot, am I—speaking well of France?

It is an odd thing about patriotism, the true love of country. A man can love his native land and never know that he loves it, though he live to be eighty—but then he must have stayed at home. You do not realize what spring means till it is winter; and the best songs of May are written behind the stove. The love of freedom is a prison flower, and only in captivity does one feel the value of liberty. And love for the German fatherland begins on the German frontier, but it waxes strong at the sight of German unhappiness in a strange land. In a book which I just happen to have at hand and which contains the letters of a departed friend, I was deeply moved yesterday by the place where, in a foreign land, she describes the impression made on her by the sight of her compatriots in the war of 1813. I will quote the dear words:

"All morning I wept bitter, prodigious tears of emotion and hurt! Oh, I never knew that I love my country so much! It is like one who may not know through science what blood is worth: if you take it from him, he will crumple just the same."

That is it. Germany—that is ourselves. And that is why I suddenly became so faint and sick at the sight of those emigrants, those great streams of blood running from wounds in the fatherland and losing themselves in the African sand. That is it; it was like a bodily loss, and in my soul I felt an almost physical pain. I tried in vain to comfort myself with sensible arguments: Africa too is a good country, and the snakes there do not wag their tongues about Christian love, and the apes there are less repulsive than the

German apes—and to take my mind off it I started humming a tune. But perchance it was the old song of Schubart's:

> We're going over land and sea
> To torrid Africa. . . .
>
> At Germany's frontier I scoop
> A bit of earth up in my hand
> And kiss it, trying thus to thank—
> For guard and care, and what I ate and drank—
> You, my dear fatherland.

These few words of the song I heard in my childhood have always remained in my memory, and every time I came to the German border they entered my mind. About the author I do not know much—except that he was a poor German poet and spent the greater part of his life in a dungeon, and loved liberty. He is dead now and long since dust, but his song still lives; for the word cannot be put in prison and left to rot.

I assure you I am no patriot, and if I wept, that day, it was because of the little girl. It was towards evening, and a little German girl whom I had noticed among the emigrants stood alone on the shore, as if lost in thought, and looked out over the wide sea. The child was eight years old perhaps; wore two neatly plaited pigtails and a short little Suabian skirt of good striped flannel; she had a pale sickly face, great serious eyes, and in a softly anxious but at the same time curious voice she asked me if that was the ocean.

Far into the night I stood by the sea and wept. I am not ashamed of those tears. Achilles wept by the sea, and his silver-footed mother had to rise from the waves to comfort him. I, too, heard a voice in the waters, but not so much consoling as rousing, commanding, and very very wise. For the sea knows all; the stars at night confide to it the most hidden secrets of Heaven; in its depths, alongside fabulous sunken empires, lie the age-old, long-forgotten sagas of the earth; at every coast it listens with a thousand curious wave-ears, and the rivers flowing down to it bring it all the news they found out in the most distant lands or overheard in the chatter of the little brooks and mountain streams. But once the sea reveals its secrets to you and whispers the great word of world redemption into your heart, then good-bye, peace—good-bye, quiet dreams—good-bye, you novels and comedies that I began so nicely and now shall scarcely finish for some time!

Translated by E. B. Ashton

The Rains of New York

Albert Camus

NEW YORK RAIN IS A rain of exile. Abundant, viscous and dense, it pours down tirelessly between the high cubes of cement into avenues plunged suddenly into the darkness of a well: seeking shelter in a cab that stops at a red light and starts again on a green, you suddenly feel caught in a trap, behind monotonous, fast-moving windshield wipers sweeping aside water that is constantly renewed. You are convinced you could drive like this for hours without escaping these square prisons or the cisterns through which you wade with no hope of a hill or a real tree. The whitened skyscrapers loom in the gray mist like gigantic tombstones for a city of the dead, and seem to sway slightly on their foundations. At this hour they are deserted. Eight million men, the smell of steel and cement, the madness of builders, and yet the very height of solitude. "Even if I were to clasp all the people in the world against me, it would protect me from nothing."

The reason perhaps is that New York is nothing without its sky. Naked and immense, stretched to the four corners of the horizon, it gives the city its glorious mornings and the grandeur of its evenings, when a flaming sunset sweeps down Eighth Avenue over the immense crowds driving past the shop windows, whose lights are turned on well before nightfall. There are also certain twilights along Riverside Drive, when you watch the parkway that leads uptown, with the Hudson below, its waters reddened by the setting sun; off and on, from the uninterrupted flow of gently, smoothly running cars, from time to time there suddenly rises a song that recalls the sound of breaking waves. Finally I think of other evenings, so gentle and so swift they break your heart, that cast a purple glow over the vast lawns of Central Park, seen from Harlem. Clouds of Negro children are striking balls with wooden bats, shouting with joy; while elderly Americans, in checked shirts, sprawl on park benches, sucking molded ice creams on a stick with what energy remains to them; while squirrels burrow into the earth at their feet in search of unknown tidbits. In the park's trees, a jazz band of birds heralds the appearance of the first star above the Empire State Building, while long-legged creatures stride along the paths against a backdrop of tall buildings, offering to the temporarily gentle sky their splendid looks and their loveless glance. But when this sky grows dull, or the daylight fades, then once again New York becomes the big city, prison by day and funeral pyre by night. A prodigious funeral pyre at midnight, as its millions of lighted windows amid immense stretches of blackened walls carry these swarming lights halfway up the sky, as if every evening a gigantic fire were burning over Manhattan, the island with three rivers, raising immense, smoldering carcasses still pierced with dots of flame.

I have my ideas about other cities—but about New York only these powerful and fleeting emotions, a nostalgia that grows impatient, and moments of anguish. After so many months I still know nothing about New York, whether one moves about among madmen here or among the most reasonable people in the world; whether life is as easy as all America says, or whether it is as empty here as it sometimes seems; whether it is natural for ten people to be employed where one would be enough and where you are served no faster; whether New Yorkers are liberals or conformists, modest souls or dead ones; whether it is admirable or unimportant that the garbage men wear well-fitting gloves to do their work; whether it serves any purpose that the circus in Madison Square Garden puts on ten simultaneous performances in four different rings, so that you are interested in all of them and can watch none of them; whether it is significant that the thousands of young people in the skating rink where I spent one evening, a kind of *vélodrome d'hiver* bathed in reddish and dusty lights, as they turned endlessly on their roller skates in an infernal din of metal wheels and loud organ music, should look as serious and absorbed as if they were solving simultaneous equations; whether, finally, we should believe those who say that it is eccentric to want to be alone, or naïvely those who are surprised that no one ever asks for your identity card.

In short, I am out of my depth when I think of New York. I wrestle with the morning fruit juices, the national Scotch and soda and its relationship to romance, the girls in taxis and their secret, fleeting acts of love, the excessive luxury and bad taste reflected even in the stupefying neckties, the anti-Semitism and the love of animals—this last extending from the gorillas in the Bronx Zoo to the protozoa of the Museum of Natural History—the funeral parlors where death and the dead are made up at top speed ("Die, and leave the rest to us"), the barber shops where you can get a shave at three in the morning, the temperature that swings from hot to cold in two hours, the subway that reminds you of Sing Sing prison, ads filled with clouds of smiles proclaiming from every wall that life is not tragic, cemeteries in flower beneath the gasworks, the beauty of the girls and the ugliness of the old men; the tens of thousands of musical-comedy generals and admirals stationed at the apartment entrances, some to whistle for green, red, and yellow taxis that look like beetles, others to open the door for you, and finally the ones who go up and down all over town like multicolored Cartesian divers in elevators fifty stories high.

Yes, I am out of my depth. I am learning that there are cities, like certain women, who annoy you, overwhelm you, and lay bare your soul, and whose scorching contact, scandalous and delightful at the same time, clings to every pore of your body. This is how, for days on end, I walked around New York, my eyes filled with tears simply because the city air is filled with cinders, and half one's time outdoors is spent rubbing the eyes or removing the minute speck of metal that the thousand New Jersey factories send into them as a joyful greeting gift, from across the Hudson. In the end, this is how New York affects me, like a foreign body in the eye, delicious and unbearable, evoking tears of emotion and all-consuming fury.

Perhaps this is what people call passion. All I can say is that I know what contrasting images mine feeds on. In the middle of the night sometimes, above the skyscrapers, across hundreds of high walls, the cry of a tugboat would meet my insomnia, reminding me that this desert of iron and cement was also an island. I would think of the sea then, and imagine myself on the shore of my own land. On other evenings, riding in the front of the Third Avenue El, as it greedily swallows the little red and blue lights it tears past at third story level, from time to time allowing itself to be slowly absorbed by half-dark stations, I watched the skyscrapers turning in our path. Leaving the abstract avenues of the center of town I would let myself ride on toward the gradually poorer neighborhoods, where there were fewer and fewer cars. I knew what awaited me, those nights on the Bowery. A few paces from the half-mile-long stretch of splendid bridal shops (where not one of the waxen mannequins was smiling) the forgotten men live, those who have let themselves drift into poverty in this city of bankers. It is the gloomiest part of town, where you never see a woman, where one man in every three is drunk, and where in a strange bar, apparently straight out of a Western, fat old actresses sing about ruined lives and a mother's love, stamping their feet to the rhythm and spasmodically shaking, to the bellowing from the bar, the parcels of shapeless flesh that age has covered them with. The drummer is an old woman too, and looks like a screech owl, and some evenings you feel you'd like to know her life—at one of those rare moments when geography disappears and loneliness becomes a slightly confused truth.

At other times . . . but yes, of course, I loved the mornings and the evenings of New York. I loved New York, with that powerful love that sometimes leaves you full of uncertainties and hatred: sometimes one needs exile. And then the very smell of New York rain tracks you down in the heart of the most harmonious and familiar towns, to remind you there is at least one place of deliverance in the world, where you, together with a whole people and for as long as you want, can finally lose yourself forever.

Translated by E. C. Kennedy

VI

Returns and New Departures

Continent, city, country, society:
the choice is never wide and never free.
And here, or there . . . No. Should we have stayed at home,
wherever that may be?

—Elizabeth Bishop
"Questions of Travel"

Frankfurt in Our Blood

Kay Boyle

IT WAS THE HALF-BOTTLES of wine that made them speak. Without them, the two women seated at a small table at the end of the dining car might have had nothing to say. Paris lay hardly twenty minutes behind them, but already the gently sloping green hills and the luxuriant fields of France were there, streaming swiftly past the windows; the villages, the feathery trees, the fluid country dimmed now to the quality of ancient murals by the veil of dusk which lay across the land. But inside the crowded diner of the Orient Express the illumination was as hard as brass, and the waiters swayed down the aisle between the tables, bearing their trays on high as if upon the current of a stream.

Behind the diner swung the nimble links of the long, racing train, the sleeping cars for Prague and Frankfurt coupled with those for Warsaw and Budapest, or with sleepers for Bratislava, Vienna, Munich, Bucharest. By morning these cars, which roared through the pastoral stillness of the continent, would have taken their separate ways, shunted off at Bar-le-Duc while the travelers slept within them, and the people who shared tables for the evening meal would have forgotten the look of one another in a little while. The two women were strangers to each other, and the one who faced in the direction in which the train was going was young and soft-skinned, and she wore a blue-cotton short-sleeved dress, as simple as a schoolgirl's dress. She sat with her face turned toward the window and her chin held in the cushion of her ringless left hand. The small, stooped, aging woman who sat opposite had also turned her head to watch the deepening twilight, her flesh, hair, clothing, eyes, all of the same worn, faded grey. But there were the half-bottles of red wine before them, and it was the faded little woman who made the first move, and who leaned forward toward the girl.

"Perhaps we could divide a half-bottle between us?" she began, her diffidence coming meekly, patiently to speech. "We could share the expense of it," she said, her accent not quite English and not quite American.

The girl turned back from the window, her wide eyes startled, and looked at the woman as if waking from a dream.

"Yes, indeed. Yes," she said, and that might have been the end of it. It was the other woman who motioned the waiter to pull the cork of one of the two little bottles of red wine. Once he had done this, and wiped the bottle's dark mouth clean, it was her hand reaching, narrow and ivory-knuckled, from the suit's grey sleeve, which poured the wine carefully into their glasses. The girl had turned to the window again, her hands clasped on the table before her, her soft dark hair hanging long across the shoulders of her dress. "How I hate it," she said, and she looked out at the sight of the fleeing country as she spoke. "How I hate going back to Germany," she said, and she reached quickly and blindly out and took her glass up, and drank down the first swallow of red wine.

"Yes, going back," said the little woman, but she did not drink. Instead, she picked up her grey cotton gloves from where they lay beside her plate, and she laid the wrinkled fingers of them carefully together, and she smoothed them gently, reflectively, out upon her knees. "Yes, going back," she said.

When the woman began to eat the split-pea soup, the girl turned away from the window again, and she pushed the metal bowl of her own soup aside. It could be seen that her mouth was bright with lipstick and blemished by discontent, and that her glossy hair was cut in a fringe above the baleful eyes. The faded little woman watched her young hand, her bare arm, lift to fill their glasses with the strong good wine.

"Every time it's a little bit harder than it was the time before," the girl was saying quickly. She sat with her arms resting on the table, turning the glass of wine between her fingers. "You see, I go to Paris perhaps once a month, just for the weekend. And every time I have to go back it's like cutting my heart out and throwing it away."

"And you can't stay in Paris?" the woman said quietly.

"Well, I have a job," the girl said, still watching the glass turn on the cloth. "I'm a War Department civilian in Frankfurt." The waiter had carried the bowls away, the full one inside the empty one, and the girl took another swallow of the wine. "I took the job just to get over. Just to get on the same continent with France," she said and she lifted one hand to the side of her face as if to shield it, as though there might be tears in her eyes and she did not want a stranger to see them fall.

"Yes, Frankfurt," said the faded little woman. "It's been a long time, but I could tell you the name of almost every street still. You know, I went there as a bride once," she said, and she lifted her glass of wine again and drank a little, trying to make it sound, even after all the years that had passed, festive and jaunty and gay. "My husband taught in the university there," she said, with a sociable smile on her lips, but her hand as it set the glass down on the cloth was trembling like a leaf in the high wind of emotion that came sweeping through her heart. She looked at the ham in gravy which the waiter set before her, but she made no move to eat. "We lived there twenty-five years together," she said.

"You have memories. That's a certain kind of wealth," the girl said, seeming to begrudge them to her. "I have absolutely nothing except the things I want to be."

"Well, let's make this into a little celebration," said the woman, and she raised her glass as if they might drink a toast together, but the girl drank quickly, without acknowledging the woman's lifted glass or the tentative smile that hung upon her mouth.

"Six months ago I didn't believe that Germany would remain for me this alien, evil thing," the girl said, and across the table the woman looked meekly up at her young face. "I thought I would be able to get close to what it really is, or was," the girl said, speaking quickly, while outside the windows the lights of the villages and the rural stations of France were cast behind them in the dark. "But I see Germany like some isolated territory, like a lepers' colony, an infected island which free men conquered, and have, because of this, become ailing and evil and no longer free."

"Yes," said the woman, "but you know, there is a strange thing that can happen to people. Or perhaps, when people get older, this is the thing that always happens." The waiter bore the plates away, and the woman sat smiling, smiling almost in apology across the cloth. "I can only think of Germany now as it was when I was a child, and of Frankfurt as I knew it as a bride," she said. And now an unexpected look of audacity, an almost devilish look of mischief came into her worn, faded eyes. "You know, I have a little French money left, not much, but enough," she said, "and I would like to spend it on another half-bottle of wine."

The waiter uncorked the second half-bottle, and wiped its mouth clean, and then put the plates of lamb and peas before them. And now that the woman's voice had ceased to speak, the girl turned to the window again, and to the sight of the deepening darkness through which the country flowed swiftly, irretrievably past. Tomorrow there would be Frankfurt, and the bomb-gutted station in the early morning, and the houses laid open to the elements still bearing within their rubble outlandish bits and pieces of what had once been comfort and security. There would be the radiator hanging by its pipes through a floor that had capsized beneath it five years before, and the bathtub standing two stories high above the dead magnolia trees, its clawed feet resting on nothing, and the paneled door behind it still standing ajar.

"Or perhaps the place you began life as a bride is a place that can never change for you," the woman was saying now, and the girl turned abruptly from the window, and she poured their glasses full with wine. "There was my husband's work in the university, and there were other professors, and there were artists, too, writers, countless friends," said the little woman, smiling as she spoke. "There we had meetings, discussions, and not only among intellectuals, but among men of free crafts, the guilds, the unions. For Frankfurt was once the heart of liberal Germany. And then, in 1934, my husband died. He was very wise to choose that year to die in," she said, still smiling, but her hand was shaking as if with palsy as she took the glass of wine. "We are a Jewish family," she said, "so in one way or another we had to go."

"And you, where did you go?" the girl asked, and the turmoil, the protest, seemed to halt within her for a moment.

"We went to China. My sons and I left for China that year," said the woman. "We carried what we could of Frankfurt in our blood with us—its culture, its wisdom, its democratic history. Or perhaps the only thing we really took with us was the sound of Goethe's words saying many things to us who were also the German people, saying very clearly that wisdom's last decree is that freedom and life are deserved only by those who conquer them anew each day." The girl and the woman both finished the wine in their glasses, and the girl sat turning the glass in her fingers while opposite her the woman's voice went on speaking gently and patiently of a town that had been Frankfurt once, and a country that had been Germany. "That was a gift I had to give my children," the woman said, "a belief in free men that free men themselves had communicated to me."

And as the girl listened to the woman's voice going on with this, the city they traveled toward took on another aspect, and the sound of the familiar German voices perished, no longer saying, as they had said to her for six months now, "I lost everything in the bombings, everything—my house, my furniture, my business," for the woman was speaking of the Taunus hills, and of the walks they had taken there in the springtime, she and the others, the professors, the artists, the writers, the free men of Frankfurt who had seen freedom die.

"And now you are going back? After fifteen years, you are going back?" the girl said, looking at her, and forgetting to turn the wine glass on the cloth.

"Yes," said the little woman. "No choice was offered. The women and children of foreigners were being evacuated. I was flown out of China last week. I am going back to Frankfurt," she said, the smile hanging on her mouth again, "because there does not seem any other place for me to go."

"How many children did you have?" the girl asked, for it was the members of this family which mattered, as the rest of Germany had never mattered. It was what they had been, and how they had spoken, and what answer they had given when the questions had been asked.

"I had four sons," the woman said, and her hand had begun to tremble again as she lifted her glass to drink. "Two of them left Germany with me, the two younger ones. We went to China together," she said, having wet her lips with the wine. "The two others . . . ," she went on after a moment, but she could not go on with it at once. "The two others," she began again, and there was no hint of crying, nothing that even resembled anguish in the words she said, "the two others died with their countrymen and women in Dachau," was what she was saying, but even the strength of the wine she drank was not enough to lean on now, and her lips, her chin, her empty hands, were trembling as if stricken with the plague.

"Now it is my turn to order another half-bottle," the girl said quickly, and she made the sign to the waiter as he passed with the *bombes glacées*. And then she reached across the table, and she touched the woman's worn, aged hand that lay, like a forgotten object, on the cloth.

"I am afraid to go back," the woman said, and her teeth bit hard into her shaking lip. "I am not afraid of my memories. I am afraid of hearing what the living now have to say."

"We can listen to other things," the girl said, and their hands held to each other's as the waiter set the plates of crackers and cheese before them and poured the fresh wine out. And then the stooped little woman shouldered the burden of patience and resignation again, and she smiled across the table at the girl.

"I shall make out very well," she said, and their hands drew apart, and they lifted their glasses and drank. "I have a widow's pension accumulated at the university. It will be enough to begin again on," she said, and an unsteady look of recklessness or tipsiness came into her face. "It will be enough to pay my way into the Palm Garden in the afternoons, and there'll still be the orchid hothouse, with orchids as different as people, with wise faces, and foolish ones," she said, and she giggled as if she were a young and giddy woman now. "I don't remember how many species there were, but I knew them all by name once. And in the tropical conservatory there'll be the camellias flowering, reddish and white and waxy, as they flowered in China so profusely—" And then she stopped talking. "Unless," she said quickly, "I mean, was the Palm Garden bombed—are the greenhouses there still?"

"Yes, they are there," said the girl, and then the two women began to laugh across the table at each other.

"I must write to my sons at once, to my two boys in China," the woman said, wiping the tears of laughter away, "and tell them how tall the banana trees have grown."

Disinheritance

An Address

Ruth Prawer Jhabvala

I FEEL GREATLY HONOURED to be here today to speak to you as a writer in commemoration of your great Scottish novelist, Neil Gunn. No two writers could, I suppose, be more different from each other than he and I; I mean, as far as background and experience are concerned. For he had everything, as man and writer, that I have lost. He had a heritage—an inheritance, whereas I have only disinheritance. You hardly need me to tell you about Neil Gunn's inheritance, by which I mean his rootedness in tradition, landscape and that inexplicable region where childhood and ancestral memories merge; that ground of being from which all great writing comes.

But what I would like to talk to you about is my own disinheritance, my own lack of any such tradition, landscape, memory (either childhood or ancestral). Yes, as I shall explain in a moment, I feel disinherited even of my own childhood memories, so that I stand before you as a writer without any ground of being out of which to write: really blown about from country to country, culture to culture till I feel—till I am—nothing. I'm not complaining—this is not a complaint, just a statement of fact. As it happens, I like it that way. It's made me into a cuckoo forever insinuating myself into others' nests. Or a chameleon hiding myself (if there were anything to hide) in false or borrowed colours.

But don't let me slide off into metaphor but start concretely at my beginnings. I was born in 1927 in Germany. My father was Polish and had come to Germany during the First World War to escape military conscription in Poland. In Germany he met my mother who was actually born in Germany—in Cologne, as I was. But her father had come from Russia—to escape military conscription there, probably. And her mother was born in Germany, in Berlin, though I don't know where *her* father—that is, my great-grandfather—came from. Probably again from Poland or Russia. Anyway, the point of all this is to show that whatever place we were in, we didn't go back into it very far. Not much rootedness—everyone having come from somewhere else; usually having run away from, or having been driven away from, somewhere else. Still, once there, once settled in a place and feeling some measure of security in it, I must say my family seem to have shown the same chameleon or cuckoo quality that I have already had to confess to in myself. And I was born into what seemed a very solidly based family who had identified with the Germany around them—had been through the 1914–18 War with them—had sung for Kaiser and fatherland. In fact, one of my mother's proudest memories was how she had been chosen to recite a poem on the occasion of her school's celebration of the Kaiser's birthday. She described the white frock she wore, the curtsey she made, the flowers she presented to whoever was the guest of honour on that memorable occasion. The school's name, by the way, was Kaiserin Augusta Schule—founded by the Empress herself, and full of pink-cheeked, blonde little blue-eyed German girls. Yet it was my mother whose name was Cohn, who had worn the white frock, presented the flowers, recited the poem in honour of the Kaiser.

My first memories then—that is, between 1927 and 1933—were of a well-integrated, solid, assimilated, German-Jewish family. We couldn't, unlike other such families, forget the Jewish part because my grandfather was the cantor in the biggest Jewish synagogue in Cologne. It wasn't an orthodox synagogue, nor was my grandfather an orthodox Jew. He prided himself on his friendship with Christian pastors—his identification with them in so far as they were all men of God, and our God was the same or at least as good as theirs (at that time). His Jewishness, his religion, was a profession—I don't mean of faith but the way a lawyer or doctor professes his profession. For the rest, he prided himself on being a German gentleman, a well-regarded citizen of Cologne. One of my family's proudest possessions for ever afterwards was a picture of the Cologne Rathaus presented to my grandfather in token of appreciation of his civic virtues. Most of all my grandfather prided himself on his beautiful baritone voice. And here I can come back to my most basic childhood memory (what should have been but never developed into my atom of delight), and that is of my grandfather, a tall imposing bearded figure in a three-piece suit with a watch chain across him and wearing laced boots, standing by the piano, clearing his throat. At the piano my grandmother who had studied at the Berlin conservatory: small, rotund, wearing a dark-brown silk dress with a deep *décolletage* and pearls around her stout manifolded neck; and her little round hands racing over the keys, her head swaying as she prepared to accompany my grandfather on his flight of song. Over the piano a picture of Rebecca at the Well; the sofa was velvet and so were the armchairs; the tablecloth tasselled; and in the corner a great porcelain stove reaching up to the ceiling, well stoked and heating the room to a temperature that I have ever since sought to recover (for a while I substituted the Delhi summers for it—but of that later). From the kitchen the delicate fragrance of a particular type of round little tea cakes that only my grandmother knew how to bake. There were aunts and uncles, all well settled, all German patriots, all life-loving, full of energy, bourgeois virtues and pleasures, celebrating every kind of festival—all the Jewish holidays, of course, but what they really liked was New Year's Eve and, especially, the annual Cologne carnival and masked ball. We all had costumes made for that every year; one year I was a chimney-sweep, and another a Viennese pastrycook. All this would be in the early 1930s—up to, but not including, 1933.

I don't feel like talking much about 1933 and after. Everyone knows what happened to German Jews first and other European Jews after. Our family was no exception. One by one all the aunts and uncles emigrated—to France, Holland, what was then Palestine, and the United States. My grandfather died, so did my grandmother. I don't know what happened to the piano or the picture of Rebecca at the Well. I never saw them again. My immediate family—that is, my Polish father, my mother, my brother, and myself—were the last to emigrate, and also the only ones to go to England. That was in 1939.

I have slurred over the years 1933 to 1939, from when I was six to twelve. They should have been my most formative years; maybe they were, I don't know. Together with the early happy German-Jewish bourgeois family years—1927 to 1933—they should be that profound well of memory and experience (childhood and ancestral) from which as a writer I should have drawn. I never have. I've never written about those years. To tell you the truth, until today I've never even mentioned them. Never spoken about them to anyone. I don't know why not. I suppose they are the beginning of my disinheritance—the way they are for other writers of their inheritance.

Anyway: England, 1939. My first entirely instinctive demonstration of my cuckoo or chameleon qualities. I took to England, and English, immediately. Up till then my language had been German. I haven't mentioned that I was writing furiously all through my childhood. It doesn't seem worth mentioning—one is just born that way: destined. One doesn't choose to become a writer. I started school at six and learned the alphabet, and then we were told to write our first composition. The subject: a hare—in German, *der Hase.* I wrote the title, 'Der Hase'. At once I was flooded with my destiny; only I didn't know that's what it was. I only remember my entire absorption, delight, in writing about—giving my impression of—*der Hase.* To think that such happiness could be! But this is an entirely different subject and I don't want to side-track myself. I'm talking about my disinheritance as a person and as a writer, not about the inheritance of my craftsman's tools. That's different, or at least I think it is. Because I have these tools—because they were given, gifted to me, happened to me—I have been a writer. The fact that I appear to have been disinherited of my 'ground of being'—that is, my childhood and ancestral memories—doesn't, oddly enough, seem to have made any difference. I have plied my tools, regardless.

So this is what happened when we went to England in 1939; I at once—within a week, I think—started to write in English. I didn't have all that much English—only what I'd learned at school in Germany—but once in England I did learn fast. And not only did I then write in the English language but also—and this is where the chameleon or cuckoo quality really came in—about English subjects. I mean, all the English life I saw around me, first in the Midlands. I first went to Coventry, then was evacuated to Leamington Spa to two maiden sisters and their caretaker father; and from there I went to London, in 1940, to rejoin my parents who had bought a house in a London suburb and who sent me to the local grammar school. And I got to know the English there and wrote about them in the stories, plays, unfinished novels that I turned out in a relentless stream all through those school years. Nothing very good, of course—at that age one's just learning one's craft. Anyway, I was. I wasn't very precocious.

By the time I had acquired enough skill to finish some of those unfinished novels, round off those formless stories, I no longer wrote about England. I never went back—either to write or to live there. But before I go on to talk about where I did live and write, I must record some of my experience of England. Which is my debt to England. England opened out the world of literature for me; what other writers have experienced and set down. Not really having a world of my own, I made up for my disinheritance by absorbing the world of others. The more regional, the more deeply rooted a writer was, the more I loved them: George Eliot, Thomas Hardy, Charles Dickens. Their landscapes, their childhood memories became mine. I adopted them passionately. But I was equally passionate to adopt, for instance, the landscape of Marcel Proust, of James Joyce, of Henry James, of the great Russians—Tolstoy, Dostoevsky, Turgenev, Chekhov (that noble roll-call). Whatever author I read last, I was ready to become a figure in that particular landscape. It was as if I had no senses of my own—besides no country of my own—but only theirs. This was the great gift, the inheritance, that England gave me: my education which became my tradition—the only tradition I had: that of European literature. It became my equipment, my baggage for the journey I didn't know I had to make: the journey to India.

Unlike so many British people, I had no connections with India: no Scottish grandfather who had built the Grand Trunk Road, or opened up canals in the Punjab, or played the bagpipes at the Relief of Lucknow. I didn't know anything about that. I'd read *Kim* and *A Passage to India*, as literature; neither made me want to go to India nor became anything more than another literary landscape to be enjoyed. Nor was I in the least attracted to anything else Indian—like, for instance, the spiritual scene. I knew nothing about it and if I had done I wouldn't have cared. I went to India as it were blind. If my husband had happened to live in Africa, I'd have gone there equally blindly; asking no questions and in fact fearing no fears. Maybe going there like that, with no preconceptions of any kind, was better than anything, in so far as it kept me completely open to receive whatever there was to receive—that is, India.

I still can't talk about the first impact India made on my innocent—meaning blank and unprepared—mind and senses. To try to express it would make me stutter. Perhaps the best way to put it would be to compare it with the effect the scenery made on Neil Gunn in his childhood: the moors, the crofts, the sea, landing the salmon and cracking the hazelnuts. Stunning, overwhelming, beyond words. I entered a world of sensuous delights that perhaps children—other children—enter. I remember nothing of it from *my* childhood. That way India was—remains till today—my childhood (though I was twenty-four when I went there). I don't know why this was so. Was it in reaction to the bleakness and deprivations of my own childhood—Nazi Germany and then wartime blitzed London (those nights and days spent in damp air-raid shelters, and queuing for matches and margarine)? Or did it go farther, and was it that whatever was Oriental within me—I mean, through my being Jewish—was opening up to buried ancestral memory? I don't know, but whatever it was, it was very strong and lasted for years. I won't go into detail. I can't; as I said, it would make me stutter. The smells and sights and sounds of India—the mango and jasmine on hot nights—the rich spiced food—the vast sky—the sight of dawn and dusk—the birds flying about—the ruins—the music—I've tried to write about it; I've spent years writing about it. At that time I loved everything there: yes—to my shame I have to say—even the beggars, the poverty, they didn't bother me then; they seemed right somehow, a part of life that had been taken out of the West (like death, which was also always present in India, carried on a bier in front of my window down to the burning ghats, or the vultures swooping over something indescribable in a ditch). It was life as one read about it in the Bible: whole, I thought; pure, I thought.

I felt like that for ten years. I didn't feel like going back to Europe—and in fact, didn't. I didn't even *know* any Europeans. I just lived there in my house in India, with my family; but really lived. All the time I was writing those early books and stories of mine. They were all about India—set in India and all the characters Indian. I was pretending to be writing as an insider, as if I didn't know anything else. As if I wasn't a European at all, had never heard of such a place. I don't know how I had the impudence to write like that—in English, in my careful, precise (maybe even prissy) prose style learned in England via English literature classes—about people who didn't even think in English, let alone speak it. But I pretended I knew them—no, more, I pretended I was them. For instance, I was always fond of writing about great big beautiful sensual Indian women, full of passion and instinct; the very opposite of myself, physically and in every other way. And yet I wrote about them, was them, wanted to be them. All this is quite inexplicable to me: those ten years of delight and immersion and more (much more) than acceptance.

What followed is more explicable. I won't call it disillusionment. I don't think it was that; it was more the process of becoming myself again. Becoming European again. The turn my life—my feelings—took is reflected in my writing. I still wrote about India, but now seen from a European point of view. I became a European sensibility again, and now I saw everything as perhaps I should have seen it from the beginning. I was no longer immersed in sensuous delight but had to struggle against all the things people do have to struggle against in India: the tide of poverty, disease and squalor rising all around; the heat—the frayed nerves; the strange, alien, often inexplicable, often maddening, Indian character. All the things that make Europeans into sahibs and (worse) memsahibs out there, make them close up and shrink into themselves, and then again shrink; making them tight, prim, self-righteous. As I said, closed-up. I became like that. I've written about that too.

Perhaps I should be a bit more specific. Let me talk about my attitude to the spiritual scene in India, or I should say the spirituality of India. I never doubted it was there—why, it was part of my delight, even sensuous delight—that sense of spirituality. It was there for me in the sight of the sky. I'd never been so aware of the sky—of there actually being a heaven with stars in it and a moon that was sometimes huge and blown and orange, like a sun and sometimes the most delicate silver sliver. Maybe it had always been too cold in England to look up at the sky, but here I slept under it all night (those great drenched Indian nights) and that made a difference. So that was another dimension, actually, physically: the world extended upward and much farther than I had thought. Then in the morning—in fact, at dawn, and what lovelier time is there—I could hear all the holy men on the banks of the Jumna singing their morning hymns, and the temple bells ringing. All that was very real: the spiritual and the physical all mixed up, all one sensuous delight. And then I loved people's simple faith: the way they could see God in a cow—let alone in a cow, in a clod of earth, in some misshapen little idol made of clay and costing a couple of pennies. And their belief in swamis and gurus and human beings actually being holy. This was the more touching when I thought of all the bad experience everyone had of human nature—like the grasping landlord, the pitiless money lender, the evil mother-in-law who tortured the little daughter-in-law (aged fourteen) for not bringing enough dowry from her father's house. All these were facts of everyday life to be lived with: one's neighbours, one's fellow human beings; and yet one could still think of human beings as being good, even perfectible, godlike. In fact, the worse the people one came into contact with, the more acceptable the notion of the holy man: a man so good he was holy. I wanted to believe in such a man too. Whenever opportunity came to visit a swami, I did so. I loved to think I was near someone holy, within the range of such wonderful vibrations.

Of course here was the richest soil for disillusionment, and I reaped that harvest in plenty. I couldn't stand those swamis any more; far from embodying human perfectibility, they embodied its corruption, degradation, lies. I loathed them. And yet at the same time always wishing: if only it could be. And those hymns still sounded so pure and beautiful (as did all Indian music, touching eternal chords); and there was absolutely no doubt about the sky being beautiful with all those stars and the moon, not to speak of the monsoon clouds and all that. It was all still there. But those terrible swamis and their terrible followers. I hated them for being what they were and not what they pretended to be, and what I wanted them to be.

I wrote a lot about that spiritual scene. I saw a lot of Western girls come to India for that. They wore saris and walked around on bare feet (and got hookworm) and took dancing lessons and meditated on the holy mantra given to them by their guru. They became vegetarians; they bathed in the holy river; they got jaundice and became very pale and worn away physically and as people, in their personalities. They had given up their personalities (as tough, thinking, fighting European or, more often, American girls). Their eyes and thoughts and souls were only for their guru. I deplored them; I wrote about them, disparagingly. I laughed at, even despised, them; but also envied them—for thinking they had found, or maybe—who am I to judge?—they had found, what I had longed to find and never could and I guess never would now.

It became time to leave India. I had spent twenty-four years there and the last twelve or so were a perpetual struggle with India: not to love it too much and not to hate it too much, one could say; but that would make it too simple. I could also say to keep my own personality and not become immersed, drowned in India; to remain European—and yet at the same time to remain open to India and not close up and wither away. Too difficult for me. I couldn't make it, not at that stage, for there was something else too—a terrible hunger of homesickness that I cannot describe it was so terrible, so consuming. Not for any specific home; I didn't have one. England wasn't it; Germany wasn't, Poland wasn't—but for Europe: to live in Europe again among people who spoke, thought, looked—it makes a difference, that—the way I did. Who were immersed in the same traditions—the same books and music and morals I suppose one could say: moral assumptions—whose soul was the same colour as mine. I wanted desperately to go.

Before I go on to what is, up to date, my last journey—or exile—or disinheritance—or search for a home—or what is it?—before I come to that, I'd like to mention those cuckoo or chameleon qualities that seem to be a part of my heritage and how they came into play in India. I've already mentioned how as soon as I got to India I did just the same thing as I had done the moment I got to England: that is, write as if I were from within that society, part of it. Later, when I began to alienate myself and to write from outside Indian society, as a European, it wasn't as the sort of person I really was myself but again adopting another alien civilisation. In fact, I identified myself as an Anglo-Saxon: I took over, that is, *your* heritage—the Scots grandfather who built bridges, canals, railways. My last novel written in India—about India—*Heat and Dust*, has come from within a double pretence: two chameleons, two cuckoos. On the one hand, as far as the Indian characters and their society and thoughts and values were concerned, I pretended to be of them; on the other hand, when I wrote about the Anglo-Indian (that is, British) characters and their traditions, I pretended to be of them. So I exited from India on a double lie—one it took me twenty-four years to manufacture.

Someone once told me that, whatever project you have in your life, whatever central concern or task or duty you set yourself (or is set to you), you should give yourself twenty years in which to bring it to its maturity and, hopefully, fruition. I consider my work—or rather, experience—in India as this twenty-year task. But I also consider the twenty years up and the task over. I'm now committed to a new twenty-year programme—in fact, I began it four years ago when I left India and also at the same time stopped writing about it.

I said that during my last years in India I became desperately homesick for Europe. Finally it got so bad that I just had to go and live there and start again—adapt myself again—leaving India behind me as I had left Germany and then England; find a new nest or world both as a person and a writer (it is no longer possible for me really to disentangle the two). And feeling so homesick for Europe, longing for it so intensely, I went to live in New York. This is not as paradoxical as it may sound, as I'll try to explain. I find myself doing a lot of explaining on this score—people are always asking me "But why New York? Why America? Why not England or some other country in Europe?" I've had to explain myself so often that perhaps I've become bit pat in my reply. Anyway, I've had to think it out, and whether the conclusion I've come to is a true one or one I've slightly manufactured to justify and explain myself, I'm really not quite sure. It might only be self-justification—perhaps I'm just fickle by nature and get tired of countries the way other women do of husbands or lovers; and then, like them, hiding my fickleness behind a screen of too many good reasons. Anyway, here are my good reasons for going to live in New York.

In a way I consider it as the place for which—like so many twentieth-century European refugees or exiles—I was destined. Certainly when I first went there, in 1966, I felt a sense of homecoming. It is the most European city I can think of, with every kind of pocket of Europe inside it—German, Czech, Polish, Italian. There are whole sections given over to these nationalities, with their languages and foods (of course there are Chinese and Indians and Puerto Ricans as well, but I was in search of Europe). And literally I met the people who should have remained in my life—people I went to school with in Cologne, with exactly the same background as my own, same heritage, same parentage. Now here they were living in New York, as Americans, in old West Side apartments, with high ceilings and heavy furniture, just like the ones we grew up in in our Continental cities (as blissfully overheated as my grandparents' flat in Cologne), and with the delicatessen at the corner selling those very potato salads and pickled cucumbers and marinated herrings that our grandmothers used to make. In fact, I haven't had these childhood tastes on my tongue since I left Germany in 1939—the exact, memory-stirring, awakening, madeleine taste that magically opens the door into one's personal and ancestral past.

But not only in New York. Wherever one goes in America, there are these pockets of Europe, of those settlers, whether they were Czech, Hungarian, Polish, Italian, who have become American and yet at the same time—in their cast of features, their physique, their food, their family structures, in all the most intimate details of their lives—have retained their origins. You can find small towns and villages with small churches and cemeteries where the names are all Dutch and so are the houses in their neatness and incredible cleanliness and the people in their square good-natured faces and bodies. The accent of the tongue may be American but the accent of the soul has retained the intonation of the European past. And for me, and maybe for others like me, this Europe that we find in America is what I can only describe as clean and wholesome. It is untouched by the events of the 1930s and '40s—an idyllic, bucolic Europe reaching far back into earlier generations, no longer to be found in Europe itself but in the pretty white houses with green shutters in (for instance) Pennsylvania or Connecticut; set in a landscape that again recalls an earlier Europe, with rivers and lakes and boys fishing in them in the summer and skating on them in the winter, and acres of pasture-land with cows and waterfalls and not a house in sight, and in the distance hills and clumps of forest with a church spire sticking up on the horizon. There is all the simplicity of a childhood landscape that perhaps I never even knew but only dreamed or read about in German fairy tales.

And yet another good reason why New York, why America. Although my longing was for Europe, can I after all these years and all this immersion into India really ever consider myself totally European again? Is there no trace of India left? I can't believe it. Certainly I find myself stirred by certain aspects of New York that are not unlike India. I can't speak about this too much as yet—it's what I want to write about so I'm still groping in the dark—but there is something bizarre about New York that appeals to me as strongly as did the bizarre in India. It might even be the cruelty of both places—the abyss for ever open. In India it is there in the dreadful poverty and physical disease, and New York too has dreadful poverty. You see sights as horrifying there as you do in India—the down-and-outs, the drunks, the drug addicts lying in the gutters or scrabbling in the trash cans, and the derelict houses in the derelict areas of New York with the boarded-up windows, and hopeless figures shuffling over the littered pavements, and miserable little shops as bankrupt and abandoned as their owners. That's in New York everywhere; and also everywhere in New York the wrecked people: talking to themselves, waving their arms in frantic gestures, tomorrow's suicides, mumbling in the deep abyss of mental sickness—everywhere as continuous a pointing to the frailty of the human condition as there is in India. You can't forget death and despair in New York any more than you can in Calcutta. And the fear everywhere—not as in India the cruelties of nature, but those of man: the muggers and the murderers that make people lock and double-lock their doors and keep their distance from strangers in the street and scuttle home at nightfall and keep clear of certain areas as though they were infested by those thugs that throttled wayfarers in the deserts of Rajasthan or the ravines of Madhya Pradesh.

And again one more—last—good reason why America. After India, can one ever really be satisfied with a country that is anything less than a continent? The way I usually put it is this: if you have for many years lived on a diet of hot spicy curries, how are you going to get used to boiled cabbage again? And as with one's sense of taste, so with all one's other senses and faculties, mental as well as physical. They become coarsened, sensationalised: you need the violent stimulation that only a big coarse country with terrible things happening in it can give you. So, after India, I find only America really big and coarse and bizarre and desperate enough.

But, as I say, all this may really only be excuses: too many good reasons for being promiscuous. Perhaps if you've been faithless once, you can never be faithful again but are committed to a life of promiscuity. Perhaps after my first disinheritance—and my calm acceptance of it, of so cheerfully pretending to be English, and then Indian, and then Anglo-Indian, changing colour as I changed countries—maybe I will just have to go on doing it, changing countries like lovers. But always totally, with total abandonment and identification, like Chekhov's Darling who, you may remember, when married to a theatre manager talked of nothing but the bad taste of the theatre public who wanted to see only clowns, and when married to a timber merchant became very knowledgeable on all aspects of wood, seasoned and unseasoned, and when she had an affair with a veterinary surgeon was entirely preoccupied by the problem of epidemics caused by the lack of veterinary inspection. Her thoughts and life were filled only by her love for a man, but always a different man; mine just so by a country, but always a different country.

Does one grow too old for this sort of thing? When I went to India I was twenty-four—plenty of time for that twenty-year stretch one has to give oneself. But now? I've only just started on my new twenty-year stretch, and it's no use pretending I don't hear time's wingèd chariot drawing near. But I think perhaps one mustn't hear it; one must just go on pretending at the end of each twenty-year stretch that there is plenty of time for the next one, or at least start off on it as if there were. That's how I feel about America. I don't know if I'll finish my twenty years there, but that shouldn't make any difference to starting it. There's a saying, and I can't (characteristically enough) remember whether it is a Jewish, or a Muslim, or a Hindu, or a Buddhist one: 'It is forbidden to grow old.' I take that to mean that one just has to go on—learning, being—throughout however many twenty-year stretches in however many different countries or places—actual physical ones or countries of the mind—to which one may be called.

Poland Revisited

Joseph Conrad

I

I HAVE NEVER BELIEVED in political assassination as a means to an end, and least of all in assassination of the dynastic order. I don't know how far murder can ever approach the perfection of a fine art, but looked upon with the cold eye of reason it seems but a crude expedient of impatient hope or hurried despair. There are few men whose premature death could influence human affairs more than on the surface. The deeper stream of causes depends not on individuals who, like the mass of mankind, are carried on by a destiny which no murder has ever been able to placate, divert, or arrest.

In July of last year I was a stranger in a strange city in the Midlands and particularly out of touch with the world's politics. Never a very diligent reader of newspapers, there were at that time reasons of a private order which caused me to be even less informed than usual on public affairs as presented from day to day in that necessarily atmosphereless, perspectiveless manner of the daily papers, which somehow, for a man possessed of some historic sense, robs them of all real interest. I don't think I had looked at a daily for a month past.

But though a stranger in a strange city I was not lonely, thanks to a friend who had travelled there out of pure kindness to bear me company in a conjuncture which, in a most private sense, was somewhat trying.

It was this friend who, one morning at breakfast, informed me of the murder of the Archduke Ferdinand.

The impression was mediocre. I was barely aware that such a man existed. I remembered only that not long before he had visited London. The recollection was rather of a cloud of insignificant printed words his presence in this country provoked.

Various opinions had been expressed of him, but his importance was Archducal, dynastic, purely accidental. Can there be in the world of real men anything more shadowy than an Archduke? And now he was no more; removed with an atrocity of circumstances which made one more sensible of his humanity than when he was in life. I connected that crime with Balkanic plots and aspirations so little that I had actually to ask where it had happened. My friend told me it was in Sarajevo, and wondered what would be the consequences of that grave event. He asked me what I thought would happen next.

It was with perfect sincerity that I answered "Nothing," and having a great repugnance to consider murder as a factor of politics, I dismissed the subject. It fitted with my ethical sense that an act cruel and absurd should be also useless. I had also the vision of a crowd of shadowy Archdukes in the background, out of which one would step forward to take the place of that dead man in the light of the European stage. And then, to speak the whole truth, there was no man capable of forming a judgment who attended so little to the march of events as I did at that time. What for want of a more definite term I must call my mind was fixed upon my own affairs, not because they were in a bad posture, but because of their fascinating holiday-promising aspect. I had been obtaining my information as to Europe at second hand, from friends good enough to come down now and then to see us. They arrived with their pockets full of crumpled newspapers, and answered my queries casually, with gentle smiles of scepticism as to the reality of my interest. And yet I was not indifferent; but the tension in the Balkans had become chronic after the acute crisis, and one could not help being less conscious of it. It had wearied out one's attention. Who could have guessed that on that wild stage we had just been looking at a miniature rehearsal of the great world-drama, the reduced model of the very passions and violences of what the future held in store for the Powers of the Old World? Here and there, perhaps, rare minds had a suspicion of that possibility, while they watched Old Europe stage-managing fussily by means of notes and conferences, the prophetic reproduction of its awaiting fate. It was wonderfully exact in the spirit; same roar of guns, same protestations of superiority, same words in the air; race, liberation, justice—and the same mood of trivial demonstrations. Once could not take today a ticket for Petersburg. "You mean Petrograd," would say the booking clerk. Shortly after the fall of Adrianople a friend of mine passing through Sophia asked for some *café turc* at the end of his lunch.

"*Monsieur veut dire café balkanique,*" the patriotic waiter corrected him austerely.

I will not say that I had not observed something of that instructive aspect of the war of the Balkans both in its first and in its second phase. But those with whom I touched upon that vision were pleased to see in it the evidence of my alarmist cynicism. As to alarm, I pointed out that fear is natural to man, and even salutary. It has done as much as courage for the preservation of races and institutions. But from a charge of cynicism I have always shrunk instinctively. It is like a charge of being blind in one eye, a moral disablement, a sort of disgraceful calamity that must be carried off with a jaunty bearing—a sort of thing I am not capable of. Rather than be thought a mere jaunty cripple I allowed myself to be blinded by the gross obviousness of the usual arguments. It was pointed out to me that these Eastern nations were not far removed from a savage state. Their economics were yet at the stage of scratching the earth and feeding the pigs. The highly developed material civilisation of Europe could not allow itself to be disturbed by a war. The industry and the finance could not allow themselves to be disorganised by the ambitions of an idle class, or even the aspirations, whatever they might be, of the masses.

Very plausible all this sounded. War does not pay. There had been a book written on that theme—an attempt to put pacifism on a material basis. Nothing more solid in the way of argument could have been advanced on this trading and manufacturing glove. War was "bad business!" This was final.

But, truth to say, on this July day I reflected but little on the condition of the civilised world. Whatever sinister passions were heaving under its splendid and complex surface, I was too agitated by a simple and innocent desire of my own, to notice the signs or interpret them correctly. The most innocent of passions will take the edge off one's judgment. The desire which possessed me was simply the desire to travel. And that being so it would have taken something very plain in the way of symptoms to shake my simple trust in the stability of things on the Continent. My sentiment and not my reason was engaged there. My eyes were turned to the past, not to the future; the past that one cannot suspect and mistrust, the shadowy and unquestionable moral possession the darkest struggles of which wear a halo of glory and peace.

In the preceding month of May we had received an invitation to spend some weeks in Poland in a country house in the neighbourhood of Cracow, but within the Russian frontier. The enterprise at first seemed to me considerable. Since leaving the sea, to which I have been faithful for so many years, I have discovered that there is in my composition very little stuff from which travellers are made. I confess that my first impulse about a projected journey is to leave it alone. But the invitation received at first with a sort of dismay ended by rousing the dormant energy of my feelings. Cracow is the town where I spent with my father the last eighteen months of his life. It was in that old royal and academical city that I ceased to be a child, became a boy, had known the friendships, the admirations, the thoughts and the indignations of that age. It was within those historical walls that I began to understand things, form affections, lay up a store of memories and a fund of sensations with which I was to break violently by throwing myself into an unrelated existence. It was like the experience of another world. The wings of time made a great dusk over all this, and I feared at first that if I ventured bodily in there I would discover that I who have had to do with a good many imaginary lives have been embracing mere shadows in my youth. I feared. But fear in itself may become a fascination. Men have gone, alone and trembling, into graveyards at midnight—just to see what would happen. And this adventure was to be pursued in sunshine. Neither would it be pursued alone. The invitation was extended to us all. This journey would have something of a migratory character, the invasion of a tribe. My present, all that gave solidity and value to it, at any rate, would stand by me in this test of the reality of my past. I was pleased with the idea of showing my companions what Polish country life was like; to visit the town where I was at school before the boys by my side should grow too old, and gaining an individual past of their own, should lose their unsophisticated interest in mine. It is only in the short instants of early youth that we have the faculty of coming out of ourselves to see dimly the visions and share the emotions of another soul. For youth all is reality in this world, and with justice, since it apprehends so vividly its images behind which a longer life makes one doubt whether there is any substance. I trusted to the fresh receptivity of these young beings in whom, unless Heredity is an empty word, there should have been a fibre which would answer to the sight, to the atmosphere, to the memories of that corner of the earth where my own boyhood had received its earliest independent impressions.

The first days of the third week in July, while the telegraph wires hummed with the words of enormous import which were to fill blue books, yellow books, white books, and to arouse the wonder of mankind, passed for us in light-hearted preparations for the journey. What was it but just a rush through Germany, to get across as quickly as possible?

Germany is the part of the earth's solid surface of which I know the least. In all my life I had been across it only twice. I may well say of it *vidi tantum*; and the very little I saw was through the window of a railway carriage at express speed. Those journeys of mine had been more like pilgrimages when one hurries on towards the goal for the satisfaction of a deeper need than curiosity. In this last instance, too, I was so incurious that I would have liked to have fallen asleep on the shores of England and opened my eyes, if it were possible, only on the other side of the Silesian frontier. Yet, in truth, as many others have done, I had "sensed it"—that promised land of steel, of chemical dyes, of method, of efficiency; that race planted in the middle of Europe, assuming in grotesque vanity the attitude of Europeans amongst effete Asiatics or barbarous niggers; and, with a consciousness of superiority freeing their hands from all moral bonds, anxious to take up, if I may express myself so, the "perfect man's burden." Meantime, in a clearing of the Teutonic forest, their sages were rearing a Tree of Cynical Wisdom, a sort of Upas tree, whose shade may be seen now lying over the prostrate body of Belgium. It must be said that they laboured openly enough, watering it with the most authentic sources of all madness, and watching with their be-spectacled eyes the slow ripening of the glorious blood-red fruit. The sincerest words of peace, words of menace, and I verily believe words of abasement, even it there had been a voice vile enough to utter them, would have been wasted on their ecstasy. For when the fruit ripens on a branch it must fall. There is nothing on earth that can prevent it.

II

For reasons which at first seemed to me somewhat obscure, that one of my companions whose wishes are law, decided that our travels should begin in an unusual way by the crossing of the North Sea. We should proceed from Harwich to Hamburg. Besides being 36 times longer than the Dover-Calais passage this rather unusual route had an air of adventure in better keeping with the romantic feeling of this Polish journey which for so many years had been before us in a state of a project full of colour and promise, but always retreating, elusive like an enticing mirage.

And, after all, it had turned out to be no mirage. No wonder they were excited. It's no mean experience to lay your hands on a mirage. The day of departure had come, the very hour had struck. The luggage was coming downstairs. It was most convincing. Poland then, if erased from the map, yet existed in reality; it was not a mere *pays du rêve,* where you can travel only in imagination. For no man, they argued, not even father, an habitual pursuer of dreams, would push the love of the novelist's art of make-believe to the point of burdening himself with real trunks for a voyage *au pays du rêve.*

As we left the door of our house, nestling in, perhaps, the most peaceful nook in Kent, the sky, after weeks of perfectly brazen serenity, veiled its blue depths and started to weep fine tears for the refreshment of the parched fields. A pearly blur settled over them, and a light sifted of all glare, or everything unkindly and searching that dwells in the splendour of unveiled skies. All unconscious of going towards the very scenes of war, I carried off in my eye this tiny fragment of Great Britain; a few fields, a wooded rise; a clump of trees or two, with a short stretch of road, and here and there a gleam of red wall and tiled roof above the darkening hedges wrapped up in soft mist and peace. And I felt that all this had a very strong hold on me as the embodiment of a beneficent and gentle spirit; that it was dear to me not as an inheritance, but as an acquisition, as a conquest in the sense in which a woman is conquered—by love, which is a sort of surrender.

These were strange, as if disproportionate thoughts to the matter in hand, which was the simplest sort of a Continental holiday. And I am certain that my companions, near as they are to me, felt no other trouble but the suppressed excitement of pleasurable anticipation. The forms and the spirit of the land before their eyes were their inheritance, not their conquest—which is a thing precarious, and, therefore, the most precious, possessing you if only by the fear of unworthiness rather than possessed by you. Moreover, as we sat together in the same railway carriage, they were looking forward to a voyage in space, whereas I felt more and more plainly that what I had started on was a journey in time, into the past; a fearful enough prospect for the most consistent, but to him who had not known how to preserve against his impulses the order and continuity of his life—so that at times it presented itself to his conscience as a series of betrayals—still more dreadful.

I put down here these thoughts so exclusively personal, to explain why there was no room in my consciousness for the apprehension of a European war. I don't mean to say that I ignored the possibility; I simply did not think of it. And it made no difference; for if I had thought of it, it could only have been in the lame and inconclusive way of the common uninitiated mortals; and I am sure that nothing short of intellectual certitude—obviously unattainable by the man in the street—could have stayed me on that journey which now that I had started on it seemed an irrevocable thing, a necessity of my self-respect.

London, the London before the war, flaunting its enormous glare, as of a monstrous conflagration up into the black sky—with its best Venice-like aspect of rainy evenings, the wet asphalted streets lying with the sheen of sleeping water in winding canals, and the great houses of the city towering all dark like empty palaces above the reflected lights of the glistening roadway.

Everything in the subdued incomplete night-life around the Mansion House went on normally with its fascinating air of a dead commercial city of sombre walls through which the inextinguishable activity of its millions streamed East and West in a brilliant flow of lighted vehicles.

In Liverpool Street, as usual too, through the double gates, a continuous line of taxi-cabs glided down the inclined approach and up again, like an endless chain of dredger-buckets, pouring in the passengers, and dipping them out of the great railway station under the inexorable pallid face of the clock telling off the diminishing minutes of peace. It was the hour of the boat-trains to Holland, to Hamburg, and there seemed to be no lack of people, fearless, reckless, or ignorant, who wanted to go to these places. The station was normally crowded, and if there was a great flutter of evening papers in the multitude of hands, there were no signs of extraordinary emotion on that multitude of faces. There was nothing in them to distract me from the thought that it was singularly appropriate that I should start from this station on the retraced way of my existence. For this was the station at which, thirty-seven years before, I arrived on my first visit to London. Not the same building, but the same spot. At nineteen years of age, after a period of probation and training I had imposed upon myself as ordinary seaman on board a North Sea coaster, I had come up from Lowestoft—my first long railway journey in England—to "sign on" for an Antipodean voyage in a deep-water ship. Straight from a railway carriage I had walked into the great city with something of the feeling of a traveller penetrating into a vast and unexplored wilderness. No explorer could have been more lonely. I did not know a single soul of all these millions that all around me peopled the mysterious distances of the streets. I cannot say I was free from a little youthful awe, but at that age one's feelings are simple. I was elated. I was pursuing a clear aim, I was carrying out a deliberate plan of making out of myself, in the first place, a seaman worthy of the service, good enough to work by the side of the men with whom I was to live; and in the second place, I had to justify my existence to myself, to redeem a tacit moral pledge. Both these aims were to be attained by the same effort. How simple seemed the problem of life then, on that hazy day of early September in the year 1878, when I entered London for the first time.

From that point of view—Youth and a straightforward scheme of conduct—it was certainly a year of grace. All the help I had to get in touch with the world I was invading was a piece of paper not much bigger than the palm of my hand—in which I held it—torn out of a larger plan of London for the greater facility of reference. It had been the object of careful study for some days past. The fact that I could take a conveyance at the station never occurred to my mind, no, not even when I got out into the street, and stood, taking my anxious bearings, in the midst, so to speak, of twenty thousand hansoms. A strange absence of mind or unconscious conviction that one cannot approach an important moment of one's life by means of a hired carriage? Yes, it would have been a preposterous proceeding. And indeed I was to to make an Australian voyage and encircle the globe before ever entering a London hansom.

Another document, a cutting from a newspaper, containing the address of an obscure shipping agent, was in my pocket. And I needed not to take it out. That address was as if graven deep in my brain. I muttered its words to myself as I walked on, navigating the sea of London by the chart concealed in the palm of my hand; for I had vowed to myself not to inquire my way from any one. Youth is the time of rash pledges. Had I taken a wrong turning I would have been lost; and if faithful to my pledge I might have remained lost for days, for weeks, have left perhaps my bones to be discovered bleaching in some blind alley of the Whitechapel district, as it has happened to lonely travellers lost in the bush. But I walked on to my destination without hesitation or mistake, showing there, for the first time, some of that faculty to absorb and make my own the imaged topography of a chart, which in later years was to help me in regions of intricate navigation to keep the ships entrusted to me off the ground. The place I was bound to was not easy to find. It was one of those courts hidden away from the charted and navigable streets, lost among the thick growth of houses like a dark pool in the depths of a forest, approached by an inconspicuous archway as if by a secret path; a Dickensian nook of London, that wonder city, the growth of which bears no sign of intelligent design, but many traces of freakishly sombre phantasy the Great Master knew so well how to bring out by the magic of his understanding love. And the office I entered was Dickensian too. The dust of the Waterloo year lay on the panes and frames of its windows; early Georgian grime clung to its sombre wainscoting.

It was one o'clock in the afternoon, but the day was gloomy. By the light of a single gas-jet depending from the smoked ceiling I saw an elderly man, in a long coat of black broadcloth. He had a grey beard, a big nose, thick lips, and heavy shoulders. His curly white hair and the general character of his head recalled vaguely a burly apostle in the *barocco* style of Italian art. Standing up at a tall, shabby, slanting desk, his silver-rimmed spectacles pushed up high on his forehead, he was eating a mutton-chop, which had been just brought to him from some Dickensian eating-house round the corner.

Without ceasing to eat he turned to me his florid *barocco* apostle's face with an expression of inquiry.

I produced elaborately a series of vocal sounds which must have borne sufficient resemblance to the phonetics of English speech, for his face broke into a smile of comprehension almost at once. "Oh it's you who wrote a letter to me the other day from Lowestoft about getting a ship."

I had written to him from Lowestoft. I can't remember a single word of that letter now. It was my very first composition in the English language. And he had understood it, evidently, for he spoke to the point at once, explaining that his business, mainly, was to find good ships for young gentlemen who wanted to go to sea as premium apprentices with a view of being trained for officers. But he gathered that this was not my object. I did not desire to be apprenticed. Was that the case?

It was. He was good enough to say then, "Of course I see that you are a gentleman. But your wish is to get a berth before the mast as an Able Seaman if possible. Is that it?"

It was certainly my wish; but he stated doubtfully that he feared he could not help me much in this. There was an Act of Parliament which made it penal to procure ships for sailors. "An Act—of—Parliament. A law," he took pains to impress it again and again on my foreign understanding, while I looked at him in consternation.

I had not been half an hour in London before I had run my head against an Act of Parliament! What a hopeless adventure! However, the *barocco* apostle was a resourceful person in his way, and we managed to get round the hard letter of it without damage to its fine spirit. Yet, strictly speaking, it was not the conduct of a good citizen; and in retrospect there is an unfilial flavour about that early sin of mine. For this Act of Parliament, the Merchant Shipping Act of the Victorian era, had been in a manner of speaking a father and mother to me. For many years it had regulated and disciplined my life, prescribed my food and the amount of my breathing space, had looked after my health and tried as much as possible to secure my personal safety in a risky calling. It isn't such a bad thing to lead a life of hard toil and plain duty within the four corners of an honest Act of Parliament. And I am glad to say that its severities have never been applied to me.

In the year 1878, the year of "Peace with Honour," I had walked as lone as any human being in the streets of London, out of Liverpool Street Station, to surrender myself to its care. And now, in the year of the war waged for honour and conscience more than for any other cause, I was there again, no longer alone, but a man of infinitely dear and close ties grown since that time, of work done, of words written, of friendships secured. It was like the closing of a thirty-six-year cycle.

All unaware of the War Angel already awaiting, with the trumpet at his lips, the stroke of the fatal hour, I sat there, thinking that this life of ours is neither long nor short, but that it can appear very wonderful, entertaining, and pathetic, with symbolic images and bizarre associations crowded into one half-hour of retrospective musing.

I felt, too, that this journey, so suddenly entered upon, was bound to take me away from daily life's actualities at every step. I felt it more than ever when presently we steamed out into the North Sea, on a dark night fitful with gusts of wind, and I lingered on deck, alone of all the tale of the ship's passengers. That sea was to me something unforgettable, something much more than a name. It had been for some time the school-room of my trade. On it, I may safely say, I had learned, too, my first words of English. A wild and stormy abode, sometimes, was that confined, shallow-water academy of seamanship from which I launched myself on the wide oceans. My teachers had been the sailors of the Norfolk shore; coast men, with steady eyes, mighty limbs, and gentle voice; men of very few words, which at least were never bare of meaning. Honest, strong, steady men, sobered by domestic ties, one and all, as far as I can remember.

That is what years ago the North Sea I could hear growling in the dark all round the ship had been for me. And I fancied that I must have been carrying its voice in my ear ever since, for nothing could be more familiar than those short, angry sounds I was listening to with a smile of affectionate recognition.

I could not guess that before many days my old school-room would be desecrated by violence, littered with wrecks, with death walking its waves, hiding under its waters. Perhaps while I am writing these words the children, or maybe the grandchildren, of my pacific teachers are out in trawlers, under the Naval flag, dredging for German submarine mines.

III

I have said that the North Sea was my finishing school of seamanship before I launched myself on the wider oceans. Confined as it is in comparison with the vast stage of this water-girt globe, I did not know it in all its parts. My class-room was the region of the English East Coast which, in the year of Peace with Honour, had long forgotten the war episodes belonging to its maritime history. It was a peaceful coast, agricultural, industrial, the home of fishermen. At night the lights of its many towns played on the clouds, or in clear weather lay still, here and there, in brilliant pools above the ink-black outline of the land. On many a night I have hauled at the braces under the shadow of that coast, envying, as sailors will, the people on the shore sleeping quietly in their beds within sound of the sea. I imagine that not one head on those envied pillows was made uneasy by the slightest premonition of the realities of naval war the short lifetime of one generation was to bring so close to their homes.

Though far away from that region of kindly memories and traversing a part of the North Sea much less known to me, I was deeply conscious of the familiarity of my surroundings. It was a cloudy, nasty day: and the aspects of Nature don't change, unless in the course of thousands of years —or, perhaps, centuries. The Phoenicians, its first discoverers, the Romans, the first imperial rulers of that sea, had experienced days like this, so different in the wintry quality of the light, even on a July afternoon, from anything they had ever known in their native Mediterranean. For myself, a very late comer into that sea, and its former pupil, I accorded amused recognition to the characteristic aspect so well remembered from my days of training. The same old thing. A grey-green expanse of smudgy waters grinning angrily at one with white foam-ridges, and over all a cheerless, unglowing canopy, apparently made of wet blotting paper. From time to time a flurry of fine rain blew along like a puff of smoke across the dots of distant fishing boats, very few, very scattered, and tossing restlessly on an ever dissolving, ever re-forming sky-line.

Those flurries, and the steady rolling of the ship, accounted for the emptiness of the decks, favouring my reminiscent mood. It might have been a day of five and thirty years ago, when there were on this and every other sea more sails and less smoke-stacks to be seen. Yet, thanks to the unchangeable sea I could have given myself up to the illusion of a revived past, had it not been for the periodical transit across my gaze of a German passenger. He was marching round and round the boat deck with characteristic determination. Two sturdy boys gambolled round him in his progress like two disorderly satellites round their parent planet. He was bringing them home from their school in England for their holiday. What could have induced such a sound Teuton to entrust his offspring to the unhealthy influences of that effete, corrupt, rotten and criminal country I cannot imagine. It could hardly have been from motives of economy. I did not speak to him. He trod the deck of that decadent British ship with a scornful foot while his breast (and to a large extent his stomach, too) appeared expanded by the consciousness of a superior destiny. Later I could observe the same truculent bearing, touched with the racial grotesqueness, in the men of the *Landwehr* corps, that passed through Cracow to reinforce the Austrian army in Eastern Galicia. Indeed, the haughty passenger might very well have been, most probably was, an officer of the *Landwehr*; and perhaps those two fine active boys are orphans by now. Thus things acquire significance by the lapse of time. A citizen, a father, a warrior, a mote in the dust-cloud of six million fighting particles, an unconsidered trifle for the jaws of war, his humanity was not consciously impressed on my mind at the time. Mainly, for me, he was a sharp tapping of heels round the corner of the deck-house, a white yachting cap and a green overcoat getting periodically between my eyes and the shifting cloud-horizon of the ashy-grey North Sea. He was but a shadowy intrusion and a disregarded one, for, far away there to the West, in the direction of the Dogger Bank, where fishermen go seeking their daily bread and sometimes find their graves, I could behold an experience of my own in the winter of '81, not of war, truly, but of a fairly lively contest with the elements which were very angry indeed.

There had been a troublesome week of it, including one hateful night—or a night of hate (it isn't for nothing that the North Sea is also called the German Ocean)—when all the fury stored in its heart seemed concentrated on one ship which could do no better than float on her side in an unnatural, disagreeable, precarious, and altogether intolerable manner. There were on board, besides myself, seventeen men all good and true, including a round enormous Dutchman who, in those hours between sunset and sunrise, managed to lose his blown-out appearance somehow, became as it were deflated, and thereafter for a good long time moved in our midst wrinkled and slack all over like a half-collapsed balloon. The whimpering of our deck-boy, a skinny, impressionable little scarecrow out of a training-ship, for whom, because of the tender immaturity of his nerves, this display of German Ocean frightfulness was too much (before the year was out he developed into a sufficiently cheeky young ruffian), his desolate whimpering, I say, heard between the gusts of that black, savage night, was much more present to my mind and indeed to my senses than the green overcoat and the white cap of the German passenger circling the deck indefatigably, attended by his two gyrating children.

"That's a very nice gentleman." This information, together with the fact that he was a widower and a regular passenger twice a year by the ship, was communicated to me suddenly by our captain. At intervals through the day he would pop out of the chartroom and offer me short snatches of conversation. He owned a simple soul and a not very entertaining mind, and he was without malice and, I believe, quite unconsciously, a warm

Germanophile. And no wonder! As he told me himself, he had been fifteen years on that run, and spent almost as much of his life in Hamburg as in Harwich.

"Wonderful people they are," he repeated from time to time, without entering into particulars, but with many nods of sagacious obstinacy. What he knew of them, I suppose, were a few commercial travellers and small merchants, most likely. But I had observed long before that German genius has a hypnotising power over half-baked souls and half-lighted minds. There is an immense force of suggestion in highly organised mediocrity. Had it not hypnotised half Europe? My man was very much under the spell of German excellence. On the other hand, his contempt for France was equally general and unbounded. I tried to advance some arguments against this position, but I only succeeded in making him hostile. "I believe you are a Frenchman yourself," he snarled at last, giving me an intensely suspicious look; and forthwith broke off communications with a man of such unsound sympathies.

Hour by hour the blotting-paper sky and the great flat greenish smudge of the sea had been taking on a darker tone, without any change in their colouring and texture. Evening was coming on over the North Sea. Black uninteresting hummocks of land appeared, dotting the duskiness of water and clouds in the Eastern board: tops of islands fringing the German shore. While I was looking at their antics amongst the waves—and for all their solidity they were very elusive things in the failing light—another passenger came out on deck. This one wore a dark overcoat and a grey cap. The yellow leather strap of his binocular case crossed his chest. His elderly red cheeks nourished but a very thin crop of short white hairs, and the end of his nose was so perfectly round that it determined the whole character of his physiognomy. Indeed nothing else in it had the slightest chance to assert itself. His disposition, unlike the widower's, appeared to be mild and humane. He offered me the loan of his glasses. He had a wife and some small children concealed in the depths of the ship, and he thought they were very well where they were. His eldest son was about the decks somewhere.

"We are Americans," he remarked weightily, but in a rather peculiar tone. He spoke English with the accent of our captain's "wonderful people," and proceeded to give me the history of the family's crossing the Atlantic in a White Star liner. They remained in England just the time necessary for a railway journey from Liverpool to Harwich. His people (those in the depths of the ship) were naturally a little tired.

At that moment a young man of about twenty, his son, rushed up to us from the fore-deck in a state of intense elation. "Hurrah," he cried under his breath. "The first German light! Hurrah!"

And those two American citizens shook hands on it with the greatest fervour, while I turned away and received full in the eyes the brilliant wink of the Borkum lighthouse squatting low down in the darkness. The shade of the night had settled on the North Sea.

I do not think I have ever seen before a night so full of lights. The great change of sea life since my time was brought home to me. I had been conscious all day of an interminable procession of steamers. They went on and on as if in chase of each other, the Baltic trade, the trade of Scandinavia, of Denmark, of Germany, pitching heavily into a head sea and bound for the gateway of Dover Straits. Singly, and in small companies of two and three, they emerged from the dull, colourless, sunless distances ahead as if the supply of rather roughly finished mechanical toys were inexhaustible in some mysterious cheap store away there, below the grey curve of the earth. Cargo steam vessels have reached by this time a height of utilitarian ugliness which, when one reflects that it is the product of human ingenuity, strikes hopeless awe into one. These dismal creations look still uglier at sea than in port, and with an added touch of the ridiculous. Their rolling waddle when seen at a certain angle, their abrupt clockwork nodding in a seaway, so unlike the soaring lift and swing of a craft under sail, have in them something caricatural, a suggestion of a low parody directed at noble predecessors by an improved generation of dull, mechanical toilers, conceited and without grace.

When they switched on their lamps (each of these unlovely cargo tanks carried tame lightning within its slab-sided body), they spangled the night with the cheap, electric, shop-glitter, here, there, and everywhere, as of some High Street, broken up and washed out to sea. Later, Heligoland cut into the overhead darkness with its powerful beam, infinitely prolonged out of unfathomable night under the clouds.

I remained on deck until we stopped and a steam pilot-boat, so overlighted amidships that one could not make out her complete shape, glided across our bows and sent a pilot on board. I fear that the oar, as a working implement, will become presently as obsolete as the sail. The pilot boarded us in a motor-dinghy. More and more is mankind reducing its physical activities to pulling levers and twirling little wheels. Progress! Yet the older methods of meeting natural forces demanded intelligence too; an equally fine readiness of wits. And readiness of wits working in combination with the strength of muscles made a more complete man.

It was really a surprisingly small dinghy and it ran to and fro like a water-insect fussing noisily down there with immense self-importance. Within hail of us the hull of the Elbe lightship floated all dark and silent under its enormous round, service lantern; a faithful black shadow watching the broad estuary full of lights.

Such was my first view of the Elbe approached under the wings of peace ready for flight away from the luckless shores of Europe. Our visual impressions remain with us so persistently that I find it extremely difficult to hold fast to the rational belief that now everything is dark over there, that the Elbe lightship has been towed away from its post of duty, the triumphant beam of Heligoland extinguished, and the pilot-boat laid up, or turned to warlike uses for lack of its proper work to do. And obviously it must be so.

Any trickle of oversea trade that passes yet that way must be creeping along cautiously with the unlighted, war-blighted black coast close on one hand, and sudden death on the other hand. For all the space we steamed through that Sunday evening must now be one great minefield, sown thickly with the seeds of hate; while submarines steal out to sea, over the very spot perhaps where the insect-dinghy put a pilot on board of us with so much fussy importance. Mines: Submarines. The last word in sea-warfare! Progress—impressively disclosed by this war.

There have been other wars! Wars not inferior in the greatness of the stake and in the fierce animosity of feelings. During that one which was finished a hundred years ago it happened that while the English Fleet was keeping watch on Brest, an American, perhaps Fulton himself, offered to the Maritime Prefect of the port and to the French Admiral, an invention which would sink all the unsuspecting English ships one after another—or, at any rate most of them. The offer was not even taken into consideration; and the Prefect ends his report to the Minister in Paris with a fine phrase of indignation: "It is not the sort of death one would deal to brave men."

And behold, before history had time to hatch another war of the like proportions in the intensity of aroused passions and the greatness of issues, the dead flavour of archaism descended on the manly sentiment of those self-denying words. Mankind has been demoralised since by its own mastery of mechanical appliances. Its spirit is apparently so weak now, and its flesh has grown so strong, that it will face any deadly horror of destruction and cannot resist the temptation to use any stealthy, murderous contrivance. It has become the intoxicated slave of its own detestable ingenuity. It is true, too, that since the Napoleonic time another sort of war-doctrine has been inculcated in a nation, and held out to the world.

IV

On this journey of ours, which for me was essentially not a progress, but a retracing of footsteps on the road of life, I had no beacons to look for in Germany. I had never lingered in that land which, on the whole, is so singularly barren of memorable manifestations of generous sympathies and magnanimous impulses. An ineradicable, invincible provincialism of envy and vanity clings to the forms of its thought like a frowsy garment. Even while yet very young I turned my eyes away from it instinctively as from a threatening phantom. I believe that children and dogs have, in their innocence, a special power of perception as far as spectral apparitions and coming misfortunes are concerned.

I let myself be carried through Germany as if it were pure space, without sights, without sounds. No whispers of the war reached my voluntary abstraction. And perhaps not so very voluntary after all! Each of us is a fascinating spectacle to himself, and I had to watch my own personality returning from another world, as it were, to revisit the glimpses of old moons. Considering the condition of humanity, I am, perhaps, not so much to blame for giving myself up to that occupation. We prize the sensation of our continuity, and we can only capture it in that way. By watching.

We arrived in Cracow late at night. After a scrambly supper, I said to my eldest boy, "I can't go to bed. I am going out for a look round. Coming?"

He was ready enough. For him, all this was part of the interesting adventure of the whole journey. We stepped out of the portal of the hotel into an empty street, very silent, and bright with moonlight. I was, indeed, revisiting the glimpses of the moon. I felt so much like a ghost that the discovery that I could remember such material things as the right turn to take and the general direction of the street gave me a moment of wistful surprise.

The street, straight and narrow, ran into the great Market Square of the town, the centre of its affairs and of the lighter side of its life. We could see at the far end of the street a promising widening of space. At the corner an unassuming (but armed) policeman, wearing ceremoniously at midnight a pair of white gloves which made his big hands extremely noticeable, turned his head to look at the grizzled foreigner holding forth in a strange tongue to a youth on whose arm he leaned.

The Square, immense in its solitude, was full to the brim of moonlight. The garland of lights at the foot of the houses seemed to burn at the bottom of a bluish pool. I noticed with infinite satisfaction that the unnecessary trees the Municipality insisted upon sticking between the stones had been steadily refusing to grow. They were not a bit bigger than the poor victims I could remember. Also, the paving operations seemed to be exactly at the same point at which I left them forty years before. There were the dull, torn-up patches on that bright expanse, the piles of paving material looking ominously black, like heads of rocks on a silvery sea. Who was it that said that Time works wonders? What an exploded superstition! As far as these trees and these paving stones were concerned, it had worked nothing. The suspicion of the unchangeableness of things already vaguely suggested to my senses by our rapid drive from the railway station, was agreeably strengthened within me.

"We are now on the line A.B.," I said to my companion, importantly.

It was the name bestowed in my time on one of the sides of the Square by the senior students of that town of classical learning and historical relics. The common citizens knew nothing of it, and, even if they had, would not have dreamed of taking it seriously. He who used it was of the initiated, belonged to the schools. We youngsters regarded that name as a fine jest, the invention of a most excellent fancy. Even as I uttered it to my boy I experienced again that sense of my privileged initiation. And then, happening to look up at the wall, I saw in the light of the corner lamp, a white, cast-iron tablet fixed thereon, bearing an inscription in raised black letters, thus : "Line A. B." Heavens! The name had been adopted officially! Any town urchin, any gutter-snipe, any herb-selling woman of the market place, any wandering Boeotian, was free to talk of the line A. B., to walk on the line A. B., to appoint to meet his friends on the line A. B. It had become a mere name in a directory. I was stunned by the extreme mutability of things. Time could work wonders, and no mistake. A Municipality had stolen an invention of excellent fancy, and a fine jest had turned into a horrid piece of cast-iron.

I proposed that we should walk to the other end of the line, using the profaned name, not only without gusto, but with positive distaste. And this, too, was one of the wonders of Time, for a bare minute had worked that change. There was at the end of the line a certain street I wanted to look at, I explained to my companion.

To our right the unequal massive towers of St. Mary's Church soared aloft into the ethereal radiance of the air, very black on their shaded sides, glowing with a soft phosphorescent sheen on the others. In the distance the Florian Gate, thick and squat under its pointed roof, barred the street with the square shoulders of the old city wall. In the narrow, brilliantly pale vista of bluish flagstones and silvery fronts of houses, its black archway stood out small and very distinct.

There was not a soul in sight, and not even the echo of a footstep for our ears. Into this coldly illuminated and dumb emptiness there issued out of my aroused memory, a small boy of eleven, wending his way, not very fast, to a preparatory school for day-pupils on the second floor of the third house down from the Florian Gate. It was in the winter months of 1868. At eight o'clock of every morning that God made, sleet or shine, I walked up Florian Street. But of that, my first school, I remember very little. I believe that one of my co-sufferers there has become a much appreciated editor of historical documents. But I didn't suffer much from the various imperfections of my first school. I was rather indifferent to school troubles. I had a private gnawing worm of my own. This was the time of my father's last illness. Every evening at seven, turning my back on the Florian Gate, I walked all the way to a big old house in a quiet narrow street a good distance beyond the Great Square. There, in a large drawing-room, panelled and bare, with heavy cornices and a lofty ceiling, in a little oasis of light made by two candles in a desert of dusk I sat at a little table to worry and ink myself all over till the task of my preparation was done. The table of my toil faced a tall white door, which was kept closed; now and then it would come ajar and a nun in a white coif would squeeze herself through the crack, glide across the room, and disappear. There were two of these noiseless nursing nuns. Their voices were seldom heard. For, indeed, what could they have had to say? When they did speak to me it was with their lips hardly moving, in a claustral clear whisper. Our domestic matters were ordered by the elderly housekeeper of our neighbour on the second floor, a Canon of the Cathedral, lent for the emergency. She, too, spoke but seldom. She wore a black dress with a cross hanging by a chain on her ample bosom. And though when she spoke she moved her lips more than the nuns, she never let her voice rise above a peacefully murmuring note. The air around me was all piety, resignation, and silence.

I don't know what would have become of me if I had not been a reading boy. My prep finished I would have had nothing to do but sit and watch the awful stillness of the sick room flow out through the closed door and coldly enfold my scared heart. I suppose that in a futile childish way I would have gone crazy. But I was a reading boy. There were many books about, lying on consoles, on tables, and even on the floor, for we had not had time to settle down. I read! What did I not read! Sometimes the elder nun, gliding up and casting a mistrustful look on the open pages, would lay her hand lightly on my head and suggest in a doubtful whisper, "Perhaps it is not very good for you to read these books." I would raise my eyes to her face mutely, and with a vague gesture of giving it up she would glide away.

Later in the evening, but not always, I would be permitted to tip-toe into the sick room to say good-night to the figure prone on the bed, which often could not acknowledge my presence but by a slow movement of the eyes, put my lips dutifully to the nerveless hand lying on the coverlet, and tip-toe out again. Then I would go to bed, in a room at the end of the corridor, and often, not always, cry myself into a good sound sleep.

I looked forward to what was coming with an incredulous terror. I turned my eyes from it sometimes with success, and yet all the time I had an awful sensation of the inevitable. I had also moments of revolt which stripped off me some of my simple trust in the government of the universe. But when the inevitable entered the sick room and the white door was thrown wide open, I don't think I found a single tear to shed. I have a suspicion that the Canon's housekeeper looked on me as the most callous little wretch on earth.

The day of the funeral came in due course and all the generous "Youth of the Schools," the grave Senate of the University, the delegations of the Trade-guilds, might have obtained (if they cared) *de visu* evidence of the callousness of the little wretch. There was nothing in my aching head but a few words, some such stupid sentences as, "It's done," or, "It's accomplished" (in Polish it is much shorter), or something of the sort, repeating itself endlessly. The long procession moved out of the narrow street, down a long street, past the Gothic front of St. Mary's under its unequal towers, towards the Florian Gate.

In the moonlight-flooded silence of the old town of glorious tombs and tragic memories, I could see again the small boy of that day following a hearse; a space kept clear in which I walked alone, conscious of an enormous following, the clumsy swaying of the tall black machine, the chanting of the surpliced clergy at the head, the flames of tapers passing under the low archway of the gate, the rows of bared heads on the pavements with fixed, serious eyes. Half the population had turned out on that fine May afternoon. They had not come to honour a great achievement, or even some splendid failure. The dead and they were victims alike of an unrelenting destiny which cut them off from every path of merit and glory. They had come only to render homage to the ardent fidelity of the man whose life had been a fearless confession in word and deed of a creed which the simplest heart in that crowd could feel and understand.

It seemed to me that if I remained longer there in that narrow street I should become the helpless prey of the Shadows I had called up. They were crowding upon me, enigmatic and insistent, in their clinging air of the grave that tasted of dust and of the bitter vanity of old hopes.

"Let's go back to the hotel, my boy," I said. "It's getting late."

It will be easily understood that I neither thought nor dreamt that night of a possible war. For the next two days I went about amongst my fellow men, who welcomed me with the utmost consideration and friendliness, but unanimously derided my fears of a war. They would not believe in it. It was impossible. On the evening of the second day I was in the hotel's smoking room, an irrationally private apartment, a sanctuary for a few choice minds of the town, always pervaded by a dim religious light, and more hushed than any club reading-room I've ever been in. Gathered into a small knot, we were discussing the situation in subdued tones suitable to the genius of the place.

A gentleman with a fine head of white hair suddenly pointed an impatient finger in my direction and apostrophised me.

"What I want to know is whether, should there be war, England would come in."

The time to draw a breath, and I spoke out for the Cabinet without faltering.

"Most assuredly. I should think all Europe knows that by this time."

He took hold of the lapel of my coat, and, giving it a slight jerk for greater emphasis, said forcibly:

"Then, if England will, as you say, and all the world knows it, there can be no war. Germany won't be so mad as that."

On the morrow by noon we read of the German ultimatum. The day after came the declaration of war, and the Austrian mobilization order. We were fairly caught. All that remained for me to do was to get my party out of the way of eventual shells. The best move which occurred to me was to snatch them up instantly into the mountains to a Polish health resort of great repute—which I did (at the rate of one hundred miles in eleven hours) by the last civilian train permitted to leave Cracow for the next three weeks.

And there we remained amongst the Poles from all parts of Poland, not officially interned, but simply unable to obtain the permission to travel by train, or road. It was a wonderful, a poignant two months. This is not the time, and, perhaps, not the place, to enlarge upon the tragic character of the situation; a whole people seeing the culmination of its misfortunes in a final catastrophe, unable to trust any one, to appeal to any one, to look for help from any quarter; deprived of all hope and even of its last illusions, and unable, in the trouble of minds and the unrest of consciences, to take refuge in stoical acceptance. I have seen all this. And I am glad I have not so many years left me to remember that appalling feeling of inexorable fate, tangible, palpable, come after so many cruel years, a figure of dread, murmuring with iron lips the final words: Ruin—and Extinction.

But enough of this. For our little band there was the awful anguish of incertitude as to the real nature of events in the West. It is difficult to give an idea how ugly and dangerous things looked to us over there. Belgium knocked down and trampled out of existence, France giving in under repeated blows, a military collapse like that of 1870, and England involved in that disastrous alliance, her army sacrificed, her people in a panic! Polish papers, of course, had no other but German sources of information. Naturally we did not believe all we read, but it was sometimes excessively difficult to react with sufficient firmness. We used to shut our door, and there, away from everybody, we sat weighing the news, hunting up discrepancies, scenting lies, finding reasons for hopefulness, and generally cheering each other up. But it was a beastly time. People used to come to me with very serious news and ask, "What do you think of it?" And my invariable answer was, "Whatever has happened, or is going to happen, whoever wants to make peace, you may be certain that England will not make it, not for ten years, if necessary."

But enough of this, too. Through the unremitting efforts of Polish friends we obtained at last the permission to travel to Vienna. Once there, the wing of the American Eagle was extended over our uneasy heads. We cannot be sufficiently grateful to the American Ambassador (who all along, interested himself in our fate) for his exertions on our behalf, his invaluable assistance and the real friendliness of his reception in Vienna. Owing to Mr. Penfield's action we obtained the permission to leave Austria. And it was a near thing, for his Excellency has informed my American publishers since that a week later orders were issued to have us detained till the end of the war. However, we effected our hair's-breadth escape into Italy; and reaching Genoa, took passage in a Dutch mail steamer, homeward-bound from Java with London as a port of call.

On that sea-route I might have picked up a memory at every mile if the past had not been eclipsed by the tremendous actuality. We saw the signs of it in the emptiness of the Mediterranean, the aspect of Gibraltar, the misty glimpse in the Bay of Biscay of an outward-bound convoy of transports, in the presence of British submarines in the Channel. Innumerable drifters flying the Naval flag dotted the narrow waters and two Naval officers coming on board off the South Foreland, piloted the ship through the Downs.

The Downs! There they were, thick with the memories of my sea-life. But what were to me now the futilities of an individual past? As our ship's head swung into the estuary of the Thames, a deep, yet faint, concussion passed through the air, a shock rather than a sound, which missing my ear found its way straight into my heart. Turning instinctively to look at my boys, I happened to meet my wife's eyes. She also had felt profoundly, coming from far away across the grey distances of the sea, the faint boom of the big guns at work on the coast of Flanders—shaping the future.

A Letter from Exile

His Love of Travel; and Unwillingness to Make a Permanent Residence in Venice

Petrarch

I HAD SUSPECTED, and now I learn from your words, that you are amazed that I keep wandering here and there, never settling down, never choosing a secure base for my existence, and that after hardly a year in Italy I migrate to France and then after two years return to Italy. As I can't deny the fact, I must report the reason, to you for your pity, to men of good will for their pardon, to the public for its information. I applaud the words of Annaeus Seneca, that "the first mark of a well-ordered mind is that it can stand still and commune with itself." But I am also aware that many who have never stepped outside of their own hometowns are nevertheless vague of mind and incoherent in thought, while some who were constantly in movement have been serious, logical thinkers. Many great generals and philosophers have been travelers, as you well recall; whereas Vatia exists as if buried alive in his country house, and Buta snores all day and lies awake all night, and never sets foot beyond his bedroom door. You know of them from Seneca's famous letters, which in mockery made them immortal. The Apostles traveled far, and barefoot journeyed to the most distant lands. One or another was sent to Ephesus, to Syria, Greece, Rome, India, Egypt. Their bodies wandered in the most rugged regions; they suffered all the misadventures of land and the wide waters; but their hearts were fixed upon heaven. Today, indeed, the bodies of our "apostles" rest on golden beds, while they send their thoughts afar over land and sea. To which group shall we adjudge the "mark of the well-ordered mind"? To those who never change their location, or to those who never change their purpose?

I must repeat what I have often said, what I still take pleasure in saying, that Homer and his great Latin follower, who are to be ranked among the first observers of human affairs, in describing the character and actions of the perfect man show him as a world-wanderer, everywhere learning something new. They thought that the kind of man they portrayed could not be formed if perpetually limited to a single spot. But since perhaps such lofty examples do not apply to me I shall omit excuses which might suggest pride and provoke to envy, and return to my statement that you should pity me.

You have always been a partisan of virtue; you have traveled far and are familiar with many places, many things; and now while still underage you have gloriously ascended to the highest post of your very noble Republic, and for the common good and common liberty you have entered the sumptuous prison of eminence. And I know that I should answer your desires if, after the long campaigns of my life, I should pitch my tent beside you, there to pass in peace the remainder of my existence. Nothing could be more pleasant for me; nothing would better fulfill my hopes, and yet nothing appears more difficult of achievement. I have long set my helm on this course, but violent seas have swept me otherwhere, despite my struggles. And since I recognize your kind condescension in lending an ear, in the midst of your occupations, to the talk of your humble friend, I shall confess that it was my purpose in youth to follow Homer's advice, to inspect "the manners of many men and their high cities," to gaze upon new lands, mountain peaks, famous seas, lauded lakes, secluded founts, mighty rivers, and all the world's varied sites. I thought that thus I might become learned, most expeditiously and briefly, and not only at little expense of trouble but with great pleasure. To know more was always among the first of my desires; and I seemed somehow to be overcoming ignorance by mere agitation of mind and body. But far enough have I wandered now; enough have I gone round and round, enough have I bowed to my desires. Now it may be time for me to say to my spirit's guide the words of the Roman centurion: "Standard-bearer, plant here the banner; here we shall do well to remain." Perhaps I am sated with travel, with rambling through many lands; perhaps my youthful ardor is relaxing and cooling, turning naturally to a love of peace, suitable for my occupations. At any rate I am losing my love of roving.

So what shall I do? You must believe me, if I have ever proved trustworthy. If I should ever find under the sun any good place—or at least not a bad place, if not perfectly awful—I should remain there gladly, and permanently. But now I keep turning over and over like a man on a hard bed, and I can obtain no rest in spite of my desire; and since I can find no softness in my bed I try to ease my weariness by constant shifting; and so I stray hither and yon and I seem to be a wanderer forever. Tired of the hardness of one place, I try another; and though it's no softer it seems so because it's different. Thus I am tossed about, well aware that though there is no resting-place for me, I must seek it out forever with pain and labor, and—this is the worst of it—with the consciousness that in all life's toils and fiery passions we must fear eternal straits and toils and everlasting fires. "Well," you may say, "where you tremble and quake, many another sits quietly and comfortably!" I reply: "How many more live there in great distress of mind, and cannot for a moment be still!"

I shan't speak of the celestial origin of souls, according to Virgil, nor shall I quote Cicero to the effect that our spirits come to us from the everlasting fires that we call stars and heavenly bodies. And Seneca has it that the changeableness of our souls, born from the rapid whirl of the celestial fires, is thereby to be excused. But I do say this: that our souls are created by God and by him are at once infused in our bodies; that God's throne is in heaven, as the Psalmist says; that the movement of the heavens is perpetual, as we see with our own eyes; so it is not surprising that we have some relation of likeness with the home of our Creator. Whatever its origin, I know that in men's minds, especially in superior minds, resides an innate longing to see new places, to keep changing one's home. I don't deny that this longing should be tempered and held in bounds by reason. Your own experience will lead you to agree with me that this taste for wandering about the world mingles pleasure with its pains, while those who sit forever on one spot experience a strange boredom in their repose. Which is the better course, in this as in man's other problems? God alone knows. If one thinks that reward is to be found not in the spirit but in some particular place, if one calls immobility constancy, then the gouty must be extremely constant, and the dead are more constant still, and the mountains are the most constant of all.

Enough of this. Perhaps I shall be accused of hunting out arguments to excuse my own diseased character. Well, I grant that I am stricken with a very serious disease—I pray it be not mortal. But I protest that I cannot blame my disease on the bed whereon I lie. I repeat, I am sick; this must be apparent to anyone, even though I should not reveal it in words. Cure me, and I shall be stronger, but my bed will be no smoother and softer. I refer to the bed of this life, on which I lie exhausted. This bed is, rather, rough, uncomfortable, foul, evil, lumpy; it tortures any occupant in the best of health. I do not know how some can rest quietly thereon, unless, in their drugged slumber, they do not feel what oppresses me, or unless they find in what tortures me some strange pleasure, to me unknown. One may of course freely presume that my mind is in fever, while theirs is healthy. I could believe this of learned men, but I can't believe that base folk are more healthy than I or than anyone else; I think rather that they are torpid and insensible. Let others ascribe their peace to what cause they will; let it suffice that I have indicated the reasons for my agitation. Unless I am much mistaken, I am not sick to such a degree that I could not find rest if freed from the inconveniences of place and circumstance. It will be well if I can apply to my own case a remedy that I have recommended to others; that is, to seek within oneself a peace one cannot find without, and to find my repose, not in this spot or that, but in the spirit, or rather in the master and enlightener of the spirit.

But more of this at another time. Wisest of rulers, you who were moved by affection to worry about my own affairs, this must be for the moment my reply. Farewell.

Translated by Morris Bishop

The Hounded Travelers

Henry de Montherlant

IN ORDER TO MEDITATE there, Barrès used to go to Portugal, "at the extreme tip of Europe." Paul Morand (*Rien que la terre*) goes to the west coast of America. One at the extremity of European lands, the other at the extremity of the white race's lands: those who like "signs of the times" may enjoy noting the difference. But, having arrived at these two extremes, both Barrès and Morand recognize that they are not happy.

"As far back as I can remember," writes Morand, "always this desire to be somewhere else, as implacable as a wound. You will change, says the *Imitation*, and will not be better off." And he applies to himself this phrase of Michelet speaking of Medusa: "In movement, she dreams of rest; inert, she dreams of movement." Yet Morand settles down, or goes through the motions of settling down. He is buying a villa on the Riviera. As for me, I have just seen here and there many a good villa for sale, and in admirable locations. But I well know that scarcely would my signature be placed on the deed than I should have an insane desire to be somewhere else, I should feel this new property weigh me down like a chain (every piece of property is one). "Settling down": the very words, if I pronounce them, nauseate me. And the word "reject" makes me younger. Reject! Reject!

Knowing this as I know it, these villas ought at least to leave me indifferent. Not at all! At the very moment when I know that such happiness would not be happiness for me, they give me a miserable uneasiness and longing for it. Thus there is no beautiful landscape, there is no beautiful creature (for it is the same with them), which does not make me doubly unhappy: the sadness of not having it and imagining the sadness that would be mine if I had it. A comedy that must be taken tragically: (this formula is perhaps valid for the whole of life) "Neither without you nor with you can I live!" The cry of the Latin poet will last as long as man.

Barrès, seeing the steamer leave for Isola Bella, did not take it, in order to exasperate his desire. That is the pleasure of a cerebral man. And in my case, having set out from the frontier for these famous lakes, at the halfway point I turned back. But my refusal is not that of Barrès. Fear is the cause of it. If the lakes are as they are said to be, the more beautiful they are, the more they will make me feel that what I live on their shores is inferior to them.

For my life on their shores will never be equal to them. The only delight in the world for me lies in its creatures. I am not made of the flesh of Barrès, who sniffs them from afar, then makes a phrase of them; I have not that sad power. Like the common man and without trying to disguise the banality of such sentiments, I seek in nomadism only opportunities to use my flesh, my heart, that indissoluble mixture of flesh and heart, in which now one now the other dominates, opportunities to be in love or rather to be charmed, drawing from human beings all their poetry in the environments whose poetry is attuned to theirs. But scarcely have I a creature in my possession than I prefer all those I do not have, the least of those I do not have. How many objects are desirable in the shop-window, that you do not know what to do with when you have them in your hands! *Everything that is attained is destroyed.* I go groping, as in a game of blind-man's buff, and what I take in my arms instantly ceases to be of interest.

In places where the ugliness of human beings never leads to intense desire, in Paris for example, this state can exist without being acute. But, where there is certain proportion of beautiful human beings, it can only be a perpetual misfortune for, as Saint Theresa says, "our desire is without remedy." Twice I have fled from Italy, confronted with the certainty of this misfortune.

Another reason: I will not go as a mere sniffer where men have lived strongly. Rome, Florence, Siena . . . , I will not satisfy curiosity where men have satisfied instincts. I prefer to deprive myself of knowing.

In a general way, the prospect of visiting museums, when the soul does not have what it desires, is nauseating. (I say: "the soul," because it is the soul, more than the body, which desires bodies. This is too often forgotten.) It is only in the absolute satisfaction of passions that I can find some interest in the world beyond them. And it seems to me that one has to have a powerful interest in the world in order to look up in a guide book the date of a Romanesque arch.

Thus I fled far from the lakes. But every change of surroundings is for me a succession of flights. I flee one after the other, like cities in flames, all the places where I am not yet happy enough. "Forward! Forward!" says desire, like death, and always the song of departure solves everything and solves nothing. Granada—I fled it impulsively, in confusion, like a man for whom a warrant of arrest has been issued. No reason, except that I was not happy enough there. I cried aloud to myself, more dead than alive in the glory of the sun: "Close your eyes, close your eyes, in order to stop seeing these places where you do not have all your pleasure." I fled it with the same mad feeling of release as in the train which carried me off wounded from the front, detesting the people so much that I spent the whole morning in the waiting room of the station, covered with flies, to avoid any further sight of the streets. . . .

"One after the other I flee all the places where I am not happy enough." And all the places where I *am* happy enough. That tribe in North Africa. Because all creatures there were desirable and all you had to do was smile to have the one you wanted. In the presence of such abundance and such facility, my desire was dispersed and finally lost. I spent the day alone, walking around outside that paradise, without being able to overcome the boredom that I felt on entering it; after the boredom of souls, an old acquaintance, the boredom of bodies, that is really amusing. I packed my bags that very evening, this time fleeing from my happiness. But, while fleeing, I had put all my hope in the neighboring country, because they told me that the people there were not beautiful. "There," I thought, "*I shall have fewer possibilities of happiness.*" Travel three thousand five hundred kilometers to say that: how can one fail to be horrified with oneself?

Morand makes this remark: if people have perceived since the dawn of the world that we are not better off simply by changing, it remained for our age to discover that during the time of the change we are better off. This is because during that time we are approaching an unknown that we have not yet exploited. It is natural to be exalted by the expectation of it. I doubt that it took ten thousand years to discover that.

You know the circus number: a cart drawn irresistibly by a donkey because the clown has attached to the end of his whip a carrot held in front of the animal's muzzle, out of his reach. He will never get it, but will always keep trotting to get it. "Forward! Forward!"

What was the matter with Granada, that it was rejected with such a feeling of nausea? Well, simply because that time I had not enjoyed a greater pleasure than the year before: I had not surpassed myself in pleasure. A painful observation, mortifying, disturbing, that with one year more of experience and daring I had not succeeded in creating for myself a new pleasure. This is the disadvantage of certain realizations achieved when too young. One drains the future.

It is not pleasure alone that is at stake here. Nomadism exasperates in us the knowledge that our soul, if one may express it thus, works "on the spot." The Vosges mountains, the flat plain of the Camargue delta, the high peaks of the Aurès, all resemble each other. I used to console myself by thinking, "Landscapes interest me only in relation to human beings. Ah, loving someone would give life to all this!" But the emotions that human beings inspire in us also sadly resemble each other. The more that places, people, customs, the material side of adventures are changed, the more we see that we in the midst of them are unchanging. We know all the reactions we shall have, all the mistakes made a hundred times over that we are going to make again, all the words spoken a thousand times that we are going to utter again: a word of tenderness, a word of promise, a word of threat. We can predict within a margin of just so many days which one of our irrational impulses will come into play, as easily foreseen as a theatrical effect. And I still have thirty years to go over and over this inexpiable self. How can I stand it till the end?

And the man who is complaining here is all mobility! But all immobile mobility. Merry-go-round horses: they go around each in its turn but there are only seven of them and an eighth one will never go by. But then what must be the horror of people who are all of a piece? However it is probable that they are very contented. The *lassata, sed non satiata* is usually understood as meaning that the Empress was physically tired of amatory exercises. Yet she was tired morally, tired of herself and of constantly beginning all over again. Her obsession disgusts her but remains her obsession. And in Hades, if she must fill the barrel of the Danaides, it too always full and always empty, or roll the stone of Ixion, it too always raised up and always falling back, she will do nothing other that what she did all her life (which once more proves the agreement of the Greek myths with the most intimate realities of the soul).

Someone says to me: "Here is peace. It is the peace of God. Fool, what are you waiting for in order to take it?" I am waiting for this peace to be my peace and not yours. A peace without human beings!

And if I did possess God? Not possessing Him, I can, in certain hours of physical fatigue, put a vague hope in that possession. But believe me, if I possessed Him, I should soon be tired of Him. And where could I put my hope at that moment, unless of necessity in everything that is not He? No, however little hope He represents, let us not spoil God. And everything that is attained is destroyed.

Morand at least is not unrestricted in his freedom. No matter how independent such an official may be, if, having arrived in Siam where he was to occupy a diplomatic post, he had conceived a horror of Siam as I did of Granada and wanted to take the first boat home in panic, I like to think that something would have prevented him from doing so. I say I like to think so for his sake. But what of the man who is totally free! At the mercy of his moods, his sudden impulses, his phobias, his impatience, he does and undoes, goes and comes back, hounded along his way. Men are known to have sacrificed everything to their independence, to a delightful carefreeness from so-called obligations and restraints, in short, to the free play of emotions alone. And yet, at certain hours, they dream of being a petty clerk with a family, subjugated and tied down with all kinds of hindrances. That is because it is almost sweet not to attain. The invalid, the poor man, the prisoner has a torment more bearable that the man who has attained. He can blame things. But everything hurts the man who has attained and is not happy: it hurts him that satisfaction does not give him happiness, and it hurts him to see that he can blame only himself. Prisons and hospitals are swollen with hope, radiant with the future, because the evil there is curable and knows it. But on luxury liners and in luxury hotels the evil is incurable and knows it. Having reached the end of one's hope, unable to continue saying "What can I hope?" having reached the point of fearing human successes (because far from arousing your joy they arouse your indifference), what is the use of struggling to have health, money, power, since they do not bring happiness? The only but sufficient condemnation of energy is that what it obtains is never worth obtaining. So now that we have cut the root of all activity, we are still farther away from men. There is nothing left to do but wait for our meals, like animals; to place our whole selves in suspension over a properly iced lemonade. Or rather to wait for sleep. Ah, may the night be long!

I feel with extreme force that when our will has worked to accumulate pleasures in our life, there comes a moment when it must reverse itself and work to make them rarer, to restrain those pleasures, in order to keep some savor in them. Yes, our will power, the strength of our soul, the word is not too strong, since, like a saint, we must resist a greater and greater part of our temptations. We come back also to life's law of alternation, and to the old victory of arrangement over accumulation: "The half is more than the whole."

Remotest antiquity is already full of neurotic kings, even completely insane, because things were so easy for them. When as a small boy, I read and reread the *Twelve Caesars*, I put too much passion into them not to be warned that the most secret threads of my temperament linked me to those men. Their eccentricities, even when I disapproved of them, seemed natural to me; it was inevitable—I recognized in me the germ which, under similar circumstances, would have flowered in them. "A thousand contradictory plans crossed his mind. To slaughter the Gauls living in

Rome, burn the city again, turn loose the wild beasts, and transport the capital to Alexandria, seemed to him a grandiose, stupefying, and easy task." Twenty years later this sentence still moves me; I rush to embrace those souls deranged by the extent of what is possible to them. When the flower of living men gives us nothing, let Xerxes and other characters invented by librarians give us the relief of seeing another ship in distress on the same sea where we are perishing without crying out for divine help.

With people of this kind, their freedom is their misfortune; yet they would rather not be than not be free. Free with the freedom that enslaves them, with the omnipotence that holds them enslaved like a clerk in his office, with the force that obliges them to carry out all their fancies and to wander forever, hunting all the big game of this world, hopeless conquerors who take their prey without enjoying it (like those wild beasts that do not eat the prey they have stalked and killed) until the day when, in death, which simplifies all things, they will at last be permitted to stop.

From afar, in the hatred, fear, and weariness they feel for themselves, they flatter themselves that they will not offer great resistance to death. But I know them well: when faced with this rest, this total settlement, this sweet release from all tension (what words of tenderness come to my mind!), will they not, on the contrary, in one last inconsistency, enter into an atrocious struggle with death?

How many hours, slumped over an empty glass in a bar on the waterfront of Tangier or Marseilles, or Genoa, leaning on my elbow, my hand wrinkling one cheek, a soft hat pulled down over my eyes, I have let well up in me floods of a melancholy that was almost despair, without any cause worthy of respect (for all this, I agree with you, deserves nothing but a kick in the pants); having arrived on the verge of great adventures, feeling disgust for those who do not carry them out, and at the same time feeling the uselessness and non-desire of carrying them out! How many hours, confined in a hotel room during the divine instant of the day—yes, because that is the one precisely that hurts the most—simply because everything wounded me without spiritual enrichment.

Notes like these are what saved me during those hours, what *killed the time*: a rather frightful expression but readily understandable to anyone who has become a vagabond. I have constantly sacrificed the ambition of building a literary work to the ambition of living; but to-day I feel less capable than ever of detaching myself from my life enough to create characters, in short, to add something intentional to the almost animal act of writing down my sensations and my moods just as they come along. Which, in any case, does not compromise the future.

From the bottom of these sinister hours arises the absurd belief that Paris will deliver me—mournful, stuffy, noisy Paris, Paris of the green teeth, of the turnip-colored complexion, with the dirty water of its concierges for blood in its veins, Paris which is repugnant to me to such an extent that I preferred to separate myself for a long time from people I loved rather than have them come there where every sensation turns rotten with intellectuality, where every love must become perversity, where there can be no joy in living.

In vain do I know everything that I find unbearable in the people of my country as soon as I have left Provence for the North, the physical disgust that I feel for their skin, their laughter, their way of speaking. Some tiny circumstance in which I was happy up there grows in my imagination, makes me believe that it is in Paris that I shall be able to realize my possibilities. I prepare my bags, buy a ticket, reserve a seat in the train . . .

Mornings of departure, when we are still in these places, when it depends only on us to stay here and still be able to do everything here, and yet we already see them as if we were far away from them, as if they were hopelessly and irrevocably lost for us; we have them and we long for them at the same time. And unexpectedly, when everything is prepared for this departure, when it will be a terrible bother of countermanding orders, making new arrangements, stupidly tiring myself if I delay it, having already become a stranger to these places, already freed from their evil spell (for all my life has preceded me to Paris, really I have already left), unexpectedly courage returns to me. The obstacle against which I had been stumbling and snorting for weeks, like a poor frightened horse—let us say that it was to go after and take back a woman who had run away from me—seems easy to overcome. Invigorated, with the sudden self-confidence of a fellow who puts on a new suit for the first time, I decided to stay and conquer.

And I conquer, of course. All that was necessary was to be a little inspired. How pusillanimous I was! And the happiness of attaining what I desired almost disappears in the deliverance of having conquered myself. Truthfully, that is all there was to be conquered.

Calm. The man who has got what he wanted. The *nobility* of those who have got what they wanted. But it remains to be seen what it will be like when last night's folly has become to-morrow's routine. The lack of this thing kept me upset for three weeks, and now I have it, I possess it, I could not possess it any more than I do—and I am still waiting for something! I perceive with a twinge of sadness that there is no very great difference between the state I was in when I was deprived of it and the one I am in when I am fully satisfied. By a conscious effort to pay attention to it, I realize perfectly well that I have obtained everything I desired, and that I am happy, obviously. But is this happiness? I have no bodily, carnal consciousness of it, the kind one has of light, of air, of music heard, of wine drunk; if I look at myself in the mirror, I can easily see from my face that I am not happy. Once again the foreign land begins to poison me, as if it were sending back to me all the non-happiness with which I intoxicated it; and my delightful hours with the creature I have found again are spoiled by those that separate them, by their dryness and their boredom in which the expectation itself is not sufficiently discernible. I have everything, everything escapes me, and this frightful equivalence is not in the world but in me, and there is no hope that I may become otherwise, that I may become another, that everything in me may be metamorphosed to its foundations. But if full equals empty, if to have equals to have not, then it is my desire, yes, it is this dreary pursuit which I drag about with me and which drags me, that is still the best thing I have, and my desire is at rest. Ah, may time, which I have "killed," kill me in its turn, but not with the kind of death where one lives again, where one is resurrected, where there is a risk (no matter what changes religions promise) that a part of the former being will subsist—but with the deadest death, dissolved into nothingness without memory and without dreams, where at last I shall finally be through with myself for good.

Thus it is that the idea of an empty heaven, which comforts us in the hours when we have a little pride, comforts us still in the hours of extreme weakness.

Italy—Provence—Morocco, 1926

Translated by Vincent Milligan

Another View of the Homestead

Christina Stead

ALL NIGHT THE SLEEPER sleeps close to a board, irons rattle, a violin played aft vibrates along the side, the body of the ship rises and falls, the engines beat on through seven hundred sleeps. The first day, yellow cliffs, blue coasts, next day, the steep green island south; a new world. Homeward bound on that ship in 1928, a Lithuanian woman in grey knitted skullcap, fifty-five, short, sour, salty; a tall English woman, eighty-four, in black, small hat and scarf, who stands for hours by the lounge wall waiting for the Great Bear to rise; a missionary woman, thirty-nine, invalided home, worn by tropical disease, her soft dark skin like old chamois; she is going back to the town, street, church she left eighteen years before, because of a painful love-affair with the pastor: his wife now dead, he has just married a girl from the choir, 'Just as I was then,' she says. There's an Australian girl, lively, thin, black hair flying, doing tricks with a glass of water, by the big hold aft, and around her her new nation, Sicilians, her husband one—they are playing the fiddle. There's a redgold girlish mother from the Northern Rivers, scurrying, chattering, collecting cronies. Three times she booked for England, twice cancelled; the third time, her youngest daughter brought her to the boat in Sydney. Three unmarried daughters, 'Oh, but we are not like other families; we cannot bear to part.' Before Hobart, she telegraphs that she will land at Melbourne, go home by train; but they telegraph, 'Go on, Mother, please.' 'They don't say how they are!' She is faded, sleepless, 'What are they doing now?' At Melbourne, the women dissuade her and she goes on. Across the surly Bight they make her laugh at herself; she laughs and turns away, aggrieved. As we approach Fremantle, she is dreadfully disturbed; the ship may dock in the night and leave before morning. She sends a message to the Captain. At Fremantle, she telegraphs, disembarks, her rose colour all back. 'I'm going home! They'll be getting ready! Oh, what a party we'll have!' 'What about the presents?' 'I'll give them back; I did before.'

There's a country minister and his wife, two dusty black bundles who conduct services in the cabin before a number of meek, coloured bundles in Sunday hats. The couple gain in stature the farther they travel, until in the Red Sea, having lost all provincial glumness, the minister shouldering tall against the railing, arm and finger stretched, explains the texts, the riddle of the Pyramids, the meaning of Revelations.

For years, I thought hazily about returning; and like that, it would be, in just such a varied society, myself unhampered, landing unknown, 'Poor amongst the poor' (a line of Kate Brown's I always liked) and would see for myself. After I had looked round lower Sydney where I walked every morning and evening of my high school, college and work life, I would go out and stand in front of Lydham Hill, the old sandstone cottage on a ridge which, from a distance looks east over Botany Bay, straight between Cape Banks and Cape Solander, to the Pacific; and the other way, due west, over a grass patch and the yellow road to Stoney Creek, to the Blue Mountains. That is how it was when my cousin and I lived there with other little ones and played in the long grass and under the old pines.

I knew all that was gone; they had driven surveyors' pegs into the gardens, the neglected orchard, before we left for Watson's Bay; and a friend in the Mitchell Library archives some years ago sent me coloured slides of the house that is. But still I would go and look at the homestead.

The other place—'Watson's'? By a magic that I came by by accident, I was able to transport Watson's noiselessly and as if it were an emulsion or a streak of mist to the Chesapeake; and truly, the other place is not there for me anymore; the magician must believe in himself. And then for long years I had a nightmare, that I was back at Watson's, without a penny saved for my trip abroad, my heart like a stone. It was otherwise. I came by air, the sailor dropped by a roc, Ulysses home without all that reconnoitering of coasts, a temporary citizen of a flying village with fiery windows, creaking and crashing across the star-splattered dark; and looking down on the horizontal rainbows which lie at dawn around Athens, around Darwin.

Unlike the ship, though close-packed as a crate of eggs, we travel with people we may hear but never see. There is only one street in the flying village and in it you mainly see children conducted up and down. Beside me, is a Greek-born mother with her Australian-born son, aged seven, she talking across the alley in English to her Greek-born neighbours, about the good life in Australia, the peace, the prospects, the education. What you hear in her tones is the good news, the rich boast delivered somewhere outside Athens to the grandparents; it is a wonderful country, we are lucky to be there, no social struggle, plenty of work, success ahead, money everywhere, no coloured people. (It turns out she thinks this.) Standing now in the alley stretching, a tall Italian proud that he has been in the country forty-two years (a year longer than my absence). There are fourteen children of all ages, three high-stomached young women hurrying out to give birth in the lucky place. Few get much sleep but all are goodtempered, it does not matter; their urge and hope is on, on. 'Are you an Australian?' 'Yes.' I am looked at with consideration.

We are a day late, mysteriously stalled at Bangkok: and the talk is of husbands, friends waiting. It is a neighbourly climate—our friendships are nearly three days old; but there is no time for histories and secrets to come out. They will be met soon, go off by plane, train and car, I will never know them.

As for me, high up, almost lunar, I could not take my eyes from the distant earth, every spine and wrinkle visible in the dry air. There did not seem to be a cloud between Darwin and Sydney. Our firebird lazily paddled (so it seemed against the motionless rush of greater vessels up there) under the broad overhang and what a sight all night!—the downpour of stars into the gulf that is not a gulf. In Australia I never lived in suburban or city streets, but with wide waters and skies and this life expanded was coming home to me; you are nearer there (in Australia) to the planets. Even more now—when we have all got a bit of the astronaut in us.

At earliest dawn, the scored and plaited land, water-rivers like trickles of mercury, sand-rivers, the olive furred hide of the red eucalypt land sprawling.

Before that, at Darwin, an airfield in reconstruction. After turnstiles and a forbidding yellow plank staircase, at the top we find a large lounge and in the centre, a small trellissed horseshoe bar, a Chinese gentleman presiding. What good sense, the Australians, what humanity! It is 3:15 a.m. and we are exhausted.

It was there, over the walls, through partitions, in the women's rooms, that there came in high, tired, bangslapping voices, 'Isn't it good to be home?' 'Yes, what a relief!' 'Better than Europe!' 'Oh, yes, I had enough of Europe.' And carolling the gladness like magpies singing with parrots, strangers behind doors, 'Yes, it is good to be home.' (One comes out.) 'How long were you in Europe?' 'Three weeks—three long weeks. And you?' 'Two months.' 'How did you stand it?' (Forty years of Europe!—I left quietly.)

Novalis said, my friend Dorothy Green remarks, that you must know many lands to be at home on earth; perhaps it is that you must be at home on earth to know many lands. A child in Australia, in the home of an active naturalist who loved the country and knew scientists, nature-lovers, all kinds of keen stirring men and women who found their home on earth, I hearing of them, felt at home; this was my first, strongest feeling in babyhood. I have had many homes, am easily at home, requiring very little. My first novel (before *Seven Poor Men of Sydney)* was to be called *The Young Man Will Go Far* and then *The Wraith and the Wanderer,* two different novels. (I still have part MSS.) The Wanderer, once he has started out in company of the Wraith, the tramp and his whisperer, does not look over his shoulder. He does not think of where to live, somewhere, anywhere; anything may happen, awkward and shameful things do happen; he does not believe it when life is good; by thirty all is not done, neither the shames nor the lucky strikes. He takes no notice, it is his equal but different fate, he marries a stranger, loves an outlaw, neighbours with many, speaks with tongues. So that if he should cross the high bridge of air sometime, going homewards, he is also on the outward path.

Now I am back in shadowy England whose pale streams are sometimes 'gilded by heavenly alchemy', they speak of 'hot summers' but there is not the pour of gold nor the fire from the open hearth. Here are white cliffs and mornings, white horses on the downs, topheavy summer trees, King Arthur in his mound, gods and Herne the Hunter in woods, green folk, little folk, squirrel-faced elves; and stranger creatures still, Langland, Wyatt, Chaucer, Ford and their pursuit of comets, the English splendour; and all this is in the people, their unconscious thoughts and their language.

Under the soft spotted skies of the countries round the North Sea I had forgotten the Australian splendour, the marvellous light; the 'other country' which I always had in me, to which I wrote letters and meant one day to return, it had softened, even the hills outlined in bushfire (which we used to see over Clovelly from Watson's Bay) were paler. The most exquisite thing in my recent life was a giant eucalypt on the North Shore as we turned downhill, the downward leaves so clear, the bark rags, so precise, the patched trunk, so bright. 'Look at that tree!' It was outlined in light. It was scarcely spring, but the lawn outside the house was crowded with camellias, magnolias in bloom, even falling; at both dawn and dusk the kookaburras thrilling high in the trees, the magpies—I had quite forgotten those musicians and their audacity—and there was even a scary fiendish cry in the bush early; it came nearer, but remained distant. It was just a bantam cockerel—I had one myself years ago in Santa Fe and had forgotten the little dawn-demon with his one-string violin. Too long in London! Everything was like ringing and bright fire and all sharpness. I was at dinner the other night, when someone said, 'What was Australia like?' 'It's the wonderful light, Bill,' I said to the Texan next to me. 'Yes,' affirmed he; and the Indian lady murmured, 'Yes.' Three exiles. No more was said; and the others, Londoners, did not even know what we had understood. It is at least the light. When people ask, I feel like saying, 'It's a brilliant country;

they're a brilliant people, just at the beginning of the leaps.' I think this is true, but it may be in part the light, the broad skies, the crowded stars, that red hide stretched out so far to cover so much land; and I do not say, because I don't really understand it, 'And there is the melancholy.' I knew as a girl that looking backward was not joy; I thought it was the waterlessness, the twenty-year droughts, the people dead of thirst, again the hatred of England, of the hulks, our black legend. But is it like the uneasiness and loneliness felt by Russians, US Americans, Brazilians, who with, at their backs, the spaces and untamed land, seek Paris, the Riviera and New York?

This brilliance one feels is not related to the present sunnyside air common to countries having a stock exchange and business boom and with money flowing into (and out of) the country; at best, an uncritical supping of splurge and at lowest, baldly expressed, 'It doesn't matter who makes us rich, as long as we get rich.' There are people in Australia who no longer believe in poverty. It has happened elsewhere; and been followed by—but we know that.

I was not long enough there to have an opinion about many things. I know about Canberra, beautiful, desolate, inspiriting Erewhon, where one can feel 'I have awakened into the future of the world'; freer because it is unfinished and all its components not yet joined; and apart, more appealing in its upland, than Washington, D.C. in its swamp; younger, closer at the twenty-first century. I don't understand the settled sadness of some intellectuals, artists and academics. The heat mystery, black shadows in the tropics, the long bright road ending in a mirage? Deserts? Not belonging to ourselves? Not united with our nearest neighbours? Smalltowners in the USA leave farm for town, town for Chicago and New York, the capitals for Paris and London. Perhaps it is just *The Beckoning Fair One* singing her faint irresistible 'very oald tune' (Oliver Onions). Well, let us be discontented then; it has never hurt art.

Good-Bye Wisconsin

Glenway Wescott

HOMEWARD BOUND AT LAST, north from Milwaukee on Christmas Eve. The red-towered station looks very German. But the stern, tattered, tall twilight is American; little by little it will change the German faces; and all that in the near future we can hope for, or fear, is resemblance. There used to be a saintly Scotchwoman in the waiting room to keep country girls from getting into trouble. In the train-shed the crowd surges against a high picket fence, sways in one piece like a boxcarful of cattle: a mixed population, returning to maternal arms, infant arms, arms in love. As the train moves north a blizzard comes south.

My life of the rest of the year being left behind, being buried beneath new impressions, trampled underfoot by resurrected ones, passing through and out of my head, bit by bit . . . The stiff carnations of the Mediterranean are in bloom. Never live in Paris: everyone there has done some harm to everyone else; the heart must be kept in fashion, there was the influence of Henry James, so it is no longer elegant to quarrel; they go on dining together, a malicious intimacy with a lump in its throat. In mid-Atlantic, a short rainbow alongside of the ship with both feet in the sea. Never live in New York either: a town in which "it is as essential to wear one's heart on one's sleeve as one's tongue in one's cheek." New York is halfway between the south of France and Wisconsin, always halfway between any two such places; that is its importance . . .

The train jerks, because the cars are of steel, I suppose. Oranges and green plush. The heat of a Turkish bath into which, through opening doors, through double windowpanes, the awful wind penetrates; nature and a comfort-loving race between them have made this the worst climate in the world. Somewhere up ahead everyone's Christmas tree, squat and dazzling.

A wild-looking youngster asks if anyone has seen his wife and baby. An old man watches over a girl as lovely as a film star. She wears in her hat a tied ostrich plume which looks as if long tresses of hair had grown on a stem; no other woman in the car is unfashionably dressed. She is a half-wit, and keeps eating sandwiches with the impressive ferocity of a monkey, clutching them with both hands. Here and there, students on their way home from college. Middle-class young men in France are less fine physically. Heads almost uniformly well-proportioned; the relaxed look that experts in dissimulation have when they are alone. Either they are blush-pink or they have that translucent dead-leaf skin, without yellowness, without whiteness, which seems peculiar to America and is said to be increasingly common, a result of American air, of the way of life and the climate. The mad girl has it, too.

Throbbing on the rails, the train begins running downhill, which means, I remember from childhood, that we have passed a town called Marblehead. That name and the mature schoolboys make me think of Greece—many-headed, marble-headed. France is its heir, eldest son in this generation of nations. I am jealous of every national glory. Not that I expect my country to become a poets' colony, a sculptors', architects', and moralists' colony. There were all sorts of Greeks . . . Heads of all complexions, even in the sculptured stone: ruddy and ivory and the very vivid brown—as if red rose-leaves had been tanned and made into a leather—which some of my friends, visiting the Mediterranean beaches, find objectionable and others do their best to acquire.

I have to change trains. The snowstorm is over, or we have passed through it. I share a corner of what is called a milk-train with a lot of baggage and two young workmen. One seems unhealthy: large hands bright with chemicals. The other has that look of sheepish melancholy which I frivolously associate with socialism. They engage in conversation about their jobs and each other's relatives which they know by name; their fathers are farmers; the yellow-handed one works in a tannery in Fond du Lac, the other is an ironworker in a Milwaukee foundry. They speak a mixture of several kinds of English—Swedish, German, Polish, Irish—immigrants' children of the second generation having inherited accents from all their parents at once, all the accents. They keep looking at my cigarette-lighter, my gloves, my tight black cap, a Basque *beret*.

The tanner : "Where d'ya work in Mulwauky?"

"I came up from Chicago."

"Yuh got some folks here?"

"My father and mother live in Claron. He was a farmer until he moved to town."

A pause, without embarrassment on their parts. The ironworker: "Wha' d'ya work at'n Chicago?"

"I don't work in Chicago. I've been in New York." I see myself retreating right round the world . . .

So I offer them cigarettes; they look at the mark; and out of timidity I open Thomas Mann's *Hochstapler Krull*. If this were Europe I could have told them that I was a writer, which would have been the end of it. One day years ago when I was wearing a rather pretentious black cape, I tipped a porter in a Munich railway station. "Thank you kindly, Herr poet," he said.

The train is making up for lost time. I know, I say to myself, what the country is like beyond the syncopated noise, the shaken light-bulks, outside the sooty windows in the dark. The state with a beautiful name—glaciers once having made of it their pasture—is an anthology, a collection of all the kinds of landscape, perfect examples side by side. Ranges of hills strung from the great lake to the Mississippi River in long, lustrous necklaces, one above another from the northern throat of the state until well below its waist. Peacock lakes of bronze weeds and vivid water, with steep shores; four or five of them to be seen at a time from certain hilltops. Fertility and wilderness in rapid succession along powdery highways: classic meadows where the cattle seem to walk and eat in their sleep, sandy slopes full of foxes, ledges where there are still rattlesnakes. Sad forests full of springs; the springs have a feverish breath. There are metallic plants which burn your hands if you touch them. All summer the horizon trembles, hypnotically flickering over the full grain, the taffeta corn, and the labor in them of dark, over-clothed men, singing women, awe-stricken children. These say nothing; their motionless jaws give an account of their self-pity, dignity, and endurance. Sheet-lightning at night, and they sleep in the grass, in hammocks, on folded blankets on the floor—the beds are too hot. They get up and work with strange, ardent motions and the obstinacies of ghosts in the heat; there is wealth in it. In the sky mocking marble palaces, an Eldorado of sterile cloud. Not sterile—for down fall large black-and-blue rains, tied with electric ribbons; they never seem to be doing much good, but the crops are saved . . .

Thus, neglecting the masterpiece which I keep in my hand to prevent the workmen from asking questions but not uninfluenced by its mood of shameless, summery confession—in which the true nature of Herr Krull is almost obscured by the bright light shed on every detail—I think of the land outside the train window as one of perpetual summer. Then the door swings open; the blown cold pounds on the nape of my neck; in spite of the coal-gas, the tobacco, the oranges, the opium-sweetness of warm bodies, I imagine that I can smell snow.

For in reality this is a sort of winter resort for storms from the North Pole; now all the half-tropic vegetation, the flesh and the fruitfulness, stripped and lying quite still, are theirs. You seem to be on a lofty plateau, and you can see with your own eyes that the world is convex. The villages are almost as lonely as the farms. It is like Russia with vodka prohibited and no stationary peasantry—strictly speaking, with none at all. The soul hibernates in the cold body; your feet ache for months at a time. I remember, at church, in my childhood, prayers that were visible, white and tenuous, and moustaches covered with frost through which the slow, discouraging hymn made its way. A good many men get drunk a great deal of the time in spite of everything. Once a month the new moon sets out like the crooked knife of a fairy story in search of a heart to bury itself in. This is the dying-season for old men and women. When the moon is full, over the crusted snow, men go rabbit-hunting . . .

The train stops at a junction and makes its presence known; with another lowing, female sound, another train replies. I have a vague remembrance of that junction, those two deep voices. I ask, and am told that we are coming into Claron.

Out of the dark run forward my young father, my small mother. Across the town in an automobile, no distance at all; home, the new house, a home in a town. On the small square of property close-pressed by other houses, collies with no more herds to tend; the color of pheasants with ruffled plumage, under the arc-light, against the snow-banks. Up the icy steps; a tumult in the doorway; energetic kisses which smell good, smell of health and warm wool; my brother, my sisters. Their courtesy a little affected but with burning eyes, breaking down repeatedly in the stress of the exuberance which they have in common, the stress of joy or disappointment, pride, contention, yearning. This is the wild fountain of friendliness. Sometimes it occurs to me that I ought to play the Ancient Mariner, but I am evidently always to be wedding guest.

There are chocolates and fruit; I remember the annual basket of grapes which my father used to bring from the state fair when we were children, a wooden basket with a wire handle and pale, elongated California grapes—each of us ate his share grape by grape, there were so few. The floors are waxed; carpets like everyone else's have taken the place of the rag rugs accumulated by my grandmothers. That fruitful, severe farmhouse of childhood, it seemed to have an immortal soul and now seems to have borne a physical resemblance to my mother—a house so cold at this time of the year that every vessel which held water had a lip of crystal. Here there is a bathroom. Progress, I think sleepily. The king is dead, long live the king; deprivation is dead . . . I rejoice, but regret some of his poetry. Fortunately, progress has not gone far enough here to deprive me of a cold bed, of the drug of zero weather, the barbaric luxury of frost, in my nostrils all night long.

Early in the morning I go out to look at the town. It is like any other not too new or too large or too small in the state—or perhaps in any state not too far east or west. Main Street down the middle—beef-red brick and faded clapboards; it is lamentably impressive. The new banks, I must admit, are of lighter brick and adorned with brief, reasonably Roman pillars. The churches have an atheistic look and must have been very cheap to build. Dry-goods stores remarkably full of luxury; drug stores which sell everything (at a glance everything seems made of paper) the most expensive cameras and the cheapest books; a windowful of superb apples. Apples are wealth in midwinter; in fact it is all wealth, though it resembles the meanest poverty. Branching off Main Street at right angles, up small hills and down gentle slopes, the other streets: short but spacious avenues, noble trees over the snowbanks, lawns under them. Actually it is one lawn, there being no hedges or fences or walls (during the burning summers, no privacy). The houses are variations on one house, a sort of palatial cottage; principally wood, you can see into most of them and through some, and they do not seem to rest solidly on the ground; the difference between them and a tent is precisely that between moving every generation and moving every month . . .

Where the houses leave off lugubrious poetry begins: never-painted landscape, chiaroscuro of twigs and snow. Framed by a puerile architecture, a patchwork of advertisements, a frieze of restless and almost beautiful men and women. The country, there it lies, a fitful and mysterious source—nothing more. The source of the sunrises, the bad weather, and the food, and of certain books already a little out of date. For the country, in the old sense of the word, has ceased to exist. Wisconsin farmers are no longer rustics; they have become provincials. The former ardent, hungry, tongue-tied life with its mingling of Greek tragedy and idyll has come to an end. Labor for the men, labor-pains for the women, elementary passions like gusts of storm moving unembarrassed in empty hearts, strong minds empty from birth until death of everything but the images of fowls in the rain, lonesome barns in the yellow sunshine—all over and done with. Now, by telephones, the radio, and automobiles, the farms have been turned into a sort of spacious, uncrystallized suburb around towns like Claron; and between the town and the suburb the contact is close. Now hired men, for example, have the privilege of being in love with Miss Garbo, whose troubling face I find on a bright poster.

Here are the humble-looking churches, half of whose faithful are farmers; many variations, both in appearance and in doctrine, on one church. I attend an elaborate pageant of the Nativity. All of the congregation's tapestries and many of its best bedsheets; rented crowns and curtains, silly angels painted on a backdrop of sky; footlights and spotlights worthy of an assembly of radio fans. A gaunt little girl in gilt and muslin represents the Angel of History; she plays theatrically, has a very modern body and a cropped honey-colored head, and even her solemnity suggests profane shows in the East. Other all too Western muses. An adolescent chokes on his words, as indeed the original shepherd probably did. One of the Wise Men has forgotten to take off his horn-rimmed spectacles. The Babe in the manger is electricity, which is moving and seems true. It is all moving and true. But as the collection-boxes on long handles are passed, rather too plaintive an appeal for generosity is made; one would suppose that there were niggardly church-goers. And a kindly deacon improvises this prayer:

"Dear Father, we thank Thee that we live in a day when men are given to enjoy many things that they never had before. Especially women—I think women's lives have been made easy and lifted out of the darkness, thanks to the right interpretation of Thy Scriptures. And dear Father, we hear at present a great deal of talk against Thy church. It has its limitations, we know, but it has done a wonderful work for mankind. And what have they found to take its place? Until another institution comes along which can do that work better, let us be faithful to it. Bless us in the name of the Son who, as we have seen, was born unto us this day. Amen." I realize that it is not blasphemous, for it is only rhetorically addressed to God, not meant to be heard in heaven but overheard in this town. Thus the religion of Calvin, holding its own in society at all costs, is helping itself cease to be a religion at all, the little churches becoming—oh, let us say, clubs.

There is a denominational college. I imagine the president of a poor school as a solicitor, a beggar of bequests, moving with anxious sociability from deathbed to deathbed, an advertiser by word of mouth, a human form-letter, praising his institution and arousing pity for it at the same time. Scandal—an indecorous dance or sometimes any dance at all, an instructor whose opinions on any subject are foolhardy or whose private life is subject to any remark—may occasion an unpleasant talk with some elderly person who has already been generous, relatively generous, or even cause a will to be revised. He has another source of revenue to keep flowing: the tuition fees, which are high. The young people are lawless, effervescent with strong ideas, insidiously persuasive; if his puritanism is tyrannical or the curriculum behind the times, friendly fathers, impatient brothers, will let them go elsewhere or try to have him removed. It is an unhappy position; he must be nobly patient and politic . . . At all events, the college reflects some such mournful reasonableness, time-serving, and trembling.

There are fraternity houses. A black upright piano rather broken by jazz and loaded with sheets of it, a phonograph as large as a pulpit, a radio-set which resembles a diamond-shaped harp—these things at least represent an art, humbly. A shout up the staircase brings the "brothers" down, single file, like jurymen. Most of them are solid and rubicund, one or two slender ones with the dead-leaf complexion: men and large men at that, but they have the blushes, the look of haunted innocence of small boys. Handsome, as a group compared with other groups; the individual faces seem too fresh and too amiable. Republican principles, false-looking gestures of affection, more than one hand laid deliberately on the next shoulder, expert joking evidently meant to create an atmosphere of intimacy: these habits will be useful in later life if they are to be, for example, travelling salesmen or ward politicians. No sign of thoroughgoing candor; almost every speech is followed by an acute glance at someone, to see how it is being taken; each is playing up to the other. Uniformly young though of various ages, the embryo without any mature bias; not a single novice doctor or lawyer or journalist or mathematician; how are they going to choose their professions? They will have to follow their noses—nothing else here to follow. The chief work of the society, I learn, is to beat out of each other all conceit and incivility; what is exceptional passes for the former, what is undemocratic for the latter. The better part of genius, if any turned up here, would be discretion. Its chief amusement is the exchange of indecent anecdotes in half-official conclave; an aimless exchange, for watch is kept and any moral slackness, however lonely, punished with a sort of paddle. Apparently a boy who procured, for instance, an unexpurgated *Arabian Nights* could make his way through school by selling it page by page. But the paddle occupies a place of honor on a hook on the wall, under a photograph of the Venus de Milo. How, with this combination of mental saturnalia and friendly *auto-da-fé*, are they to learn even to choose wives? Choosing, as a human function, does not seem to be greatly favored . . .

And what of sensual pleasure (call it love) in this town? Out of sight, fraught with dangers up to a certain age, subject to ridicule or worse thereafter. Boyish passion, that of Daphnis and Cherubino alike—its joys are restricted to Latin countries; its pains flourish anywhere. Women who live alone, in these translucent houses, are easily chaperoned by their neighbors; most people never hear of adultery except when there is a murder trial; there are only one or two charmless loose women, who fulfil their destiny, furthermore, under a cloud of specific suspicions; which leaves, for the vicious or the exasperated, girls of the poorest families, hired girls: obscure nights in motor-cars which are like rudderless boats, a handful of touches, farewells charged with resentment, finally an unpleasant reputation among other men. Americans like what is public, feel cheated by what some other races especially enjoy, the illicit; they dislike obliging their relatives to defend them; they dislike danger. To the young man with ambition enough to matter, premature marriage is the worst of dangers. It means earning a living by whatever is at hand; beggars of jobs cannot experiment, ought not to be far-sighted or fastidious. It means Wisconsin forever, with never any wholesome dissipation of a thousand chimeras—travels, ambitions, curiosities. That illusions should come to grief is the first step toward contentment; early marriage keeps as many hopes as are left intact, embalms them in a safe irreality, and keeps the young husband too young at heart. And almost any girl may spring, under the feet of a beau who suits her, any sort of man-trap. In general the young men mind this danger as well as the others. But fright is a strong stimulant; after dark there is a vibrant atmosphere of pleasure—worried, adored, and left to its meager resources. Fever takes the wheel of the autos. In the round of sufficient amusements, a more or less alert suspicion of their sweethearts and themselves; they must keep their self-control, must keep their bodies safe and sound, must keep from proposing. Under the soft maples, nervous teasing and erotic songs whistled and shrubs jetting their moist flowers and a lump in every throat. Syncopated bewilderment on the dance-floors; the music melts their hands and knees, but nothing is any easier. In the motion-picture theaters, thanks to the disastrous and vacillating ease in Miss Garbo's face—more fever.

A modest theater, shaped like a garage; but it is the imagination's chapel in this town, the small temple dedicated to licentiousness, aspiration, ideals. On the brick wall, on easels on the sidewalk, samples of what it has to offer: the abnormally large and liquid eyes of a beauty; the ridicule and pity of ill-fitting shoes; distant crystal and iron seas; foreign luxury, fashion shows, garden parties white with diamonds and swans. Every plot is founded on restlessness and good luck; every film is a documentary film, fantastic only in relation to its subject—realistically true to the imaginations to which it is addressed. There they all flock to see, not really a world brought to their door, but themselves in every foreign and domestic disguise; themselves as they might be, convincingly photographed where they are not—the variable bodies of other Narcissuses on other mesmerizing streams. And in the dark and pleasant silence, unreasonable music smooths their troubled foreheads. What might be a stimulant is another narcotic. Their restlessness is merely played upon, to pass the time—played upon and just enough, from day to day, appeased. Meanwhile the time does pass.

One would think of Wisconsin as the ideal state to live in, a paragon of civic success, but for the fact that the young people dream only of getting away. And there are already a fair number of Middle-Westerners about the world; a sort of vagrant chosen race like the Jews. It is our better luck to leave behind in our Palestine a teeming, prospering family, to fall back on in case of disaster and to save us, meanwhile, from the nervousness of vagabonds who really have no native land left. But we are more than likely to call New York, that palace-hotel, home; the midland gets little glory and even less entertainment from our activities. A great maternal source of, among other things, ability and brutal ardor and ingenuity and imagination—scarcely revisited, abandoned, almost unable to profit by its fruitfulness in men.

Upon these renegade children, voluntary exiles, adventurers and emigrants, brothers, cousins, or acquaintances—the others, those who have not yet taken flight, even those who never will, speculate a great deal in their own interest. They envy our apparent moral emancipation, our pocket money literal and otherwise, the gaiety which, if nothing more, we bring home to show them. They dread risks we seem to have run, suspect abnormalities which may have abetted us. What they admire most is our good luck; we are the favorites of chance, goddess whose mythology the films have spun. They ask question after question and prefer not to take advice. Most of them will remain what they are, where they are—reality only a little poisoned by notions of themselves freed and perfected, of pleasanter societies and facile foreign cities.

For those who dare not go east to meet the future, there is the hope that it may little by little be coming to them. Dreading isolation, most of them keep in line in spite of any eagerness; they do regret that the Middle West is so slow to change, but there is no comfort in anything unless all act together. That Basque *beret* at which the two workmen in the train stared—my brother asks me not to wear it in the street; but having seen in a New York magazine widely circulated out here a recommendation of such headgear, I can assure him that he will have to buy one for himself presently. The same law applies to manners and morals. The peculiar juvenile debauchery which in the East resulted from prohibition, that very Western law, has already crept westward; aided by drink, certain young married sets have begun to make the simplest experiments in immorality; every irregular problem ever thought of may well be on its way.

By birth the best of these young people are Protestants of some sort; by accident, or thanks to their own efforts, the classic Protestant rules have given way to an almost equally scrupulous open-mindedness. The doctrine of their elders imposes on them a certain lack of candor; they are wonderfully adroit; the danger is that in an admirable maze of diplomacy, discretion, and amiability they may lose track of their impulses. They are eminently reasonable, and wish neither to be hampered by old nonsense laid down as law nor to be exposed to the least persecution, but to be informed about the consequences of daring which is greater than their own; so that when the time comes they need not court disaster in the way that others have done. Individually they have few fundamental prejudices; the intolerance of Western society as a whole now seems to rest upon timidity about talking to each other. Their heresies are all hypothetical and they are in a certain sense courtiers, perfectly willing to compromise, to manoeuvre, to turn about as the wind blows, and meanwhile to do the greater part of their experimenting in imagination or vicariously.

Hence their enthusiastic appetite for a certain type of very rare fiction in which, in so far as the author has them, the keys to personal liberty, the ledgers of genuine revolutions, shall be given. A literature of fresh convictions and agility in avoiding sorrow, of caprice, intoxications, and tenderness without shame; offering—to the new generation on stock-farms, in suburbs and sleepy colleges—the advantages of travel, the advantages of recklessness at a distance and vicarious trial flights; unexpurgated reports from the laboratories in which the future of conduct, their conduct, is being experimented upon; some tart breath of the sumptuous though menaced time to come; some sort of *Chanson de Geste* to provoke and ravish this imaginative soldiery to violent effort, to an intelligent looting of liberties, to a final ripe and amused peace . . . They do ask for a certain cheerfulness; one cannot expect those who seek the future in literature to wish to be altogether discouraged. I have not hitherto believed that the search for the future in literature often leads to good literature; be that as it may. No more weather-bound farmers, they beg; no more of the inarticulate, no more love limited to unfortunate stables and desperation growing faint between rows of spoiled corn, no more poverty-striken purity, no more jeering or complaining about lamentable small towns . . . They or their fathers have had enough of all this. Who can blame them?

I at least do not, as in my mother's spare room I try to put in final order the manuscript of the book of which this diary, this stock-taking, is to form a part, and which scarcely seems inspiring or prophetic. It is no eagle for these ambitious, often heavy-hearted Ganymedes. Nor can it be very instructive: how could I expect natives of Wisconsin to see in the first story in the collection or the last my comment on, let us say, their flight or desire to fly to such questionable utopias as New York and Montparnasse?

It does represent, the whole collection, be it Wisconsin's fault or my own, a strangely limited moral order. Drunkenness; old or young initiations into love; homesickness in one's father's home for one's own, wherever it may be, or the more usual sort with its attendant disappointment; the fear of God; more drunkenness. Roads and piazzas and lawns (always out of the corner of one's eye the haunting landscape, the haunted sky, the brindled fields, the four seasons with their over-ornate weather) small houses and small towns and other tiresome roads. That is all there is to it. And set beside a complicatedly unfolding reality, it seems little or not enough: too formal, as one's view of something which in one's childhood one did not expect to see change; now too squalid and now too noble; painted with too rudimentary a rainbow.

Then, with a sense of an immortal task and a mortal weariness, it comes time to return to New York, which is halfway back to the south of France. How much sweeter to come and go than to stay; that by way of judgment upon Wisconsin. The dark red railway station reminds me of Germany, the dim country into which the polished tracks lead away, of Russia—that is, of a place I have never seen. The orchards on the horizon look like black crêpe; there is a little lacquer sunset; useless and uselessly somber things, vainglory of God. Just as a child finds omens all about, I feel glad that I have never written a line for which there is any earthly use. Above the sunset the evening star blazes away superfluously, Mars or Venus in a sky composed of frost—though there is fighting only once a lifetime and, I suppose, less love-making than anywhere else in the world . . .

The train scarcely leaves the dim roofs and yellow windows behind before I feel my imagination beginning to be drawn away elsewhere, to several places irrelevant to each other at once; it is as if half the world were made of magnets. I fight against these charms and suspiciously close Gide's *Les Nourritures Terrestres*, which I had begun to read; my life of the rest of the year will get under way all too soon. Two young women across the aisle try to discover what my book is; theirs is a novel about Helen of Troy. They are workingwomen; I know because I hear them talking about a raise of their wages; but they are as arrogant and delicate as if they were kept. At present the West is a women's world; their bright minds make up its heart. But men's hearts suffer, in 1927, a strangely intellectual ferment . . .

I change trains, and throbbing on the rails the engine climbs up toward the town called Marblehead, which starts the same train of thought as before. It is the Greeks and Romans and the traditions preserved in Europe by the translators of Plutarch and by Montaigne and Goethe which, if one is an American, exasperate the imagination. Traditions of the conduct of life with death in mind . . . Few Americans are reasonable enough even to demand of seventy years their entire sweetness; the fame of too few will outlast, anywhere except in heaven, their mortal bodies. For various reasons we are, in 1927, the dominant nation in the world; there are, nevertheless, in 1927, more Frenchmen than Americans whose lives are to be memorable. (For Lindbergh and Isadora Duncan God be praised . . .) But I believe that American youngsters are equal in force, elasticity, beauty, and other natural gifts to the Greeks. In the fourth university year, let us say; not much longer. Something happens to them; the flower turns out to be seedless. Now all the causes, the mysterious stamens, are undergoing subtle transformations, perhaps for the better, perhaps not. It is a grave situation; and I believe that in the near future descriptive writing about average American destinies must inevitably be that of a reporter, an analyst, a diagnostician.

What may be called honest portrayal of a period of transition, of spiritual circumstances changing for an entire race, requires a fastidious realism, minute notation of events in their exact order, and the special sobriety of doctors or of witnesses at a trial. The more such an author has in common with his characters the better; typical trivialities surpass in significance the noblest feelings; an immediate report is more valuable than reminiscences. The rest is lyricism: the hero's shameless ode in praise of his own fortune or, even in the great, dim, half-attentive courtyard of the Mississippi Valley, a sort of serenade . . .

For fiction may combine in various proportions poetry and journalism. Poetry dispenses with chronology; it offers object or emotion as an end in itself during one moment which is assumed to be eternal, or under conditions as unfluctuating as those of the golden age; it must have some sort of immutability as a foundation. So I decide that the novelist who is or wishes to be anything of a poet will avoid such problems as, for example, Wisconsin is now likely to suggest; and will try to contribute to the appetites which make themselves felt there rather than to portray the confusion in which they arise. And no judicious novelist, however prosaic, will strive to outdistance life; he will choose problems which only seem insoluble, which in some corner of society, on some small illustrative scale, have been solved. The future of American civilization is a genuine riddle. The riddle of a sphinx with the perfect face of a movie star, with a dead-leaf complexion which is the result of this climate, our heating system, our habits . . .

Over many little bridges the train makes a soft thunder. A piece of moon has come up. In front of it a grove of naked trees, a flat expanse of dreary silver tarnished by weed-tops thrusting through it, a broken-looking house, a town, a living but icy river, rapidly give place to each other; as in the foreground of a writer's attention possible subjects for a book vary and shift before that waxing, waning, one-sided radiance which is his own spirit and about which alone he has no choice.

An English friend of mine once took to visit her father in the country a young American painter of some note. A year or two later he had an exhibition in Paris; she told the aging gentleman about it and asked if he remembered the American. "Ah yes, yes. That was the young man who didn't know where he was born. I thought it very curious."

"Now what made you think that, father? You misunderstood. He was born in the Middle West."

"But that's just it! I asked him, and that is precisely what he said—all he could tell me."

That, I believe, is a parable. A place which has no fixed boundaries, no particular history; inhabited by no one race; always exhausted by its rich output of food, men, and manufactured articles; loyal to none of its many creeds, prohibitions, fads, hypocrisies; now letting itself be governed, now ungovernable . . . The Middle West is nowhere; an abstract nowhere. However earnestly writers proud of being natives of it may endeavor to give it form and character, it remains out of focus, amorphous, and a mystery. And by attempting to be specific as in these notes of my visit I have done, one over-particularizes, inevitably. What seems local is national, what seems national is universal, what seems Middle-Western is in the commonest way human. And yet—there is the sluggish emotional atmosphere, the suavity of its tedium, the morbid grandeur of its meanest predicaments; or are these illusions of those who take flight, who return? There is no Middle West. It is a certain climate, a certain landscape; and beyond that, a state of mind of people born where they do not like to live. A certain landscape? All the landscapes, except the noblest: the desert, the alp, the giant seas. One of its climates, one of its anarchic aspects clings to every memory, and deforms or charges with excessive lyricism the plain facts; so the winter, dazzling and boring as it is, has brooded too much over this account. There are other aspects, other seasons. In recent years I have not been at home except in midwinter or midsummer; next time I shall try to come in the fall . . .

A season which cannot be nationalized; wherever there are carts of gathered food, rumpled skirts, laborers, there is Breughel. Overhead, the gray and blue of the iris of an eye, a calm clear gaze now animated by sensitive winds, now short-sighted with raindrops. The season of the eye, of supreme decoration: maroon with gun-metal, canary-yellow with silver, mahogany with pewter. About sundown farm-hands sing—what matter whose songs? The five senses saying good-bye; a whisper in the girls' ears, "Next summer we'll do it again." Out of the rags of husk comes the necessary corn; the hands, hard and flushed, wear beaks of steel for this work. Tobacco, butternuts, apples, and bitter grapes—the mouth is keen because it is getting cold. Harvest is the second or third oldest human contentment. It is never great enough, fortunately. Perennial disappointment to keep hope alive; so one is carried on from year to year. The last sunshine of every year is as bright as a wasp.

Perhaps I should enjoy myself more in the spring. There can be no disappointment then, for one expects nothing but promises and illusions. Sorrow is merely desire and all the joy promiscuous. Hepaticas under the rags of snow, blood-root, arbutus, and deadly nightshade, violets, mandrake, famished-looking lilies, iris, and cinnamon roses. Fruit trees: first, bony branches with negro skin and in due time their metamorphosis—angels' flesh, soft, mauve, milky, scented, roseate. In the sky other multiple branches, trailing vines, and wet sunken shadows: a colorless Everglades of cloud. The grass is like a sponge dipped in vinegar and perfume. Persian lilacs lay wreaths on the girls' shoulders as they pass in the lanes. Even the funerals are ragged with wild garlands; even the dead marry the ground; even the weddings sparkle with tears of rain. Rainbows and a profusion of birds. A wedding profusion of strange flowers, from the breast to the thighs of Wisconsin a rain of bouquet . . .

I realize that there are also mediocrities and spavined horses and tuberculous men, misery and streaks of madness, just as there were on the last farms before automobiles and electricity; but my mind leaves them out. One thing is certain: Wisconsin is no longer a wilderness. But I now know that a garden is better than any wilderness. Men and women have human stature in it and feel a greater number of satisfactions and disappointments; there is less cruelty, less involuntary cruelty at least.

I should like to write a book about ideal people under ideal circumstances. No sort of under-nourishment, no under-education, nothing partial or frustrated, no need of variety or luxury—in short, no lack of anything which, according to its children, Wisconsin denies. Only the inavertible troubles, all in the spirit, and only those characteristic of a period in which, here and there, certain bans have been lifted, certain jealousies appeased. The ease of mature and healthy plants in a well-kept garden, but an indoor book, in which human beings alone, not the weather or swamps or the beasts of the field, shall have parts to play. I am content that it shall pass for tragedy; even the arias of Mozart, the love-making of Daphnis and Chloe, hurt. And when that is done, I shall have to ask myself whether, like Emerson and Whitman, I lack the vision of evil . . .

A little Italian brakeman, hurrying through the train, shouts, "Milwaukee! Milwau-kee!" giving back to the syllables their red-Indian sound. I have some time before a train goes on to Chicago and climb up into the little park beside the station. Snowy bluffs over the fresh-water sea. On the other side of the real sea I shall miss this exciting air, which is to make a new race of us if nothing else does. Indeed it is melancholy leaving this land in which democracy is coming to a climax, in which a whole uneven generation is beginning to claim as its right, not merely the rewards, but the powers of supermen. The moonlight is brilliant because the windows of the thick-set Germanic buildings are not too close, because of the ice drifting on the water or attached to the shore. The bluish stars have horns. There are no boats in the harbor.

Then, wishing like Gide in his youth "to have been born in a time when, to celebrate all things, the poet had only to enumerate them," I remember the ports which seem to me more beautiful than this: the Hudson River whose lowing steamships send into your sleep flocks of great marine cattle; the Pool of London, a hollow and perhaps criminal cave under the fog of amber; the port of Marseilles shaped like a drinking bowl, wreathed with nets and rigging, and giving off an odor of poison in spite of the dates, sea-chestnuts, sea-potatoes, lemons and olives; the bay of Naples over which, on roofs, balconies, and perilous streets like tree-branches, figures out of the *commedia dell'arte,* beaked, ragged, clear-eyed as birds, gesticulate and play evil tricks and sing; and the roadstead of Villefranche. The latter lies in a broken ring of dim olive-trees; and between the lemon-white quay and the battleships, sailors signal to each other with an alphabet of outstretched arms and small flags like handkerchiefs on sticks, their faces gone blank with concentration. For another book I should like to learn to write in a style like those gestures: without slang, with precise equivalents instead of idioms, a style of rapid grace for the eye rather than sonority for the ear, in accordance with the ebb and flow of sensation rather than with intellectual habits, and out of which myself, with my origins and my prejudices and my Wisconsin, will seem to have disappeared.

An Apartment in the City

Janet Frame

IT WAS A BASEMENT apartment with windows looking out over two streets, the large sitting room and kitchen facing the busier streets, the large bedroom beside the quieter 'place', with the bathroom enclosed in the hallway. The pebble garden at the back was planted with spiked shrubs of the kinds that, growing by the sea, suffer the salt spray and winds by bending their backs and heads forward away from the storm, and, growing in a city, adopt the same pose to avoid the fumes, soundwaves and odious smells, and in both cases they survive and bloom with thorn crowns and small blue and pink flowers. When the trucks passed along the back street the apartment shuddered with grindings, slammings, squealing of brakes, while outside the bedroom the traffic though quiet, was unceasing.

The apartment was luxurious for me. For the first time since I had been in London I had hot running water and a bath and bathroom and kitchen to myself. The furnishings were luxurious also, with striped Regency sofas and chairs with round bun-like seats, and dark polished chests of drawers. The double bed had sheets and blankets wide enough and long enough to tuck in and the mattress was as level as a wooden shelf and as unyielding, while some of the towels in the linen cupboard were labelled *Bath Sheets.*

At first I arranged my workplace in the bedroom only to find the room was too dark and I felt I was missing events in the sitting room, therefore I tried typing there beside the inner wall but the sounds of traffic intruded. I was also intimidated by the fine furniture. In a half-hearted way I leafed through the poems I had written during my East Suffolk days, and the book I had begun but my mind was occupied by the publication of *Scented Gardens for the Blind* and the sentence from a review that I could not ignore: 'This book is unreadable in the worst sense.' I struggled against losing my small supply of confidence. In another journal someone had described the book as 'likely a work of genius.' The two opinions, extreme yet balancing, shifted from me like alternatingly oppressive and buoyant waves, leaving me a damp survivor, jetsam of yet another flow of reviews.

In South Kensington I learned more about life in London, of the ease of living in SW7 compared to SE5, for a miracle seemed to occur in libraries, museums, shops as soon as I gave my address: I was treated with kindness,

I was offered credit; and could they call me a taxi? The tendency to questioning and suspicion by the keepers of Camberwell had vanished. And when I walked along the streets of Kensington and Knightsbridge, jostled by the beautiful and the rich, I found myself remembering the dream of my Aunt Polly in Petone, New Zealand, to be 'someone'. 'I'd like to be somebody,' she'd say, reminding herself that she had relations, town clerks or mayors, lawyers or doctors, who were 'somebody'. In Kensington I too was 'somebody', but not because of my actions or works or some remarkable personal trait: I was 'somebody' because my address was South Kensington SW7. I had a luxury apartment with a bathroom, a white entry phone as well as an 'ordinary' telephone, a tradesman's entrance and a private entrance . . . I was out of step, however, with the dwellers of South Kensington. In Grove Hill Road SE5, getting up very early and starting work, I'd know a feeling of being at home as I saw the lights in the houses and imagined the hasty breakfasts, and watched the workers hurrying through the half-dark to catch their buses, and, later, the groups of children on their way to school, swishing and tapping and knocking their sticks in an unknowing rehearsal of age. Here in Kensington few appeared to be awake before ten in the morning. The mail was delivered late. If there were children they were driven silently to school in large dark cars. I might have felt stranded had I not known that other writers lived in Kensington. I liked to think they were working near, unseen, never forgetting or abandoning the Mirror City.

In the centre of my dining table I put the bowl of planted flowers sent by the Gouldens to welcome me on my first day in the apartment. They had also sent an invitation to their home to meet the author Alan Sillitoe and his wife, Ruth, at afternoon tea, and on the day, in spite of the heavy rain, I chose to walk to their place in Mayfair, planning a route where I might arrive fairly dry. The rain persisted. I did not find the verandahs I had hoped to find. My shoes filled with water, my stockings, the lower part of my dress, the back of my cardigan were soaking when at last I stood outside the Gouldens' apartment and watched the Sillitoes arriving warm and dry by taxi. I was hot, red-faced, flurried; my bladder was full, and my visit was just beginning. I waited 'in the shadows' as it were until the Sillitoes had gone into the building, then I took the lift to the top floor, rang the bell, and was admitted by Mrs Goulden, tall, dark, regal, (with a remarkable resemblance, I thought, to the Queen of Spades in the film I had lately seen, *The Manchurian Candidate*). She wore black and had an air of having lived inside her skin as if it were a house, polished, prepared daily, with herself the mistress in total possession. She was not an immediate person; there was a porch, an entrance hall where one waited to be received. She introduced me to Alan and Ruth Sillitoe. ('I've read your books . . . etc.')

The introductions over, there was consternation that my clothes and shoes were saturated. Mrs Goulden took me to a bedroom where she found dry clothes and shoes for me to wear while mine dried, and so I began my visit wearing a tight-fitting black dress and black evening shoes with gold borders, peep toes and two-inch heels.

Presently Mrs Goulden rang a silver bell and a servant, a darkhaired buxom woman named *Columba*, appeared with the afternoon tea and when she had left the room, Mrs Goulden explained that Columba had been brought from Portugal and spoke little English. This caused excitement between the Sillitoes—Alan, the latest star of the northern writers, deep in realism, poverty, struggles for food, work and sex in the slums of the north, had been living in Morocco and had brought a servant home with them, they said, but when they arrived in England, they discovered they had purchased and paid for her as if she were a slave.

Oh, the servant problem!

I listened, quietly amazed, while Mrs Goulden and the Sillitoes ranged from the servant problem to the au pair and back to the servant problem; there in the Mayfair apartment with its Persian rugs, Turkish cats, exquisite paintings, dark knobbly furniture.

I had little to say. I smiled a lot and said 'Yes, yes.' My evening shoes were pinching. And when the time came to leave and I changed into my dry clothes and shoes Mrs Goulden parcelled up the black dress and evening shoes.

'You're welcome to keep them,' she said.

The rain had stopped. No, I said, I'd walk home and not get a taxi. As I left, carrying my new black dress and evening shoes, I thought, with excitement and satisfaction, I have met Alan and Ruth Sillitoe. My second *real* writer. (The first had been John Silkin who had given me a poem inscribed to me, but that is another story.)

Living in South Kensington I could not rid myself of the idea that I was playing house, playing at being someone who lived in an apartment with a white entry phone and a white telephone in the bedroom, beside the bed, for me to answer calls in the middle of the night, 'Oh is that you darling. Don't bother me now.' Playing at having a real bathroom and bath with hot water and cupboards full of linen and huge towels labelled *Bath Sheets* for me to wrap around me when Nigel or Gerald came (opening the door with their private key) and I called, 'Just a minute, *hunny*, I'm in the bath,' with the imagined dialogue the same as that used when I and my sisters played Hollywood with our kewpie dolls. The apartment was a game, beginning with my role as tenant to the unrealistic rent that I would never have money to pay.

And each day I sat at my table trying to write my new novel, *Letters to a Sculptor*. Then I'd get up and walk around the apartment and gloat over it as I used to gloat over the garden in Suffolk, as if producing it had been 'all my own work'. And instead of returning to my typewriter and shaping a batch of sentences, I'd experiment with the new stove in the kitchen, producing an unusual dish from *Aunt Daisy's Recipe Book* sent to me by my father for my last birthday. He'd also sent me a case of New Zealand butter which, after giving some away, I had packed in the snowy refrigerator.

Then one day a friend of Frank Sargeson, Paula Lincoln, who had left New Zealand after thirty years and bought a cottage in a small village in Norfolk, wrote to say that she and her sister Rachel who were ardent cricket fans were coming to London to see the cricket at Lords and they'd like to accept the invitation I had given them to 'stay any time'.

I met them at Liverpool Street Station. They were to sleep in the bedroom while I slept on a folding bed placed half in and out of the hall cupboard with just enough room for passing into the kitchen. I found both Paula and Rachel overwhelming, eager, enthusiastic, moving abruptly in what seemed like a physical attack on the space around them; and as they were sisters who did not see each other often, their voices were high-pitched with excitement and their Oxford accents, sharply edged, sliced through the apartment, furniture, fittings, air and my ears. At Lords I sat watching a tedious game that I knew nothing about, and when a newcomer whispered urgently to me, 'I say, who's first man?' and I echoed meekly, 'First man?' the woman looked at me with disgust.

Halfway through the morning I left Paula and Rachel and returned to Kensington where I found a letter from my sister in New Zealand telling me that my father, cycling to his work as boiler attendant 'out the North Road' had collapsed near Willowglen, our home, and had been admitted to hospital where a diagnosis was not made at once, and the next day he was being x-rayed, still in a state of collapse, when he died. He had been suffering a haemorrhage from a stomach ulcer.

Poor difficult, bullying, loving Dad, I thought, sighing my tears. Later when Paula and Rachel came home from Lords, I told them my news. What could they say? They began to reminisce about their father, a distant man who when they were children had visited them occasionally in the nursery. They remembered his 'twinkling, kindly eyes' and his shyness.

They had called him 'Father'. He was a clergyman at a girls' public school, and because he was employed there the Lincoln family was educated there, and, later, they were at school in Switzerland. They had called their mother, 'Mother'. Their parents came rarely to the nursery, they said, and it was their elder sister to whom they looked for guidance and help.

'Poor Mother,' they said. 'Poor Father.'

And they said to each other, 'Do you remember? . . .' using words and phrases that were of the nineteen twenties and before and that I'd read only in books. Some of the girls at school had fathers who were 'rotters', they cried. 'Rotters and cads. But Father was tophole, wasn't he?'

That evening as I lay in my foldaway bed I thought of Dad alone at Willowglen and I remembered Aunt Polly's criticism of me for going 'overseas'—'You are single and it's your place to stay home and look after your father.' Poor Dad with his five-shilling postal notes, and his stinking fish-bag, the inside covered with old fish scales, hanging inside the back door, and his trouser clips for his bike hanging on their hook behind the door, and his face wobbling with tears when he said goodbye at the Wellington wharf.

A few days later I had a letter from the lawyer in Oamaru to say that my brother and I were now joint owners of Willowglen and that I had been left all the contents of the home, and would I be returning to New Zealand as I was the sole executor of my father's estate? My father's estate! There were the home and its contents, enough money for the funeral, a small sum of money for my sister, and a bank book containing six shillings and fourpence. The cash for the funeral and the small bequest came from money won a week earlier in a lottery or on a racehorse, otherwise there would have been nothing.

I consulted Dr Cawley whom I still visited regularly. Should I return to New Zealand? A shocked angry letter from my brother said that Willowglen had been locked up and no-one would let him in, and although he was not living at Willowglen, he was hurt by the idea of not being allowed into his old home.

Should I return? Perhaps I had already made up my mind. The opinion was that it might be unwise to live in New Zealand after my past experience there, and that I might even be in danger from the mistaken diagnosis for few there had questioned it, and now that my books were being published there was constant reference to me as 'unbalanced, insane' with a tendency to ally this to my writing and even make it a reason and explanation for my writing. Perhaps I had already made up my mind, for I realized that I wished to return to live and work in New Zealand. Although I was now being referred to as an 'expatriate' writer, my reasons for leaving New Zealand, apart from the desire to 'broaden my experience', had not been literary or artistic. My reason for returning was literary. Europe was so much on the map of the imagination (which is a limitless map, indeed) with room for anyone who cares to find a place there, while the layers of the long dead and recently dead are a fertile growing place for new shoots and buds, yet the prospect of exploring a new country with not so many layers of mapmakers, particularly the country where one first saw daylight and the sun and the dark, was too tantalising to resist. Also, the first layer of imagination mapped by the early inhabitants leaves those who follow an access or passageway to the bone. Living in New Zealand, would be for me, like living in an age of mythmakers; with a freedom of imagination among all the artists because it is possible to begin at the beginning and to know the unformed places and to help to form them, to be a mapmaker for those who will follow nourished by this generation's layers of the dead. I was strongly influenced in my decision by remembering, from time to time, Frank Sargeson's words to me 'Remember you'll never know another country like that where you spent your earliest years. You'll never be able to write intimately of another country.'

My argument had always been, 'What of the writers forced into political exile who never had or have the choice of returning, who live and work and bring new insights to the language of their adopted country? And what of those who have had to go more deeply into the unknown by changing their language? Conrad, Nabokov . . . and what about James Joyce . . . and Samuel Beckett . . . ? All writers—all beings—are exiles as a matter of course. The certainty about living is that it is a succession of expulsions of whatever carries the life force . . . All writers are exiles wherever they live and their work is a lifelong journey towards the lost land . . .'

The fact is that when I was about to go home to New Zealand I did not need reasons for returning; but others needed to know why, to have explanations. I could have said that, sitting at my sewing machine table looking out at the fields of East Suffolk, I had known a sensation of falseness, of surface-skimming . . . the feeling, perhaps, when after writing a letter and sealing it and writing the address on the envelope one might find that the stamp won't hold, there's nothing to glue it to the envelope, and no matter how hard one tries, the stamp keeps coming unstuck—so what use, except as a self-confirming exercise, was a letter that stayed with the writer?

Whatever my reasons for returning to New Zealand, I knew I would try to make them sound as elevated as possible; but I did experience this unease in Suffolk, knowing that thousands of miles away there was a cabbage tree or a clump of snowgrass or a sweep of sky that I had not examined as carefully as I examined the ninety-foot lilac hedge; and a nation of people that I had never learned to know as well, as during my short stay in Suffolk—or in Ibiza or Andorra—I felt I knew the inhabitants, their landscape, their history and was beginning to know their language.

Now that writing was my only occupation, regardless of the critical and financial outcome, I felt I had found my 'place' at deeper level than any landscape of any country would provide. In New Zealand Frank Sargeson had saved my life by affirming that I could spend my time writing, although to him, I think, I was always the 'mad, sane' person; here in London writing had been affirmed as a way of life without psychiatric qualifications. I now felt, inhabiting my 'place', that day by day I could visit the Mirror City and ponder questions that only those trying to practise a form of art have time for: artists, monks, idlers, any who stand and stare. I could journey like a seasoned traveller to the Mirror City, observing (not always consciously), listening, remembering and forgetting. The only graveyard in Mirror City is the graveyard of memories that are resurrected, reclothed with reflection and change, their essence untouched. (A truthful autobiography tries to record the essence. The renewal and change are part of the material of fiction.)

Having advised against my returning to New Zealand, and accepting that I chose to return, Dr Cawley reminded me that I should live as I wished and not as others wished, that I had no obligation to 'mix', that he agreed with me that living alone was my ideal way of life if I chose it to be. And writing.

He did advise that I buy a return ticket.

I knew, finally, that leaving one's native land forever can be a strength or a weakness or both, depending on the artist, to be used to add to the store of material processed in Mirror City, and that for the writer of fiction being an exile may be a hindrance, especially if the writer is from a country just beginning its literary tradition. The writer (if there is ever such a person as 'the writer') may find herself spending a lifetime looking into the mists of distant childhood, or becoming a travel writer who describes the scene, then leaves it, pocketing the uprooted vegetation, erasing the sea and the sky without hearing the cries of a world that has been torn from itself into the fictional world, from people whose very skin is left hanging in the centuries-old trees; the unmistakable cry of a homeland truthfully described and transformed.

I know that unless the writer embraces the language of the new land there are constant betrayals of language. (Language may betray the writer but the writer must not be the betrayer.) When I had returned to New Zealand and wrote *The Adaptable Man* set in Suffolk, a sharp-eyed critic noted my inaccurate reference to the *Orwell River* instead of the correct, *River Orwell*, my usage being the New Zealand idiom—the Rakaia River, the Waitaki River, the Clutha River—and not the English—River Thames, Humber, Orwell.

Wherever one lives, in the growing necessity for a 'world view', living or not living in one's native land may give equal advantages and insights, and from whatever land, the truth is always painful to extract and express whether it be the truth of fact or fiction.

I had written a few chapters of *Letters to a Sculptor*. Although my return fare to New Zealand had been guaranteed by 'an anonymous donor' whom I suspected (correctly, I think) to be Charles Brasch (the poet), I preferred to receive money from an institution rather than an individual. I had enough to pay my return fare and my proportion of the rent of the Kensington apartment, but there were no prospects of my being able to have funds in New Zealand. I therefore applied either for a Literary Fund Grant or for the Scholarship in Letters for 1964.

I booked my passage, a single cabin on the *Corinthic*, a one-class ship sailing from London through the Panama Canal to Auckland. I knew I had been advised never again to travel by sea but I was ever hopeful of becoming a good sailor.

Where had my London years gone? Why had I never been to Stratford-on-Avon? To the Brontë country? To Hardy country? Stonehenge, Tintagel Castle, Tintern Abbey? I had spent a week in the Lake District camping out for one night beside Sour Milk Force on the route through to Buttermere. I had roamed the Fells all day visiting places known to Wordsworth, Coleridge, Shelley.

I had absorbed much from living in London. I had seen the rise and strength of the Campaign for Nuclear Disarmament, the Easter Marches to Aldermaston; the Suez crisis; the Hungarian Revolution, the Parliamentary scandals. I had seen the arrival of the 'kitchen sink' playwrights and painters, the West Indian novelists, the North Country novelists and I had found my favourites to take their place beside those already there—I read the Beat Poets of City Lights Press; Ted Hughes, Sylvia Plath (recently dead); William Golding; Samuel Selvon; Iris Murdoch, Albert Camus, Sartre, Duras, Sarraute, Robbe-Grillet . . . I had seen *Last Year in Marienbad* and the new films from India. I had attended a performance of *Three Sisters* in Russian . . . I had listened in St Pancras Hall to the London Mozart Players, the Bach Players . . . and Kathleen Ferrier, dead. I had interesting correspondence with Bertrand Russell's first love. The librarian at the Kentish Town flat had sponsored me for a ticket to the British Museum Reading Room. Well, my London days were full of experience—museums, galleries, libraries, people; and underlying all was a gradual stengthening of me in my place through my talks with Dr Cawley as if he was a *bespoke* tailor helping to reinforce the seams of my life and now I was putting on my own garment to try it. And woven into the garment were my experiences in Ibiza and Andorra. (I'd had a loving postcard from the fur shop in the south of France, from El Vici Mario, but the address was illegible and I therefore excused myself from replying.)

There were many people I knew whom I do not describe here; they are living and I have tried to restrict myself to my own story without presuming to tell the stories of others. Writing of the dead is a different matter, for the dead have surrendered their story. There is a danger, however, in living at a distance from the source of one's fiction, for one so easily equates distance with death, and, rejoicing over the freedom of a story, one is suddenly faced with the curtailing effects of facts that have never undergone the necessary transformation in Mirror City; the writer has supposed that staying safe in this world and sprinkling a potion of distance-death upon a chosen ingredient of fiction, can result in the same transformation that occurs within the harsh lonely places of Mirror City. Instant fiction is as contradictory as instant future.

I said goodbye to London where living had been for me like living within a huge family with London our house. I looked forward to the terrible winters of frost, ice, chilblains. I watched the leaves turning and falling and drifting against the black iron railing of the parks. I saw the sun change to blood-red and stand on end upon the winterbeaten grass of the Common; I watched the people with a new urgency in their gait, hurrying to their homes, if they had homes to escape the dark and the cold; and those with no homes depending for warmth and shelter on the doorways of peopleless places like banks and insurance buildings and (before the great railway stations were demolished or remodelled and rebuilt without seating) on the seats of the railway stations and bus terminals and down from the Strand, by the river, underneath the arches. Then after dark the new life of London, the glitter, the people in taxis and dark polished cars . . . wandering misfits shouting at the sky . . . the dark January days . . . the appearance of spring . . . June, dusty July, August, the cycle again. The seasons in the city of millions became my relations as they had been in the countryside of New Zealand. Here there was the evidence of lives shared with the human power of destruction and creation; the irreparable mistakes that are part of the construction of a city, no matter how carefully it has been planned, the effect of the mistakes, some disastrous, the illumination of the way of human beings, shafts of light not originating in the sun; while the seasons, modified, damaged, but recurring, continue to regard the city, they too in a sense at home, acclimatized to themselves. The effect of London as a vast city gives only a hint of the complexity of Mirror City, yet it filled my life with thoughts and images that have stayed and will stay until I, as a season, accept inevitable change, when leaves of my own memory drift downward to become part of the rich earth of Mirror City.

My departure from London was sad and strange. With scenes in my mind of my journey from New Zealand, of my father, Uncle Vere and Aunty Polly waving goodbye from the shelter of the wharf sheds in Wellington; streamers, the ritual playing of *Now is the Hour*, the fearful apprehension that came over me when I watched the hills receding, the rising sense of adventure when I realized there was no turning back. I tried to imagine how it would be now, leaving London. The wharf, the embarkation, sailing down the Thames to the open sea . . . but where were the people to say goodbye in a city where my only family was the city itself?

I had spent seven years away from New Zealand with my past few years occupied entirely with writing, dividing my time between writing, solitary walking, dreaming in cinemas. I had no close friends who might wish to stand on a London wharf waving a sad goodbye. Unable to face a solitary departure I asked the librarian who had secured me a ticket to the Reading Room, would she mind 'seeing me off'. She agreed. The literary agent, Patience Ross, farewelled me at Victoria Station, and when the train arrived at the East London docks there was Millicent the librarian, who had taken an extended lunch hour to say goodbye. We had afternoon tea on board ship. I thanked her. She returned to her work. And as the engines started and the last farewells were made, and the ship began to move down the Thames, I looked about me at the sober, subdued passengers. There had been no band playing, no streamers. Some of the passengers had the air of being about to sail to their doom; many, no doubt, were emigrants who had said last goodbyes and would never return; faces showed anxiety rather than anticipation, a certainty of a journey away from rather than a journey towards.

Recovering from my own brief self-pity (all those years in London and I need to ask someone to say goodbye to me!) I looked with interest at the dock buildings and the dark dampness of 'dockside' and I thought of my father and his Sexton Blake paperbacks, half-sized pocketbooks on mottled paper, and their scenes of crime in London's dockland; and the character, Tinker's, 'Right, guv.' I thought how much Dad would have relished a description of the docks, and how grateful he would have been, like one who feels the movement of a telephone wire although there is no distinct message, had I written to say that I could just imagine Tinker and Sexton Blake at the docks meeting some unsavoury character, a 'nark' who would give them the 'tip-off'.

And so it was not the buildings of London, the Tate Gallery, the new literature, the excitement of living in London, that I thought of as the ship sailed towards the open sea, it was the girlhood sharing with my father of the cheap, poorly-written detective stories with their pulp-soaked racist stereotypes, Tinker and Sexton Blake and their 'guvs' and 'm'lords' and 'm'luds' who were yet fictional characters whatever their literary deficiencies; and it was not even Dickens or Lamb or Samuel Pepys, it was Sexton Blake and Tinker, his faithful servant, who farewelled me from London while I, in my turn, was waving goodbye for the last time to my father, he too perhaps sheltering in fiction, huddled by the docks in the company of Tinker and Sexton Blake of Baker Street.

Pencilled Notes

Isabelle Eberhardt

A SUBJECT TO WHICH few intellectuals ever give a thought is the right to be a vagrant, the freedom to wander. Yet vagrancy is deliverance, and life on the open road is the essence of freedom. To have the courage to smash the chains with which modern life has weighted us (under the pretext that it was offering us more liberty), then to take up the symbolic stick and bundle, and *get out*!

To the one who understands the value and the delectable flavor of solitary freedom (for no one is free who is not alone) leaving is the bravest and finest act of all.

An egotistical happiness, possibly. But for him who relishes the flavor, happiness.

To be alone, to be *poor in needs*, to be ignored, to be an outsider who is at home everywhere, and to walk, great and by oneself, toward the conquest of the world.

The healthy wayfarer sitting beside the road scanning the horizon open before him, is he not the absolute master of the earth, the waters, and even the sky? What housedweller can vie with him in power and wealth? His estate has no limits, his empire no law. No work bends him toward the ground, for the bounty and beauty of the earth are already his.

In our modern society the nomad is a pariah "without known domicile or residence." By adding these few words to the name of anyone whose appearance they consider irregular, those who make and enforce the laws can decide a man's fate.

To have a home, a family, a property or a public function, to have a definite means of livelihood and to be a useful cog in the social machine, all these things seem necessary, even indispensable, to the vast majority of men, including intellectuals, and including even those who think of themselves as wholly liberated. And yet such things are only a different form of the slavery that comes of contact with others, especially regulated and continued contact.

I have always listened with admiration, if not envy, to the declarations of citizens who tell how they have lived for twenty or thirty years in the same section of town, or even the same house, and who have never been out of their native city.

Not to feel the torturing need to know and see for oneself what is there, beyond the mysterious blue wall of the horizon, not to find the arrangements of life monotonous and depressing, to look at the white road leading off into the unknown distance without feeling the imperious necessity of giving in to it and following it obediently across mountains and valleys! The cowardly belief that a man must stay in one place is too reminiscent of the unquestioning resignation of animals, beasts of burden stupefied by servitude and yet always willing to accept the slipping on of the harness.

There are limits to every domain, and laws to govern every organized power. But the vagrant owns the whole vast earth that ends only at the nonexistent horizon, and his empire is an intangible one, for his domination and enjoyment of it are things of the spirit.

Translated by Paul Bowles

Acknowledgments

THIS ANTHOLOGY WOULD NOT have been completed were it not for the efforts of a remarkable quartet. April Bernard cajoled me into reviving the project many months after I had lost hope and stored it away. Her advice continued to sustain me as I was gathering, editing, and writing about the book's contents. Gloria Loomis, my agent, was always generous and considered with her own suggestions; her instincts were unfailing. Caryl Phillips responded to this collection in a particularly heartening way—as an exile himself, eager to read about the varieties of his condition. He also introduced me to my editor, Fiona McCrae. The anthology benefited immensely from her adventurous thinking and shrewd criticism.

Since some of the writing I considered has not been translated into English (or not translated adequately), I have relied on the advice of a number of other people: I'm thankful to Richard Howard, James Magruder, Patricia Simpson, and the three translators who completed work especially for this book—Catherine Ciepiela, Jeanine Herman, and Douglas Langworthy. Richard Gilman, Elana Greenfield, and Maggie Paley all offered close readings of the introduction. Several other people helped type the manuscript; thank you to Stephanie Coen, Charles McNulty, Silvana Tropea, and (again) Douglas Langworthy. Assistance of various kinds has come from Hilton Als, Peter Cipkowski, Laurence Davies, Bonnie Marranca, Paul Schmidt, and Alisa Solomon. A valuable source of information for many of the biographical notes has been the reference work *Literary Exile in the Twentieth Century,* edited by Martin Tucker. Nicole Aragi at Watkins/Loomis has been tremendously helpful with practical matters large and small. Finally, my work on the anthology was partly supported by a Griswold Faculty Grant from the Whitney Humanities Center at Yale University and by the MacDowell Colony.

My deepest gratitude goes to the writers. I'm especially in the debt of Darryl Pinckney and Austin Clarke, whose essays were commissioned for this volume. All of these exiles, of course, have given generously of themselves in the observations, outcries, and celebrations collected here. I hope *Altogether Elsewhere* honors their efforts to feel at home.

For permission to reprint copyrighted material the editor and publishers gratefully acknowledge the following:

Vassily Aksyonov, from *Salmagundi* magazine, no. 72, copyright ©1986 by Vassily Aksyonov and Skidmore College; reprinted by permission of *Salmagundi* and the author.

Fernando Alegría, from *Review: Latin American Literature and Arts*, no. 30, copyright © 1982 by the Center for Inter-American Relations, Inc. Reprinted by permission of the publisher and the author.

Hannah Arendt, from *The Menorah Journal*, January 1943, copyright © 1943 by The Menorah Association, Inc.

James Baldwin, from *Esquire* magazine, July 1961, copyright © 1962 by James Baldwin. Collected in *The Price of the Ticket*. Used by arrangement with the James Baldwin Estate.

Stanislaw Baranczak, from the *University of Toronto Quarterly*, no. 58, copyright © 1989 by the University of Toronto Press. Reprinted by permission of the University of Toronto Press, Incorporated, and the author.

Kay Boyle, from *Words That Must Somehow Be Said*, copyright © 1985 by Northpoint Press. "Frankfurt in Our Blood" originally published in *The Nation* in 1949. Reprinted by permission of the Watkins/Loomis Agency.

Breyten Breytenbach, "A Letter from Exile, to Don Espejuelo" from *End Papers*, copyright © 1986 by Breyten Breytenbach. Reprinted by permission of Farrar, Straus & Giroux, Inc. "The Exile as African," excerpted from essay originally titled "The Long March from Hearth to Heart," from *Social Research*, Spring 1991, copyright © 1991 by New School for Social Research. Reprinted by permission of *Social Research*.

Joseph Brodsky, from *The New York Review of Books*, January 21, 1988, copyright © 1988 Nyrev, Inc. Reprinted with permission from *The New York Review of Books*.

Albert Camus, from *Lyrical and Critical Essays*, ed. P. Thody, trans. E. C. Kennedy, copyright © 1968 by Alfred A. Knopf, Inc. Copyright © 1967 by Hamish Hamilton, Ltd., and Alfred A. Knopf, Inc. Reprinted by permission of Alfred A. Knopf, Inc.

E. M. Cioran, from *The Temptation to Exist*, trans. Richard Howard, published by Seaver Books, copyright © 1956 by Librairie Gallimard. Translation copyright © 1968 by Quadrangle Books, Inc. Reprinted by permission of Seaver Books.

Austin Clarke, "Exile," copyright © 1994 by Austin Clarke. Printed by permission of the author.

Joseph Conrad, from *Notes on Life and Letters*, copyright © 1921 by Doubleday. Used by permission of Doubleday, a division of Bantam Doubleday Dell Publishing Group, Inc.

Julio Cortázar, from *Review: Latin American Literature and Arts*, no. 30, copyright © 1982 by the Center for Inter-American Relations, Inc. Reprinted by permission of the publisher.

Belkis Cuza Malé, from *Contemporary Women Authors of Latin America*, Brooklyn College Humanities Institute Series, copyright © 1983 by Brooklyn College Press.

Hilde Domin, from *Aber die Hoffnung*, copyright © 1982 by S. Fischer Verlag. Reprinted by permission of S. Fischer Verlag, Frankfurt am Main. Translation copyright © 1994 by Douglas Langworthy. Printed by permission of the translator.

Isabelle Eberhardt, from *The Oblivion Seekers and Other Writings*, copyright © 1975 by City Lights Books. Translation copyright © 1975 by Paul Bowles. Reprinted by permission of City Lights Books.

Janet Frame, from *The Envoy from Mirror City*, copyright © 1985 by George Braziller, Inc. Reprinted by permission of George Braziller, Inc.

William H. Gass, from *Salmagundi* magazine, nos. 88–89, copyright © 1991 by Skidmore College and the author. Reprinted by permission of *Salmagundi* and the author.

Witold Gombrowicz, from *Diary,* volume 1, originally published in France under the title *Dziennik,* copyright © 1957 by Instytut Literacki. English translation copyright © 1988 by Northwestern University Press. Reprinted by permission of Northwestern University Press.

Eva Hoffman, from *Lost in Translation,* copyright © 1989 by Eva Hoffman. Used by permission of Dutton Signet, a division of Penguin Books USA Inc.

Victor Hugo, from *Pendant L'Exil: 1853–1861,* published 1883 by J. Hetzel and Co. Translation copyright © 1994 by Jeanine Herman. Printed by permission of the translator.

Ruth Prawer Jhabvala, from *Blackwood's* magazine, no. 1965, July 1979, copyright © 1979 by Ruth Prawer Jhabvala. Reprinted by permission of Harriet Wasserman Literary Agency, Inc., as agents for the author.

Leszek Kolakowski, from *The Times Literary Supplement,* October 11, 1985, copyright © 1985 by Leszek Kolakowski.

Mary McCarthy, from *Occasional Prose,* copyright © 1985 by Mary McCarthy. Reprinted by permission of Harcourt Brace and Company.

Czeslaw Milosz, from *Books Abroad,* vol. 50, no. 2, Spring 1976, copyright © 1976 by the University of Oklahoma Press. Reprinted by permission of the editor.

Henry de Montherlant, from *From the NRF,* copyright © 1958 by Editions Gallimard. Reprinted by permission of Georges Borchardt, Inc.

Es'kia Mphahlele, from *Daedalus, Journal of the American Academy of Arts and Sciences,* from the issue entitled "Black Africa: A Generation After Independence," Spring 1982, vol. 111, no. 2, copyright © 1982 by the American Academy of Arts and Sciences. Reprinted by permission of *Daedalus.*

Lewis Nkosi, from *Home and Exile,* published 1965 by Longman Group Ltd., copyright © 1965 by Lewis Nkosi.

Jan Novak, from *The New York Times Book Review*, April 2, 1989, copyright © 1989 by Jan Novak. Reprinted by permission of the author.

Petrarch, from *Letters from Petrarch*, trans. Morris Bishop, copyright © 1966 by Indiana University Press. Reprinted by permission of Indiana University Press.

Darryl Pinckney, "How I Got Over," copyright © 1994 by Darryl Pinckney. Printed by permission of the author.

Augusto Roa Bastos, from *On Modern Latin American Fiction*, ed. John King, copyright © 1987 by John King. Reprinted by permission of Hill and Wang, a division of Farrar, Straus & Giroux, Inc.

Jean-Jacques Rousseau, from *The Reveries of the Solitary Walker*, trans. Charles E. Butterworth, copyright © 1979 by New York University Press. Reprinted by permission of New York University Press.

Edward W. Said, from *Granta* magazine, no. 13, Autumn 1984, copyright © 1984 by Edward W. Said. Reprinted by permission of the author.

George Santayana, from the *Virginia Quarterly Review*, Winter 1964, copyright © 1964 by the *Virginia Quarterly Review*. Reprinted by permission of the editor.

Madame Germaine de Staël, from *An Extraordinary Woman: Selected Writings of Germaine de Staël*, ed. and trans. by Vivian Folkenflick, copyright © 1987 by Columbia University Press, New York. Reprinted by permission of Columbia University Press.

Christina Stead, from *Ocean of Story*, copyright © 1985 by the Estate of Christina Stead. Reprinted by permission of Penguin Books Australia Ltd.

Marina Tsvetaeva, "An Emigré from Immortality" from *Art in the Light of Conscience*, by Marina Tsvetaeva, selected, translated, and introduced by Angela Livingstone, Cambridge, Mass.: Harvard University Press, copyright © 1991 by Angela Livingstone. Reprinted by permission of Harvard University Press. "An Insistence of Memory" from *Izbrannaia proza v dvukh tomakh*, by Marina Tsvetaeva, translation copyright © 1994 by Catherine Ciepiela. Printed by permission of the translator. "A Hero of

Labor" from *Znamia*, by Marina Tsvetaeva, translation copyright © 1994 by Catherine Ciepiela. Printed by permission of the translator.

Miguel de Unamuno, from *Our Lord Don Quixote*, copyright © 1967 by Princeton University Press. Reprinted by permission of Princeton University Press.

Glenway Wescott, from *Good-Bye Wisconsin*, published by Harper and Row in 1928, copyright © 1955 by Glenway Wescott. Reprinted by permission of Harold Ober Associates, Inc.

A persistent effort has been made to trace all the copyright holders, but if any have been overlooked the publishers should be contacted.

Biographical and Textual Notes

Vassily Aksyonov was born in 1932 in Kazan, USSR, emigrated to the United States in 1980, and now lives in Washington, D.C. He is the author of numerous novels, including *The Burn* (1980), which provoked Aksyonov's expulsion from the Soviet Writers' Union and eventual exile. The essay collected here was originally read in January 1986 at an International PEN Conference in New York City devoted to "The Writer's Imagination and the Imagination of the State."

Fernando Alegría was born in 1918 in Santiago, Chile. In the 1940s, he moved to the United States to attend graduate school; he remained to teach and, for a short time, to serve as Chilean President Allende's cultural attaché in Washington. After Allende's government was overthrown in 1973, Alegría chose permanent exile in the United States, where he has written numerous essays, poems, and novels, including *The Chilean Spring* (1980). The essay collected here was written in 1981. He now lives in California.

Mary Antin was born in 1881 in Polotzk, Russia, and died in 1949 in Suffern, New York. In response to the policies of both the czarist government and the orthodox Jewish community, Antin's family emigrated from Russia to Boston in 1891. Her memoir *The Promised Land*, from which the essay collected here is excerpted, appeared in 1912. Another autobiography, *From Polotzk to Boston*, had appeared in 1899.

Hannah Arendt was born in 1906 in Hannover, Germany, and died in 1975 in New York City. In 1933 she fled Germany, moving first to Prague, then Paris, and finally, in 1941, to New York, where she wrote her most influential works, including the monumental *Origins of Totalitarianism.* The essay collected here was first published in *The Menorah Journal* in January 1943.

James Baldwin was born in 1924 in New York City. He moved to Europe in 1948, traveling to and living in Paris, the South of France, and Switzerland through 1957. In these years he wrote *Notes of a Native Son*, *Go Tell It On the Mountain*, and *Giovanni's Room*. In the 1960s and 1970s Baldwin traveled widely in the United States, Turkey, Africa, and the Middle East. He died in 1987 in St. Paul de Vence, France. The essay published here was written in 1962.

Stanislaw Baranczak was born in 1946 in Poznan, Poland. In 1981, after numerous unsuccessful attempts to get an exit visa, Baranczak left Poland to accept a position at Harvard University, where he still teaches. Among his many books of poetry and criticism the best known are *Selected Poems: The Weight of the Body* (1989) and *Breathing Under Water and Other East European Essays* (1990). The essay collected here was written in 1989.

Kay Boyle was born in 1902 in St. Paul, Minnesota, and died in 1992 in San Francisco. She moved to Paris in 1923, lived in England, Austria, and Switzerland in the 1930s, and finally moved back to the United States in 1941. After the war, Boyle returned to Europe, living in Occupied Germany from 1946 to 1953. In 1963 she became a professor at San Francisco State University. Her many books include *Crazy Hunter*, *My Next Bride*, and *Fifty Stories*. The essay collected here was written for *The Nation* in 1949.

Breyten Breytenbach was born in South Africa in 1939 and now lives in Paris. Considered South Africa's most important Afrikaans poet, he is perhaps best known in the United States for his prose, including *The True Confessions of an Albino Terrorist*, a memoir of his imprisonment in South Africa between 1975 and 1982, and his recent *Return to Paradise*. "A Letter from Exile" was written in 1985. "The Exile as African" is adapted from "The Long March from Hearth to Heart," an address delivered in New York City in 1990; this adaptation originally appeared in *Harper's* magazine.

Joseph Brodsky was born in 1940 in Leningrad and went into exile in 1972. He now lives in Massachusetts and New York City. His books of poetry include *A Part of Speech* and *To Urania;* his prose collections include *Less Than One*. He was awarded the Nobel Prize for Literature in 1987. The speech collected here was delivered at a conference on writing in exile held in Vienna in 1987.

Albert Camus was born in 1913 in Mondovi, Algeria. Persecuted for his politics, he moved to France in the early 1940s, where he wrote his major works of philosophy and fiction. He died in France in 1960. The selection collected here, originally published in *Formes et couleurs*, dates from Camus's trip to the United States in 1946.

E. M. Cioran was born in 1911 in Rasinari, a village in Rumania. In 1937, he traveled to Paris on a scholarship, and eventually settled there permanently. He began writing essays and aphorisms in French in 1947; his best-known books include *The Temptation to Exist*, *The Fall into Time*, and *A Short History of Decay*. The essay collected here was originally published in 1956.

Austin Clarke was born in 1934 in Barbados and now lives in Toronto. His books include the novels *The Prime Minister* and *Amongst Thistles and Thorns*, and an autobiography, *Growing Up Stupid Under the Union Jack*. The essay published here was written especially for this volume.

Joseph Conrad was born in 1857 in Berdyczow, Poland. He went to sea for the first time when he was seventeen, spending four years abroad. In 1886, Conrad became an English citizen. He died in 1924 in Bishopsbourne, England. The essay collected here was written in 1915 for *The Daily News*.

Julio Cortázar was born to Argentinean parents in Brussels in 1914. In 1918, the Cortázars returned to Argentina, where Julio eventually became an outspoken opponent of Juan Perón. Cortázar moved to Paris in 1951, and began publishing his stories and novels, including the well-known *Hopscotch* (1963). He died in Paris in 1984. The essay collected here was written in 1978.

Harry Crosby was born in 1898 in New York. In 1922, he moved to Paris, where he published numerous books of poetry, became closely involved with the émigré magazine *transition*, and began what would become a three-volume diary, eventually published under the title *Shadows of the Sun*. Crosby returned to the United States in 1929; he killed himself in New York that December. The selection published here is excerpted from Crosby's response to a questionnaire, "Why Do Americans Live in Europe?," sponsored by *transition* in 1928.

Belkis Cuza Malé was born in 1942 in Guantánamo, Cuba. In 1971, she and her husband, the poet Heberto Padilla, were imprisoned for "subversive writing." Censorship and periods of house arrest followed their release. In 1979 Cuza Malé and her husband went into exile in the United States. She is the author of numerous novels, essays, and poems (the latter of which have been translated into English). The essay collected here originally appeared in *Contemporary Women Authors of Latin America* in 1983.

Hilde Domin was born in 1912 in Cologne, Germany. In 1931 she left Germany, living for a time in Santo Domingo, where she began to write poetry. In the late 1950s, Domin returned to Germany, settling in Heidelberg. Her *Collected Poems*, published in 1987, solidified her reputation as one of Germany's leading poets. "Heimat," translated for the first time for this anthology, was delivered as a radio address in 1975, as part of a series called "Verbal Taboos."

Isabelle Eberhardt was born in 1877 in Geneva. In 1897, she and her mother fled from Isabelle's father and moved to Algeria, where Isabelle converted to Islam and adopted the habits and dress of the Arab men. She spent the rest of her life as a nomad, traveling widely in southwest Algeria and writing extensive journalism and memoirs. She died in 1904 in Ain Sefra, Algeria. It is impossible to date precisely the essay collected here; it is believed to have been written between 1901 and 1904.

Lion Feuchtwanger was born in 1884 in Munich, and died in 1958 in Pacific Palisades, California. In 1933, with the success of his best-known novel, *Jew Süss* (1925), behind him, Feuchtwanger fled Nazi persecution and went into exile, first to France, then to Moscow, then to France again, then to Spain and Portugal, and finally to the United States. Feuchtwanger's other books include *The Oppermanns*, the *Josephus* trilogy, and *Success*. The address collected here was delivered in California to a Writers' Congress sponsored by the Hollywood Writers' Mobilization and the University of California in October 1943.

Janet Frame was born in 1924 in Dunedin, New Zealand. As a young woman, she was mistakenly committed to a hospital as a schizophrenic and underwent numerous shock treatments; she was released only when her story collection *The Lagoon* (1951) won an award. When Frame was thirty-two, she traveled to London, where she lived for the next eight years before returning to New Zealand. Her other works include the novel *Faces* *in the Water* and the autobiographies *To the Is-land, An Angel at My Table,* and *The Envoy from Mirror City.* The selection included here, excerpted from *The Envoy from Mirror City,* was originally published in 1985.

William H. Gass was born in 1924 in Fargo, North Dakota, and now lives in St. Louis, Missouri. He is the author of the novel *Omensetter's Luck,* the story collection *In the Heart of the Heart of the Country,* and the essay collections *Fiction and the Figures of Life* and *The World Within the Word,* among numerous other books. The essay published here was written in 1991.

Witold Gombrowicz was born in 1904 in Maloszyce, Poland, and died in 1969 in Vence, France. Vacationing in Buenos Aires at the outbreak of World War II, Gombrowicz remained in Argentina until 1963, when he returned to Europe. After a year in Berlin, he settled in France. His plays and novels include *Ferdydurke* (1937), *Marriage* (1947), *Trans-Atlantyk* (1953), and *Pornografia* (1960). This response to E. M. Cioran is excerpted from Gombrowicz's 1953 *Diary.*

Heinrich Heine was born in Dusseldorf, Germany, in 1797 and died in Paris in 1856. His interest in the July Revolution and his frustration with the limited opportunities in Germany for publication and work led him to Paris in 1831, where he remained for the rest of his life. In 1835 a German federal decree condemned his writings as subversive; he made his last visit to Germany in 1844. "A German Poet" is excerpted from Heine's *Memoirs* (1854). "They Were Emigrants" is excerpted from Heine's preface to the first volume of *The Salon,* written in Paris and dated October 17, 1833.

Eva Hoffman was born in 1945 in Cracow, Poland, and moved with her family to Canada in 1959, eventually settling in Vancouver. She traveled to Texas to attend college and Massachusetts to attend graduate school. After taking her degree, she moved to New York City, where she worked primarily as a literary critic and editor. She now lives in England. The reflections collected here, "Obsessed with Words" (the title is borrowed from the text), originally appeared in Hoffman's memoir, *Lost in Translation* (1989). Hoffman's latest book, *Exit into History,* appeared in 1993.

Victor Hugo was born in 1802 in Besançon, France, and died in 1885 in Paris. In 1851, after organizing a failed resistance to Louis-Napoleon's coup d'état, Hugo went into exile, first to Belgium, then in 1853 to Jersey, and finally in 1855 to Guernsey, where he stayed until a triumphant return to Paris in 1870. The essay collected here, appearing in English for the first time, is excerpted from "Ce Que C'est Que L'Exil," written in November 1875 and published as an introduction to Hugo's *Pendant L'Exil: 1853–1861.*

Ruth Prawer Jhabvala was born in 1927 in Cologne, Germany. Fleeing the Nazis, her family moved to England in 1939. In 1951 she and her Indian husband moved to New Delhi. She now lives primarily in New York City. Her novels include *Heat and Dust* and *Poet and Dancer*; her screenplays include *A Room with a View* and *Howard's End.* The address published here was originally delivered in 1979, when Jhabvala was awarded the Neil Gunn International Fellowship by the Scottish Arts Council. The phrase "atom of delight," mentioned by Jhabvala, refers to the title of one of Gunn's books.

Leszek Kolakowski was born in 1927 in Radom, Poland. For political reasons, he was dismissed from his post as professor of philosophy at the University of Warsaw in 1968; later that year he moved to Montreal, where he taught until 1969. In 1970, after an academic year at Berkeley, California, he accepted a position at Oxford University. Kolakowski's major work is the three-volume *Main Currents of Marxism* (1978). The essay collected here originally appeared in the *Times of London* in 1985.

Mary McCarthy was born in 1912 in Seattle and died in New York City in 1989. After her marriage to James West in 1961, she moved to Paris; for the next two decades she divided her time between Paris and Maine. Her books include *The Group, Memories of a Catholic Girlhood, Venice Observed,* and *How I Grew.* The essay collected here was written in London in 1972.

Thomas Mann was born in 1875 in Lübeck, Germany, and died in 1955 in Zurich. In 1933, vacationing in Switzerland after a European lecture tour, he decided not to return to Germany. In 1936 he became a Czech citizen; in 1938 he moved to Princeton, New Jersey, where he remained until 1941. He then moved to Pacific Palisades, California, became an American citizen in 1944, and remained in the United States until 1952, when he returned to Switzerland. The address collected here was delivered in California to a Writers' Congress sponsored by the Hollywood Writers' Mobilization and the University of California in October 1943.

Czeslaw Milosz was born in 1911 in Lithuania, worked in New York, Washington, and Paris in the 1940s and 1950s, and finally settled in Berkeley, California, in 1960. The recipient of the Nobel Prize for Literature in 1980, Milosz is the author of *Bells in Winter, The Captive Mind,* and *Collected Poems 1931–1987,* among many other books. The essay collected here was written in 1976.

Henry de Montherlant was born in 1896 in Paris. Beginning in the 1920s, Montherlant spent ten years traveling widely in Europe and Africa, especially in Spain and Morocco, thereby setting a pattern of nomadism he would celebrate for much of his adulthood. In the 1930s he began writing his major novels, including *Pity for Women* (1937); his most successful play, *Port-Royal,* was written in 1954. After Montherlant committed suicide in 1972, his ashes were scattered over the forum in Rome. The essay collected here was written in 1926 in Italy, Provence, and Morocco. Of the figures Montherlant mentions, Maurice Barrès (1862–1923) is the author of a trilogy of novels known as *Le culte du moi,* among other books.

Es'kia Mphahlele was born in 1919 in Pretoria, South Africa. In 1957, in reaction to the growing pressures of apartheid, he began a peripatetic exile spent in Nigeria, Kenya, Zambia, France, and the United States. During this time he published short stories, a novel, and an autobiography, *Down Second Avenue.* He returned to South Africa in 1977. The essay collected here is excerpted from a longer article first published in 1982.

Lewis Nkosi was born in 1936 in Durban, South Africa. After he traveled to the United States to accept a fellowship in 1961, the South African government barred him from returning. He lived in England and California before moving to Lusaka, Zambia, where he began teaching at the University of Zambia. Nkosi's books of nonfiction include *Home and Exile* (1965) and *Tasks and Masks* (1981); his first novel, *Mating Birds,* was published in 1986. The essay published here, collected in *Home and Exile,* was written in 1964.

Jan Novak was born in 1953 in Kolin, Czechoslovakia. In 1970, after a year in an Austrian transit camp, he and his family emigrated to the United States, settling in Chicago. Novak now lives in Oak Park, Illinois. His novels include *The Willys Dream Kit* (1985) and *The Grand Life* (1987). The essay collected here was written in 1989.

Petrarch was born in 1304 in Arezzo, Italy. His family had already been exiled from Florence; in 1312 they finally settled in Avignon. Petrarch spent much of his life traveling between Italy and his home at Vaucluse, in the French countryside. He died in Arquà, near Padua, in 1374. Of the writings collected here (all of which are excerpts from longer letters), the "Protest to a French Friend" was written in Padua to Philippe de Vitry in 1350; the "Proposal for a Long Stay" was written in Vaucluse to Olympius in 1351; the letter about his "Love of Travel" was written in Vaucluse to Andrea Dandolo, Doge of Venice, in 1352.

Darryl Pinckney was born in Indianapolis in 1953, attended college in New York City, moved to Berlin in 1987, and now lives in England. He is the author of a novel, *High Cotton*, and is a frequent contributor to the *New York Review of Books*, among other publications. The essay published here was written especially for this volume.

Plutarch (c. 46–c. 120) was not an exile himself; "To a Young Exile," originally titled "On Exile," was written for a man named Menemachus, banished from Sardis and living in Athens. Scholars have been unable to date the essay conclusively, but believe it was begun sometime after 96. The selection published here is excerpted and adapted from a longer essay collected in *Moralia*.

Augusto Roa Bastos was born in 1917 in Iturbe, Paraguay. An easy target for the right-wing forces in Paraguay's civil war, Roa Bastos went into exile in 1947—primarily in Argentina and France. He returned to Paraguay in 1989, after the fall of General Stroesser's government. Roa Bastos is best known for his novel *I, the Supreme* (1974); he is also the author of numerous short-stories and essays. The essay collected here was first published in English in 1987.

Jean-Jacques Rousseau was born in 1712 in Geneva and lived in Annecy, Turin, Chambéry, Paris, and Venice, among numerous other cities. After the publication of *Émile*, Rousseau was censured by the Sorbonne and the Parliament and threatened with arrest. He left Montmorency, France, for Switzerland in 1762, where he met further persecution from Genevan and

Bernese officials. He finally settled in Môtiers in the Val-Travers near Neuchâtel. In 1765 his writings angered the Neuchâtel clergy, and Rousseau fled to St. Peter's Island in Switzerland's Lake Bienne. (It is this part of his internal exile described in the selection published here.) Several weeks after his arrival, he was ordered to leave by the Bernese authorities; a short stay in England followed, before Rousseau returned to France in 1767. He died in Ermenonville near Senlis in 1778. The "Fifth Walk" printed here (from *The Reveries of the Solitary Walker*) was written in 1777.

Edward Said was born in 1935 in Jerusalem, moved with his family to Cairo in 1947, and then settled in the United States in 1951. He now lives in New York City. The author of numerous books of literary and cultural criticism, including *Orientalism* (1978) and the recent *Culture and Imperialism* (1993), Said also remains active in Palestinian politics. The essay collected here was originally published in 1984.

George Santayana was born in Madrid in 1863, moved to the United States when he was eight, and died in Rome in 1952. Before settling in Rome in 1920, he lived in Cambridge, Massachusetts; Oxford; and Paris. His best-known works of philosophy are *The Life of Reason* and *Realms of Being.* The essay collected here was discovered after Santayana's death; it was probably written around 1912.

Seneca was born in 4 B.C. in Cordoba, Spain. He was raised and educated in Rome, where he wrote his major essays and plays, served as a senator, and held a position at Claudius's court. In A.D. 41 he was falsely accused of intrigue with one of Caligula's sisters and exiled to Corsica; eight years later he was summoned back to Rome by Agrippina, where he became her son Nero's tutor. He committed suicide in A.D. 65. The selection published here is excerpted and adapted from a longer consolation to his mother, written between 42 and 43, and gathered in his *Moral Essays.*

Madame Germaine de Staël was born in 1766 in Paris and died there in 1817. In 1792 she moved to Coppet, in Switzerland, returning to Paris in 1797. As a result of her outspoken opposition to Napoleon, she was exiled three times: in 1803, 1806, and, after she published *On Germany,* in 1810. She spent her exile at Coppet and traveling through Europe. In 1814 she returned to Paris. "On Exile" is excerpted from her *Considerations on the Principal Events of the French Revolution,* published after her death.

Christina Stead was born in 1902 in Sydney, Australia. In 1928, she left home to live in England; shortly thereafter she moved to Paris. In 1937 she moved to the United States with her American husband. While in the States, she wrote her major work, the novel *The Man Who Loved Children.* Stead next lived in the Netherlands, France, Switzerland, and England. She returned to live in Australia in 1974, and died in Sydney in 1983. The essay collected here was written in 1970, after Stead paid a brief visit to Australia in 1969.

Marina Tsvetaeva was born in 1892 in Moscow and died in 1941 in Elabuga, USSR. In 1922 she left Russia to reunite with her husband, Sergei Efron, who had fled to the West with the defeated White Army. She moved to Berlin, and shortly thereafter emigrated to Prague, where she lived for the next two and a half years and where she wrote some of her most important poetry. In 1925 Tsvetaeva moved to Paris; in 1939 she followed her husband and daughter back to the Soviet Union, where they were arrested not long after her arrival. During the 1941 German invasion, Tsvetaeva was evacuated from Moscow to the small town of Elabuga, where she hanged herself.

"An Insistence of Memory" (as with the two other Tsvetaeva selections, the title has been borrowed from the text) is Tsvetaeva's answer to a questionnaire from *By Our Own Paths,* a Prague émigré journal, which published these remarks in 1925 under the title "Russian Writers on Themselves and Contemporary Literature." This English translation appears here for the first time. Among the figures Tsvetaeva mentions, Aleksei N. Tolstoy (1883–1945) was the author of several famous historical novels. Prince Igor was the earliest Kievan prince (913–945). Nikolai S. Gumilev (1886–1921) was a distinguished Acmeist poet (and first husband of Anna Akhmatova). He was executed for alleged counter-revolutionary activities. Tsvetaeva's term "social relic" is a borrowing of Soviet rhetoric: It broadly designates former members of the hereditary nobility and the bourgeoisie. (Tsvetaeva belonged to the latter.)

"An Émigré from Immortality" is excerpted from Tsvetaeva's essay "The Poet and Time," written in France in 1932. "A Hero of Labor" is from her 1931 notebooks (also written in France); it appears here in English translation for the first time. Tsvetaeva's two parenthetical clarifications prefaced by "Note!" were added in 1938. The phrase "a hero of labor" is, of course, another ironic use of Soviet rhetoric: Workers who overfilled their quotas received this title.

Miguel de Unamuno was born in 1864 in Bilbao, part of Spain's Basque country, and died in 1936 in Salamanca. An essayist, novelist, playwright, and poet, he was banished in 1924 by Primo de Rivera, whose military government he had opposed, and went first to the Canary Islands, then to Paris, and finally to Hendaye, on the French side of the border with Spain. He returned to Spain in 1930. When the essay collected here was first published, in 1917, Unamuno was already out of favor with King Alfonso XIII, soon to be a supporter of Primo de Rivera. According to the essay's translator, the word *salido* means "one who has gone out," and was coined by Unamuno as an equivalent to émigré. The words *saudade*, *morriña*, *señardá*, *anyoransa*, and *soledad* are all variations on loneliness, melancholy, nostalgia.

Glenway Wescott was born in 1901 in Kewaskum, Wisconsin. He moved to Europe in 1925, living in England, Germany, Paris, and the South of France until 1933. During these years, he wrote his most important fiction, including the novel *The Grandmothers* (1927) and the story collection *Good-Bye Wisconsin* (1928). He died in Rosemont, New Jersey, in 1987. The essay collected here, which details Wescott's visit home to Wisconsin (via New York) and swift return to Europe, was written in 1927 as an introduction to the book of the same name.